Advertising & Promotion

SAGE | 50 YEARS

SAGE was founded in 1965 by Sara Miller McCune to support the dissemination of usable knowledge by publishing innovative and high-quality research and teaching content. Today, we publish more than 750 journals, including those of more than 300 learned societies, more than 800 new books per year, and a growing range of library products including archives, data, case studies, reports, conference highlights, and video. SAGE remains majority-owned by our founder, and on her passing will become owned by a charitable trust that secures our continued independence.

Los Angeles | London | Washington DC | New Delhi | Singapore

Advertising & Promotion

Chris Hackley *and* Rungpaka Amy Hackley

3rd Edition

SAGE

Los Angeles | London | New Delhi
Singapore | Washington DC

Los Angeles | London | New Delhi
Singapore | Washington DC

SAGE Publications Ltd
1 Oliver's Yard
55 City Road
London EC1Y 1SP

SAGE Publications Inc.
2455 Teller Road
Thousand Oaks, California 91320

SAGE Publications India Pvt Ltd
B 1/I 1 Mohan Cooperative Industrial Area
Mathura Road
New Delhi 110 044

SAGE Publications Asia-Pacific Pte Ltd
3 Church Street
#10-04 Samsung Hub
Singapore 049483

Editor: Matthew Waters
Assistant editor: Nina Smith
Production editor: Sarah Cooke
Copyeditor: Elaine Leek
Proofreader: Dick Davis
Indexer: Judith Lavender
Marketing manager: Alison Borg
Cover design: Francis Kenney
Typeset by: C&M Digitals (P) Ltd, Chennai, India
Printed and bound in Great Britain by Ashford
Colour Press Ltd

Library of Congress Control Number: 2014937946

British Library Cataloguing in Publication data

A catalogue record for this book is available from
the British Library

ISBN 978-1-4462-8071-3
ISBN 978-1-4462-8072-0 (pbk)

At SAGE we take sustainability seriously. Most of our products are printed in the UK using FSC papers and boards.
When we print overseas we ensure sustainable papers are used as measured by the Egmont grading system.
We undertake an annual audit to monitor our sustainability.

Contents

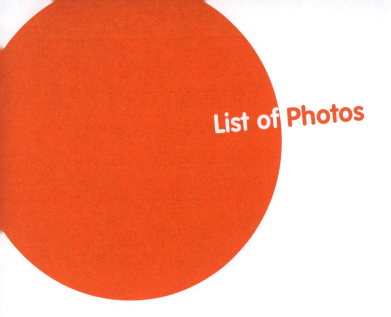

List of Photos

Photographs appear in the full colour section of the text between p. 152 and p. 153.

About the Authors

Chris Hackley was the first Chair in Marketing to be appointed at Royal Holloway University of London, in 2004. Prior to that he was head of the Marketing subject group at the University of Birmingham, UK. His PhD from Strathclyde University (AACSB), Scotland, focused on the creative development process in top advertising agencies. He teaches and researches in advertising, marketing, and consumer cultural policy. Chris has published his work in some 200 books, research articles, features, reports, conference papers and presentations. He has consulted on UK alcohol policy with the UK Government Cabinet Office and the Department of Health, and with commercial organisations such as ITV, Sky Media, Channel 4 TV, New Media Group and the Huffington Post on topics including product placement and native advertising. Professor Hackley is a regular contributor to print and broadcast media on marketing and consumer policy topics with more than 100 media appearances and mentions. He has been interviewed on alcohol policy and media policy for BBC TV, ITV, BBC Radio 4 and Channel 4 TV, and his joint research has been mentioned in most UK national newspapers, and also in some overseas publications such as the *Melbourne Age*, *Harvard Business Review* and *The Times of India*.

Rungpaka Amy Hackley is Lecturer in Marketing at Queen Mary, University of London. Prior to that she was Lecturer in Marketing at Durham University, and before that, she lectured in marketing at the University of Surrey. Dr Hackley's teaching and research focuses on advertising, branding, marketing and consumer culture theory research. Her PhD entailed a cross-cultural study of young consumers' experiences of TV product placement, and her first publication from her PhD research was the only UK paper cited by the ITV companies in their response to the UK government's first consultation on UK TV product placement regulation. She also holds a first degree in Mass Communication and a Master's in Marketing. Dr Hackley has presented her research at international conferences in Asia, North America, Australasia, Europe and the UK, and her work has been published in journals such as the *International Journal of Advertising, Journal of Business Research, Journal of Marketing Management, Marketing Theory, Asian Journal of Business* and *Proceedings of the Association for Consumer Research,* among others.

Preface

Our memory of this edition will be of writing it in Newport Beach, California, with the view of the glistening sea and dolphins from our balcony and our baby, Dulcie-Bella, playing by our feet. Professor Alladi Venkatesh at The Merage Business School at the University of California, Irvine, kindly invited C.H. to be a Visiting Researcher for Spring 2014, and we took the opportunity to have a close look at the biggest advertising market in the world, in the world's most dynamic advertising environment, from the vantage point of one of the most prestigious universities in the region. Our thanks go to Alladi, to the business school, and to the university. We also thank the School of Management at Royal Holloway University of London, for granting C.H. the sabbatical that made it all possible.

The first and second editions of this book have been successful core texts for under- and postgraduate advertising courses in the UK and worldwide. One of the intentions of the book was and remains to bring out the creative/account planning perspective more strongly than is typical in managerial advertising and marketing communications texts that approach the topic from a client/account management position. As well as offering a more evenly balanced treatment of the managerial issues in managing advertising and promotion, the book seeks to offer a broader intellectual treatment of the subject, drawing on perspectives from anthropological and sociological consumer culture research as well as managerial marketing concepts. Finally, the book anticipated the way that divisions between promotional communications would gradually break down under convergence, and the new edition follows through with this logic, focusing on the way that all advertising and promotional genres are being subsumed under the category of 'content'. The third edition retains this synthesis and is thoroughly updated with new examples, cases and vignettes. It brings out the changing managerial issues of advertising and promotion in greater depth and detail, focusing on the broader skill set that is now demanded in advertising and promotional agencies.

Arguably, the most profound shift occurring in advertising and promotion is toward non-advertising promotion, especially branded content on digital media, both as a free-standing strategy and also as an essential dimension of integrated campaigns. Advertising remains at the centre of promotional communication for its strategic importance, but it is now part of an ever-expanding media landscape. This shift has many implications, not least for brand communication strategies, for media planning, campaign development, and for the design of creative strategies in advertising. The book as a whole is written to reflect the profound influence of this shift on contemporary advertising in particular and marketing and branding in general.

The third edition is updated throughout with much re-written text, new practical examples, new cases, academic references and revision questions, and one entirely new chapter. This new edition includes:

- a new chapter on creativity, strategy and planning
- new case studies with increased global coverage including emerging markets
- increased coverage of the internet and its effects on advertising
- enhanced website materials including videos, journal articles and multiple choice questions

Chapter 1 sets the tone for the book by outlining the economic and cultural power and influence of advertising communication as a whole. As a unique hybrid communication form, advertising communication occupies a contested place in cultural life. Traditional, mass media advertising remains important, in spite of predictions of its demise, but is now seen by professionals as one aspect of a holistic brand communication approach that embraces all media channels. The chapter describes the broad scope of the book and its ambitious agenda. Chapter 2 sets out the theoretical frameworks that will guide the student through this complex and challenging field. It is important for students of advertising to appreciate the richness of its theoretical background. Advertising communication is conceived as science, as art, as literature, and as a practical and pragmatic managerial tool. Theory in advertising is important, since it underpins all action, even though those theoretical assumptions are seldom explicitly articulated in practice. Advertising strategies are laden with implicit assumptions about the nature of consumers, the nature of communication and the motivating forces of human behaviour. Paying attention to theory enables us to make some of these implicit assumptions of practice explicit, and hence available for closer critical scrutiny. Chapter 3 looks at the business of advertising in the service of brands, and deals with some of the things advertising communication can accomplish for brands. Chapter 4 looks at the people, processes and practices of advertising agencies. Since the invention of print, advertising agencies have been at the centre of commercial communication, using their unique vantage point across many industry sectors to develop expertise in many related fields, including consumer research, media strategy, creative execution and artwork, typography and copywriting, market research, brand positioning, audience research. This accumulated expertise remains important as advertising agencies typically operate at the hub of major consumer marketing campaigns, keeping the strategy coherent across all media.

Chapter 5 looks in greater depth at several aspects of this role, especially the uses and role of creativity in advertising, the techniques of developing communication strategy in the service of the brand, and the art and science of communication planning. Chapter 6 moves on to explore media planning and its evolving role in the convergent media era, including the planning issue raised when digital media move to a central role in campaign planning. Chapter 7 looks at the rapidly developing field of non-advertising promotion in integrated marketing communications. Chapter 8 focuses on the challenges advertisers face in addressing a global audience, including the issues of cross-cultural communication and co-ordination of brand values across international markets. Chapter 9 is concerned with advertising ethics and regulation with a focus on the contradictions that arise through advertising's dual character as an essential economic tool communicating offers, facilitating competition and generating demand, and as a unique and powerful form of social communication that inflects everyday life. Chapter 10 may be last but is by no means least, as it looks at the complex and contested but vital role research plays in the advertising business. This role embraces not only pre-testing (often called copy-testing) of creative executions and post-campaign evaluation but also the equally important consumer and market research that feed into the creative advertising development process.

Chris Hackley and
Rungpaka Amy Hackley
Newport Beach, California, March 2014

Guided Tour

Chapter outline

Chapter 1 sets the scene for the
the book. It opens by outlining
environment, especially the co
and mobile access, and the con
a result of these changes, adv
in emphasis from traditional
toward brand storytelling th
discusses the evolution
media environment.

Chapter outline provides an outline of what the chapter will cover and what the reader will learn from the chapter.

Key chapter content provides a clear set of key contents for each chapter.

Key chapter content

- The changing global adv
- The challenges for adverti
- What is advertising?
- Studying advertising: mana
- Functionality, symbolism an

SNAPSHOT 1.1

Video-sharing and chann

Video sharing websites have had
defining features of mass media
advertisement, and the identi
placed in designated media
ted in-between and d

Snapshot boxes
feature issues and topics
of interest through
examples and critical
discussion in boxed
sections throughout the
chapters.

Review questions
help develop the
reader's analytical
and critical
thinking skills by
reflecting on a set
of questions either
individually or with
classmates.

Review Questions

1. Make a list of all the forms of adver
   heard of in the last month. Does the
   that have not yet been exploited by

2. After reading this chapter, has y
   of arguments in favour of a
   advertising. Convene a s
   ints be reco

rand? Why was th

material you can for two brands
the typography and the other features
preted differently by different people?

CASE STUDY

Content marketing – the new frontier

ten look like movies, movies look like advert
stories, and PR, well, PR is *everything*. Con
e internet is acting like a sort of black h
genres are merging too: movies are
advertisements for the brand
beyond the dreams of

Case study
provides a full in-depth
example from the real
world of advertising
and promotion, with
reflective questions
at the end to test the
reader's understanding
of the case study.

onal companies ,
u Yu Hsu and Gina G.
Chinese and American telev
Gazette, 75 (8): 695–714.

■ ■ Further reading ■

Dholakia, N. (2012) 'Being critic
    macro perspectives', *Journal of*
Hackley, C. (2013) *Marketing in*
    Macmillan.
ckley, C. (ed.) (2009)
    3 volumes: Vo

Further reading provides suggestions for other reading sources about the chapter topic from both books and academic journals.

Companion Website

Advertising and Promotion, Third Edition, is supported by a **free** companion website for students and lecturers.

Visit **study.sagepub.com/hackley** to take advantage of these extra learning and teaching resources.

For Lecturers

- **PowerPoint Slides:** Chapter-by-chapter slides for use in lectures in support of the textbook.
- **Tutor Guide:** A chapter-by-chapter guide to the textbook with additional materials for teaching.
- **IMC Jeopardy Game:** An interactive team game based on the popular TV show which informally tests students in groups in the classroom. Ideal for the last week of term!

For Students

- **SAGE Journals Online:** Free open access to full, author-selected SAGE journal articles featured in each chapter to help students engage with relevant research literature for higher grades.
- **Video Links:** Links to relevant videos for each chapter to help students and lecturers easily find fun, visual, real-world examples.

(Continued)

(Continued)

- **Weblinks:** Links to relevant websites for each chapter to help students make links to industry and find practical examples for assignments.
- **Author Blog:** Visit www.hackleyadvertisingandpromotion.blogspot.com to view an author-maintained blog that accompanies the textbook. Read posts on current advertising examples and related topical items from the news including popular culture and current affairs.

(S)SAGE

Instructor Resources   Student Resources   Contact us   Help   User menu

Third Edition

Advertising and Promotion
by Chris Hackley and Rungpaka Amy Hackley

Student Resources

1. Introducing Advertising and Promotion
2. Theorising Advertising
3. The Brand and Integrated Marketing Communications Planning
4. Advertising Agencies – Organising Creative Work
5. Strategy and Creativity
6. Promotional Media in the Digital Age
7. Non-Advertising Promotion
8. International Advertising
9. Advertising and Promotion – Ethics and
10. Research in Advertising

Advertising and Promotion

Advertising and Promotion, Third Edition, is supported by a **free** companion website for students and lecturers.

This website offers a range of extra teaching and learning resources, including:

For Lecturers

- **PowerPoint Slides:** Chapter-by-chapter slides for use in lectures in support of the textbook.
- **Tutor Guide:** A chapter-by-chapter guide to the textbook with additional materials for teaching.
- **IMC Jeopardy Game:** An interactive team game based on the popular TV show which informally tests students in groups in the classroom. Ideal for the last week of term!

For Students

- **SAGE Journals Online:** Free open access to full, author-selected SAGE journal articles featured in each chapter to help students engage with relevant research literature for higher grades.
- **Video Links:** Links to relevant videos for each chapter to help students and lecturers easily find fun, visual, real-world examples.
- **Weblinks:** Links to relevant websites for each chapter to help students make links to industry and find practical examples for assignments.
- **Author Blog:** Visit www.hackleyadvertisingandpromotion.blogspot.com to view an author-maintained blog that accompanies the textbook. Read posts on current advertising examples and related topical

Authors: Chris Hackley and Rungpaka Amy Hackley
Pub Date: November 2014

Buy the book

Order Review Copy

1 Introducing Advertising and Promotion

Chapter outline

Chapter 1 sets the scene for the third edition by noting some key themes of the book. It opens by outlining major changes taking place in the advertising environment, especially the convergence of media channels via the internet and mobile access, and the consequent changes in media funding models. As a result of these changes, advertising practice is also changing, with a shift in emphasis from traditional broadcast 'spot' and print display advertising toward brand storytelling through 'content' and 'native' advertising. The chapter discusses the evolution of advertising and promotion in this new, digitised media environment.

Key chapter content

- The changing global advertising environment
- The challenges for advertising agencies
- What is advertising?
- Studying advertising: managerial, consumer and societal perspectives
- Functionality, symbolism and the social power of brands

The changing global advertising environment

As this book is being written, advertising is undergoing a time of change and disruption as the industry tries to respond to new media funding models and changing patterns of media consumption. Advertising agencies are thinking laterally as never before to place their creative stamp on new forms of content that are attractive to clients. The somewhat mythologised creative revolution in advertising of the 1960s occurred in the context of a classic media funding model. Paid-for advertising generated the revenue to fund media channels. In other words, the spot advertising in the intervals paid for television shows, while the classified and display advertising paid for print publications, with a small contribution from the cover charge. As circulation and viewing figures grew, so did advertising revenue. This funding model set the parameters for advertising, since advertisements had to fit particular genre conditions in order to be suitably differentiated from the 'editorial' content in traditional media vehicles such as newspapers and commercial television or radio shows. Back in those days, the advertising agencies earned revenue from commission on the media space they bought, before their media buying departments were hived off as separate businesses. In the West, and especially in Madison Avenue, the epicentre of American advertising, the agencies grew fat on this system and the clients paid for what were seen as great creative ideas to motivate and inspire the newly affluent consumers.

Today, the traditional media funding model is no longer the natural order of things. In fact, the world of old media has been turned on its head by digital communications technology. Now, media professionals often talk about 'content' as a category of promotional communication covering a vast range of genres and media, including but not confined to traditional advertising.

'Content' (see Chapter 1 Case Study) could be a set-piece advertisement that is shared on social media, but it could also be any media form, such as a 'vine' (a 6 second movie clip on social media), a viral ad, a clip of news, documentary or opinion, a blog article, a print media feature article, indeed any communication form at all which has the potential to generate audience engagement. The idea of content is partly driven by the emergence of new media funding models that are forcing advertisers to be more innovative in how they conceive of advertising. These new media funding models are being driven by various pressures, including the fragmentation of media audiences under the influence of new communications technology, and de-regulated media markets.

'Spot' advertising during commercial breaks on television or radio, classified and full-colour advertising spreads in press publications, out of home (OOH) and cinema advertising all retain their high profile, audience reach and dramatic impact. But the advertising landscape is changing. For example, it is becoming pitted with many new media vehicles as digital technology reduces start-up costs for print, internet and broadcast media. There are more magazines, television and radio channels than ever before. But the audience reach of each individual media vehicle has shrunk under increased competition and changing patterns of media consumption. This trend is evident all over the world. Some of these new media vehicles are not funded by the traditional model, social networking websites being the most striking example. Their business model has been to build 'traffic', that is, to elicit millions of users, without conventional advertising, and then to try to devise forms of paid-for promotion that fit the ways their users consumer the service. So, for example, you have the use of algorithms that monitor Facebook users' patterns of use and target individualised promotions into their newsfeed. Other digital media brands, especially news brands, are creating sponsored content that is 'native' to the page: called native advertising, it takes the conventional 'advertorial' and makes it even less easily distinguished from editorial.

The fragmentation of media audiences

Another pressure on the traditional funding model for media is the fragmentation of media audiences as viewing, listener and readership figures for traditional television, print and radio fall, and advertising revenues consequently collapse. For example, in the UK and the USA, newspapers established for over 100 years may cease to exist in the not-too-distant future as advertising revenue falls to unsustainable levels. Underlying the reduction in advertising revenue for traditional media, fewer consumers are paying for print media and more consumers are viewing, and interacting with, media content on mobile phones, PCs, laptops and other wireless devices such as netbooks, iPads and e-book readers. We can watch television programming or read news on digital devices without having to watch the ads. Even more problematic for conventional advertising, the internet offers massive potential audience reach for cheaply made and easily targeted 'viral' advertisements which cost nothing to place on video sharing websites such as YouTube. Finally, when 'convergence' is achieved between television and the internet, and the mass market begins to watch all of its TV on PC screens with wireless broadband capability, the advertising revolution will be in full flow and advertising agencies will face a very different environment to the one in which they evolved. Already, a huge proportion of under-35s in developed economies access all their news, information and entertainment via the internet. They rarely watch live TV or buy paper publications and, therefore, they are not in the habit of regularly watching traditional advertising.

All these changes mean that what we understand by 'advertising' as a genre of communication is changing, and this has as yet uncertain implications for the advertising industry. Advertising has always been a fluid industry in which creative 'hot shops' and talented individuals could thrive, but the core organisational actors in the advertising environment have consistently been the major 'full-service' advertising agencies. Over nearly 400 years, since the development of mass consumption print publications in the Western world, advertising agencies have proved to be the most flexible and astute of organisational forms in adding skills and techniques to retain their central place in an evolving media environment. They are well used to having to explain exactly what it is they do to add value, and why the client ought to pay for that. But can they deal with the challenges of new media and the digital revolution? What will the advertising agency look like in twenty years? Will it be a hybrid media/advertising agency? Will there be fewer big agencies but hundreds of teams of specialists all working under in-house brand managers or specialist brand consultants? Will agencies re-organise to re-focus around creative, digital and integrated media planning, and strip away layers of account management? Or, on the other hand, will the big agencies expand to embrace a wider range of skills, including scriptwriters, animators, bloggers, novelists, film directors, PR and events specialists, digital creatives and more, to become all-purpose, multi-media branded content creators?

SNAPSHOT 1.1

Video-sharing and channel entrepreneurs

Video sharing websites have had a striking effect on the advertising environment. Once, the defining features of mass media advertising were that it was paid-for, it was identifiable as an advertisement, and the identity of the sender was known. Normally, paid-for advertising was placed in designated media spaces set aside solely for the purpose, such as the intervals created in-between and during television or radio shows on commercial channels, or the classified pages or lifestyle sections of print publications. Today, many advertisements are placed on video sharing websites or brand web pages as well as, or instead of, being placed on mass, paid-for media channels. A successful ad on the internet can be viewed and shared by millions of people in just a few weeks, giving an audience reach greater than that possible via television advertising alone, and at far lower cost.

Authenticity is contested in viral content. Some videos now appearing on the internet have been made by advertising agencies to look as if they were made by private citizens. The rationale for this is that privately made content might look more authentic, and therefore be more enthusiastically shared, than commercially sponsored content – although the fact is that most popular shared video content now is commercially made. Even the videoed responses to these virals, called 'video blogging', have sometimes been paid for by advertisers. Not only professionals have been advertising in this way: individuals have even started to use sites such as YouTube as a personal platform by developing content for their own channel. They might post comedy sketches, clips of their activities or video blogs on their specialist topic. If they can build up a significant number of users, they can sell advertising and earn revenue from their channel. The viral possibilities of these sites mean that uploads which people like can spread to millions of viewers in just a few days. For advertisers, this kind of 'earned' media is far cheaper than 'bought' media such as television spot advertising. The difficulty is that it is hard to produce a hugely popular piece of video content to a formula.

Advertising and broadcast 'media convergence'

The convergence of television, print media and the internet has been predicted for more than a decade (Jenkins, 2008). There is increasing momentum toward media convergence, since television shows, radio shows and movies are being made available and viewed on computers, pads and mobile devices, whilst print publications are shifting their business models toward internet and mobile presence. In the near future, technological convergence will move closer as combined television and PC units reach the mass market. In the longer term, the mobile phone industry will generate a technology platform that will enable mobile devices to fulfil all a person's communication, entertainment and work needs.

The economic impetus behind broadcast media convergence comes, on the one hand, from the shrinking audiences for traditional mass media including television, and, on the other, the increasing audiences for televisual forms of entertainment via the internet and PC or mobile communication. The internet has powerful potential as a platform for television content and advertising because of its massive audience reach and its capacity for targeting, instant response and audience measurement. The problem for internet sites is that, while they are attracting an increased proportion of advertising spend, the sums are still relatively small compared to television advertising. There is a mutual need driving convergence: traditional media need to find ways to access the huge audience traffic of the internet, while internet sites need to tap into some of the platform impact and (still) higher total advertising revenues available from television exposure.

The implications of convergence for advertisers, are profound. Mobile advertising is growing rapidly although it still remains a small sector relative to mass media. There are still obstacles to be overcome. These include the lack of common software and hardware platforms to carry video, text and audio on all mobile devices, and the fact that consumers don't really like receiving overt advertisements on mobile social media platforms. Mobile phones are carried everywhere, they are always on and they are highly personalised, which gives them obvious potential for carrying advertising. In the longer term, the convergence of mobile and internet delivery with traditional media will generate new media funding models, though advertising will still play a major part in this, in adapted forms.

The challenges for advertising agencies

The aforementioned scenario, then, could eventually result in an advertising environment quite different from any that has gone before. Conventional advertising, in the form of a striking 30 second television spot or stunning print display, is not going away any time soon. But the dynamics of making money out of this communication form for brand clients and agencies is certainly changing. Today, audiences for live TV have dwindled since viewers can record, stream and buy on-demand service to watch their favourite shows whenever they like. As a result, big televised sports events offer the last large-scale, real-time media audience for advertisers. The attraction of live audiences of many millions is driving sports business through bigger and bigger sponsorship and TV viewing rights deals.

Live audience events on mass media are rare today as media audiences fragment across multiple media vehicles and channels. As noted above, if ad agencies want to keep their place at the centre of the marketing world, they have to respond to the new reality of the convergent media environment creatively by reorganising, by evolving new skills and techniques, and by developing new ways to get business. For example, according to some visionaries, web blogs have become the most important source for new agency business, as clients and agencies struggle to find time for the traditional pitching process. Blogging has, in fact, become a key marketing strategy (Hackley, 2009a) and many agencies have embraced this trend on their own websites. Many others are placing digital communication at the centre of their planning process by hiring digital account planners in response to the demand from internet providers for many forms of creative content. Still others are adapting to the logic of branding and proclaiming their ability to craft brand stories that will resonate with the relevant consumers and can be shared across social media.

It isn't easy for advertising agencies (or even for specialist digital agencies) to generate revenue from original digital content. Clients don't like to pay for it, at least they don't like to pay much. Where digital comes into its own, in the form of branded microsites, games, apps and other branded media content, it can be difficult to offer clients a clear return on investment (ROI) calculation. What is more, the 'freemium' business models so prevalent in internet brands means that consumers often resist advertising on free-to-use social media websites. Freemium refers to giving away a basic level of information and service in the hope that this will attract clients willing to pay for a higher level of service. *LinkedIn*, the professional networking site, is one example of this approach. Many advertising agencies themselves are using a partial freemium model by offering case studies and other information sources free of charge via their website in the hope that clients will be attracted to pay for a deeper engagement with the agency. Social networking sites like Facebook and YouTube have tried to get their user traffic to accept a certain level of click-through or banner advertising, and increasingly they are turning to forms of 'native' advertising, that is, sponsored content that is 'native' to the page and looks much like normal, non-sponsored content.[1]

Many agencies have re-organised their account teams, for example by incorporating digital planners, or in some cases by cutting out a layer of account management. Others have crossed into new areas, for example some direct mail agencies have expanded their service offer, even producing broadcast advertising. Increasing numbers of media agencies are also trying to move into advertising. As advertising morphs into 'content' they see an opportunity to leverage their specialist expertise in media to encroach on the ad agencies' field of work. Some advertising agencies have developed new revenue streams by re-positioning themselves as ideas companies and developing creative projects as diverse as comics, movies and stage plays. There are ongoing experiments with new agency forms, such as the 'social-media' agency that attempts to handle all the brand communication via the internet.

From the client side, non-traditional styles of advertising are taking a greater share of promotional spend because of the need to engage consumers in ways that offer a more clearly defined return on investment (ROI) than traditional advertising. In particular, clients need their agencies to offer an integrated communications solution that offers value and impact by using different communication channels in a single campaign. For example, this may take the form of a television advertisement supported with dedicated brand microsites containing consumer forums, games, access to company information, and creating presence for the brand in other areas through media coverage, sponsorship, branded apps, direct marketing or sales promotion activities. Within the flux of change in the advertising environment, advertising agencies cannot be expected to be the experts in every communication channel but they are in a prime position to generate and to co-ordinate new models of creative and brand communications strategy.

SNAPSHOT 1.2

New funding models needed for new media

The concept of freemium, giving away free basic content to encourage consumers to pay for enhanced services, has become associated with second-generation interactive services. Their defining features are new models of business and communication. Lateral thinking is required

(Continued)

(Continued)

to creatively harness the interactive properties of the web for social and commercial purposes, and new ideas are evolving every day. Social networking and video sharing websites, blogs and wikis exemplify web-based business concepts that are enriched by open access and user participation. In many cases, such sites generate huge user traffic but have struggled to monetise this other than by trying to get users to accept a certain amount of paid-for advertising. Twitter, for example, founded in 2007, gained 7 million users in the USA alone in the first two years, a figure that has grown to around 250 million worldwide users today. It is a free service that generates relatively small revenues from sponsored 'tweets' yet it was valued at $250,000,000 when it raised money in 2007, and more recently its market value was estimated at some $35 billion.[2] It remains to be seen how Twitter might be able to turn its audience traffic into substantial revenues to justify that market capitalisation. Other sites, like *LinkedIn*, utilise the freemium concept to add value to services that can only be acquired by customers paying a premium. The advantage of freemium is that it can generate considerable audience reach through word-of-mouth (WOM) very quickly. The difficulty of translating this audience reach into large revenue streams – in other words, the problem of how to monetise audience traffic – is the key problem of internet business models. Traditional mass media brands such as TV shows and newspapers have a double problem: firstly, how to shift their resources to the internet site to make up for losses in print sales and reductions in viewing figures, and secondly, how to generate revenue from their web traffic. A small number of media brands, for example UK newspaper site *MailOnline*, seem to have cracked this particular issue with an astute combination of sensational news coverage and showbusiness gossip (Hackley, 2013a).

Can ad agencies survive in the convergent media landscape?

If advertising agencies are to survive into the next century, they have to engage with new client priorities and broaden their skills in developing creative branded content, including advertising, that can translate across new media channels. Of course, it is easier to say that ad agencies need to acquire expertise in unfamiliar, non-advertising promotional disciplines, than it is for them to do so. They sit alongside other communication disciplines such as public relations (PR), sales promotion, digital and direct mail, out of home (OOH) advertising and so on. Nonetheless, difficult as it may be, the logic of media convergence dictates that the disciplines of promotional communication will also need to converge. The battle is on as to which form of agency turns out to be the most fluent at developing brand storytelling and other creative craft skills that address clients' needs for integrated campaigns. Promotional communication now entails brand storytelling that resonates with consumers and translates across media platforms. For example, whiskey brand *Jack Daniel's* in its storytelling of American's hillbilly sub-culture romanticises the sub-culture of 'hooch' distilling in a small Tennessee distillery and the ideology of masculinity and anti-industrialism that it supports (see Holt and Cameron, 2010). Brand storytelling demands creative craft skills such as scriptwriting, narrative development, characterisation, screenplay development and visualisation that span analogue and digital media.

What will result from the current changes in the advertising environment is anyone's guess, but advertising agencies might well retain their importance. Since they began as brokers of classified advertising space in the early press publications, they have added many new skills and techniques such as copywriting, creative production, business strategy, brand strategy, consumer and market research and media planning. They have been at the centre of the evolution of marketing as a discipline and they remain in a positive position to continue their evolution into the new, convergent, media environment.

What is advertising?

This is a question with two possible responses – a short one and a long one. The short one is that advertising is a paid-for promotional message from an identifiable source transmitted via a communication medium. Advertising is conventionally seen as one sub-element of promotion, which is itself one of the four elements of the marketing mix, the others being product, place (distribution) and price. The marketing mix element of 'promotion' embraces any promotional communication, and includes advertising, public relations, personal selling, corporate communications, direct mail and other direct marketing techniques, point-of-sale (or point-of-purchase) and merchandising, sales promotions, exhibitions, SMS text messaging and other forms of mobile marketing, email advertising, internet banner advertising, social media advertising and more.

There are many forms of advertising execution, and we will explore numerous examples of these in the book. In order to create effective advertising transmitted via print in newspapers, magazines or on out of home (OOH) street billboards, on vehicles or on bus shelters, ad agencies need to deploy a range of medium-specific creative craft skills. TV advertising still presents the highest profile platform for advertisers, with live sports events offering large real-time viewing audiences to advertisers. As seen in Chapter 6 Case Study, page 179 one of the last major real-time TV advertising opportunities is the American football season finale, the Super Bowl. *Fox Sports* were reported to be charging up to $4,000,000,000 for a 30 second spot for advertisers to reach the 100,000,000 audience.[3] Production costs can be even higher, and much thought and planning goes into making a big budget TV ad.

Television is by no means the only medium for short advertising films – there is advertising shown in cinemas before the main feature, and, of course, advertising that is produced and aired over the internet and on video sharing websites. Then, there is advertising that integrates intertextually with TV and social media. For example, the *Yeo Valley* yoghurt brand created a TV ad using a specially created boy band, 'The Churned', who sung an original song in a spot during the UK TV talent show *The X Factor*. The item became a world-wide trending topic on Twitter and a viral hit on YouTube, and the song was an *iTune* chart hit.[4]

Forms of advertising and promotional communication such as these are very flexible and can be used for many different kinds of creative execution and many different kinds of appeal. This is where the creativity comes in, to make one ad stand out and get viewers' attention by being resonant, whether that is because it reflects an insightful truth for its audience, because it is beautifully made and diverting, or because it is funny, striking or challenging. Some advertising may be designed specifically for direct mail or direct response campaigns, whilst radio advertising is yet another category that demands complex and medium-specific craft skills in order to effectively reach the desired target audience and convince them to take a second look a the brand.

And that was the short answer. The longer answer will take the rest of this book to explore. There are two reasons why the longer answer is important. One is that, to most people, advertising is a word that covers any kind of pro-motion whatsoever. To professionals in the field, the various promotional disciplines are important because individuals might spend an entire career in one of them as a professional in, say, PR, direct mail, sales promotion, or indeed, advertising. But for laypeople, for consumers, it's all advertising, of one kind or another (Percy and Elliott, 2009). That in itself isn't a good enough reason to conflate the various disciplines of promotional communication under one heading, but along with the next reason, it may be. As noted above, the media infrastructure for advertising is undergoing profound changes driven by digital communication, and this is changing the very way advertising is conceived. Advertising remains an important discipline, but integration is now the watchword, and major campaigns are now typically expected to embrace a number of different media channels, especially digital channels, with differ-ent but thematically connected creative executions. In many cases, large organisations treat the different communication disciplines as separate func-tions with different departments handling, say, corporate communications, direct marketing, advertising or sales. Yet, in the new advertising environment, and from a management point of view, the logic of integration is compelling. Media audiences now access more channels than ever before, and in different proportions. Newspapers and television still retain their place in the advertis-ing scene, but they have given up a lot of ground to the internet and mobile communication. In response, brand clients want promotional campaigns to be integrated across media channels and across promotional sub-categories. Given the entrenched professional and organisational separation of the various mar-keting communication techniques and channels, the ideal of fully integrated marketing communication (IMC) management remains only partially realised. As we have touched on above, there is a shake-out going on in the promotion industry which includes not only advertising agencies but direct mail, sales promotion, media and branding agencies, and even creative hot shops and digital agencies. The winners will be the ones that adapt most successfully, and most profitably, to the logic of IMC.

Under the influence of IMC, advertising creative executions are changing and moving towards a broader category of 'content'. The goal is no longer only to create short-term sales but to maintain long-term brand presence and market share. Hence advertising is moving closer to publicity and entertainment as brand owners seek to activate the recognition of consumers across different media platforms in ways that are likeable, challenging and engaging, and that generate social media sharing and brand engagement. Brand owners want to create content that is subtly branded but that will engage consumers, whether that is in the form of a 30 second TV advertisement that is then shared on social media, or a tweet or a viral video, or a piece of branded content on YouTube, or a branded game that can be downloaded as an app on a mobile device ... the list is limited only by the digital imagination, and as varied as the technology. In this book, then, the term 'advertising and promotion' is used as an umbrella category for all forms of promotion communication on all media channels. The book is intended to reflect the changes in technology, in advertising practice and in consumer behaviour that are blurring the lines between the traditional categories of marketing communication.

Blurring the definitions of advertising and promotion

The ingenuity of advertisers and the flexibility of advertising as a communication form often render attempts to define it in one sentence trite, or tautologous. As noted in Snapshot 1.2, the internet is creating new forms of advertising that don't conform to the old definitions. Advertising often sells something, but often does not, since a great deal of advertising promotes not only branded products and services but political candidates and political parties, public services, health and safety issues, charities or other non-profit issues. Advertising is often an impersonal communication, distinguishing it from personal selling, but there are many ads that are eye-to-eye sales pitches delivered by actors or celebrity endorsers in a mediated imitation of a personal sales encounter. Advertising is usually paid-for, appearing in a media space set apart for promotional communication. But, increasingly, as noted above, advertisements may be put on internet sites such as YouTube with no fee involved at all, because viewers actively search out advertisements they may find entertaining or amusing. In other cases, video sharing is utilised to expand the audience for the ad. For example, UK TV aired a novel ad break in which all the scheduled ads were enacted by *Lego* characters, as a promotion for a forth-coming *Lego* movie.[5] The ad break was posted on YouTube[6] with a view to sharing for cross-promotion of the ads, the *Lego* brand and the movie. This is a novel twist on advertising that is extended through social media, but, increasingly, the mass media advertising is being ignored as promotional budgets are being turned to forms of non-advertising promotion that are implicit rather than explicit, such as sponsorship, advertainment, or product placement. Consequently, attempts to define advertising in concrete and exclusive terms are usually more notable for what they leave out than for what they include.

Advertising can sometimes be distinguished by genre elements that set it apart from other forms of mediated communication. Overheated sales pitches from improbably coiffed spokespersons, deliriously happy housewives singing irritatingly catchy jingles at the kitchen sink, unfeasibly attractive models excited by chocolate confections all spring to mind as advertising clichés. But then again, many advertisements contradict advertising stereotypes. Just as American advertising guru Bill Bernbach created the ironic or self-deprecating ad in his iconic *Volkswagen* campaign of the 1960s, many advertisements now subvert conventional genres and eschew the rhetoric of over-selling in favour of postmodern irony, understatement or narrative designed to create presence and generate word-of-mouth for the brand, as opposed to trying to sell it. Bernbach was credited with starting the advertising 'creative revolution'. Some in the industry today feel that creativity in advertising faded away along with the swinging sixties. Others feel that creativity is still around in advertising, but the way it is conceived has to change along with the changes in media infrastructure. Consumers today sometimes like to be passive consumers of entertainment, but often take a much more active part in advertising campaigns, adapting, criticising, re-making, and even contributing to story development when brands crowd-source ideas. In such a scenario, creativity in advertising has to be seen as something that is no longer a matter of individual creative genius, if it ever was, but as something that is collaborative, dynamic and subjective.

So, a narrow definition of what advertising is can obscure consideration of what advertising does. We might categorise a given piece of communication as an advertisement in terms of its parallels with a vague and fuzzy mental prototype of what an ad should look or sound like (see Rosch, 1977, cited in Cook, 2001: 13), but the norms of advertising media, genres and payment methods are being revised by changes in the industry. Advertising may be a communication that at some level has a promotional motive, but this doesn't prepare us for all the kinds of promotional messages we are likely to encounter. Neither can it prepare us for the subtlety of motive that underlies many hybrid promotional forms, such as a post-match interview with a logo-wearing sporting star, a free download of a trial version of a new computer game, free content from a magazine's website you can download to your mobile phone, or a 'courtesy' phone call from your bank. Each can be regarded as a promotional communication, or might be regarded by a lay person as a piece of advertising. Textbook definitions of advertising are being outpaced by innovations in digital communication technology and by hybrid promotional genres. A realistic study of advertising and promotion cannot hope to put all the parts in neatly labelled packages. Advertising takes the enquirer on a journey that is all the more fascinating because it defies boundaries.

Studying advertising – managerial, consumer and societal perspectives

The consumer perspective

In this book, then, we try to take a 360 degree look at advertising and promotion by taking in three distinct perspectives: these are, the consumer perspective, the managerial perspective and the socio-cultural perspective. Advertising and promotion are inherently important to study for the influence they exert on consumer culture (Powell, 2013). It is important for us to educate ourselves about this decidedly contemporary form of communication because of the influence it might have on our lives. Of course, advertising and promotion are also powerful managerial tools and students of social science and business and management might want to learn something of how, why and when this tool is deployed. The managerial perspective is also important, though, to assist the consumer and socio-cultural perspectives, since our understanding of advertising is incomplete without an insight into the material conditions from which it emerged (McFall, 2004).

As a consumer, take a moment to think about the advertisements you have seen or heard this week. At whom do you think they were aimed? What, exactly, were they trying to communicate? How did they make you feel? Did you immediately rush to buy the brand? Did you tell your friends about the ad or share it on social media? Which medium conveyed the ads? Did you see them on a passing vehicle, on outdoor poster sites, on the television, hear them on the radio, read them in the press, see them on your Twitter feed or on some other website? Did you see other forms of promotion on your clothing, smell them in a promotionally enhanced shopping environment, see them on product packaging, on an air balloon in the sky or on the back of a bus ticket? It is difficult to remember more than a few of all the hundreds of promotions we experience each week, at least if we live in urban areas and have access to televisions, mobile phones, tablets and computers. Advertising has become such a feature of daily life that sometimes it seems as if we hardly notice it. Advertising often seems to pervade our cultural landscape and we carry on our lives taking it for granted.

We are struck, then, when particular promotional campaigns become topics of general conversation, whether that conversation is critical or approving of the campaign. For example, *Coca-Cola* aired a TV ad during Super Bowl 2014[7] in which people of many ethnicities were filmed to a soundtrack of 'America the Beautiful', sung in different languages. The ad caused a storm on social media with many supporters lauding its multicultural theme, but many others claiming that it did not reflect their idea of a predominantly white, English-speaking America. Advertising is often dismissed as a trivial, mendacious and irritating form of communication, yet there are times when it catches the cultural zeitgeist and articulates issues of social importance in ways that other media simply cannot do. Of course, one can ask how important this debate is, since, ultimately, this is about selling fizzy drinks. Yet, the fact that, through advertising, the business of selling fizzy drinks can become entwined with the most pressing social issues of our time says something about the cultural force of brands, and of advertising. It is at times like this we realise that advertising occupies a contradictory social space – we take it for-granted, and yet it is a profoundly influential form of cultural communication.

Advertising is, of course, so powerful precisely because it is taken for granted. There are frequent press features that reflect our puzzled fascination with the latest iconic or controversial ad. The TV show dedicated to the funniest or most outlandish ads has become a mainstay of popular TV programming in many countries. Advertising has become part of mainstream entertainment, while entertainment media make use of advertising styles and techniques, reflecting advertising's dynamic character as a perpetually evolving form of social communication (Leiss et al., 2005). The hard-sell ads remain, but there are also new narrative advertising forms of ever-greater subtlety, variety and penetration. Sometimes, deliberately or through serendipity, these advertisements tap into and articulate acute cultural conflicts and, as Holt (2002) suggests, these can sometimes be understood conflicts of identity. The *Coca-Cola* ad discussed above clearly touched a nerve as regards some Americans' sense of national identity.

SNAPSHOT 1.3

New narrative forms of advertising – from 'advertising' to 'content'

Contemporary advertising often departs from the conventional sales narrative to tell a story that may be only tangentially linked to the brand. The reasoning behind this may be that a given audience at a given time needs to be amused or enchanted rather than beaten over the head with a sales message, or it might be that the strategy is about long-term brand recognition and positioning, in which case the branding in the content can be quite understated, and there may not be any overtly promotional element at all. For example, in 2009, a series of television ads for mobile supplier *T-Mobile* showed what appeared to be a 'flash mob' of several hundred people breaking spontaneously into a choreographed dance in the middle of London's Liverpool Street Station.[8] Incredulous commuters reach for their mobile phones to film the event and share it with their friends. The *T-Mobile* tune played briefly at the end and the spoken line 'life is for sharing' are the only things indicating that it is an advertisement. There have been countless variations on this since, some of them branded as corporate content, many not. One of the former was for a brand of mints shot in France in 2012,[9] while a non-commercial example was by the United States Air Force Band in late 2013.[10] Flash mobs going viral does make a good story, and one needs to be a little cautious, since flash mobs are essentially an exercise in public relations and getting the story out is the major part of the project. There are no clear criteria of what constitutes 'going viral'.

In many countries other new narrative forms have been developed which depart from the traditional genres of advertising. Some of these might be called advertainment since the ads are presented simply as entertainments. If people like them, they attract press coverage and media shares, and the lack of a direct and explicit product pitch lends them a stronger sense of authenticity than one feels with a conventional advertisement. In mid 2013 David Beckham starred with digital reproductions of himself in a piece of promotional content for *Sky Sports*,[11] and car brands *BMW* and *Jaguar* have made slick movies that achieved considerable numbers of 'earned' media views (see also Chapter 1 Case Study below).

The managerial perspective

For organisational managers, advertising and promotion are tools for supporting a wide variety of marketing, corporate and business objectives. There are many professionals on the client side who are deeply sceptical about the claims made for advertising as a business tool, unless they are backed up by statistical evidence of attitude change, recall, or, preferably, sales response. Brand managers are usually under pressure to account for their advertising budgets by linking them to sales or market share in the short to medium term. They often have little use for theories of advertising based on building long-term brand equity. This is understandable, because in the long term, they are in a different job, or out of a job. Many others in the marketing business feel that they have to match competitor promotion levels for fear of losing market share if they don't. Even though much advertising activity is driven by organisational politics and competitive neurosis, there is an acknowledgement that the world's major brands would be inconceivable without advertising.

Neither can it be doubted that the commercial fortunes of some brands, and in some cases the size of entire markets, have been transformed through powerful and creatively compelling advertising campaigns. Even so, there are persistent questions hanging over advertising's effectiveness and the genuine return it delivers on investment. As a consequence, the advertising budget is often the first to be cut in difficult economic times and mutual insecurity can colour the relationships between clients and advertising agencies. Like a star-crossed relationship, business can't live with advertising, and it can't survive without it.

The managerial uses of advertising and promotion

Industry professionals tend to regard advertising as a powerful if imprecise marketing tool, a means of persuasively communicating with (or to) large numbers of customers and potential customers, along with other interested stakeholders. But advertising's ability to persuade people to buy product in the short term is often overstated. Instead, it is often used much in the same way as publicity, to generate and maintain market presence and to reassure consumers (Ehrenberg et al., 2002), while also reminding shareholders, employees and competitors that the brand remains salient.

A strategy of long-term brand building may not always grab the imagination of the brand manager who has weekly sales charts waved in his or her face at the regular board meetings, but soft sell can translate to sales simply by being remembered in the right way by enough consumers. Human beings have a short-term memory capacity of about six or seven items (psychologists call this Miller's magic number seven, after George A. Miller's theory about short term memory). Most purchases are not researched exhaustively, so we will often choose from the six or seven brands of which we have heard, and we can recall without effort, and which are easy to find. Factor in consumer markets of many millions of people, and it seems self-evident that the most memorably, and the most persistently, advertised brands will take the top few places in the market, provided they are readily available, competitive in quality, and reasonably priced. Given the possibility that sales dynamics might conform to some degree to this kind of loose model, the aforementioned shift from advertising toward non-advertising branded content is easily explained.

It must be acknowledged that the purposes advertising serves may differ somewhat under different economic and cultural conditions. In the USA, for example, TV advertising seems to serve its economic function to communicate offers with typically direct and forthright advertising, because of the huge size of the country, the competitiveness of its markets and the fragmented nature of its media markets. In the UK, on the other hand, TV advertising tends to be less direct and more of a soft sell: it tells branded stories, and that may be because UK consumers know the offers, they just want them to be made to seem interesting. The UK, of course, is much smaller, it has a less dynamic consumer market than the USA, and state-controlled, non-commercial media outlets occupy dominant positions, limiting the capacity for advertising.

The problem with this informal theory of advertising as a matter of getting into the 'evoked set' of six or seven recalled brands, though, is that it implies that the creative content of the ads is not necessarily of critical importance. There will always be examples of ads that capture the public imagination and build brand presence out of all proportion to their budget, and of branded content that achieves millions of social media shares in days, but these are rare. The truth is, much advertising needs only to be good enough in order to maintain market share and brand presence, and it is quite rare for entirely new brands to break into the top few places in established product or service markets because of the barriers to entry. While all this is a simplification, it might help explain the popularity of some leading brands of fast food and household detergent whose ubiquitous advertising campaigns are often excoriated for their cliché-ridden narratives and deplorable creative standards, but they are hard to forget and they seem to play a part in the success of the brand.

Social marketing and advertising

The managerial perspective in advertising and promotion is not confined to profit making activities. 'Social marketing' (Kotler and Roberto, 1989; Kotler and Zaltman, 1971), touched upon earlier in the chapter, is a genre of promotion that addresses issues of social concern, and is typically funded by charities, lobby groups, or by the state. Many public services, charities and government departments use advertising campaigns to try to promote their causes or to change behaviour with respect to, for example, alcohol or cigarette consumption, safer driving, sexual practice, domestic violence or social prejudice towards disability or ethnicity. Social marketing, and specifically social advertising, can sometimes shout louder than commercial advertising. In terms of impact, it can do so by shocking audiences into paying attention, at least for the duration of the first ad. Social campaigns are allowed by the regulatory authorities, at least in the UK, to push the boundaries of tasteful depiction further than brand advertising, because of their ostensibly virtuous motives (also see Chapter 9). Ads on UK television depicting car crashes, child abuse and drug taking have been pretty hard-hitting, but their aims of reducing car crash injuries, reducing violent or sexual abuse of children and reducing addiction to illegal drugs are deemed by the UK advertising regulator, the Advertising Standards Authority (ASA), to be worth supporting and therefore they are allowed to be quite shocking. Whether or not shocking social advertisements are actually effective in achieving their aims, or in merely getting PR profile for the cause, is a difficult question to answer.

In some cases, social marketing and advertising have been turned to commercial use, where a brand decides that linking its values with a cause or a particular charity might help its commercial brand positioning. For example,

Unilever's *Dove* brand in the UK has created a long running and successful campaign based around the idea that women are misrepresented in cosmetics and personal care products advertising. The *Dove* 'campaign for real beauty'[12] includes a charitable foundation supporting women's interests and promoted the idea that 'real' women need not try to conform to the idealised stereotypes of typical, photoshopped cosmetics advertising (see Chapter 10 Case Study).

Questions of what kinds of advertising 'work' and deliver the best value to shareholders, taxpayers and other stakeholders depend for their answer on one's perspective. But no one has a definitive answer. The effectiveness of a campaign invariably depends on many factors, including its objectives, its audience, its budget, its timing and media channel, the quality of the creative execution, and many other environmental factors such as market price and competitive behaviour. In Chapter 2 we will examine some of the many theories of advertising that have been developed to try to find answers to the question of how, and if, advertising 'works'.

The socio-cultural perspective

Advertising is regarded by many people as a communication form that is inherently deceitful and debased, and occasionally offensive. Yet, considering the tenaciousness with which corporations pursue profits, remarkably few ads tell literal untruths. Of course, some do, but most advertising satisfies typical social conventions, and regulatory requirements, of tact and truthfulness. The interaction of consumers with advertising and promotional communication is usually too complex and subtle to be thought of as, simply, a matter of either fact or fiction. If an ad implies that a man's sexual attractiveness and social status will be enhanced by shaving with a *Gillette* razor or deodorising with *Lynx* body spray, surely this is merely preposterous rather than untrue? Who would possibly take such an idea seriously? To be sure, consumer perceptions and beliefs about brands are self-sustaining to some degree: we believe what we want to believe, sometimes in the face of contradictory evidence. Do smokers really cough less using low-tar cigarettes? Are we slimmer because we put calorie-free sugar substitute in our coffee? It can hardly be denied that there is an important element of wish fulfilment in what we choose to believe in advertising. The advertisers provide the suggestion, and, as consumers, we complete the gestalt. Gestalt psychology refers to the way people complete the circle of meaning from partial cues or prompts. In other words, our inference goes beyond the evidence. Advertising plays with the grey area of meaning, using implicit connotation and suggestion as well as making explicit claims. The socio-cultural perspective attempts to delve beneath the literal interpretation of advertising messages to access their symbolic codes and generate insight into their cultural meaning.

The social power of advertising

The nice thing about teaching advertising is that it is such an immediate part of daily experience it is relatively easy to get a sense of student engagement with the subject. Few people do not have opinions on advertisements they have seen. This can give the subject of advertising great resonance as a subject of study that is suitable for a wide variety of practical and theoretical treatments. Beyond the classroom, advertising can occasionally have an astonishing power to grasp widespread attention and, in a few celebrated cases, change entire markets. The legendary 'Laundrette' ad that agency Bartle Bogle Hegarty created in the 1982 campaign for *Levi's 501* jeans[13] used American provenance to revolutionise the denim jeans market in general and sales of *Levi's* in particular for the following decade. It has been claimed that the campaign increased sales of denim jeans by some 600%. Other campaigns have become so talked about they have changed language, for example when a campaign for *Budweiser* beer increased market share for the brand and earned valuable free publicity simply because they added a word ('Whassup')[14] to the vernacular of American English (and even earned a listing in *Longman's Dictionary of Contemporary English*).[15] Advertising has always had the potential to capture the popular imagination in a way that feels a very intimate part of peoples' lives. Social media now leverage this aspect of advertising, the potential to be talked about, adding an air of cultural charisma to advertising as the most enigmatic of creative industries.

Advertising and promotion, then, constitute a vivid cultural presence in capitalist economies, influencing and inter-penetrating social and cultural values. This is important – too many academic studies conceive of advertising in terms of a narrow cognitive influence on individual consumer decision making, but advertising does not exist in a cultural vacuum. It is ineluctably a form of social communication (Leiss et al., 2005) and the socio-cultural perspective draws on concepts and theories from semiotics, cultural anthropology, literary studies and sociology to try to articulate the various ways in which advertising mobilises, exploits and contributes to cultural meanings. Advertising agencies know this, and most duly employ people from many disciplinary backgrounds, including cultural anthropology, ethnography and sociology, alongside history, philosophy, psychology, literature, art, aesthetics and business graduates (Hackley, 2013b).

Interpreting advertising: humour and hyperbole

One peculiarity of advertising is that consumers are expected to be able to distinguish between untruth and humorous hyperbole, but the advertisers make every effort to blur this distinction. This is just one reason why this sophisticated communication form is rightfully a part of literary academic study. Advertising performs an essential economic function in capitalist economies. It communicates offers to facilitate consumer choice and market competition and stimulate demand, but for it to perform this function well, it demands a relatively sophisticated level of discernment from consumers who have learned the reading strategies demanded by advertising (for example, see O'Donohoe, 1997). Advertising is rarely a significant part of the school curriculum, yet negotiating a way through the advertising landscape is important to the economic and social competence of citizens. Advertising is often accused of exploiting the vulnerable, the less educated, the very young, the very old and those with access to fewer resources. But the ways in which advertising communicates are still relatively poorly understood and under-examined, especially as regards the roles of implicit meanings, such as irony and humorous hyperbole.

Take, for example, a long-running campaign theme used by the male personal care brand *Axe*, known as *Lynx* in the UK, which implies that men who use *Lynx/Axe* become instantly irresistible to women. The ads assume that the viewer will understand that it is all just a joke: the plots are clearly intended to be funny. *Lynx* is pointing at the narrative conventions of male grooming brands and laughing at them with the viewer. But the high production standards of the ads show viewers that, in fact, the marketing campaign is deadly serious. Viewers agree – *Lynx* is the leading brand in several male grooming product segments. Could it be that knowing the ads are not serious strengthens rather than weakens the message, that using *Lynx* deodorant might just make the user more sexually alluring to the woman of his dreams? According to some theorists, it is enough that audiences are aware of the implied message in an ad for the communication to be persuasive – they do not have to believe it. The area of implied meaning in advertising is very difficult for regulators, since this is exactly the area advertising exploits. It is conventional wisdom that 90% of face-to-face communication is dominated by implicit signals, body language, facial expression, tone, gesture and so forth. Why, then, do advertising regulators often focus on the literal message in advertisements, ignoring the other 90%?

The issue highlights the problem advertising regulation has with implicit meaning in advertising. In many cases, especially in areas of public concern such as alcohol advertising, the ASA has made judgements on the implicit meaning that could be read into advertisements, even though the explicit content of the ads did not contravene any of the ASA codes of practice. Researchers have drawn attention to the rhetorical force in advertising of what is implied rather than explicitly stated. For example, Tanaka (1994) argues that 'covert' or implicit communication allows advertisers to make claims that they could not get away with making explicitly. The point here is that implicit communication is not accidental or incidental to advertising but a carefully considered element of advertising creative strategy. McQuarrie and Phillips (2005) suggested that advertisers can use 'images to imply messages that cannot be legally verbalized'. Crucially, researchers say that we do not have to consciously believe implied meanings in ads for them to register with us: we only have to understand what the implied message is in order for it to cast its spell over us.

Advertising's contested cultural status

Advertising is a topic that often inflames public debate, dissent and disagreement. Advertising is blamed, by some, for many social evils. It is blamed for causing obesity, for causing anorexia, for causing bad manners, reckless driving, excessive drinking – the list is long. Yet, paradoxically, advertising is also widely regarded as trivial. It tends to occupy a lowly status in our cultural hierarchy, beneath popular art, literature, movies, even stand-up comedy performers. Yet its lowly cultural status is belied by our fascination with it. We enjoy TV shows about the funniest ads and we often talk about the latest ads in our daily conversations. Cook (2001) notes this duality about advertising's cultural status. It is regarded as both trivial and powerful, banal and sinister, amusing and degrading. Even though advertising is a familiar form of communication in developed economies, we still struggle to come to terms with its contradictions. In spite of its putative triviality, it is clearly a powerful cultural presence.

Although the level of popular interest in advertising is great, there is little consensus about its role in society. Some argue that it corrupts cultural life with its insistent, hectoring presence cajoling us to buy ever-greater quantities of goods and services. Advertising intrudes into ever more social spaces, both public and private. Many schools, especially in the USA, now accept fees to give exclusive rights to commercial organisations to advertise and sell their goods on campus. Even religious observance is not immune from advertising's influence. Advertising-style slogans in brash colours promoting religious observance can be seen outside many places of worship. Evidently, advertising influences the communication norms of the very culture of which it is part. But while some have a political objection to advertising in all its forms, many people are irritated not by advertising in general but by what they see as its excesses, whether these are to do with its ubiquity or with the offensiveness of particular creative executions. Even acknowledging advertising's unique ideological force in promoting consumerism, legitimising capitalism and framing everyday experience (Elliott and Ritson, 1997) does not necessarily imply an anti-advertising stance. Few can deny that advertising is intrinsic to the creation of wealth and many would argue that it has an equally important role in the free and untrammelled expression of ideas, a socially progressive exchange of 'ideas for living', to adapt John Stuart Mill's phrase.[16] In the USA, advertising is protected under the first amendment of the constitution as a branch of free speech.

For many who accept the economic inevitability of advertising, though, its forms and styles provide particular sources of annoyance. 'Pop-up' internet ads, uninvited SMS texts and email 'spam' are a continuing irritation for many internet users. Unwanted junk mail annoys millions of householders daily. Roadside poster sites are sometimes accused of polluting the urban environment or even of distracting drivers and causing road accidents. Even conventional spot advertising is intolerable to many people because of its 'interruptive' nature – it interrupts the flow of the entertainment or news programming we were watching. In addition to the intruding on our private time and visual amenity, advertising can be a source of ethical transgression. Organisations are often accused of using advertising unethically for commercial advantage. There is persistent criticism of advertising's role on children's health and moral development, a topic discussed at greater length in Chapter 9. The rise of 'pester power' as a marketing technique and the distortion of childhood values into those of adults are two of the trends that ad agencies have been accused of initiating, or at least exploiting. All these issues reflect concern with the social responsibility, ethics and regulation of advertising.

The diversity of views advertising attracts reflects its role at the centre of what Wernick (1991) called 'promotional culture' (see also Powell, 2013). Within promotional culture, we grow accustomed to spending significant sums of money on items that are not essential for survival. We associate happiness with consumption, indeed, in many ways we define our existence in terms of consumption. As advertising and promotion make continuous consumption of branded items a culturally normal practice, other competing cultural values that encourage abstention from consumption are relatively reduced in status. Today, at least in advanced economies, over-indulgence is the norm and waste is everywhere. Changes in cultural norms and practices of consumption in some countries (such as, in the UK, the move towards eating 'fast' food and away from the family-based social ritual of the home-cooked meal) to some extent may reflect the influence of promotional culture. Deeply held values and practices are undermined and finally overthrown, partly, though not entirely, under the influence of advertising. Advertising's apparent triviality as a sub-category of popular art should not distract us from its profound cultural influence in framing and changing, as well as reflecting, the way we live.

According to some critics, advertising offers the illusion that one can live 'the good life' by buying material goods (Belk and Pollay, 1985). Yet advertising is also an easy target to blame for the weaknesses that have characterised humanity since its beginnings. Advertising and promotion are, in the end, necessary to economic growth, competition and consumer choice. How we manage the advertising that we make and see has deep implications for the wider world in which we live and it is incumbent on consumers, managers, advertising practitioners and policy makers to have a better understanding of the ways in which advertising wields its influence, in order to make informed choices about advertising policy, regulation and practice. Advertising is both a managerial discipline with profound implications for the wider economy and for the general standard of living, and (arguably) one of the most far-reaching cultural forces of our time.

The role of advertising in brand marketing

It is important to appreciate advertising's place within an inter-connected tissue of mediated communication. Marketing communications in general, and advertising in particular, are now seen as the major source of competitive advantage in consumer markets (Shimp, 2009). Other elements of the marketing mix occur prior to promotional communication, yet it is the communication that stamps the brand identity on a market. In a world of near-instant communication and rapid technology transfer, it is difficult for brand owners to police their global intellectual copyright. The brand has to stand out as a communication, so that consumers will recognise it and actively seek it out for the symbolic values it represents (Gardner and Levy, 1955). In this way, successful branding creates a quasi-monopoly and a basis for earning what economists call 'super-normal' (i.e. higher) profits. In a sense, it is a mere tautology to draw an equivalence between brands and their promotion. After all, many people have never owned a *Mercedes*, or shaved with *Gillette*, or walked in *Jimmy Choos*, but many of those people would be able to describe the brand values if asked, and they might buy it if they had the means to do so. All the totality of communication about and around a brand informs the way people think about it, and in some mysterious way this communication percolates through to balance sheets.

Decisions on pricing, design, packaging, distribution outlet and even raw materials are taken with one eye on the brand's core values and how these might be perceived in the light of media coverage of the brand. As we note, the term media coverage now includes citizen journalism, internet publications, weblogs and chatroom dialogue, Twitter and Facebook threads and scores of other social media forums, as well as copy produced by professional journalists for established print publications. It is an overstatement to argue that communication is all there is to brand marketing (but see Schultz et al., 1993; Wells, 1975), but it is a truism that advertising and marketing communications have assumed a key importance in the destiny of brands and their producing organisations.

Advertising alone does not make the brand but the successful consumer brand is, nevertheless, closely identified with its portrayal in advertising and other marketing communications media. The brand 'image', its symbolism (Levy, 1959) has come to represent a dynamic and enduring source of consumer interest (and company revenue) that brand management are keen to try to shape or control. Marketing communications do not simply portray brands: they constitute those brands in the sense that the meaning of the brand cannot be properly understood in separation from the consumer perceptions of its brand name, logo, advertising, media editorial, its portrayal in entertainment shows, peer comment on social media and the other communications associated with it. Whether brand A is better designed, more attractive, easier to use, or more useful than brand B is frequently something that cannot be decided finally and objectively. It is usually, to some degree, a matter of opinion. This is where advertising acquires its suggestive power. It occupies a realm in which consumers are actively seeking suggestions to layer consumption with new social significance. Advertisers offer us this symbolic material. Consumers are not passive dupes being taken in by exaggerated claims, we are complicit in our own exploitation. We get something out of being sold intangible dreams and unrealisable fantasies. We find that life becomes more interesting when our choice of deodorant or sugar substitute becomes a statement of personal identity and lifestyle aspiration. We must do, or we wouldn't buy this stuff.

Functionality, symbolism and the social power of brands

In order to understand the role of advertising in brand marketing it is important to focus not only on the promotional sales message but also on the symbolic meanings incorporated into the brand (Levy, 1959). Brands have functionality – they do something for consumers, they solve problems. They also have a symbolism that is largely articulated through advertising and promotion. Brands communicate symbolically in the sense that they are signs or combinations of signs (words, music, colours, logos, packaging design, and so on) that convey abstract values and ideas. For consumers, the world of marketing is a kaleidoscope of communication, the component parts of which are impossible to disentangle. When commentators say that marketing, and marketing communications, are inseparable (Leiss et al., 2005; Schultz et al., 1993: 46; Shimp, 2009: 4), they are making an important point. Every aspect of marketing management (price, distribution, product design) can carry powerfully suggestive symbolism. In an important sense, consumers occupy a symbolic economy in which the meaning of symbols is negotiated and traded through a mediated market. Marketing in general can be understood as the management of meaning (McCracken, 1990), and marketing meanings are mobilised primarily through advertising and promotion, in all their forms.

Anthropologists have long noted the importance of ownership and display of prized items for signifying social identity and status in non-consumer societies. In economically advanced societies, brands take this role as a 'cultural resource' (Holt, 2002: 87; see also Belk, 1988; Elliott and Wattanasuwan, 1998; McCracken, 2005) that enables and extends social communication. The influence of brands is such that even resistance to brands has become a defining social position. The 'social power' of brands (Feldwick, 2002: 11) refers to the meaning that goes beyond functionality and is a symbolic reference point amongst consumers and non-consumers alike. This symbolic meaning is powerfully framed by advertising and sustained through other forms of communication such as word-of-mouth, public relations, product and brand placement in entertainment media, sponsorship and package design, and through the brand's presence in social media.

Those marketing professionals more concerned with logistics, supply chain management, order fulfilment, customer service operations, quality management, production engineering and the many other concrete and prosaic activities that bring products and service to the market might not experience marketing in such terms on a daily basis. Brands are material entities and they have functional attributes. But they operate in a consumer plane in which the functional and the symbolic interpenetrate. We might convince ourselves that our purchases are based on a cold-eyed appraisal of a brand's material and functional qualities, but the market dominance of some brands over other, equally functional but less symbolically resonant ones, tells a different story. One marketing legend holds that *Pepsi* consistently beats *Coke* in blind taste tests. Whether or not this is true, it articulates the truism that a brand is far more than a tangible product.

The functionality of a brand, then, refers to what it does: the symbolism of a brand refers to what it means. One is not necessarily implied in the other. Advertising and promotion are central to the creation and maintenance of the wider symbolic meaning of brands. This wider meaning can give brands a cultural presence that goes beyond purchase and ownership. Brands such as *Marlboro*, *Mercedes–Benz*, *Gucci*, *Prada* and *Rolls–Royce* have powerful significance for non-consumers as well as for consumers. Branded items are recognised, and they carry a promise of quality and value. But the symbolic meaning the brand may have for friends, acquaintances and strangers cannot be discounted as a factor in its appeal. For example, a simple item of clothing such as a shirt will sell in far greater numbers if it is bedecked with a logo that confers a symbolic meaning on that item. Wearing a branded shirt, as opposed to an unbranded one, can be said to confer a symbolic status on the wearer because of the values of affluence and social privilege and taste the brand represents (Schor, 1998: 47, cited in Szmigin, 2003: 139). As with implied meaning in advertisements, we may be fully aware that this, seen literally, may be a risible or preposterous notion, but that does not necessarily undermine the communicative force of the brand's symbolism. Brands have a cultural resonance (Campbell, 2013; Schroeder and Salzer-Morling, 2005) that is not limited to their materiality.

Marketing is replete with symbolism in many forms. Marketing activities of all kinds can be seen to combine signs that resonate with cultural meanings (Barthes, 2000; Umiker-Sebeok, 1997; Williamson, 1978). The futuristic design of a *Dyson* vacuum cleaner or the clean, aesthetic lines of an *iPod* have the powerful appeal of implied values that are very important to the consumer. A *Rolex* watch might be a well-made jewellery item with time-keeping utility but the *Rolex* brand is best known as an ostentatious symbol of wealth. Rodeo Drive in Beverly Hills, California, Madison Avenue, New York, and Knightsbridge, London, are home to many designer stores because these locations have become culturally identified with prestige retail outlets. The location and architecture of the retail outlet, as well as the price, can often carry a powerful symbolism for the brands.

Brands and integrated marketing communication

Many other aspects of organisational activity not usually categorised as communication can carry particular meanings. Perhaps the most visible aspects of commercial communication for consumers are advertisements placed in above-the-line media such as TV, outdoor, the press, cinema or commercial radio. But organisations know that consumers' experience of brands is integrated in a powerful sense: consumers will not normally distinguish between different communication channels when they think of a brand or an organisation. So, organisations need to be conscious of the way that their various communications can be interpreted and of how consistent these interpretations may be with those from other communication sources. This is the logic of the integrated marketing communication (IMC) process (Schultz et al., 1993).

For example, as consumers encounter corporate communications through vehicle liveries, letterhead design, corporate advertising, staff uniforms, telephone conversations with organisational staff and press coverage of the organisation's activities, they will assimilate these experiences into their overall understanding of the brand. They will also assimilate news coverage, social media chatter, blog comment, press and PR and any number of other sources into their aggregated idea of a brand. Corporate identity is a distinct field of research and practice (Melewar and Wooldridge, 2001) but much of its importance lies in the connection consumers make between corporations and their brands in an IMC landscape. More broadly still, in advanced economies, marketing activity can lie behind a huge majority of the images we see. The ways in which we interpret, understand and use them are central to our experience of marketing and consumption (Schroeder, 2002). In a promotional culture (Powell, 2013) media brands interpenetrate each other and commercial logic permeates media content. It is in this multidimensional mediascape that brand management have to try to maintain some kind of stability of meaning for their brands. Social media have facilitated consumer activism and engagement around brands as never before, and control over the brand image is now a highly nuanced and iterative process. To this end, the integration of different but thematically linked brand communications across a number of media channels is now a default position for most promotional campaigns.

There are yet more subtle dimensions of communication to consider. In the Veblen effect (Veblen, [1899] 1970), demand for a product reacts inversely with price changes. Price signifies the quality positioning of the brand and this can be an important influence on demand for very expensive, prestige items. Although it is anti-competitive for manufacturers to enforce prices on retailers, nonetheless many brand owners do not like to have their product discounted because of the potential threat to consumers' perceptions of quality. The high price of prestige brands is an essential part of their brand positioning, although, increasingly, even prestige brands are broadening their markets by supplying stock of slightly inferior quality for 'discount' outlets.

The architecture and floor design of retail stores can also carry heavy signification. In the early 1900s US department store retailers were well aware of the power of impressive architecture in creating environments that inspired consumers to consume (Marchand, 1998). The interior design of retail outlets is also a powerful signifier in the marketing process. Retail organisations often commission detailed research into in-store consumer behaviour in order to help the design to cohere with the brand image of the store and to enhance sales per square foot of floorspace. For some fashion retail brands, such as fading clothes brand *Abercrombie and Fitch*, every detail, from the volume of in-store music (60 decibels) to the look of the 'models' (i.e. retail assistants), is part of the brand symbolism. At the time of writing, A&F is said to be losing its position in its target markets of under 25s, and the fact that one of the authors has been known to buy A&F clothes *for their comfort* (in size XXL) probably isn't helping.

As consumers, then, we understand brands holistically by assimilating meanings from many diverse channels of communication. Media editorial, direct mail shots, customer service encounters, television and press advertising and retail store displays, brand logos, social media and website news and opinion, product design and price relative to competition all converge to inform the consumer's understanding of a given brand. Include word-of-mouth and personal experience of brand usage, and it becomes clear that we cannot normally remember which particular communication or experience was significant in forming our enduring impression of a particular brand. Brands subsist symbolically as a nebulous and mutable, yet enduring, memory of many kinds of consumer experience. Brands have a tangible, concrete reality, of course; they are created through human and technological processes, they require resources and they usually (though not always, as in the case of virtual corporations) occupy office or factory space. But, most importantly, a brand also has a secret life, as symbolic abstraction. This abstraction, sometimes called the brand image, in ad man David Ogilvy's term, acts in concert with its more tangible dimensions to frame and support the overall idea of that brand.

The integrated perspective of this book does not conflate disciplines or media channels that are, rightly, considered by managers to be separate and distinct. Rather, it acknowledges the blurring and convergence of communication media sources in consumers' outlook. It also acknowledges that communications act interdependently: ideas can be reinforced through more than one channel, providing more than one route to consumer activation. The assimilation of brand advertising and marketing into mainstream entertainment media, discussed in detail in Chapter 6, is perhaps the most telling aspect of marketing in the era of media convergence (Hackley, 2003a, 2013a).

Chapter summary

This chapter has introduced the topic of advertising and outlined the key themes of the book. It has discussed major changes in the advertising environment that are driving new forms of advertising. These changes are behind a radical shift in advertising management as advertising agencies try to think of process innovations that will keep them at the centre of the brand and marketing communications world. The changes they face focus around the impact of social media, mobile and the convergence of media channels via the internet, and the accompanying changes in media consumption patterns. Consumers are drifting away from traditional mass media, and newspapers, magazines, TV and radio channels are all trying to develop new business models based around web presence and digital communication. Advertising isn't going away, but what we understand as advertising is broadening. The chapter also discussed general issues of advertising concerning its economic, social and business function. Finally, the chapter looked at the nature of brands and the importance of advertising and promotion in framing brand symbolism. Now the topic has been introduced, Chapter 2 will look at the long history of theorising about advertising.

■ Review Questions

1. Make a list of all the forms of advertising and promotion that you have encountered or heard of in the last month. Does the list surprise you? Can you think of any social spaces that have not yet been exploited by advertisers?

2. After reading this chapter, has your view of advertising's social role changed? Make a list of arguments in favour of advertising and contrast it with a list of arguments against advertising. Convene a study group to discuss their implications: can the opposing viewpoints be reconciled?

3. List all the communication sources you can think of that might potentially influence your perception of a brand. Can you think of ways in which your perception of three brands has been so influenced? In your view, which communications channel was most influential in forming your impression of the brand? Why was this?

4. Gather all the promotional material you can for two brands. What meanings do you feel are implied by the imagery, the typography and the other features of these promotions? Could the meanings be interpreted differently by different people?

CASE STUDY

Content marketing – the new frontier

These days, adverts often look like movies, movies look like adverts, adverts refer to news events, brands are news stories, and PR, well, PR is *everything*. Convergence is the term used to describe the way that the internet is acting like a sort of black hole, sucking in all traditional media channels. The media genres are merging too: movies are being made by brands, some movies are effectively extended advertisements for the brands placed within them, and some viral videos achieve exposure that is beyond the dreams of most movies or advertisements. The new frontier of marketing is *content*, the catch-all term that dissolves genres and media channels into one, seamless, media experience, viewed on any of a number of wireless connected devices. The common thread is the presence of brands, in, around or behind the content. Here are some examples.

Jaguar financed a movie to accompany the launch of its new *F Type* model in 2012. The *F Type* is Jaguar's first new sports car in fifty years, according to *Advertising Age*. The makers of the 12 minute film, called *Desire* and directed by a chap who has *Dr Who* amongst his credits, deny that it is merely a pale repeat of *BMW*'s famous series of short movies a decade ago. *Desire* stars *Homeland* actor Damian Lewis and the plot revolves around a car chase through a Chilean desert. To top off the tie-ins, Lana Del Ray, no slouch in viral marketing herself, sings a new song to go with the movie. Ms Del Ray, or Ms Grant, as she was formerly known, launched her career with a huge YouTube hit. *Desire* airs through video sharing on social media, principally YouTube, and the plot includes no promotion at all, other than the presence of the car as the real star.

This type of movie was kicked off by *BMW*'s 2001 effort *The Hire*, directed by Guy Ritchie. The plot entails pop star Madonna being driven erratically to a gig by movie actor Clive Owen.[17] Films like these have probably generated as much newsprint and social media sharing as a product placement in a Bond movie, with the added advantage of total creative control.

(Continued)

(Continued)

In content of a different style, pop star Miley Cyrus created a huge media splash with a clip of a performance at the 2013 VMA awards show that went viral and turned Miley, formerly widely known by the name of her TV character Hannah Montana, into a global star. This kind of content is very much a marketing entity – it was carefully staged and planned, and the clip was soon followed by a record release that rode to number 1 on the publicity wave. Social media content tends to be dominated by corporate interests, but there are still examples of autonomous content uploaded by consumers that keeps a vague sense of authenticity in social media. The Miley phenomenon was voted top content of 2013 by the Huffington Post UK and Ogilvy PR.[18]

Media content of any kind can be turned to a marketing purpose, but the term is typically used with reference to entertainment, news or spectacle that is branded in some way, and is shared spontaneously. This 'earned' media (as opposed to bought advertising spots) is valuable to brands because it reflects genuine consumer engagement (though not, necessarily, sales). The logic is often that a brand can earn favour with its audiences and cultural 'share of voice' by giving away entertaining stuff for free. Perhaps a more sinister aspect of content marketing is the development of 'native' advertising. This term is usually reserved for digital promotion that is 'native' to the page, so that the consumer does not treat it as promotion. In fact, some critics argue that native advertising is advertorial without the 'advertorial' heading.

At its best, content evinces all the things marketing should be about. It's a blank slate, or a blank screen, waiting to activate consumers through great writing, creativity, wit, technical adroitness and visual and musical imagination. Confusingly, advertising itself often looks more like content, with entertaining narrative forms and no hard sell. If you think of a continuum with editorial in the middle, entertainment on the left and advertising on the right, you can see the whole line collapsing into each other. Which is good, if you want your media content to entertain. If you want disinterested information, though, it could be confusing. It's a world designed by and for the quicksilver minds of well-informed, media-savvy, cynical consumers. Most readers, though, don't reflect critically on the way we respond to a text. We just respond.

Case Questions

1. List all the examples of media content your group can think of. Is the category of promotional communication described as 'branded content' helpful, or too vague? Can you think of a better label?

2. Social media shares have become more than merely an extension of viewing or reader figures for an advertisement, but a proxy for consumer engagement. In what ways do you feel that social media shares of ads might reflect benefits to brands?

3. Bought media space refers to advertising on bought media. Earned media space refers to social media shares of a piece of promotional content, such as a viral ad. Compare and contrast the benefits to advertisers of bought media space and earned media space.

4. Design a concept for a social networking website. How would you make your concept popular, and, if you were successful in building significant traffic, how do you think you could monetise that traffic ('by selling the site to Google' isn't an acceptable answer).

Useful journal articles

(These Sage articles can be accessed on the book website)

Stephanie O'Donohoe (2001) 'Living with ambivalence: attitudes to advertising in postmodern times', *Marketing Theory*, 1 (Mar): 91–108.

Anne M. Cronin (2004) 'Currencies of commercial exchange: advertising agencies and the promotional imperative', *Journal of Consumer Culture*, 4 (Nov.): 339–60.

William E. Kilbourne (2004) 'Sustainable communication and the dominant social paradigm: can they be integrated?', *Marketing Theory*, 4 (Sept.): 187–208.

Mark W. Stuhlfaut and Craig Davis (2010) 'The teaching of advertising management: essential, elective, or extraneous', *Journalism & Mass Communication Educator*, 65 (3–4): 265–82.

Lynne Ciochetto (2011) 'Advertising and value formation: the power of multinational companies', *Current Sociology*, 59 (2): 173–85.

Siu Yu Hsu and Gina G. Barker (2013) 'Individualism and collectivism in Chinese and American television advertising', *International Communication Gazette*, 75 (8): 695–714.

■ ■ Further reading ■

Dholakia, N. (2012) 'Being critical in marketing studies: the imperative of macro perspectives', *Journal of Macromarketing*, 32 (2): 220–25.

Hackley, C. (2013) *Marketing in Context: Setting the Scene.* Basingstoke: Palgrave Macmillan.

Hackley, C. (ed.) (2009) *Advertising.* Sage 'Library in Marketing'. London: Sage. 3 volumes: Volume 1: *Advertising Management*; Volume 2: *Advertising Culture*; Volume 3: *Advertising Science.*

Jenkins, H. (2008) *Convergence Culture: Where Old and New Media Collide.* New York: New York University Press.

O'Reilly, D. (2006) 'Commentary: Branding ideology', *Marketing Theory*, 6 (2): 263–71.

Powell, H. (ed.) (2013) *Promotional Culture in an Era of Convergence.* Abingdon: Taylor and Francis.

Notes

1. www.huffingtonpost.co.uk/2013/10/21/guide-to-the-native-age_n_4136861.html accessed 8.2.2014
2. http://247wallst.com/media/2014/01/31/twitter-market-value-tops-target-and-cbs/ accessed 8.2.2014

3. http://america.aljazeera.com/articles/2014/1/31/a-football-game-withoutcommercials notonthissideoftheatlantic.html accessed 7.2.2014
4. www.independent.co.uk/arts-entertainment/tv/news/if-you-want-to-watch-x-factor-youll-have-to-watch-the-churned-2368637.html accessed 19.3.2014
5. www.theguardian.com/media/2014/feb/07/lego-movie-itv-ad-break-lenny-henry accessed 8.2.2014
6. www.youtube.com/watch?v=HSbYBzUEQlc accessed 8.2.2014
7. www.latimes.com/entertainment/tv/showtracker/la-et-st-coca-cola-super-bowl-ad-stirs-controversy-20140203,0,1361331.story#axzz2sbl6JaIo accessed 6.2.2014
8. www.youtube.com/watch?v=VQ3d3KigPQM accessed 19.3.2014
9. www.hollywoodreporter.com/news/tic-tac-worst-breath-on-earth-viral-video-310973 accessed 6.2.2014
10. www.kake.com/home/headlines/Hutchinson-native-produces-viral-holiday-flash-mob-235168221.html accessed 6.2.2014
11. www.huffingtonpost.co.uk/2013/07/15/david-beckham-sky-sports-advert-video_n_3597268.html accessed 6.2.2014
12. www.dove.us/social-mission/campaign-for-real-beauty.aspx accessed 7.2.2014
13. www.youtube.com/watch?v=wT4DR_ae_4o accessed 2.2.2014
14. www.youtube.com/watch?v=UDTZCgsZGeA accessed 4.2.2014
15. www.ldoceonline.com/dictionary/wassup accessed 5.2.2014
16. Mill, John Stuart. *On Liberty*. London: Longman, Roberts & Green, 1869; Bartleby.com, 1999. www.bartleby.com/130/ accessed 8.2.2014
17. www.youtube.com/watch?v=TNquj6HTA78 accessed 6.2.2014
18. www.huffingtonpost.co.uk/2013/12/11/best-of-2013_n_4425766.html accessed 8.2.2014.

2 Theorising Advertising

Chapter outline

This chapter is organised around three overlapping traditions of advertising theory. One concerns theories that have been developed by and for advertising practitioners. Another, labelled as linear information processing theory, draws its methods and assumptions mainly from the cognitive and communication sciences. The third tradition, referred to here as socio-cultural theory, draws on disciplines such as cultural anthropology, sociology and literary theory for its key concepts and perspectives. The chapter highlights some of the continuing contradictions raised by advertising theory as it plays out both in academia and professional practice.

Key chapter content

- Why theorise advertising and promotion?
- Practice-based advertising theory
- Information processing theory in advertising
- Socio-cultural theory in advertising
- Levels of explanation in advertising theory – cognitive, social and cultural

Why theorise advertising and promotion?

Business people, marketing and advertising professionals included, rarely have much time for theory. Theory is popularly understood as a synonym for the complex, esoteric, or abstract. The term 'in theory' is often used in a pejorative sense to refer to ideas that are seen as irrelevant, impractical or obscure. But theory can be seen in another, more constructive way. It can be viewed as a form of everyday understanding that allows us a sense of control over our world and, sometimes, helps us to predict outcomes based on previous experience or well-grounded assumptions. Rudimentary theories allow us to understand our world in ways that are not possible if we are solely concerned with concrete experience.

In this chapter, theory is considered in terms of a rough guide to practical action, rather than in terms of formal social scientific criteria. The terms theory and model are mis-used a lot in business studies, and we will not try to put that right here. For our purposes, we will treat theories, or models, as devices that enable some degree of explanation and prediction. We all live by implicit theories: knowing that rain gets you wet therefore you should put on a coat before you leave the house may strike you as obvious, but it involves an abstraction from particular experiences of getting wet and it informs our behaviour. It may not be as complex as a theory of relativity but it is the kind of theorising that most of us are familiar with. Practical theory guides behaviour and action in the workplace even though it may be implicit rather than explicit. Noted advertising man turned academic Arthur Kover (1995) studied the implicit theories of communication used by creative professionals in New York advertising agencies. They each had their own implicit theory of communication and this guided their problem solving strategies in addressing creative briefs. In another study (Hackley, 2003b) account team professionals in London agencies worked to differing implicit models of the consumer. These models implied quite different ways of understanding, and therefore of communicating with, consumers.

Theorising informally allows us to use our imagination to move from the concrete to the abstract and to attempt to generalise from the particular. We can compare and combine ideas and speculate on new ways of understanding the world. Our understanding of any social phenomenon requires some theoretical dimension in order to raise it beyond the trivial. One can say without fear of contradiction that books are made up of printed words, but to compare different books and to offer views on their qualities one has to invoke informal theories of literary criticism on matters of, say, prose style ('this book is well written'), theories of narrative ('the plot was exciting') or theories of dramatic characterisation ('the characters were not believable'). We have an opinion of what constitutes good writing or effective characterisation even though we may not be at all familiar with intellectual traditions of literary criticism.

Advertising is a field particularly concerned with human communication, thought and behaviour. It can be seen as applied psychology (Hackley, 2013b), or perhaps applied cultural anthropology. As we shall see in this chapter, academic theory in advertising has drawn on the disciplines of cognitive and social psychology, sociology, anthropology, cybernetics, mathematics, communication science and literary theory, to name just a few. Advertising professionals are practical people who develop experience in particular areas and know what works for them in given situations, but advertising as a category can hardly be spoken of at all without some implicit theoretical assumptions to guide us. In this book, then, theory is not considered as a byword for obscurity. At a rudimentary but decidedly non-trivial level it simply allows us to articulate the world in ways that go beyond the unimportant or the obvious.

Different stakeholders in advertising theory

Clients would like proof that their investment in advertising gives them a good return. Ad agency account planners would like theories that give them strategic insights into consumers (Hackley, 2003b). Agency creatives would like theories that show why their idea should get made. Regulators, consumer groups and policy makers would like theories that help them to understand the effect advertising has on socially problematic phenomena such as drinking alcohol or eating healthily.

Unfortunately for all these stakeholders, advertising remains an enigma in spite of its 100-year history of practice, thought, theory and research. There is no lack of theory – it's just that there is lack of agreement around it. As consumers, we do not agree about what advertising means, what it does, or how it does it. From the practitioner side, too, there are stark disagreements about how, and indeed if, advertising 'works' (see Hackley, 2010; Heath and Feldwick, 2008;[1] Vakratsas and Ambler, 1999); in what ways it influences consumers (or doesn't) (Ehrenberg et al., 2002); what role creativity plays in effective advertising (Smith and Yang, 2004[2]), how advertising strategy should be generated for best effect, and on how advertising budgets should be spent most efficiently. Advertising agencies would really like to be able to prove definitively to clients that their campaigns achieve their objectives. They cannot, because there isn't a theory that allows them to do so. What they can do, is to write up case studies of their campaigns that marshal circumstantial evidence that is sometimes quiet compelling. However, scientific proof it is not. Spending money on advertising and promotion remain, to some extent, a leap of faith for clients.

The advertising industry has enjoyed global growth and influence on a huge scale in spite of uncertainty about its theoretical foundations. It is, perhaps, unrealistic to seek a general theory of advertising, given the complexity of this communication form. Advertising has to serve many stakeholders, including main board executives, shareholders, advertising agencies, consumers, regulators, governments and citizens. It applies in many different situations. As a communication form it is complex, since it can combine music, visual imagery and written or spoken words in a huge variety of narrative forms and on a wide range of media channels. Even tiny elements of an advertisement, such as the choice of font, the colour of a background, or the intonation with which an actor recites a script, could potentially be decisive in the interpretation of that communication. Advertising speaks to a huge variety of quite different demographic, ethnic, national socio-economic and sub-cultural groups. The idea that advertising 'works' in one way in all conditions to all people is clearly an oversimplification. Theories serve different vested interests, depending on what they want to argue about advertising – that it sells product, that it doesn't, that it operates on consumers in unethical ways, that it doesn't, that it causes social ills, or that it doesn't, and so on. Theory is essential to understanding, but it is equally essential that we understand the limitations of theory.

Practitioners seem to manage well enough without formal theories, although they do use them in an ad hoc and often implicit way to guide research (Hackley and Kover, 2007). Agencies are always looking for a competitive edge and theory often lends itself to claims that one agency can deliver better value for the client's advertising budget. Cornelissen and Lock (2002) have argued that theoretical developments in advertising do influence practice, not always by changing it but by supplying new conceptual vocabularies to articulate practice. For their part, agencies are quick to latch on to the latest buzzy concept, whether that it semiotics, psychographics, neuro-marketing or another, to help convince clients that they, unlike other agencies, have the inside track on how advertising works.

SNAPSHOT 2.1

Interpreting advertising

The strategies consumers bring to reading and interpreting advertising are still relatively under-explored by researchers. One old story illustrates the intractable problem advertisers face in trying to predict how consumers will interpret an advertising communication. A 1950s cigarette brand was advertised in the UK with cinema ads. The ads featured an actor alone on London Bridge at night, mock heroically lighting up a *Strand* cigarette to the accompanying strapline, 'You're never alone with a *Strand*'.[3] The print version of the ad is reproduced as ad number 3 in the colour section of the book. The brand failed to sell and it transpired that cinema audiences felt that the user was a lonely soul who couldn't find friends. To ad agency types familiar with

Hollywood movie heroes such as Humphrey Bogart, it seemed inconceivable that cigarette smoking could be seen as anything but the act of a streetwise tough guy whose heroic destiny was to be alone. The audience decoded a different meaning from the one the agency had planned to encode into the message. The reason for the miscommunication was not known: it may have been the actor was unconvincing as a hero, or the clothes, the set or the props – all may have undermined the intended effect. Today such a mistake would be unlikely to happen. Most major advertising campaigns are carefully pre-tested on trial audiences before launch. The story reveals the subtlety and indeterminacy of meaning in advertising communication. It also illustrates the truism that the people who make advertisements are from different milieux to the audiences at whom they are aimed.

Implicit and explicit communication in advertising

The importance of the implicit in communication may seem self-evident, yet the concept that has dominated research in advertising has been the idea of a clear, explicit, verbalised and unproblematic 'message'. Of what, though, this message is comprised is hard to say. As noted in the previous chapter, advertising can be seen as a form of 'social communication' (Leiss et al., 2005) that operates on many dimensions. As a complex communication form, advertising can be understood not only in terms of an engineering model of 'information' transmission, but also in terms of a vehicle of meaning which is interpreted in symbolic ways by different audiences (McCracken, 1987; Sherry, 1987).

One problem facing advertising theorists has been finding a popular and accessible way to theorise both its explicit and implicit elements. Human face-to-face communication has been shown to be about the gestures, vocal tone, emotional timbre, poise and gravitas, facial expression and social context, as well as about the verbal content. Words are important; they are the infrastructure around which persuasive arguments are built. But what listeners take from such communication is not determined solely by the words, by any means. Advertising theory, both practitioner and academic, has tended to privilege the verbalised content of promotional 'messages', the explicit communication, and underplay the elements of communication that are implicit, or those to which conscious attention is not paid (Heath and Feldwick, 2008).

One reason for this is that it is, simply, easier to conceive of advertising as a verbal message that is processed consciously by individual receivers. Another reason is that acknowledging the implicit elements of advertising and promotion opens up controversial issues of 'subliminal' or hidden influence. Much advertising theory has been conceived with one eye on the latent public unease articulated by Vance Packard's (1957) idea of advertisers as 'hidden persuaders' engaged in sinister and underhand manipulation (Hackley, 2007).[4] A focus on the rational, the conscious and the verbal, deflects the charge of manipulation quite neatly, but at the considerable price of over-simplifying the subject matter.

So, having outlined some of the problems and possibilities of advertising theory, Chapter 2 will now begin to explore the topic in terms of three traditions of theory: practitioner theory, information processing theory and socio-cultural theory (Hackley, 2010).

Practice-based advertising theory

'Reason why' and 'USP' advertising

The surprising thing about advertising theory is that, in spite of the huge volume of academic and practitioner research, significant elements of it have changed little in a century. Early advertising theory was based on direct experience, though informed by psychological studies. It was focused mainly on improving practice. John E. Kennedy (1904) is credited with one of the earliest attempts when he wrote that advertising was 'salesmanship in print'. Kennedy was at the Lord and Thomas agency, later to become the biggest agency of its era in the world. This was where American advertising pioneer Albert D. Lasker started the first school of advertising copywriting, applying Kennedy's principles. The idea that a direct analogy could be drawn between face-to-face selling and advertising on a medium appeared self-evident to advertisers of the time.

Kennedy subsequently developed the 'reason why' approach to copywriting (Fox, 1984), a technique that led to Rosser Reeves's idea of the Unique Selling Proposition (USP) some decades later (McDonald and Scott, 2007). The USP is the single thing that gives the consumer a reason to buy. Advertising agencies today often refer to the 'proposition', by which they mean the premise of an advertisement, the single idea that they want consumers to get from the ad. The 'proposition' is still the key concept in the creative advertising development process today (Heath and Feldwick, 2008). Kennedy's (1904) analogy between (print) advertising and personal selling has proved equally enduring.

Other well-known developments in practitioner theory for advertising include Bill Bernbach's emphasis on creativity, David Ogilvy's 'brand personality' and Leo Burnett's use of dramatic realism, using images of housewives at the kitchen sink, but looking impossibly glamorous, in advertising that reached out to consumers' daily experience. Creativity in advertising is a contentious topic, since there is little agreement on what it is or on whether it is useful. For some hard-headed practitioners, the idea of creativity smacks of the kind of self-indulgence that can lead agencies to try to make advertising that forgets about the client and instead make advertising that is 'arty' for its own sake. For others, creativity is the fundamental contribution advertising agencies make to business: they are, after all, ideas factories, and creativity is the stuff they sell, however it may be conceived. For still others, creativity is a component of the best advertising that must be used judiciously alongside more pragmatic considerations. After all, countless ads today turn out to have been copied from internet videos, or they use the latest photographic or animation technique for visual effect – advertising certainly need not always be creative in the sense of being original. On the other hand, for many creative professionals in advertising, the purpose of advertising is the same as the purpose of art – to activate the audience, to inspire them and make them think (Hackley and Kover, 2007).

One commonplace distinction that is often used with regard to advertising is between 'hard' and 'soft' sell. Sometimes, compelling creativity is thought to establish and build the brand equity, anthropomorphising the brand in value terms that stimulate responses of affection and perhaps loyalty, from consumers. The other side, the 'hard sell' theories, follow the tradition of Kennedy and Reeves, and the equally noted Claude Hopkins (McDonald and Scott, 2007), and are not associated with stunning creativity. They tend to be direct sales appeals that rely more on rational persuasion than creative activation, in keeping with their objective of generating a spike in sales in the short term.

Other practitioners in advertising soon began to burnish their informal theories with academic work. Of these, Edward Strong (1929) and Harry D. Kitson (1921) can probably claim the longest legacy. Strong's book *The Psychology of Selling and Advertising* and Kitson's (1921) *The Mind of the Buyer* melded psychological principles to the evolving work in theories of personal selling. Their work was influential and added some scientific starch to a rudimentary theory of persuasive communication known as AIDA that is still repeated in almost every textbook on advertising and marketing, including this one. The Attention–Interest–Desire–Action (A–I–D–A) model for personal selling, adapted to advertising, remains by far the most influential theory in the field. AIDA is often cited alongside the 'transmission' model of mass communication from mathematical communication science, also known as linear information processing theory. Both are described below.

Another important academic influence on advertising theory that is worth mentioning here came from one of the originators of the behavioural psychology, John B. Watson. Watson (1924) was a psychology professor who left academia and applied his theories of learning and reinforcement to a successful career in advertising with J. Walter Thompson and later the William Esty agency. Watson's ideas may have fallen out of vogue long ago, but of all the advertising theorists, he is possibly the most well known and his approach can be seen today in some learning systems.

Information processing theory in advertising

The Shannon–Weaver communication model

'Information processing' is a term that sums up a vast tradition of advertising theory. It encompasses not only a theory of communication but an implied theory of human cognition. The information processing model was originally devised to model the mathematical efficiency of technical communication channels (Shannon, 1948; Weaver and Shannon, 1963) but was applied to mass communication (Katz and Lazarsfeld, 1955; Lasswell, 1948; Lazarsfeld, 1941; Schramm, 1948). Applied to human communication, the theory assumes that humans 'process' data much in the same way as computers or other machines. It is also called the 'transmission' model since data are transmitted to the receiver. It is linear, in the sense that it can be modelled as if there is a straight line from sender to receiver and back.

There are many variations on the model but its basic components remain the same in most applications. There is a sender, or a 'source', and a receiver. The message is encoded into a form that allows transmission, and then is sent via a medium or channel of communication to be decoded by the receiver. There is a feedback loop in the model, so that it can be determined whether or not the message was efficiently delivered. If the message was encoded accurately, and transmitted via the correct medium, the only reason for miscommunication would be 'noise', which refers to anything that interferes with the transmission or decoding/encoding process.

Whether or not the classic information processing model (Figure 2.1) is appropriate for human communication is a highly contested matter. Nevertheless, in most marketing textbooks and those of many other disciplines including communication studies, it is reproduced faithfully and presented as if none of its key elements nor its founding metaphor are in any way problematic.

It is easy to see how the analogy between machine communication and human communication could be applied to a simple model of advertising. An advertisement can be conceived as a message, especially if one refers to the ideas of Kennedy and Hopkins. The message has to be encoded by the sender (the advertising agency creative team) into a form that will be decoded successfully by the receiver, who is of course the consumer. Encoding will put the message into a form in which communication is possible on the available media channels. In Kennedy's day, this would consist of print advertising. With the development of broadcast media it would be possible to include sound and, later, moving pictures. The challenge for the advertising creative is that they want the receiver to decode the same message that the advertisers encoded into the communication in order to retrieve the meaning intended.

The surrounding environment may have 'noise' of various forms that distracts from the message. Noise can be construed metaphorically as anything

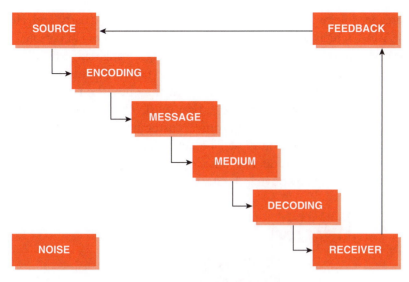

Figure 2.1   The classic transmission model of communication

that might disrupt the communication by, say, distracting the attention of the receiver, or confusing their decoding process. In an aural communication it may be literal noise that disrupts the communicative process. With visual communications such as roadside advertising poster sites, noise may be all the activities of an urban road that might distract a person's attention from the poster, such as pedestrians, cars, shops, stray dogs, or anything else. This simple conceptualisation of advertising communication has many descriptive uses. It has been a mainstay of marketing communications and advertising texts because of its economy and descriptive scope. It can be applied to almost any communications scenario and will have a degree of superficial applicability. The idea of the advertising 'message' still drives much thinking in advertising, and as a practical construct the linear information processing model has proved useful. But as a theoretical explanation for what is happening in advertising communication it has serious limitations.

The AIDA (Attention–Interest–Desire–Action) model

A theoretical model is no more than a textual representation that captures by analogy some, but by no means all, of the features of the phenomenon it purports to represent. In other words, models as theoretical representations have weaknesses. Before discussing these in more detail, though, we will revisit the AIDA model of persuasive advertising communication. This maps easily onto the classic information processing model of communication because of its linearity and its cognitive focus, and it has generated a host of variations that fall under the category 'hierarchy-of-effects theories' in advertising (Barry and Howard, 1990). AIDA, which, as noted above, was designed as a theory of personal selling before it was co-opted to model mediated selling through advertising, is based on a simple set of sequences that are supposed to take the consumer from a state of indifference to one of commitment, when they buy the product or service that is being advertised. Firstly, the advertiser must get the consumer's attention. An indifferent consumer will not become a customer. Following that, the ad has to generate the consumer's interest. The next stage in the persuasive process is to elicit desire for the product or service being sold. Finally, the consumer is moved to take action, by buying the item (see Figure 2.2).

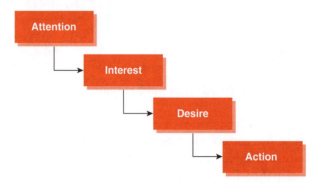

Figure 2.2   The Attention–Interest–Desire–Action (AIDA) model of persuasive advertising communication

The AIDA model assumes that consumers are essentially indifferent to the offer and need to have their attention grabbed. After that, they (and we) have to be pushed along a continuum of persuasion until we buy the product. When the AIDA model is conceived in terms of mass communication to thousands or millions of potential consumers through advertising, this process can be seen in terms of a gradual and incremental effect. As consumers we have many communications competing for our attention. If an advertiser wants to sell us a new product or service, then on this model they first have to get our attention. This could take many attempts – we might view an advertisement many times before we find ourselves sufficiently interested to pay explicit attention to it. Once we have done that it may take many more exposures, or even many more campaigns, to elicit our interest, evoke our desire for the brand, and finally to provoke us into actually acting on the message by purchasing the advertised brand.

Hierarchy-of-effects

The logic of AIDA, extended from a face-to-face sales conversation to a mass mediated advertising market, takes the human consumer as an entity that is resistant to persuasion but susceptible to a successive accretion of persuasive inputs. In other words, we are gradually persuaded to accept the sales message as our resistance is undermined by the accumulation of messages. The 'hierarchy-of-effect' theory represents 'compounding probabilities' (Percy et al., 2001), as each step in the process is a necessary condition for the subsequent step. The 'hierarchy-of-effects' tradition has spawned many theories that are designed to improve the efficiency and effectiveness of campaign planning (Barry and Howard, 1990; see also Lavidge and Steiner, 1961; Rossiter et al., 1991; Vaughn, 1986). Most importantly, they all conceive of advertising persuasion as a rational and self-conscious process through which an individual consumer can eventually be persuaded to buy by the force of the message. The assumption is that any advertisement can be reduced analytically to the notion of the univocal 'message'. There is no scope in AIDA or information processing theories for implicit communication or contested interpretations of advertising.

Cognition, affect and conation models

Some variations on advertising theory have incorporated emotion, humour or other intangible elements into an over-arching information processing scheme. One well-known generic model incorporated emotionality into purchase decisions by using a three-stage conceptualisation: cognitive, affective and conative, known colloquially as 'think–feel–do' (for discussions see Bagozzi et al., 1979; Barnard and Ehrenberg, 1997; Lutz, 1977). The cognitive element persuades the consumer on a rational level by including facts about the product or service qualities. The affective dimension gets the consumer to respond emotionally to the appeal, by, say, including images of attractive, happy families or by making the consumer laugh, and therefore encouraging affection toward the brand. Finally, conation refers to the behaviour elicited by the advertisements, for example by including a direct-response coupon or telephone number for the customer to call.

Many automobile advertisements seem to conform to the cognitive (thinking) affective (feeling) and conative (doing) model when they picture a beautiful car to strike at the prospect's sense of aesthetics and aspiration, slot in an attractive driver or happy family to promote projective identification and elicit desire, underpin the picture with detailed information about petrol consumption and speed, and finally add a direct response mechanism for the consumer to send off for a brochure or apply for a test drive.

The think–feel–do scheme tells us why many ads combine rational with emotional appeals. It cannot tell us which of those appeals will prove more powerful or what the right balance of rational–emotional appeal should be to create a successful advertisement. In other words, like many theories and models in marketing it may have some explanatory value, but no predictive or normative value.

It cannot tell which ads will be successful and which will not, and it cannot tell us how to construct a successful ad. Consumers do not conform to convenient textbook models. Some drivers buy a car for its colour, some for its speed, some for its practicality. Many are influenced by the brand image, and many drivers buy the same brand of car repeatedly even though there are many others from which to choose which perform equally well. More and more car ads like to play with the 'emotional realm' (Percy and Elliott, 2009), examples include *Honda*'s 'Choir', *Skoda* and *VW* ads.[5] Clearly, there is no formula that fits every model or every buyer.

Advantages of information processing theory

The information processing model and its associated theories of persuasion, notably AIDA and the other hierarchy-of-effect family of theories, have some advantages. One is that they allow the complexity of advertising communication to be reduced to a simplified and easily recollected model that appears to fit any communication scenario. The shared assumptions of AIDA and information processing theory means that any construct of cognitive psychology can be the subject of research into 'intermediate' advertising effects. For example, attention is a sub-field of psychological research and theory with relevance for this model. So are the psychological research fields of memory, attitude, emotion and behaviour. Research into intermediate advertising effects focuses on the elements that appear to be sequentially necessary in order for persuasion to take place. For example, it is assumed that if consumers like an advertisement because of its humour they are more likely to respond emotionally to the brand, and therefore more likely to change their attitude from negative or indifferent to positive. The assumption is that purchase is then more likely to result. Many studies are conducted on consumer memory to try to understand which advertising formats prompt the best recall scores, on the assumption that remembering an ad is a stage in the process leading to purchase.

Criticisms of information processing theory

The use of information processing models of communication in advertising, and related linear theories of persuasive communication such as AIDA has been criticised on many grounds (see Stern, 1993a, for an overview, and also Heath and Feldwick, 2008; Hackley, 2010). Plausible as they may seem, their usefulness as a teaching device for advertising and marketing education has also been questioned (Buttle, 1994) because of the extent to which they seem to oversimplify the ways in which, as consumers or viewers, we engage with advertising. They rest on many assumptions that tend not to be made explicit.

For example, do these theories correspond in any meaningful way with the way human communication actually happens? Do we process information serially or one piece at a time, and consciously, so that we are fully aware of each piece of communication we encounter? Advanced research in artificial intelligence has modelled serial as opposed to linear information processing: computers can process input data through more than one channel at a time. Intuitively, we know that paying attention to more than one sensory input at a time is difficult for a human, but it is certainly possible. It is easy to argue that most advertising is screened out at the attention stage. But is it really? Do advertisements occupy some part of our peripheral vision and hearing, even if we are paying more explicit attention to something else? Or, rather, might advertisements deliberately attempt to seduce our unconscious mind and by-pass our conscious reasoning altogether, as Robert Heath (2012) suggests?

Advertising and the social context

AIDA and the hierarchy-of-effects models of advertising persuasion tend to focus on a single advertisement seen by an individual consumer, which is not surprising given that they were developed from a model of face-to-face sales communication and later adapted to mass advertising communication. Some authors (e.g. Ritson and Elliott, 1999) have pointed out that advertising is seldom viewed by an individual in an experimental viewing booth. More typically, advertisements are seen in social contexts, in the company of other communications and, often, in the company of other people. What is more, they are often the subject of social interaction. Indeed, long before social media sharing became so important for advertising, it was acknowledged that one of the key elements of success for an ad is to get it talked about (Dichter, 1949, 1966). Consequently, some researchers have argued that advertising is better understood as a social, rather than a cognitive phenomenon. Theories that posit one sender and one receiver of an advertising message, then, lack naturalistic validity in the sense that they do not necessarily reflect the way that consumers consume advertising.

Another much-criticised aspect of the linear information processing approach to theorising advertising is its assumption that advertising communication occurs mainly in one direction towards a passive consumer who will be acquiescent toward an unambiguous message if they process it correctly. This leads to another criticism, which is that these theories assume that the message and the meaning of the advertisement are synonymous. In other words, there is no theoretical scope for different consumers to interpret the ad in unexpected ways. Finally, there is a key assumption that the object of any advertisement is, always, a sale. As we have noted, sales, at least in the short or medium term, may not always be the best measure of a campaign's success.

'Strong' and 'weak' theories of advertising effect

Before discussing socio-cultural theories, there is another informal theory of advertising which is relevant here. The distinction between advertising and promotion that is designed to sell product, and advertising that is designed to build brand presence, has been expressed in terms of 'strong' and 'weak' theories (Jones, 1990). A popular analogy we have already noted expresses the same idea in terms of 'hard sell' and 'soft sell'. Theories of advertising that assume its main purpose is to persuade a potential customer (a 'prospect' in sales jargon) to buy, are called strong theories. AIDA falls into this category, since it is premised on the assumption that an advertisement is designed to persuade the viewer to change their behaviour and buy the product, and so on. Theories that take a less sales oriented view and allow that advertising may have a similar effect to publicity as a long-term builder of brand presence and brand positioning, are called 'weak' theories.

Strong theories are more compelling to many clients of advertising agencies who really want to see the sales graph spike upwards within a few days of the campaign launch. The problem is that a direct causal relationship between an advertisement and a sale cannot be proven beyond doubt, however persuasive the circumstantial evidence, because sales can be affected by other variables such as trends, fashions, weather events, seasonal sales, or changes in disposable income. To add to the difficulties for strong theories, even if there is a sales increase as a result of the campaign, the time lag between advertising exposure and sale is impossible to predict.

Advertising as publicity

As we have noted, many contemporary ads eschew the 'strong' sales pitch format in favour of a less direct narrative that is designed to build long-term brand equity, and to remind or to reassure existing customers. Ehrenberg et al. (2002) have suggested that advertising seldom actually persuades a non-buyer to buy in the short term, but more typically acts like publicity to reassure existing buyers that the brand remains relevant and current. Many car brand ads for, say, *BMW* or *Mercedes–Benz*, evince general brand values as well as promoting particular models because consumers may only buy that car brand once or twice in a lifetime, if at all. They need to be consistently reminded of the brand's relevance and values for the time when they might be in a position to buy. For example, *Mercedes*'s innovative Twitter campaign YOUDRIVE, first launched during the *The X Factor* TV show in 2012, gave viewers a chance to engage inter-actively in a driving game.[6] The *X Factor* audience might not be the primary market for *Mercedes* sales, and there was no sales pitch as such, the campaign was just a fun way for a wider audience to engage with the brand.

A great deal of theory in advertising has been devoted to understanding persuasion (O'Shaughnessy and O'Shaughnessy, 2004). But there is a question of what persuasion in advertising entails. Does it entail directly changing someone's attitude or behaviour through the force of reasoning? Or does it mean presenting brands in a generally persuasive light by inferring that they enhance personal lifestyle and act as symbolic resources for the production of social identity (Elliott and Wattanasuwan, 1998)? Weak theories of advertising assume that the advertising cause and the sales effect are linked, but over a much longer time period and through different mechanisms to strong theories. An important function of branding is that it is a badge of reassurance for the consumer (Feldwick, 2002). Consumers are often insecure about making difficult purchase decisions. None of us wants to get our purchase home to find that it is defective in any way or that our peers regard it with disdain. Brand names offer reassurance for the consumer that the purchase we have made is safe in the sense that the brand is credible and the quality good. Brand advertising, then, supports this sense of reassurance by reminding consumers that the brand is current, relevant and successful.

SNAPSHOT 2.2

'Weak' advertising appeals

John Philip Jones's (1990) 'strong' vs 'weak' advertising appeals roughly maps on to the popular distinction between, respectively, 'hard sell' and 'soft sell'. Hard sell is perhaps best understood as a direct and forceful appeal to purchase. Examples might be ads that focus on price, quality or superior value over competitors. The narrative structure of these ads would typically follow a personal sales conversation, in which the salesperson is trying to anticipate and answer the prospect's/consumer's objections to purchase. Weak advertising appeals, on the other hand, would cover a wide variety of ads that tell brand stories rather than trying to persuade the consumer to buy the product or service by reason, argument and evidence. One of the most popular ads in the UK in the last decade was a 2007 *Cadbury's* ad (by agency Fallon, London) featuring a man in a gorilla suit playing the drums.[7] The ad went worldwide and formed part of an integrated campaign with print, TV and social media. There was subtle branding on the ad but no sales appeal or product features. It was all for fun. It was reported that the *Cadbury's* brand image was enhanced and market share increased. It is probably fair to say that the most popular ads do tend to be fun and like-able,[8] in other words they appeal to emotion, rather than conforming to a sales pitch narrative. Cadbury followed up 'Gorilla' with several more 'feel-good' ads, including their hugely successful 2009 film 'Eyebrows', the 'Not-so-secret secret' and their *Crispello* ad, 'A lovely little naughtiness' in 2013.[9]

Socio-cultural theory in advertising

AIDA and other hierarchy-of-effects theories remain influential in advertising, but advertising agencies also make considerable use of socio-cultural theory in their practice. Many agencies employ account planners with backgrounds in cultural anthropology, sociology, literature, psychology or ethnography. Academic studies of advertising often have different aims to professional practice, but there are many to be found in all these disciplines (e.g. Cronin, 2008; Mick and Buhl, 1992; Scott, 1990, 1994a; Schroeder, 2002; Sherry, 1987; Stern, 1993b; for an overview, Hackley (ed.), 2009).

For example, the implied passivity of the consumer as a receiver of a one-way advertising message has been a criticism of the information processing models. This assumption is left unstated in 'transmission models' of mass communication but nevertheless implies that audiences 'receive' information, much as a computer receives data. In contrast, drawing on literary criticism, advertisements can be understood as texts, like other reading matter, to be read, with the same elements of judgement and interpretation. Academic studies applying reader–response theory to advertising (e.g. O'Donohoe, 1994; Scott, 1994a) suggest that audiences actively interpret, critique and/or resist advertising messages. Consumers are by no means passive receivers of advertising. This, of course, is truer than ever in the age of social media.

Critiques of the passive consumer assumption have engaged with the transmission model of communication. For example, Stern (1993a) undertook a thorough critique of static transmission models of communication in advertising, arguing that the model over-simplifies the communication process. Other work that has indirectly opposed the idea of a passive consumer posits the consumer as an active reader of text, as noted earlier (Scott, 1994b), or an interpreter of signs (Mick, 1986). Researchers working from the standpoint of linguistics have pointed out that what is implicit in communication is often more persuasive than what is explicit. When this principle is applied to advertising communication, the limitations of a focus on explicit messages become all too apparent. For example, Tanaka (1994) analysed advertisements in detail to illustrate the rhetorical force of implied connotation and denotation in advertising.

Economic rationality and emotion in buying behaviour

A further criticism of linear models of advertising persuasion is that they overplay the role of economic rationality in the consumption of advertising and ignore the role of emotion. Subsequent models have incorporated stronger elements of consumer emotionality not as a mediating influence but as a guiding motive in the buying process (Elliott, 1998; Holbrook and Hirschman, 1982; Holbrook and O'Shaughnessy, 2006[10]), reflecting the often irrational and quirky motivations behind consumer behaviour (Dermody, 1999).

Many of us go shopping when we feel down. Buying things can be therapeutic. Rationality plays little part in addictive or mood shopping, or in compulsive or impulsive consumer behaviour like excessive drinking (Hackley et al., 2012).

Our rationality as consumers can also be challenged by unconscious contextual effects (Hackley, 2013a). We can be swayed in our interpretation of communications through the other communications that are juxtaposed with an advertisement. The medium influences the way that the message is interpreted and understood (Cook, 2001; McLuhan, 1964). Our perceptions can be framed by the wider context, and the ways we 'read' marketing signs can be influenced by environmental cues. Advertisements are interpreted in the light of the context in which they are viewed, including the medium, the media vehicle, the other ads wrapped around the ad in the slot, the programming and so on. Advertising acquires meaning not only by its content but also its context.

Cook (2001) suggested that the contexts of advertising include the following:

- the physical material or medium which carries the text (such as the cathode ray tube, newsprint or radio waves)
- the music and pictures that may accompany the text
- the gestures, facial expressions and typography that constitute the 'paralanguage' of the text (in the UK, TV ads for Nescafé *Gold Blend* instant coffee featured romantically linked characters who created a sexually charged atmosphere, while interacting in settings that suggested affluence and social poise)
- the location of the text in time and space, on an outdoor poster site, in a magazine or during a commercial TV break
- the other texts that connect to that text such as the other ads in the same magazine or the other brands appearing or mentioned in a TV show
- the connections with other social discourses implied in the ads (for example intertextuality)
- the participants, that is, the intended audience, the apparent originator or sender of the ad and their respective assumptions, intentions and communicative idiom (Cook, 2001: 2) (ads sometimes have a particular 'voice' designed to confer authority, such as when ads for children's toys feature adults speaking the voice-over in the tone and patois of children).

Clearly, this list of the contexts of advertising implies that research studies which analyse the recall and attitude of an individual consumer to a single promotion by exposing the consumer to the ad in a viewing booth risk ignoring some of the most powerful influences on how ads are interpreted and understood. The contextual influence on advertising interpretation can have serious implications for advertising regulation.

Emotion and advertising

Advertising theory has been focused mainly on consumer reasoning and decision making, and this seems odd when one considers that marketing began as a discipline that dissented from the economist's fixation with consumer rationality. Some thinkers felt that microeconomics lacked the conceptual penetration to assist in clearing markets because consumers were far less rational and more variable in their wants and needs than the economist's notion of utility allowed. Hence, marketing was born as a university discipline at the turn of the twentieth century (Hackley, 2009a). And yet, marketing itself, along with advertising, seem both to have largely forgotten the founding principle of the discipline, since so much research and thinking assumes that consumers buy with conscious reason, rather than with unconscious emotion. In the 1980s there was a movement in consumer research that revived the sense of consumption as something motivated not solely by cold reason but by a need for feelings, fantasies and fun (Holbrook and Hirschman, 1982). The advertising world has, from time-to-time, also remembered the importance of emotion in consumption. A 2013 article in *The Economist* magazine[11] credited Nobel prize-winning psychologist Daniel Kahneman with turning advertisers onto the notion that emotion could be more important than reason for consumers. Or, to be more accurate, some advertisers have picked up on Kahneman's ideas to justify what many in advertising knew already. Kahneman posits that human brains operate in two systems: system 1 is an intuitive and emotional system, while system 2 is rational. According to his (very simplified) theory, our behaviour is governed by system 1 to a far greater extent than system 2. This might explain why many of the most popular advertisements are just feel-good pieces with no rational product appeal, and also why so much market research that asks consumers to explain their thoughts and feelings around a particular brand or advertisements turns out to be wrong.

Meanings and messages in advertisements

Information processing models tend to focus on the communication of a message, whilst socio-cultural theories of advertising communication focus on meanings rather than messages. The difference is important, since the idea of a message emphasises the power of the sender to control the way that a communication is received, while the idea of meaning in communication emphasises the power of the receiver. In literary theory, this difference is sometimes referred to in terms of hegmonic readings, that are intended to be accepted unconditionally, and negotiated or resisted readings, in which the reader/consumer might re-interpret or dissent from the message as it is intended. The concept of a message is often used broadly to refer to the content of an ad, that is, to the creative execution, but in advertising theory it is often used more narrowly to refer to a communication in terms of a single, unequivocal and uncontested meaning. In other words, in AIDA and similar linear schemes of advertising communication, meaning and message are assumed to be identical. Alternative theories of communication challenge this notion.

A similar distinction can be made between advertising as meaning, and advertising an information (McCracken, 1987).[12] An advertising 'message' would typically be conceived as some information that is intended to constitute a persuasive argument that will appeal to the rational (Kanheman's system 2 – see Snapshot 2.3) part of a consumer's brain. If, on the other hand, an advertisement is conceived as a vehicle for meaning, this indicates a broader but deeper conceptualisation that taps into the consumer's need for meaning within a cultural system.

Polysemy in advertising

Advertisements carry meanings that may be interpreted differently in different situations, or by different consumers. The capacity for a communication to have more than one possible interpretation is called polysemy. The meaning of some ads is indeterminate: none of the meanings in a given ad is necessarily prior to, or stronger than, the others. There is an interpretive space through which consumers can engage creatively with the ad. This gives advertising a particular power. It is us, the audience for advertising, who impose particular meanings on a given ad, helped, of course, by the cues placed in the ad by the creative people. This freedom to interpret advertising and to use it creatively in our own lives gives advertising communication a dynamic and iterative character that is particularly suitable for social media engagement. If people enjoy an ad they might want to discuss its possible meanings through social media and video sharing. All this engagement benefits the brand.

Advertising agencies, far from being limited by the complexity of advertising meaning, exploit the ambiguity of advertising (Pateman, 1983, in Forceville, 1996) to create an intimate and personal engagement with consumers. In other words, polysemic advertising can be a deliberate strategy rather than a failure of communication. Ads can be artfully designed so that the curiosity of a designated target group of consumers is excited. Ads that are deliberately obscure can seem inaccessible to older consumers and, by implication, aimed at younger consumers. Ambiguity of meaning in ads can be used as a deliberate strategy to engage a target group by allowing them to feel part of an in-group who 'get' the ad. In addition, carefully coded ads can create a sense of conspiracy by communicating in a way that excludes non-targeted groups. As we note throughout the book, there is a shift in advertising toward polysemic content that does not hammer out a sales message, which people would find uninteresting, but instead seeks to engage by being entertaining, intriguing or simply fun. The more an ad is discussed and shared on social media, the wider the audience it reaches.

Open versus closed advertising texts

As we have noted, advertisements can be understood in literary terms as texts that have to be read. We look at an ad and try to read and interpret it just as we would a poem, a novel, a comic strip, an art object, a movie or a piece of graffiti on a wall. Some ads attempt to create a hegemonic reading by hammering home a clear message that the advertiser hopes will be interpreted in the same way by all readers/consumers who encounter it. Other ads are less determinate, like a piece of art they actively solicit the reader's involvement in interpreting the meaning of the ad. This can be termed as closed versus open advertising texts (Yannopoulou and Elliott, 2007).[13] Open advertising texts have more than one possible interpretation – they are polysemic (Scott, 2012).[14] The ways in which open advertising texts might be interpreted need not be entirely arbitrary. The creative team can encode certain cues within the ad to appeal to a particular sub-cultural group or consumer community. For example, there is a long tradition of polysemic ads for the clothing fashion brand *Diesel* that are open to many possible interpretations, but are also targeted at a young, style-conscious in-group. Many of its ads, including the 'Be Stupid' campaign, have won industry creative awards.[15] *Guinness* is another brand famous for the open text character if much of its advertising over many years[16] (see Colour Section, photo 4). *Guinness* ads have been deigned to inspire with visual spectacle and heartwarming stories of human creativity and achievement. They focused on creating pieces of entertaining content long before the term 'content' came into fashion in marketing and advertising.

Covert and ostensive communication

The examples of polysemic and open text advertising we have noted above make their point by using implicit as well as explicit communication. The presence of both explicit and implicit elements in advertising communication has complicated the task of theorising advertising. Forceville (1996: 105) refers to a distinction made by Tanaka (1994: 41) between 'ostensive' and 'covert' communication in advertising. This distinction allows us to theorise what is implied in ads, as opposed to what is clearly and unambiguously claimed. The ostensive communicator makes the intention of the communication clear. The covert communicator does not. Many ads combine both ostensive (or explicit) and covert (or implicit) elements.

As we have noted, it is the capacity of advertising to deploy implicit communication that gives it its cultural force as a system of communication. This important dimension is neglected by linear theories of advertising communication and persuasion. The implicit dimension creates a problem for advertising regulators. Advertisements under industry regulation are strictly constrained from making claims that are untrue or preposterous. They get around this inconvenience by implying covertly those claims that could be seen as ridiculous or would open them up to criticism if they were made explicitly. The

Lynx/Axe campaigns mentioned in Chapter 1 make absurd claims about how men's sexual attractiveness is increased by using the product, but this is implied in the narrative of the advertising, not stated explicitly as a feature of the product. In this particular case what is implied is clearly intended as a joke, although, as Tanaka (1994) notes, even if a claim made about a brand is absurd, the fact that it is understood makes it persuasive on some level.

Advertising cannot compel us to believe particular claims or to accept that certain values are embodied in a given brand. Rather, advertising suggests, implies and hints. It places images and words in suggestive juxtaposition to imply that consuming a given brand will symbolically confer certain qualities and values. If you use a *Gillette* razor you are enjoying 'The Best a Man Can Get' (at least, according to the ads), and you might even acquire some of the characteristics and lifestyle of the actor in the ads (see Colour Section, photo 5). Driving a prestigious motorcar brand such as a *Toyota Avensis* will (we are invited to infer from the TV ads), confer a symbolic social status on us that reflects our success and desire. The ads don't actually say these things: they merely imply them, hoping that viewers will read the desired implication.

Ads frequently imply that consumers will be more sexually attractive, more powerful, more happy, or will appear more materially successful if they consume a given brand. Where branded products are juxtaposed with images of attractive, happy and successful people, the link between the two is implied but not stated. Most importantly, knowing that these suggestions are absurd does not necessarily undermine their force. Watch brand *Omega* (see Colour Section, photo 6), for example, is well known for pairing the brand with celebrities such as Nicole Kidman and Bond stars Pierce Brosnan and Daniel Craig in movie product placement and advertising, and it sponsors major events, such as the London 2012 Olympic Games, with its precision timekeeping. *Omega* also deploys feel-good advertising with aesthetically beautiful images in its advertising.[17]

Visual metaphor in advertising

Covert meaning is often conveyed in advertising though pictorial, auditory or linguistic metaphor. If a branded bottle of alcoholic drink is pictured juxtaposed with scenes of fit, young, affluent people, then the metaphoric link is clear. For example, alcohol brand *Martini* used to be advertised in the UK as a drink enjoyed by swimsuited young men and women diving from a yacht moored at a tropical island. The juxtaposition of a branded alcohol drink with apparent wealth, attractiveness and physical fitness is exactly the opposite of what one might reasonably expect, since alcohol drinking is quite likely to make exponents fat and unfit, and may also make them poor if they drink enough. The covert communication in this campaign was preposterous but was nevertheless clear. The *Martini* brand was used as a metaphor for sexual attractiveness and the good life. It matters little that the drink may often be consumed in social contexts that are, on the face of it, as far from the good life as one might wish to be. One can see the same implied suggestions in countless ads for alcohol, cigarettes and cosmetics.

Consumption is, significantly, not only a verbal phenomenon but a visual one. Images can communicate with great economy and force, and advertising is pre-eminently a visual phenomenon. Yet the particular qualities of visual communication have been very much under-theorised in the field. One notable exception comes in the work of Jonathan Schroeder (2002), who draws on art history and aesthetics to help us understand the complex ways in which advertising communicates visually. Schroeder (2002) argues that we do not only consume the branded products and services that are advertised, we also 'consume' the visual images of advertising and promotion.

For example, many perfume ads in lifestyle and fashion magazines make no direct reference to the odour; instead, they juxtapose sensuous images with an enigmatic strapline or slogan that evinces some abstract notion of the brand. The visual organisation of image and copy is carefully designed to rhetorically support the implicit claims made about the brand. A UK press ad for an Estée Lauder perfume portrayed a woman with flowing hair against images of waves, scattered flowers and sunlight with the copy 'Introducing the new fantasy in fragrance' and the brand 'beyond paradise' with the explanation that it offers 'an intoxication of the senses'. The ad had visual impact: it made a striking image when placed in a double-page section immediately inside the magazine cover. By its size and page location the ad was rhetorically declaring that its subject matter was important, more important, perhaps, than the magazine's editorial. The woman's face engages the reader eye to eye with a questioning and provocative expression that seems to be asking 'Dare you join me in paradise?' The face rhetorically supports the idea that this brand transports the ordinary woman from the everyday to a different world in which she can be free to be any self she chooses. The French brand name draws on the cultural idiom of style and sophistication to imply that the perfume has those qualities and so, by association, will the reader who buys the brand. Of course, consumers will decide if they like the odour, but the odour is designed to be pleasant. Once again, the powerfully suggestive aspect of this ad is not only in its message but in its creativity. The ad is rhetorically organised to support certain implied meanings.

The visual rhetoric of ads is not, then, confined to the copy. An ad is an argument, a persuasive communication. Every part of it must support the main argument, must be persuasively suggestive. A press ad for *Retinol Actif Pur* face cream used a clever visual metaphor to support a claim that the cream reduced facial wrinkles. The ad featured two juxtaposed images of a beautiful (Caucasian) woman. She was wearing what seemed to be a white robe, folded over one shoulder like a Roman toga. In the background was a pure blue sky and a suggestion of white pillars, of the kind found in a Greek temple. One picture was cracked, like the surface of an old oil painting. The other was smooth. The metaphoric reference was clear: the cracks suggested wrinkles, but in an elegant way that was complimentary, not demeaning, to age. Old paintings are things of classical beauty, but the paint does tend to crack with age. The ad was designed to draw the eye across aesthetically appealing images while giving the reader heavy hints about the classic beauty they might aspire to if they were to consume the brand.

Advertising and the cultural context

Advertising is not merely a force acting upon us from some other place. It is part of our cultural scene – we draw on our cultural knowledge to interpret and understand, to 'read', advertising, just as advertisers draw on the very same cultural milieu to find ways to articulate brand stories visually and verbally. Research studies have drawn attention to the ways in which advertising occupies the same cultural space as consumers. In other words, advertising does not simply do things to consumers – consumer also do things with advertising. This insight was perhaps a more novel one twenty years ago when most advertising theory within academic marketing took a linear communication approach. Today, in the context of social media, the active involvement of consumers in adapting, re-making, discussing, re-interpreting and satirising advertising seems impossible to ignore.

Theorists such as Stephanie O'Donohoe (1994) and Grant McCracken (1986) and, before them, Ernest Dichter (1966), point out that advertising is ineluctably a cultural as well as a cognitive communication phenomenon. We consume and discuss advertising in a social and cultural context, not in an individually isolated experimental viewing booth. Ritson and Elliott (1999) showed how important advertising can be in the everyday conversation of adolescents. By expressing preferences and finding certain ads funny or enjoyable the researchers found that the adolescents were also expressing their sense of social identity and group membership.

Advertising's meaning, then, draws on the cultural environment within which it is framed. A key concept in understanding this aspect of advertising as social communication is intertextuality (also discussed in the Chapter 2 case below). Intertextuality refers to the ways in which one text refers to other texts (e.g. O'Donohoe, 1997). Intertextuality might be invoked when, say, an ad uses a style of cinematography more commonly used in news or documentary filming, or when an ad includes a visual or verbal reference to a TV show, a movie, or a topical event. When celebrities are used in ads it can be seen in terms of an intertextual reference to the celebrity's persona outside of advertising, as, say, when a former sporting star is used as a spokesperson for a brand.

Intertextuality can also be invoked as a discourse, that is, a particular way of talking about or representing things, say, where an ad takes on the stereotypical sales conversation style of a company representative talking direct to camera, or an authoritative grey-haired man in a white lab coat invoking the representational style of science to make claims about the scientific properties of a product. Intertextuality is far from an arcane literary concept but a typical way that advertisements communicate with their target audiences (some examples can be seen on the link in note).[18] Most importantly, though, consumers must have the relevant cultural knowledge to decode the intertextual references in advertisements – they must know about the movie, the topical event, the actor, to which the ad refers in order to *get* the ad. By the same token, advertising agencies must understand the cultural reference points of their target consumers in order to design creative executions that are loaded with relevant cultural cues.

Our understanding of ads, then, and the brands they promote, is formed in the light of the social contexts within which such communications subsist. This inherently social aspect of human understanding reflects a broader concern with the socially constructed character of social reality (Berger and Luckman, 1966) and of individual psychology (for introductions see Burr, 1995; Nightingale and Cromby, 1999). In important respects we maintain that brands and their advertising cannot be properly understood simply as self-sustaining entities. They must also be understood as entities that exist in the realm of social interaction, sustained through the way they are talked about and used. In other words, brands can be seen as social constructions. A great deal of marketing activity can be seen to have a socially constructed character (Hirschman, 1986, cited in Hackley, 2000: 47) in the sense that it has an existence that is sustained in the social world beyond the tangible realities of product features, packaging and price. A brand's meaning as portrayed or implied in advertising subsists in the social space between the organisation, the advertising and its interpretive communities of consumers. In the convergent media era, this truism plays out in very tangible ways and consumers actively participate in the negotiation and renegotiation of brand meanings.

up into a poster and featured on roadside billboards it elicited such a large number of complaints that even though the campaign was launched in 2000, in 2012 it still ranked in the top ten ads most complained about to the UK Advertising Standards Authority (ASA).[19] The magazine ad was, presumably, seen as sensuous and witty in the context of many such ads for perfume in fashion and lifestyle magazines. The same ad on posters was widely considered to be obscene. The complaints to the ASA were predominantly from young women, exactly the readers of the magazines in which the press ad had featured. The meanings we impute to ads are, it seems, highly influenced by the interpretive context in which the ad is placed.

Advertising and semiotics

Semiotics deserves a brief mention because of its considerable influence in studies of advertising (Mick, 1986; Mick and Buhl, 1992). Semiotics is the study of signs and their meaning. American influence (particularly that of Charles Sanders Peirce) has broadened the field from the study of linguistic signs, also called semiology (de Saussure, 1974) to include the study of any signs whatsoever (Peirce, 1958; introductions in Danesi, 1994; Hackley, 1999). Advertising and marketing have attracted much attention from semioticians (Barthes, 2000; Williamson, 1978). Ads are seen as 'strings of signs' (Umiker-Sebeok, 1997) in the service of the brand. Such signs (copy, typeface, soundtrack, positioning, image, colour, objects) rhetorically support the subtextual or covert meanings that are central to the persuasive force of advertising. The meaning of a given sign depends on the context, the receiver and the communication codes that form the cultural expectations of the sender and receiver.

The sales message, if one can be discerned among the cacophony of signification in many ads, is only one part of the complex process of communication that is going on when a consumer engages with an ad and attempts to interpret its meaning. For example, another way of analysing polysemic ads is to look at the signification properties of each part of the ad. These will include the copy and the other visual elements; colours, print quality, actors, props in the scene, the clothes, the juxtaposition of images, the intertextual references, and so on. Semiotics seeks to recover the communicative codes through which we receive messages from word, visual, auditory or other signs.

Marketing as a whole is a rich source of symbolism (Sawchuck, 1995) that reaches into the most intimate areas of our lives to transform the meaning of everyday signs. The acts of shaving, washing, even personal cleanliness are superimposed with marketed values. Advertising lies at the fulcrum of marketing's semiotic mechanism, symbolically articulating the brand values contrived by the strategists. We will return to some of these concepts as the book progresses through its account of the advertising and promotion field.

Levels of explanation in advertising theory: cognitive, social, and cultural

In the book we hint at the vast range of theory in advertising. To conclude Chapter 2 it is worth briefly discussing the role and purpose of theory in the context of social science, given that scholarship and research in advertising is concerned both with managerial issues and matters of social policy. The difficulty of this is that theory and research in management and business is derivative. It does not have its own theories and methods but borrows them from social science. This creates problems of ecological validity. To express this with an example, why should a theory of emotion developed in general psychology be appropriate for advertising? All too often, social scientific theories are bolted on to advertising contexts without any adaptation.

The marketing field in general has a tendency to use theories without reference to their original context. It has adapted, and often bowdlerised, theoretical and conceptual developments in many other social disciplines, such as economics, psychology and sociology (Foxall, 2000; Gronhaug, 2000; Hackley, 2003c, 2009a; O'Shaughnessy, 1997). Theoretical work in advertising has, as we have seen, similarly adapted work from other fields. Much advertising research draws on assumptions from mass communications research which had, in turn, borrowed ideas such as linearity and the concept of the internal mental state from early research in artificial intelligence and computing.

Much research into advertising has drawn on the arts and humanities, for example, literary theory (Scott, 1994a, 1994b), feminism (Stern, 1993b), anthropology (Sherry, 1987), ethnography (Ritson and Elliott, 1999), applied linguistics (Cook, 2001), critical theory (Elliott and Ritson, 1997), and so on. All this diversity begs the question of whether one can fairly evaluate a social theory without also understanding the assumptions about the audience for the research and the rightful aims of that research. To try to accommodate something of the diversity of theory in advertising in a way that reconciles the different kinds, it will be useful to draw on the notion of 'levels of explanation' in social research, which has been used in social psychology education (Stevens, 1996) to integrate differing kinds of theory.

The cognitive level of explanation

Advertising works at a cognitive level in that it influences the individual cognitive functions of perception, memory and attitude. Theories that focus on the cognitive levels of explanation also emphasise rational, conscious consumer thinking. The scope of explanation in such theories extends to the internal mental state of the individual and the assumed connection between those internal states and observed (consumer) behaviour. Copy-testing, experimental research designs and attitude research attempt to isolate the internal mental states that act as causal variables that motivate consumers to act on the advertising they see. This level of explanation offers succinct and measurable results, but its weakness is that it risks distorting the way consumers engage with and understand advertising to fit a set of convenient research methods.

Much cognitive research into advertising has taken the individual consumer as the unit of analysis (Hackley, 2002: 214; Holbrook, 1995: 93, citing McCracken, 1987: 123; Ritson and Elliott, 1999: 261). Unlike computers, humans depend heavily on social interaction for meaning. People born blind who have sight restored in middle age have to learn to perceive structures and images from a jumble of visual sensory data. In other words, they have to learn how to see. People who are raised in social isolation cannot naturally learn speech and people who live in a culture without mediated communication cannot 'read' advertising. The way that we understand advertising is deeply informed by the cultural understanding we can only acquire in social interaction. The experimental research paradigm that attempts to isolate individual physiological or attitudinal responses to advertising cannot easily capture this dimension.

The social level of explanation

The social level of explanation offers an account of advertising that accommodates its social character. Advertising is not encountered in a social vacuum but in a given social context, and it occupies a place in public discourse. How we think about advertising is strongly influenced by what we hear others say about it. How many times has someone asked you if you have seen this or that ad? As ads become part of social discourse they assume the characteristics of social constructions, in the sense that Berger and Luckman (1966) described. Research and theory that focus on internal mental states (such as memory or attitude) fail to grasp the essentially malleable nature of these states. One's attitude towards an ad is not arrived at in isolation but is constructed in a social context. Social constructionism (see also Burr, 1995; Hackley, 2000) disputes the validity of the internal mental state as a construct and suggests that such states subsist in social discourse. In practical terms, this implies that it not sufficient to measure memory or attitude in experimental laboratories; rather, advertising research needs to look at consumer thinking and behaviour in its normal social context, in interaction.

It is hugely significant that advertising agency professionals understand this intuitively. But politically, many agencies still struggle to justify this form of understanding to clients and account managers who are concerned with measuring consumer attitudes to advertising. This fundamental difference of mentality is a central issue in advertising and promotional management (Hackley, 2003d), but many existing research approaches perpetuate the differences instead of providing possibilities for reconciliation.

The cultural level of explanation

We have seen that advertising can be regarded as a form of cultural text. It takes the symbolic meanings and practices of non-consumer culture and recreates them in juxtaposition with marketed brands to suggest contrived brand values and to portray a brand personality. For advertising to be construed in this way there needs to be a symbolic aspect to the way consumers engage with advertising. We must understand advertising in terms that transfer symbolic meanings from our broader cultural experience to advertised brands (Belk, 1988; Mick and Buhl, 1992). This level of analysis broadens a socially constructed notion of advertising to accommodate the wider cultural influences that are the preconditions for local social discourse.

At this level of analysis power is an inevitable part of the picture. Brand marketing corporations have the economic and political power to impose contrived meanings upon cultural practices. Brand advertising, cleverly designed and expensively produced and exposed, can work to normalise particular social practices (such as cigarette smoking, alcohol drinking for females, fast-food consumption for children) and invest these practices with symbolic values such as personal independence, power and coolness. In this way advertising can be seen to operate as an ideology (Eagleton, 1991) or, indeed, as the 'super-ideology' of our time (Elliott and Ritson, 1997).

An exposition of advertising as ideology lies beyond the scope of this book. It is worth pointing out, though, that an intellectually viable appraisal of how advertising works is incomplete without an understanding of advertising's ideological power to render consumption practices normal and everyday in an infinite variety of appealing portrayals, to invest these practices with rich cultural significance and to place the interests of brand marketing organisations in the forefront of social life. If marketing as a whole can be seen as a vast semiotic vehicle constituting experiences and identities (Brownlie et al., 1999), then advertising is its engine, providing a continuous stream of new images, ideas and portrayals of consumption in juxtaposition with marketed brands.

Chapter summary

This chapter has discussed the importance of theory in advertising and outlined three overlapping but contrasting traditions: the practitioner tradition, the information processing tradition, and the socio-cultural tradition (Hackley, 2010). It reviewed practice-based advertising theory, some of which is still well known in the advertising world, such as the idea of the Unique Selling Proposition (USP). The chapter then discussed linear information processing theories of persuasive communication and the hierarchy-of-effects theories that they underpin, most notably AIDA. Finally, it reviewed a number of concepts from what it broadly labels as socio-cultural theory. The key distinction in the chapter reflects a contentious and long-running debate in marketing studies as a whole. Can marketing best be conceived as art, or as science? (See Brown, 2001[20], for an overview.) There is a parallel debate in advertising, although the two perspectives achieve a tense but largely productive co-existence in most advertising agencies. This topic is explored again in Chapter 10 on research in advertising. For the present purpose, Chapter 2 has attempted to present an outline of some of the complex though highly influential issues in theorising advertising. These issues have very practical implications for advertising and promotional strategy, and are therefore central to the book.

■ Review Questions

1. Choose three print advertisements and three TV ads. For each, construct descriptions that distinguish the covert from the ostensive meanings in the ad. Compare your interpretations with colleagues: do they differ?

2. What is meant by polysemy? What is its importance in advertising? Collect several magazines: can you find ads that appear to be polysemic?

3. Choose one print ad and form a group with three collaborators. Try to pick out all the individual signs that might carry meaning in the ad. These might include the copy (the words, the position of the copy in the visual and the typeface or font that is used), the models, the props in the set, the background, the relation of objects and bodies to each other, the gestures, the quality of paper and use of colour and the other brands advertised in the magazine. What is the meaning of each in its context?

4. What is a message? To what extent is meaning carried unequivocally within an advertisement? Compare three ads to discuss this.

5. Choose three ads. Try to discern the message and conceptualise the ad in terms of the stages of AIDA. How effective is your conceptualisation in explaining how the ad might 'work'?

CASE STUDY

Intertextuality and the interpreting consumer

Advertising is 'parasitic' (Cook, 2001) in the sense that it draws from, and refers to, styles, genres and discourses of textual and visual representation that are not exclusive to advertising but subsist in other cultural areas. Julia Kristeva's concept of intertextuality refers to the idea that no text is entirely original or autonomous but consists of references, conscious or not, to other cultural texts. The idea of intertextuality, originating with Kristeva and the

(Continued)

(Continued)

French poststructuralists, has been adapted to advertising by O'Donohoe (1997). Intertextual references reflect advertising's derivative character by evincing other, non-advertising discourses. For example, television ads have evoked the discourse genres of, say: scientific reports (with a white-coated, male actor as 'objective' spokesman for the proven qualities of the brand); the face-to-face sales pitch (delivered by a man in a loud tie and check jacket); and the confidential piece of advice from the older woman experienced in house-hold management to the younger (examples are taken from Cook, 2001: 194). Intertextual references in advertising tend to be implicit, they are there to be noticed, or not, by an interpreting consumer.

In research with young British consumers, O'Donohoe (1997) has shown how advertising can use intertextuality to engage particular audience groups. A piece by Catherine Langan[21] shows some good examples of how cigarette brand *Silk Cut* used intertextuality cleverly to get around regulations on cigarette advertising in the UK. Other examples can be seen on YouTube.[22] Advertisements can evince certain values and ideas by linking the brand with the discourses of, say, sport or movies, with TV quiz shows, news announcements, fashion photographs, court-room dialogue or TV situation comedies. In many cases, ads deploying intertextual references are then featured on compilation TV shows of funniest ads, completing the circle by drawing ads into mainstream entertainment. The intertextual references are 'read' by the relevant target audience who recognise that the brand is speaking to them.

Creative professionals may use intertextuality as a tactic to try to engage consumers with points of shared cultural reference. Intertextual references are often used in a spirit of parody to break down consumer resistance to advertising appeals. In such cases the marketing message is predicated on the target consumers getting the reference and appreciating the wit. As noted earlier in the chapter, in order to design intertextual references into an ad, the ad agency creatives must understand the cultural references their target audience will recognise, and also the value they place on them. This aspect of advertising creativity is seldom analysed, but it is central to advertising development. One famous advertising person said that his agency staff must know 'what the man on the Clapham omnibus is thinking'. In other words, effective advertising professionals must be curators of everyday culture, they must have a sense of their target audience's cultural milieu in order to communicate with them.

Case Questions

1. **Choose any three print or broadcast advertisements. Can you identify the intertextual elements in each? What does this tell you about the intended target market segment?**

2. **What kinds of cultural knowledge do you feel are required in order to identify the intertextual elements in your chosen advertisements?**

3. **Is one implication of intertextuality that advertising cannot be interpreted in the same way by people from different cultures? If this is so, how can you explain, for example, the global success of the Diesel brand, which often uses the same campaign globally without adaptation?**

Useful journal articles

(These Sage articles can be accessed on the book website)

Xiaoli Nan and Ronald J. Faber (2004) 'Advertising theory: reconceptualizing the building blocks', *Marketing Theory*, 4 (Jun.): 7–30.

Barbara J. Phillips and Edward F. McQuarrie (2004) 'Beyond visual metaphor: a new typology of visual rhetoric in advertising', *Marketing Theory*, 4 (Jun.): pp. 113–36.

Chris Miles (2007) 'A cybernetic communication model for advertising', *Marketing Theory*, 7: 307–34.

Adriana Campelo, Robert Aitken, and Juergen Gnoth (2011) 'Visual rhetoric and ethics in marketing of destinations', *Journal of Travel Research*, 50 (1): 3–14 (first published March 19, 2010).

Stefan Schwarzkopf (2011) 'The political theology of consumer sovereignty: towards an ontology of consumer society', *Theory, Culture & Society*, 28 (3): 106–29.

Bernard Cova, Pauline Maclaran, and Alan Bradshaw (2013) 'Rethinking consumer culture theory from the postmodern to the communist horizon', *Marketing Theory*, 13 (2): 213–25.

■ ■ Further reading ■

Arnould, E. and Thompson, C. (2005) 'Consumer culture theory (CCT): twenty years of research', *Journal of Consumer Research*, 31: 868–82.

Danesi, M. (2006) *Brands*. London and New York: Routledge.

Hackley, C. (2003) *Doing Research Projects in Marketing, Management and Consumer Research*. London: Routledge.

Hackley, C. (2010) 'Theorizing advertising: managerial, scientific and cultural approaches', in Pauline MacLaran, Michael Saren, Barbara Stern and Mark Tadajewski (eds), *The Sage Handbook of Marketing Theory*. London: Sage. pp. 89–107.

Holt, D. (2004) *How Brands Become Icons: The Principles of Cultural Branding*. Boston, MA: Business School Press.

Notes

1. www.paulfeldwick.com/images/pdf/Feldwick%20and%20Heath.pdf   accessed 10.2.2014
2. www.alexandujar.4t.com/generaltheoryofcreativeadvertising.pdf accessed 10.2.2014
3. www.youtube.com/watch?v=WjBHUQEiTPw accessed 18.3.2014

4. www.thepsychologist.org.uk/archive/archive_home.cfm?volumeID=20&editionID=150&ArticleID=1228 accessed 10.2.2014

5. Examples of emotional car ads are: *Honda*'s 'Choir' see www.youtube.com/watch?v=gjyWP2LfbyQ
   Skoda Fabia's ad 'how to bake a car- full of lovely stuff' see www.youtube.com/watch?v=k_uyUAR8nZE
   Volkswagen's 'stay in safe hands' see www.youtube.com/watch?v=3WPZGLSjB08

6. www.youtube.com/watch?v=VXO_WKe54jY&list=PLv2mhXe6zUJuEuoh0T8Le5j8eOes_NwxD accessed 19.3.2014

7. http://vimeo.com/73564800 accessed 11.2.2014

8. http://metro.co.uk/2010/01/19/cadburys-takeover-top-5-tv-adverts-gorilla-milk-tray-man-and-more-39960/ accessed 11.2.2014

9. Following the gorilla ad, *Cadbury's* launched a couple of adverts that appeal to emotion such as the 2009 ad 'eyebrows' featuring two kids moving their eyebrows up and down to the beat of the song. See www.youtube.com/watch?v=TVblWq3tDwY, Cadbury's dairy milk 'The not-so-secret secret' see www.youtube.com/watch?v=aAymavc19Zs, and Cadbury's Crispello 'A lovely little naughtiness' in 2013 (www.theguardian.com/tv-and-radio/2013/may/18/new-cadbury-crispello-advert),

10. http://onlinelibrary.wiley.com/doi/10.1002/mar.4220010206/abstract   accessed 10.2.2014

11. www.economist.com/news/business/21591165-admen-have-made-marketing-guru-daniel-kahneman-prizewinning-psychologist-nothing-more accessed 11.2.2014

12. www.acrwebsite.org/search/view-conference-proceedings.aspx?Id=6667   accessed 11.2.2014

13. http://138.38.0.49/criac/publications/pdf/21_advertisng.pdf accessed 11.2.2014

14. Polysemy in Advertising Linda M. Scott Advertising & Society Review Volume 13, Issue 2, 2012 | 10.1353/asr.2012.0016

15. www.creativeadawards.com/diesel-be-stupid-advertising-campaign/ accessed 11.2.2014

16. www.youtube.com/playlist?list=PL015E38B3CC988F4B accessed 11.2.2014

17. www.youtube.com/watch?v=ctj-RDbTBMU accessed 18.3.2014

18. www.google.com/search?q=intertextuality+in+advertising&client=safari&rls=en&tbm=isch&tbo=u&source=univ&sa=X&ei=F9f6UtmZBsTr2QXAt4CQCw&ved=0CCYQsAQ&biw=1229&bih=645 accessed 11.2.2014

19. www.huffingtonpost.com/2012/05/30/sophie-dahl-ysl-opium-asa-banned_n_1555478.html accessed 11.2.2014

20. www.cfs.purdue.edu/richardfeinberg/csr%20331%20consumer%20behavior%20%20spring%202011/readings/marketing%20as%20science.pdf accessed 11.2.2014

21. www.aber.ac.uk/media/Students/crl9502.html accessed 11.2.2014

22. www.youtube.com/watch?v=J2quHgLgepQ accessed 11.2.2014

3 The Brand and Integrated Marketing Communications Planning

Chapter outline

The brand is the central concept of consumer marketing, and integration of promotional campaigns across different media channels, both on and offline, is the key theme of contemporary advertising. This chapter describes the integrated marketing communications planning process in relation to the brand. It explores distinctions between marketing strategy and advertising strategy, and it examines the ways in which communication can support brand marketing objectives.

Key chapter content

- The communicating brand
- What advertising and promotional communication can do for brands
- Marketing and communication planning
- Integrated marketing communications
- Limitations to IMC

The communicating brand

In Chapter 3 we turn from the complexities of theorising advertising and promotion campaigns to the uncertainties of planning them. Planning is the area where the art of advertising is assimilated into management tools and used in the strategic or tactical interests of the brand. A plan can help to guide, control and co-ordinate the many tasks that are involved in the management of a brand's marketing and communications. In Chapter 2, we noted a number of theoretical perspectives on advertising that illustrated how difficult it is to impose meaning on an individual consumer through an advertisement. Part of the enigma of the advertising business is that we may not fully understand how it works, but it does, nevertheless, seem to do so and there are many striking examples. Indeed, it is impossible to conceive of the world's most prominent brands without advertising. It is important to analyse advertising, but if it is to be used as a management tool to achieve something, it is also useful to have a plan, even if that plan eventually acts as a point of departure for a more interesting destination. In this chapter we will take integration as a basis for discussing management issues of the planning and co-ordination of advertising and promotion as part of integrated marketing communications campaigns. Firstly, however, it is important to reflect a little on the central concept of integrated advertising and promotion – the brand.

The brand is a badge of origin, a promise of performance, a reassurance of quality, and a transformation of experience (Feldwick, 2002: 4–9; de Chernatony et al., 2010). The brand is, though, not a fixed entity but a cultural construction that subsists in the social spaces between people. To be sure, there is a concrete materiality in the brand, but the symbolic extension of it is far less tangible. The value of consumer brands lies substantially in their symbolism, and brand symbolism can be influenced by advertising and promotion.

Brands are valuable (see Snapshot 3.1) because consumers seek them out, recognise them and buy them instead of alternatives. Branding enables consumers to take a short cut through extended product searches and simply buy with assurance. Brands act as a symbolic vocabulary that enables and facilitates consumption. In effect, a successful brand acts as a quasi monopoly, because a proportion of consumers will seek out a particular brand, while ignoring the claims of other brands. As a result, brands allow companies to charge higher prices and make higher profits. They also enable the same companies to sell longer production runs and lower marginal costs. In competitive markets, this can mean lower consumer prices. Branding, marketing and advertising are not necessarily costs born by the consumer. They can underpin economies of scale by improving productive efficiency.

The relational brand

Consumer brands may have a concrete materiality but they are, nonetheless, a phenomenon of communication. They subsist in the minds of consumers and other stakeholders as sets of nebulous and iterative associations. There is a great deal of cognitive psychological research into visual identity, logo design and brand loyalty, but a brand can also be understood as a cultural entity (Holt, 2002; Schroeder and Salzer-Morlig, 2005) that has a relational character. A brand's qualities and characteristics subsist in relation to other brands, in relation to consumers' subjective perceptions and in relation to cultural conditions. The cultural meaning of a brand does not remain eternally the same but shifts with cultural movements. Brands have to work hard to retain their cultural meaning.

SNAPSHOT 3.1

Advertising and global brands

Brand consultant *Interbrand* compiles a list of the top global brands each year by value.[1] In 2013 they placed *Apple* and *Google* at number 1 and number 2, with values of $98,316 million and $93,291 million respectively. The rest of the top ten were *Coca-Cola*, *McDonald's*, *Samsung*, *IBM*, *Microsoft*, *Intel*, *Toyota* and *GE. Forbes*[2] magazine produces its own list with a different methodology, and also puts *Apple* at number 1, with *Microsoft* at number 2. Few would claim that advertising built these companies, but it played a part in most of them. For *Coca-Cola* and *McDonald's*, advertising has been a central pillar of their growth strategies. For some of the other brands, advertising has been important in distinguishing their corporate brand, or in maintaining product marker share for particular lines or models under the corporate brand umbrella. The combined value of the top 100 global brands is astonishing, and if advertising can claim merely a proportion of the credit for this, it is still a vast figure. Advertising and promotion are central to brands, and it is no accident that most of the brands in the list are familiar to consumers through the promotional communication they have seen.

Brands are inherently social phenomena. They communicate values, attitudes, identity positioning and discernment, and hence they constitute a shared symbolic cultural vocabulary. We would get little out of owning and displaying brands as symbolic objects if we did not know that others also speak the same vocabulary. Advertising and promotion are essential for spreading knowledge of this cultural vocabulary. For example, many men were greeting each other with the word 'whasssup' in 1990s before *Budweiser* used it in a series of TV ads. The ads made the term a much more widely understood phenomenon and linked it with the brand. The term fitted the brand positioning for a beer that recognised no social or ethnic divisions but brought men together in a spirit of informal camaraderie. The ads responded to an existing cultural event, the growing popularity of 'whassup' as a greeting signifying male camaraderie and leisurely down-time, and leveraged it through a major campaign that became a huge social media phenomenon.

Advertising and promotion can lend many qualities to a brand in the form of perceived attributes that can confer upon it a brand 'personality'. The notion of brand personality reflects the attempt to generate a sense of affinity between consumers and brands by anthropomorphising the brand, giving it human characterics (a 'personality') in order to stimulate affective and emotional responses from consumers towards the brand. Many brands are anthropomorphised through fictional characters (Brown and Ponsonby-McCabe, 2013) whilst others use celebrity spokespeople. The goal overall is to make it easier for a consumer to respond affectively to the brand as if it were human, by liking, not liking, being loyal to, being fond of or even loving, the brand.

In-keeping with the importance of brand anthropomorphism, social media and convergence mean that brands can respond in a dialogue with consumers in order to reinforce the sense of interactive communication. Some brand communication, such as advertising and promotion, can be controlled. Other elements of brand communication, such as social media sentiment and press coverage, are far more difficult to influence and brands have, instead, to react and respond. Brands have to ride cultural currents and respond creatively to shifts in the popular sentiment or to topical events. Brands have to work hard to maintain their cultural resonance and remain relevant to their target audiences, and advertising and promotion, in all their forms, lie at the heart of the way brands can manage their cultural meaning. The key issue for brand management is for the brand and their advertising agencies to continuously work to understand the cultural milieu of their consumers so that their brand communications are cast in the same cultural idiom used by their consumers, so that they can make a connection with their consumers' cultural experience.

That experience is not only reflected in the choices of preferred brands but is also transformed by it. Brands transform experience from something functional into something that symbolically represents aspirational values, identity and lifestyle. Advertising leverages the cultural meaning of brands. The ways in which brands transform consumer experience are often suggested by advertising that builds in layers of meaning to prosaic activities such as washing one's hair, drinking coffee, or even cleaning the toilet.

For some, advertising that encourages us to think that our choice of detergent is important to our sense of social status, our identity, even our happiness, is ridiculous. It may be absurd, but through advertising, brands acquire this strange power to transform an everyday activity into something more meaningful that connects it to the wider symbolic world, at least if we suspend our scepticism for a little while. The brands themselves are often competing with similar commodities for our attention and our repeat purchases, and they will try to be as alluring as possible to us in order to be able to compete with their market rivals. Advertising and promotion are central to the realisation of the cultural resonance and market potential of brands. In a fundamental sense, communication doesn't simply pass on messages about the brand – it constitutes the brand.

In spite of countless books and research studies about branding there is still a great deal of mystique about what goes into a successful brand. Writing about brands can be a little overblown – some authors declare that brands are 'gods' with 'personalities' – they even have 'souls'. This reflects the limits of managerial analysis of brands, which generally fails to grasp the degree to which brand anthropomorphism extends. The gap between management understanding and brand success lies in the enigmatic currents of everyday consumer culture. To some extent, brands are cultural constructs, and management of them requires a nuanced and processual orientation. Brands are not gods, or persons, but they can be highly enduring. Cadbury's *KitKat* in the UK had been the leading 'countline' for more than fifty years, and many of the European luxury brands now booming in sales in the East have histories of more than 100 years. Indeed, this history is part of what appeals about many luxury brands (Lu, 2008).

SNAPSHOT 3.2

IMC trends

IMC (integrated marketing communications) trends include a shift away from traditional advertising to non-traditional promotion and, in particular, toward branded content that works on multiple media platforms: well-conceived content strategy (especially on video) will prove central to IMC success: great creative ideas founded on genuinely penetrating consumer insight still cannot be beaten in advertising and promotion: digital will continue to increase in importance through the ubiquity of smartphones and tablets, and internet advertising in general will continue to grow apace in relation to other media: journalism jobs will continue to migrate to PR and brand blogging, reflecting the shift to 'native' advertising as the decline in spot advertising continues to challenge traditional media funding models.

What advertising and promotional communication can do for brands

Advertising's role in marketing is often under-emphasised. It is easy to see why. Advertising and promotion are, too often, the very last things marketing or brand managers think about, after product development, market testing, business analysis, production planning, material sourcing, distribution and so on. Yet it is a mistake to assume that the sequence of managerial activities involved in bringing a market offering to the consuming public reflects their relative importance. Advertising and other forms of marketing communication are not in themselves sufficient for successful consumer brand marketing, but in most cases they are necessary to the success of the venture. From a managerial perspective advertising and promotion are the final step in bringing an offering to market. From a consumer perspective advertising is often the only step that they see before consumption. Advertising is the typical consumer's point of entry into the long chain of brand marketing planning and co-ordination. The advertising helps to establish a set of assumptions that the consumer will bring to all other aspects of their engagement with a given brand.

Advertising and promotion are also important for the confidence and morale of other parties who have a stake in the success of a brand, such as shareholders, sales staff and other employees, and suppliers. Advertising provides tangible evidence of the financial credibility and competitive presence of an organisation. Corporate communication is a distinct discipline in itself. But in a broader sense every ad is a reflection on the corporation that sponsored it because of the cumulative influence on its commercial credibility. Tangible benefits from this credibility might include longer supplier credit periods, greater influence over suppliers' prices, better employee retention and more effective recruitment, and greater confidence among stockmarket players.

Advertising's corporate influence can spread far beyond the brand. As a device of marketing strategy, advertising and promotion can also be both subtle and precise. The UK Institute for Practitioners in Advertising (IPA)[3] claims that among other business aims, advertising can:

- Defend brands against own-label growth
- Effect change internally as well as externally to the company
- Increase the efficiency of recruitment
- Transform entire businesses by generating new markets for a brand
- Revitalise a declining brand
- Reinvigorate a market
- Stop line extensions cannibalising existing sales
- Change behaviour
- Influence share price
- Make other communications more cost-effective
- Generate rapid sales increases
- Increase growth of a mature brand in a declining market
- Address crises in public relations.

With creative ingenuity and careful targeting, advertising can support many kinds of marketing objective. It must be remembered that advertising itself is communication: ads cannot sell anything as such, neither can they in themselves create a successful brand. What they can do is to place particular ideas in the public realm to make consumers aware of brand offerings, to create a favourable predisposition towards a brand, to explain things about the brand and to tell a story of uniqueness about the brand. Advertising can also support more closely specified marketing techniques such as positioning and repositioning, market segmentation, launch and relaunch, raising brand awareness or rebranding, and fulfilling corporate communication objectives.

Consumer marketing is not alone in using integrated marketing communication planning. Advertising has been extensively deployed in the case of socially important causes and non-profit organisations such as charities, care organisations and political parties (Peng and Hackley, 2007, 2009). Organisations that promoted causes of social welfare, such as the UK Labour Party and the trade unions, were historically unsympathetic to advertising because they associated it with a sell-out to capitalism. As a result, such organisations were unable to promote themselves effectively. A change of viewpoint eventually emerged, significantly because of the involvement of DDB London Chairman at the time, Chris Powell. This change of view about using advertising to promote left-wing politics and issues coincided with the political revival of the Labour Party. One poster campaign called 'Labour Isn't Working' produced by Saatchi & Saatchi for the UK Conservative Party for the 1979 general election has been described as the most successful political advertisement of all time,[4] since it was credited with winning the election for the Conservatives.

Non-profit advertising including charities, public sector, health services and public safety and information campaigns have collectively become a significant sector of the advertising business The use of advertising in public service campaigns, though, can be seen as problematic, and it is questionable how effective it is in public health issues such as alcohol consumption (Szmigin et al., 2011). Campaigns in these areas are subject to similar planning processes as commercial advertising and promotion. The differences lie in the fact that each sector serves different stakeholders and, therefore, has different objectives to fulfil and different expectations to meet.

Advertising and segmentation

Marketing management texts have popularised the term 'segmentation' to refer to the need for categories of consumer to be broken down for easy identification, surveillance (through consumer research) and targeting. We consumers are often complicit in this categorisation (Hackley, 2002), since we eagerly seek out ads and images that we feel cohere with our sense of social identity and resonate with our individual aspirations and fantasies. Most importantly, this entails creating a sense of otherness towards categories of consumer that are not us. The distinctions between categories of consumer open up the possibility for consumer discretion and choice. In a given TV or poster ad the casting, the set, the scene props and the dialogue are all powerful signifiers of the kind of human that is supposed to favour a given brand.

It is a cliché in advertising that half the budget is wasted, but no one knows which half. The value of segmentation to organisations is that it can make marketing effort appear more cost-effective by reducing the amount of the marketing budget that is misdirected at undesired consumer groups. Clearly there is a potential drawback to targeting a given segment. If the target group is wrongly identified then there is a risk that the entire marketing budget might be misdirected, instead of only half of it. As we have seen, brand planners might see sales increases as a long-term consequence of a strongly sustained brand personality. An over-emphasis on targeting might neglect to project the brand personality to non-consumers. This could be an important omission given that the brand personality depends as much on the perceptions of non-consumers as of consumers.

Brand communication and differential advantage _____

In many competitive markets commodities are relatively undifferentiated in terms of product qualities and characteristics, but through advertising and promotion the brand can be differentiated, resulting in a competitive advantage. Innovations of design, process, pricing, distribution and manufacture can be quickly copied. Manufacturing technology or service operations can often be transferred to countries with lower labour costs and overheads. This means that a tangible competitive advantage is hard to achieve and even harder to sustain over long periods under competition. Intellectual property and patent rights confer some protection on innovators but rival businesses can succeed in making their offering appear to be identical to that of an innovator in important respects. In many countries, intellectual property rights are difficult or impossible to police. Furthermore, in developed economies consumer markets are increasingly sensitive to the actual or perceived links between public events, personalities and news stories, and brands. This makes the brand vulnerable to unexpected changes in public taste.

For these reasons and others, advertising communication is an essential component of brand marketing. A brand lives on through consumer perceptions that are formed in engagement with advertising communication. The distinctive positioning, segmentation and targeting that is so difficult to achieve and sustain through other means can be achieved symbolically through advertising and promotional communication. The point that communication is integral to how consumers understand and engage with marketed brands does not necessarily imply that a brand is all about superficial 'puffery' and short-term publicity. 'Puffery' is the name given to advertising copy that is so clearly hyperbolic that no reasonable person would take it literally. It is also sometimes used as a derogatory term for advertising in general. Most advertising conveys something about a brand's values and characteristics, but this is not all there is to brand marketing. Brand managers will normally argue that communications are like the tip of an iceberg, just visible above the waterline with a far more substantial structure, unseen, beneath. This invisible structure includes production, staffing, training, operations, logistics, supply and material sourcing, and all the other activities without which a branded product or service could not reach a marketplace. The communications dimension, the tip of the iceberg, is all that the general public can see and that is why it is so important.

Most brands have a concrete existence as businesses with plant, machinery and personnel, but they also have another existence as an idea in the collective public mind. Some brands, such as *Virgin*,[5] exist primarily as an abstract entity covering many diverse businesses (an airline, a cable TV and phone supplier, music production company, tourism and space travel operator and many more). In some cases, such as *Virgin*, corporate brands act as a family branding system, even if there may be no connection between those different businesses, other than the corporate branding. In other cases, such as *Unilever* or *P&G*, the corporate branding may often be invisible and individual product market offers are branded as distinct entities.

Brand advertising and communication, then, should not be thought of as a trivial or superficial activity in a marketing context. It is central to success in consumer, and increasingly industrial, marketing. For consumers the brand image or personality, the values and associations linked with the brand, the way the brand is talked about by friends and acquaintances, the way the brand is represented in press editorial and TV coverage, and the memory of personal experience of consuming the brand, are all aspects of a holistic engagement with this entity, the brand. A consumer brand is a fine exemplar of the notion of social construction (Berger and Luckman, 1966) since a brand is more than the sum of its parts, it is the ways in which it is understood, perceived and talked about. What is more, the perceptions of the brand become reality in the world of mediated communication, just as, in Berger and Luckman's (1966) example, a book can assume a separate but parallel existence through the way it is perceived and talked about. Influencing the way this abstraction is thought and spoken of is clearly a task in which communication is a primary tool.

Brand positioning and integrated communication

Positioning refers broadly to the values and associations, both tangible and intangible, that are linked with a given brand in relation to its competition. This positioning differentiates the brand from its rivals. Positioning can be conceived graphically, as a positioning 'map' in which competitors are mapped according to two dimensions, say, price and quality. Positioning can also be conceived linguistically in terms of metaphors that connect the brand to its values and associations. Brand marketing organisations take great care to articulate the positioning of brands so that the necessary values and associations can be reproduced through all levels of communications and marketing. Some, such as Unilever, who market some 1,000 brands globally, undertake detailed analysis of some of their brands to delineate its 'essence'. The components of this essence include: an analysis of the competitive environment; the target consumers; the key insight that makes the brand distinctive; the consumer benefits (tangible or intangible) conferred by the brand; the values and personality of the brand; the way the brand supports those values and why consumers should believe them; the features that differentiate the brand from its competitors; and the single concept that sums up the brand 'essence'. Unilever would need to draw out these issues for brands such as *Colman's* mustard, *Pot Noodle* snack food, *Birds Eye* processed foods, *Surf* detergent, *Domestos* bleach and numerous others. Each would differ depending on the brand positioning and the competitive conditions in each particular market. All major brand organisations use brand planning conceptual frameworks to emphasise the distinctive characteristics of each brand they market, and to enable them to maintain the same brand values and positioning through all their integrated communications.

Brand positioning

'Positioning' (see Snapshot 3.3) normally refers to the abstract psychological attributes and associations that a brand may evoke for consumers. It is inherently a relational concept since the positioning is relative to other brands in that marketspace. Positioning can also refer to more tangible characteristics of a brand that ostensibly differentiate it from others, such as the logo, packaging colour, frequency of and reason for use, and any other characteristic. Positioning is linked to the benefit, tangible or intangible, the manufacturer wishes to associate with consumption of the brand. For example, the chocolate countline *KitKat* has been positioned for many years as a reward for hard work, epitomised in the famous strapline 'Have a break – have a KitKat'. In contrast, rival countline brands such as *Bounty* bars or Cadbury's *Flake* are positioned as sensuous indulgences, not rewards for hard work but rewards for just being you. The differentiation is echoed in all advertising and brand communication since it is this differentiation which is essential to maintaining the brand's market share.

Positioning can also refer to the usage occasions appropriate for a brand. For example, advertising can be used to signal to consumers that a brand can be used in an alternative way or by different people in relation to the previous norm. The chocolate snack *Mars Bar* was advertised for many years with the strapline 'A Mars a Day Helps You Work, Rest and Play'. This reflected the brand's positioning as a tasty snack that gave one energy to cope with a busy life. Like many chocolate snack ads it was presented as a solitary pleasure rather than a social one. A later advertising campaign showed a group of happy-go-lucky young people pushing a broken-down car to a garage, cheerfully chomping on *Mars Bars*, thus repositioning the brand's somewhat dated image for a younger and more socially oriented consumer. *Mars Bar* consumption was now positioned as a social event and re-positioned to a younger audience. The breakfast cereal *Kellogg's Cornflakes* was the subject of an ad campaign that showed people enjoying cornflakes in non-breakfast scenarios. A couple enjoyed a romantic late-night bowl of cornflakes, and another consumer used the brand as a TV dinner. The aim was to increase sales to existing consumers by showing that you can eat cornflakes at any time. The brand was thus re-positioned as an anytime snack as well as a breakfast cereal.

Marketing and communication planning

There can be confusion between brand clients and advertising agencies about what, exactly, can be achieved through advertising communication. There is certainly some overlap between marketing and communication, but they are not the same. For example, a marketing plan might set an objective of achieving a 3% increase in market share over 2 months. A communication cannot deliver market share, because it is a communication. What it can do is to support the marketing objective by, for example, motivating consumers by giving them a reason to buy the desired brand instead of its rivals. This distinction may be nuanced but it is important. Exactly how a communication might motivate consumers would depend on the consumer target group characteristics, the product or service market in which the brand is operating, the distribution channels, the current competitive conditions, and so on. The relation between a marketing objective and a marketing communication objective is important and closely linked, but it can be subtle.

As an example, in one long-running campaign for car manufacturer Volkswagen, a London agency, then known as DDB Needham, devised a campaign based on the creative idea that Volkswagen cars were not as expensive as people thought. The qualitative research revealed that consumers perceived *VW* as high quality, and high price. In fact, the prices of the models were competitive with rivals in each car class. The marketing objectives were to increase market share by 3% in each class (family saloon, small car and executive saloon) across Europe, and to refresh the brand. The communication objective was to persuade consumers that they could have *VW* reliability and prestige without having to pay a high price. The advertising strategy had to put across the idea that *VW*s were not as expensive as people thought. The agency found amusing and low-key creative executions that informed consumers that, in fact, *VW*s were indeed less expensive than they thought. One ad showed an audience at a tennis match, losing focus on the ball when they see a *VW* poster. Another showed workmen wrapping up a lamp-post with a rubber cover because a distracting *VW* billboard has been placed by it, just as a man is about to walk into the lamp-post because he's looking at the billboard.[6] The market share increase was indeed achieved and the campaign ran for many years, winning many industry awards for creativity and for effectiveness. In this case, the marketing objectives, the communication objective and the advertising strategy were not exactly the same but they were mutually supportive. Naturally, the objectives would not have been achieved if the other elements of the marketing mix, the product (including service and after-sales, warranties, reliability, image and performance) and the distribution through the service centres, had not been up to scratch.

There is a great deal of scope for confusion and misunderstanding between the marketing plan and the marketing communication plan. This is one reason why client–agency relations is such a fraught advertising area. The problems can be managed if there is frequent dialogue and a mutual appreciation of the differences between marketing and communication. One of the key elements of integration in marketing communication is to ensure that all communications portray consistent and coherent brand values through all media and across all product ranges. So it is essential that the marketing planning and the communications planning do not conflict. For example, if an advertising campaign builds a high level of awareness and anticipation for a new brand launch in the chewing gum market, all that effort and resources will be wasted if the chewing gum has not made it into the stores by the time the campaign is launched, as happened in one instance. As another example, if the brand is positioned at the low cost, low quality end of the market, it would not be useful for the advertising to imply that the quality is excellent.

Strategic and tactical planning

It is useful to note a semantic distinction that can be important in brand planning. This is the distinction between strategic and tactical planning. Broadly, strategy refers to longer-term objectives that demand significant resources, while tactics refer to shorter medium-term objectives demanding fewer resources. However, the distinction between strategy and tactics is not always so clear-cut. Promotion is one quarter of the marketing mix, along with physical distribution, price and product, but it can command extensive resources and can also be the most important element of competitive success in some circumstances. Management is, after all, as much art as science, and the use of terms is far from precise or universally agreed. In the *VW* example above, the use of advertising clearly had a strategic implication since it represented a major and long-term investment (the campaign helped achieve strategic corporate goals in European market share). The distinction between strategy and tactics is typically based on timescale and importance to the overall profitability of the organisation. It is a mistake to assume, as some marketing texts do, that all promotional effort is merely tactical just because it is promotion. Advertising and promotional campaigns have, in many cases, attracted substantial resources and achieved strategic objectives for brands and for whole companies.

For example, a marketing strategy might be to achieve market dominance by being the high-quality supplier, and the promotional communications would have to find a way of supporting that. A marketing tactic might be to spoil a rival's promotional campaign by having a short-term, 10% price discount offer. Again, the communications would have to support the price-based promotion. In many organisations, the ideal plan would have strategic aims and objectives operating at the level of the corporation, with operational plans designed for each individual product market. The various levels of business and marketing objective would, ideally, dovetail into each other. So, for example, if the corporation was dealing in motor cars and positioned itself as the innovator in the market, then the various car brands it sold in each motor car segment (family saloon, small car, utility sports vehicle, etc.) would have different plans tailored to their particular target market and competitive conditions, though all would need to have a degree of fit with the overall corporate strategy. *Honda* and electronics giant *Sony* have become known for expensive, entertaining and high profile advertising campaigns that focus on the corporate brand values of quality and innovation, while they also have individual campaigns for particular models. The corporate level of communication sets the tone for the product–brand level of communication in advertising.

Integrated marketing communications (IMC)

The phrase 'integrated marketing communications' or IMC (Schultz et al., 1993, 1996) reflects managerial interest in co-ordinating different media channels to optimise the effectiveness of brand marketing communications programmes. If brand communications reflect coherent values, themes and imagery that have a connecting thread through differing media channels, then, the hope is that these might act in a mutually reinforcing way. Not only that, but using different media channels in a co-ordinated campaign might also reach much larger potential audiences. A third perceived advantage is control. The portrayal of the brand has become the dominant issue in marketing communication, and IMC holds out the hope that brand representatives might be able to control the way the brand is portrayed from the centre of communication strategy, instead of having to cede some of that control to different media specialists. In practice, IMC is far from realised for reasons that we will discuss below, but it remains a useful descriptive tool for marketing education.

Brands clients often want to see the brand values communicated across several platforms simultaneously in 'through-the-line' or 'integrated' campaigns. Above-the-line (ATL) media are mass media: TV, radio, press etc. Below-the-line (BTL) refers to media that did not attract commission payments from media owners, such as sales promotions, logo-bedecked balloons, pens, direct mail, OOH etc. Through-the-line (TTL) campaigns use both, in an integrated way. Interest in IMC has developed partly because of the view that marketing communication offers the 'only sustainable competitive advantage of marketing organizations' (Schultz et al., 1993: 47). IMC places the brand at the centre of strategy, rather than on the periphery as an afterthought. Once, advertising and promotional communication was conceived on a linear model as an effort to create one-way communication that would influence the attitudes and behaviour of target audiences (Shimp, 2009). In the convergent media environment, in contrast, brands are considered in relational terms as nodes of interaction between brand owners, consumers and other stakeholders. IMC represents the attempt to co-ordinate brand stories and content through all media channels, especially social media.

There have been pressures in the industry pushing ad agencies toward integration. Advertising agencies consider traditional advertising to be their core activity, but the larger, full-service agencies are increasingly finding that clients expect them to offer expertise across the marketing communication disciplines. Consumers, moreover, do not generally make a strong distinction between the differing media that carry advertising. As Percy et al. point out, 'people generally look at all marketing communications as "advertising"' (2001: v). The rise of brand marketing makes the advertising medium secondary to the brand personality (to use ad man David Ogilvy's expression), an entity that can be expressed through many differing forms of creative execution and communicated through different media. Integrated advertising campaigns utilise the qualities of different media in a communications effort designed to maintain consistent brand values regardless of whatever communication source the consumer encounters.

The blurring of the lines between marketing communications disciplines is part of a radical change in the media infrastructure coming from developments in electronic communications technology and the rise of global business.

Global brands now cross borders and resonate with the consumers in many countries. Mass media, above-the-line advertising is often regarded as the strategic element of marketing communications, the one communication technique that can transform the fortunes of corporations, create brands and change entire markets. Although there are still good reasons for holding this view, there is also a strong case for managers to consider advertising from a strategic, integrated and media-neutral perspective which acknowledges that the rationale for brand communications drives the pragmatic development of integrated creative executions and media strategies. On this logic, mass media advertising is not necessarily the centerpiece of every campaign.

The idea of integrated marketing communications, then, reflects the need to take a global view of the brand and to ensure that brand communications across all media are consistent in terms of the brand image, values and personality, and that the media channels used are complementary with regard to segmentation, positioning and targeting. IMC has become more popular because of various factors, notably the fragmentation of media audiences and changes in the media consumption patterns of these audiences in the light of an explosion of new media channels and vehicles. Concomitantly, IMC reflects a shift in power from manufacturers to consumers, a shift from mass to niche media channels and vehicles, the emphasis on data-driven marketing and the move to 24/7 consumption.

Integration of media implies the use of online and offline media channels. Offline media channels could include the traditional 'old media' of television, print (newspapers, magazines), radio, cinema advertising and also outdoor advertising, direct marketing, public relations, personal selling and sales promotion. Online channels could include dedicated websites, optimisation of search engine results, email, banner and click-through advertising, podcasts, blogs and other web-based exposure.

SNAPSHOT 3.4

Integration and the creative execution

A major challenge for IMC is to devise a creative approach, the creative execution, that will translate across different media channels. Many creative approaches are channel-specific in the sense that they will work best on a particular medium. For example, one of the major creative movements in advertising since the 1960s has been dramatic realism. Ad agencies use imagery and metaphors from classical art and literature to create aesthetically inspiring dramatic portrayals of the product along with 'an account of … the social benefit that the consumer

(Continued)

(Continued)

could be expected to derive' (Leiss et al., 1997: 79). Demonstrating the social benefit is most effective if the consumer can be portrayed in their everyday circumstances, but with the heightened dramatic effect contributed by portrayal in a medium with high production values such as a glossy magazine or TV ad. This takes consumers' daily activities and portrays them in an altogether more dramatically interesting light. Marchand (1985) describes the advertising technique used to accomplish this effect as 'dramatic realism'. For example, an everyday situation such as dirt on clothes might be portrayed as a problem that the model housewife solves with the help of a branded detergent. The picture accompanying the advertising text would be carefully drawn as graphic art, perhaps with an attractive model in a striking pose, in juxtaposition with the brand logo and packaging. Dramatic realism helps the consumer identify with the creative themes in the ad. Advertising agencies recognised consumers' needs for aesthetic stimulation and symbolic self-expression and bridged the gap between manufacturers and creative artists. In this way the design of American advertising and the products themselves was improved (Leiss et al., 1997: 81). Consumers were treated to advertising that was aesthetically attractive and a product that could express something about consumer personality and social identity. Mass media were especially suited to this kind of execution, so part of the challenge for IMC has been to adapt creative executions into new media channels.

Two dimensions of integration for brand communication: themes and channels

It is important to understand the rationale behind integration of marketing communications. One key issue has been noted above: that is, the primacy of the brand as the concept that drives marketing activity. All marketing activity is designed to support, enhance and reflect the brand as a symbol of certain values and characteristics that differentiate it in the market. Consumers seek out brands, we recognise them and we pay more for the reassurance that quality brands offer. The brand may comprise many tangible things, and consumer preferences may be developed through the direct experience of buying it. But there is also a powerful element of communication involved since brand image is built up not only through direct personal experience of the brand's utility but also through less tangible attitudes and perceptions which are influenced by the communication we read, hear, see and express about the brand. The management effort to ensure a co-ordinated and coherent approach to integrated brand planning rests on two overlapping and connected dimensions: (1) brand themes; and (2) media channels.

The first, the themes, concerns the need to manage the distinctive brand values and personality as they are expressed through all communication, from corporate to product–market communication. This focuses on the visible elements of the brand, including its colours, logo, typeface, and other aspects of the visual representation. So there should be particular themes which reflect and portray the brand positioning that can run through all marketing communication for a given brand, and which ensure that the brand is recognised and its positioning is distinctive. This is no easy task when campaigns may have many parts, perhaps designed by different sub-contracted agency specialists. Nevertheless, it is the key task of brand planning to ensure that the brand retains its integrity whatever the medium or creative execution may be. The second dimension concerns channel integration. We live in a world of integrated and interlocking media. If we have a favourite TV show we don't just watch the show. We can read weblogs posted by fans or critics, we can go to the show website for stories about the characters and the actors or to buy merchandise. We can even download episodes via the internet, to listen to by podcast or on a mobile device. We can buy magazines that carry articles for fans of the show, follow the show's Twitter feed and like its Facebook page. And so it goes, a given brand, whether it be a car, a watch, or a clothing range of a movie or syndicated TV show, can be exposed on many different media channels. It is therefore incumbent on the brand management to utilise these different media channels in promotion of the brand, and to try to manage the brand image through these channels.

The integrated marketing communications plan

There is no definitive formula for planning or implementing IMC. The precise composition of an IMC plan will differ according to the particular market and communication context, and according to the custom and practice of particular organisations. A plan is not a prescription nor is it a checklist. It is a guide for action. Typically, an IMC plan would have the following general elements. There are many possible variations on the IMC plan.[7]

- Executive summary
- Brand research and competition analysis
- Target audience
- Communication objectives
- Advertising strategy
- Creative approach
- Media plan
- Action plan and tactics
- Budget estimates
- Effectiveness evaluation

Brand research and competition analysis

It is rare for brands to require a radical re-positioning that distances the brand from its earlier manifestations. In most cases, the brand needs some continuity from one campaign to the next to reflect the coherence and stability of the brand personality. This is why it is so important for the agency to research the brand and the client organisation in order to try to fully understand its history and values. This includes looking at previous promotional campaigns. In addition, it is important to thoroughly understand the competitive context in which the brand is operating. Brand values and personalities must be understood in the context of alternatives – the reason for the brand is to differentiate the offer from competitors, so it must be understood in relation to competitors. This differentiation expresses the brand's positioning, and it reflects the attitudes and values that consumers project onto the brand. So for integration in brand communication to be achievable, it is a prerequisite that the advertising agency has a deep understanding of the brand.

In many cases, the agency will take two or three weeks over this research and analysis stage. The account team will rely mainly on secondary sources but they may also make use of primary sources in the form of focus groups with consumers and in-depth discussions with the client staff. After all, if a client thinks its brand values are different to those the consumers thinks it has then there is a fundamental communication problem to address. Advertising agency staff are fond of relating stories about clients who didn't understand their own brand. It is easy to understand that internal organisational values and politics might make it difficult to face reality if, for example, consumer perception of a brand personality has been distorted through negative media coverage. Sometimes a dispassionate agency view can highlight incoherence between the brand values as envisaged by the client and those as perceived by the consumer. Whether the client can accept such advice is another matter. Either way, the first element in the process of creating an integrated marketing communications campaign is for the agency to gain a thorough and insightful understanding of the brand, its history and values, and its competitive context.

Target audience

Advertising agencies need to know to whom the client wants them to speak. This refers to the tasks of segmentation and targeting. But knowing who the target audience is, is not enough. A conscientious agency will also want to understand the lifestyle preferences, consumption habits, media consumption patterns, values, attitudes, drives, aspirations, income, priorities and influential peer groups of its target segment. Qualitative research in the form of discussion or focus groups, or surveys, can be of assistance in this stage of the process.

Secondary data sources detailing demographic and other information important to segmentation and targeting can also be invaluable. If the mentality, lifestyle, demographic characteristics and buying preferences of the target group are understood, then this can form the basis for a creative execution which speaks to its members in a way they will recognise. Defining the target audience is a difficult task with major implications. Once the audience is defined, this will drive the media plan and advertising schedule. It will also heavily influence the advertising strategy and creative execution. Get it wrong, and all the effort is wasted. If the defined audience is too narrow then opportunities for consumer engagement will be lost and the campaign will not yield the desired return on investment. If the target group definition is too wide, then impact may be lost or the campaign might be scheduled on a medium that the real targets don't use.

Communication objectives

Building on the above information and insights, the account team will be ready to formulate communication objectives. These will guide the overall approach and should dovetail into the client's marketing plan objectives. Communication objectives are key because they will form the bridge between the marketing plan and the integrated marketing communications campaign. They will clarify how communication can support the marketing objectives. Life in brand marketing and advertising agencies consists of a lot of meetings at which every step in the planning process is debated and discussed. Each element of the IMC plan will be interrogated for coherence and viability. The elements of the brand personality and its 'essence' are so difficult to pin down that this kind of process is necessary in order to keep attention focused on the key brand values and personality and to ensure that they are superimposed throughout all communication channels and mix elements. Communication objectives might, for example, be to engage the interest of the target audience and inform them about the kinds of problem-solving challenges entailed in active army service. Whatever the objectives are, they should be something that can be achieved through communication and which supports the marketing objectives.

Advertising strategy

Advertising has to have a purpose in order to succeed. If no one knows what they want to achieve by a campaign, then success is not possible because there will be no yardstick by which to measure it. The advertising strategy is important because it guides the creative team and encourages them to produce creative work which can motivate the desired consumers in a way that supports the overall communication objectives. To be effective, the advertising strategy should be expressed in simple terms without jargon, so that creatives (who have no patience with marketing jargon) can understand it.

The advertising strategy should explain what the ad is to do. For example, should it motivate an immediate response? Does the client want people who engage with the ad to pick up the phone or go on the internet to contact the company? Or is the aim to encourage an emotional response from the viewer in the interest of building long-term brand equity? Is it to persuade the consumer to trial the product, or to convince them that it is better value/cooler/higher quality than competitors? Is the strategy to change consumer attitudes or buying habits? The advertising strategy will inform the creative brief which is the document the creative team has to work from. It is therefore essential that the advertising strategy, the reason for advertising, is clear, coherent and consistent with the overall brand personality and communication objectives.

Creative approach and creative brief

Once the marketing and communication objectives have been decided and the advertising strategy devised, the most important part of the whole process is undertaken – this is the creative approach (also called the creative execution). The creative approach can undo all the careful planning and waste the budget, or it can leverage the brand and generate benefits of positive publicity far in excess of expectations. A campaign that is talked about and shared on social media will receive unsolicited attention that spreads the brand values and reinforces the brand presence. A creative execution that is ignored because it's regarded as boring might lack impact and resonance for the target group. On the other hand, with some campaigns and some brands it is more important to portray the brand values in a clear and coherent way than it is to be creatively striking. As with all other elements of the IMC plan, the precise marketing and communication objectives in the context of the brand's values, positioning and competitive position, inform the creative approach.

The creative approach is decided with reference to the creative brief. The creative brief is an important document that is discussed in detail in Chapter 5. It is the guide from which the creative team will work and it represents an agreement between the agency and the client regarding what the advertising should achieve. The brief disciplines the creative work to ensure that the creativity is not over-indulged simply because it looks great or because it's so funny. The aim of advertising is not to win awards for creatives or to gratify their creative urges but to generate business for clients. The creative brief is the document that represents the client and agency interest in the campaign. It is the creative expression of the communication strategy.

The creative team must express the brand values and the advertising strategy in a way that attracts the right kind of attention from the target group. The creative approach also needs to consider practical issues such as the budget, length or size of ad, medium or channel. Most importantly, it needs to be focused according to the particular type(s) of person to whom the advertisement must speak. Creatives tend to claim that if they know their audience, whatever kind of person that is, they can produce a piece of work which motivates that audience. So the brief has to be based on careful research and clear commercial reasoning.

Media plan

In any advertising campaign there are important decisions to take regarding media, and many issues to consider. Most media buying agencies are now independent of advertising agencies, but media should have been kept in mind from the beginning of the IMC process because media and creative execution are interdependent. How can the target group be reached most efficiently and with the greatest impact? Do media choices have to accommodate a direct response element? Does the budget allow for broadcast media, or does it confine the campaign to local print media?

The media plan (discussed more extensively in Chapter 6) is an important document that directs the campaign to the right target audience with the maximum impact and reach, at the lowest possible cost per thousand consumers reached. Some campaigns burst onto the scene saturating all media channels for a week, and then disappear. Others are planned to drip the communication into consumers' consciousness in short exposures at longer intervals over a protracted period of time. Still others are focused on seasonal demand issues, such as where chocolate manufacturers spend a large proportion of their advertising budget in the UK over the Christmas period because of the high concentration of chocolate sales at that time. The media schedule depends not only on the budget but also on the brand, the market, the target audience or segment, and the campaign objectives.

Budget and effectiveness

In reality, in many cases, the budget has been set by the client before the first stage in the IMC planning process has begun. Where the agency does have scope for action is in accounting for the success, or the failure, of the campaign. Any campaign can be assessed against the objectives set for it, though doing so is not always a simple task. Calculating return on investment (ROI) is a difficult but important task in marketing and advertising since it reflects the effectiveness of different kinds of marketing intervention and the implications go straight to the bottom line of profitability. The ROI is also important in deciding in the future what budget to allocate to particular forms of advertising.

As noted above, well-planned campaigns have clear and achievable objectives precisely so that their achievement (or lack of it) can be judged. For example, if the communication objective of a campaign were to change attitudes towards eating a brand of breakfast cereal so that consumers would start to eat it in the evening as a snack, it would be relatively easy to conduct a street survey asking respondents when they ate this brand of breakfast cereal before and after the campaign. Before and after surveys of attitudes or behaviours are common methods of measuring campaign effectiveness. Another common approach is to use internal company records to look at sales patterns or new customer enquiries that might be linked in principle to advertising exposures. Many measures of effectiveness rely on long-term data regarding market share or sales volume, so the true effect of an advertising campaign can often not be fairly judged until many months after the campaign.

SNAPSHOT 3.5

Tracking the effectiveness of BT's 'It's Good to Talk' campaign

One example of effective campaign tracking involved the use of a statistical technique called multivariate analysis to try to establish a strong correlation between a campaign and a change in customer behaviour. A famous UK campaign (called 'It's Good to Talk') conducted for British Telecom (BT) attempted to change the telephone usage habits of domestic British customers. The advertising agency's consumer research had established that the average length of British domestic telephone conversations was significantly shorter than those in other countries such as the USA, Italy and Germany. It seemed that there was a British mentality that saw talking on the telephone as a cost that should be minimised. In fact the cost was and is small as a proportion of household income. In many other countries (such as Germany, Italy and the USA) domestic telephone users seemed to regard telephone conversation as a necessary expense and spoke for far longer on average on each call. This consumer research insight formed the basis for the campaign. A series of TV ads dramatically portrayed the typically succinct British phone user as someone lacking in empathy and warmth. The message was that it was kinder to talk at greater length, especially when talking to loved ones. The ads also suggested that telephone communication could strengthen bonds of family and friendship if people used it generously. It was claimed that the campaign resulted in a major social change: domestic telephone usage habits in the UK were substantially altered. A near 60% increase in call revenues to BT was claimed. The agency used multivariate analysis to correlate the electronic data on telephone conversation length with the exposure of the TV ads.

Limitations to IMC

IMC has made a big splash in academic journals but its resonance for practitioners is variable (Eagle et al., 2007). Carolyn Ray, a Director of Integrated Communications Planning at consultants Interbrand, has written of the reasons why the industry feels that IMC has not lived up to its hype. IMC, however, isn't going away, because of the potential benefits it holds. As Ray puts it:

> IMC is based on the principle of integration, which holds that all communications emanating from a single strategic platform will generate a significantly greater return on the communications investment than would be the case with traditional independent media executions. In a client–agency relationship, the theoretical benefits are clear. For the client, there is the potential for significant synergies and stronger connections with their customers. For the agency, there is the promise of a more complete partnership with the client that provides a greater share of the total marketing communications budget. [8]

On the one hand, practitioners tend to agree that integration is a given in contemporary advertising planning. The use of new media is essential if clients are to fully leverage the promotional budget. On the other hand, many professionals dispute whether it is possible or desirable to formalise IMC. This intersects debates within strategy and marketing on the virtues and practical difficulties of planning per se. In many cases, business plans are created through an internal process that focuses minds and helps to disburse resources, but often departs more than somewhat from what actually takes place. Plans tend to rest on assumptions, the full implications of which only become apparent when the action is under way. This is not to argue that planning is irrelevant in business and administration, it is merely to point out that while planning is a necessary and fundamental part of managerial processes it does have its limitations.

With regard to IMC, many industry professionals ask whether it can ever be more than partially achievable. Media integration is something that depends very much on the circumstances of the brief, on the creativity and lateral thinking of the teams involved, and on the objectives for the campaign. How can there be general theories or principles of IMC if each brief is so very different? What is more, from a practical perspective, should there be an assumption that IMC is a necessary virtue for any campaign?

It is by no means clear that integration will benefit every brief. Some twenty years after IMC became a popular buzz term in marketing, some leading ad agencies still handle a large proportion of business in which they are asked to produce an advertising campaign without any digital component. It is a standard part of advertising planning that there is an evaluation of media channels in terms of segmentation and targeting, audience reach, resonance and cost per thousand target consumers. In this regard, some practitioners argue that IMC is nothing new. The media channels have changed and the media vehicles have multiplied, but advertising has always been subject to such changes and has adapted accordingly. It has always been conventional wisdom in advertising that media channels are used selectively: why use every channel just because they are there?

One reason might be that media consumption patterns have changed in such a way that reaching a target consumer through all possible channels is now feasible, where it wasn't before. But even this is dubious. The ideal of controlling the message through every medium through which the target audience might access brand communication is all very well in principle, but there are many barriers. Firstly, absolute control of brand communication is not possible – there will always be leakage between media, say through media editorial coverage. User-generated content such as blogs and wikis, twittering, and so forth, occupies much internet space and neither this, nor everyday news stories connecting with the brand, can be controlled. They can be reacted to and incorporated into communication plans, but this is a reactive process largely charged to the media relations function.

Furthermore, absolute control over brand communications on every medium may not even be desirable, even if it were possible. Brands are products of culture. They result from the interactions of consumers in the social context in which they are seen and used. They are not entirely the creation of the brand owner. Many brands, indeed, are building user-generated content into their strategies through social media consumer engagement initiatives. For example, in 2011 *Coca-Cola* posted a video demonstrating their content marketing strategy through 2020 on YouTube, and a central part of this is to engage consumers in brand storytelling and to incorporate consumer ideas into future strategies.[9] Arguably, this is less about a top-down, one-way model of brand communication control and more about a collaborative style of opening up the brand to consumer engagement, which, in turn, feeds back into brand and communications planning.

Where there is less argument is around the need for advertising and promotional planning to integrate creative themes across different media platforms. This is dictated by the logic of branding – a brand must represent distinctive values and these are linked with certain conventions of visual and auditory representation. Put more simply, a brand ought to be distinguished by the same colour scheme or signature tune whatever the medium, so that consumers recognise it as that brand. But many professionals regard this as a given, a default position, and no more than professional commonsense, rather than a theoretical or formal planning principle. IMC is undoubtedly an area that professionals in communication cannot ignore. It is perhaps not surprising that academic and scholarly research focuses around trying to gather general principles or theories, while professionals are focused more pragmatically on client briefs that can be utterly different from day to day.

Naturally, if academics can generate a theory of IMC that helps practitioners get more out of their clients' budgets then there would be less scepticism and much applause from the industry. But like so much research and theory in business and management, the ambition of IMC scholarship and research isn't yet realised in terms of its relevance and effectiveness for practice. Nonetheless, several factors will ensure that IMC as an idea continues to receive attention from all sides. One factor concerns the possibilities for greater efficiency and accountability opened up by digital advertising media applications and the increasing advertising potential of mobile. While this area may not be accessible to a general theory, it is certainly one in which practitioners will be open to any useful general insights or principles. In particular, the economic recession and the consequent squeeze on promotional budgets will mean that greater attention will be paid to cost-per-thousand and return on investment criteria. These returns can be measured most effectively through new media.

Another important factor driving integration of campaign planning concerns the fragmentation of media audiences and changes in media consumption patterns that mean that advertising and promotional planners often have to deploy integrated campaigns simply in order to reach sufficient numbers of their desired market segment. Finally, the increased attention being paid to consumer engagement with brand communications also pushes planners towards new media that facilitate such engagement in cost-efficient and user-appealing ways.

Chapter summary

This chapter has introduced the integrated marketing communication process. It discussed the central role of the brand in this process, and explained the distinctions between marketing objectives, communication objectives and advertising strategy. It also discussed distinctions between marketing strategy and tactics, and noted that advertising and promotion can be strategic as well as tactical. The two main dimensions of integration were explained, these being integration of brand theme across channels, and integration of media channels in advertising campaigns. The chapter then listed the basic stages in a typical IMC plan. Each stage in the plan has been outlined in Chapter 3 while many of them are developed in greater detail in other parts of the book. Finally, limitations and caveats around the somewhat fashionable notion of IMC were discussed. Chapter 4 will move on to discuss the internal processes and roles of advertising agencies engaged in this process.

■ Review Questions

1. Collect ten video, radio or print advertisements and divide them between two groups. Each group should try to ascertain what each of their ads was intended to accomplish. In other words, what was the planning rationale behind the ads? Then the two groups should swap ads and perform the same exercise on the other group of ads. The two groups combined should discuss their respective analysis of each ad and decide which analysis seems the most likely to be accurate. The intention behind the ads should be considered in the light of such issues as: (a) the likely target audience for the brand; (b) other possible stakeholders; (c) the apparent brand positioning indicated by the ad's creative approach; (d) the choice of medium; and (e) other marketing issues concerning this brand.

2. List as many examples as you can of marketing objectives that might be supported with advertising and promotion. Be prepared to justify your choice with examples or reasoning.

3. Is the role of communication in marketing primarily tactical or strategic? Give reasons for your answer.

4. Develop a scenario in which your group has been asked to offer outline creative ideas for the launch of a new brand of chocolate confection called 'Slick'. Focus on the segmentation, targeting (especially media) and positioning issues.

CASE STUDY

Toyota Corolla and IMC

The new model 11th generation *Toyota Corolla*, the biggest selling car brand in the world, launched in 2014 accompanied by an integrated marketing communication campaign called 'Elevate' from Saatchi & Saatchi Los Angeles. The campaign was targeted at the 'Millennial generation, while still appealing to Baby Boomers'. The campaign press release[10] claimed that their research has shown that Millennials ('also known as Generation Y') were looking for their first 'real' car, and the company is hoping that the redesign of the car will make it fit the bill. The key broadcast ad is a 60 second spot called 'Style Never Goes Out of Style' shown on TV and in cinemas. The ad places the *Corolla* at the hub of pop culture since its launch in 1968. The print campaign shows crowds of people cheering the car, while content clips of battling DJs and a hip-hop music producer were shown on digital. LED highlighted OOH signs and billboards in major US cities had a built-in chip that enabled consumers to go on a virtual test drive via their smartphone. An advergame mobile app adds to the excitement, whilst 6 second Vine videos and 15 second Instagram videos showed dance styles including the signature 'Elevated' dance from the broadcast commercial. The agency hopes that viewers will share content via the hashtag CorollaStyle. Access to the campaign via mobile is particularly important for the Millennial target group.[11] Experiential and activation included events and games at cinema showings of the ad, and opportunities for test drives.

There are certainly plenty of media involved here, and lots of variety, but the advertising strategy failed to ignite the enthusiasm of some industry bloggers.[12] The *Toyota Corolla* has always been regarded as a reliable, trustworthy workhorse of a car – it has never been about style. Agency creative briefs typically feature the question 'what must the consumer believe as a result of seeing the ad?' followed by the supplementary question 'why will they believe it?' Is it believable that *Corolla* was a style-leading car for young people through the decades? Is it believable that it will be so in 2014? Then again, could the strategy be a double bluff, appealing to the anti-style consumers but allowing them to pretend that they're cooler than they really are?

For some industry experts, IMC requires the same things good advertising has always required – a strong creative idea based on a genuine consumer insight. *Nike* is touted as an example of this by one expert[13] for its 2014 'Find Your Greatness' campaign, as were *Snickers* 'you're not quite you when you're hungry' and a campaign for *Foster's* lager that played on laddish humour. In each case, the writer claimed that the foundation was a great idea based on a consumer insight. Just as with an advertising campaign, the platform for success for an IMC campaign is the creative idea. The difficulty in IMC is in finding ways to craft an idea that works well on broadcast to also work well on digital, print and so on. Then again, as noted in Chapter 2, for some brands, in some markets, perhaps the creative idea doesn't need to be great, perhaps it only needs to be not too terrible, provided the campaign makes enough noise to alert the market to the presence and intent of the brand.

Case Questions

1. In a small group, design an IMC campaign for a new brand of car. The name, brand positioning and target market are your choice. Try to integrate as many media channels as possible, and unite them with a key idea. Do this in half an hour. What are the key problems that emerged in this task?

2. Does IMC re-write the rules of marketing, or merely offer increased opportunities for good marketing practice to reap rewards?

3. By the time this book goes into print, the verdict will be out on the *Toyota Corolla* 2014 campaign. What are the industry and bloggers saying about it, and how successful do they feel it was? What were the components considered most successful?

4. List all the circumstances you can think of in which an IMC campaign would not be appropriate for a brand. Give reasons to justify your list.

Useful journal articles

(These Sage articles can be accessed on the book website)

Diana L. Haytko (2004) 'Firm-to-firm and interpersonal relationships: perspectives from advertising agency account managers', *Journal of the Academy of Marketing Science*, 32: 312–28.

Harlan E. Spotts, David R. Lambert and Mary L. Joyce (1998) 'Marketing dèjá vu: the discovery of integrated marketing communications', *Journal of Marketing Education*, 20: 210–18.

Yesim Kaptan (2013) '"We just know!": Tacit knowledge and knowledge production in the Turkish advertising industry', *Journal of Consumer Culture*, 13 (3): 264–82.

Neil O'Boyle (2012) 'Managing indeterminacy: culture, Irishness and the advertising industry', *Cultural Sociology*, 6 (3): 351–66 (first published December 14, 2011).

John R. Rossiter (2012) 'Advertising management principles are derived mostly from logic and very little from empirical generalizations', *Marketing Theory*, 12 (2): 103–1.

■ ■ Further reading ■

Belch, G. and Belch, M. (2011) *Advertising and Promotion: An Integrated Marketing Communications Perspective*. New York: McGraw-Hill.

Hackley, C. and Hackley née Tiwsakul, R.A. (2013) 'From integration to convergence – the management of marketing communications', in H. Powell (ed.), *Promotional Culture in an Era of Convergence*. Abingdon: Taylor and Francis, pp. 70–87.

Holt, D. (2004) *How Brands Become Icons: The Principles of Cultural Branding*. Boston, MA: Harvard Business School Press.

Percy, L. and Elliott, R. (2009) *Strategic Advertising Management*, 3rd edn. Oxford: Oxford University Press.

Schultz, D. (2003) *IMC – The Next Generation*. New York: McGraw-Hill.

Schultz, D. and Kitchen, P. (1997) 'Integrated marketing communications in US advertising agencies: an exploratory study', *Journal of Advertising Research*, September/October: 7–18.

Notes

1. www.interbrand.com/en/best-global-brands/2013/Best-Global-Brands-2013.aspx accessed 11.2.2014
2. www.forbes.com/powerful-brands/list/ accessed 12.2.2014
3. www.ipa.co.uk/ accessed 13.2.2014
4. http://backspace.com/notes/2002/09/the-poster-that-won-the-election.php accessed 13.2.2014
5. www.virgin.com/ accessed 13.2.2014
6. www.campaignlive.co.uk/thework/920833/ accessed 12.2.2014
7. For example, see www.brandchannel.com/papers_review.asp?sp_id=650 accessed 13.2.2014
8. www.brandchannel.com/papers_review.asp?sp_id=650 accessed 13.2.2014
9. www.youtube.com/watch?v=LerdMmWjU_E accessed 13.2.2014
10. www.prnewswire.com/news-releases/integrated-marketing-campaign-elevates-2014-toyota-corolla-to-new-heights-222503921.html accessed 13.2.2014
11. www.mobilemarketer.com/cms/news/strategy/16115.html accessed 13.2.2014
12. http://adage.com/article/cmo-strategy/toyota-s-ad-2014-corolla-shows-sell-cars/244201/ accessed 13.2.2014
13. www.theguardian.com/best-awards/powerful-integrated-campaigns-secret accessed 13.2.2014

4 Advertising Agencies – Organising Creative Work

Chapter outline

Chapter 1 explained that advertising agencies are operating in an uncertain environment. New media funding models are being driven by media convergence and audience fragmentation, and one consequence of this is that advertising has been displaced by new, hybrid promotional genres, most strikingly by the superordinate concept of branded 'content'. The demands on agencies for creativity, strategic thinking and media craft skills have never been greater, and agency working practices are evolving to face the new environment. New knowledge, new disciplines and new work processes are being mixed with tried and tested methods. Chapter 4 uses traditional agency account team roles as a starting point for an exploration of how advertising is made.

Key chapter content

- Advertising agencies as cultural intermediaries
- The advertising agency in evolution
- Advertising agencies and the pitch process
- Account team roles and responsibilities

Advertising agencies as cultural intermediaries

Advertising and promotion are the primary means by which brands acquire their cultural resonance. The mechanisms through which they do this tend to be largely ignored in marketing texts and courses. To be sure, a great deal of advertising seems to lack much depth or complexity – what is there to analyse in a 10 second broadcast ad making a price appeal for a local car retailer, or a print ad declaring that the kumquats from one supermarket chain are always fresh and juicy? But as we have noted, there are deeper aspects to advertising. For one thing, the aspects of communication we take most for granted are often the most enigmatic, once we start to notice them. In particular, what is not expressly stated but implied in ads can often be the most powerful. For another, it seems clear that a lot of advertising is not merely a cheaply made and simply conceived sales pitch, but is thoroughly planned and conceived at an abstract level to subtly perpetuate brand values and associations. Advertising agencies are regarded as key institutions in twentieth-century capitalism, and they have collectively been and continue to be a major influence on contemporary consumer culture. As we have seen, most global brands cannot be conceived without the advertising that is central to their success. Not only what they do but how they do it are important topics in marketing and advertising.

Advertising agencies have been described as 'cultural intermediaries' (e.g. Cronin, 2004) in the sense that they seem to take elements of culture such as art, language, music, fashion and popular trends, and they use them in juxtaposition with brands to make up new forms of communication aimed at a selected audience. Culture in this sense is meant broadly to mean not only high art, classical music and serious literature, though these are very much part of the advertisers' vocabulary, but also aspects of everyday culture such as current affairs and media news stories, popular fashions, fads and trends, and anything else that might feature in the habitus of the consumer. Advertisements take culture and reflect it back at itself, marketising the most mundane of daily routines by adding symbolic value. At least, that is one way of conceiving of the role of advertising agencies.

Certainly, ad agencies are deeply interested in everyday consumer culture, and cultural theorists have been very interested in ad agencies, although there have been surprisingly few studies of the social dynamics of advertising development (exceptions include Blake et al., 1996; Cronin, 2004, 2008; Deuze, 2007; Kelly et al., 2005; Alvesson, 1998; deWaal Malefyt and Moeran, 2003; Fowles, 1996; Leiss et al., 2005; Hackley, 2000; McCracken, 2005; Nixon, 2003; Svensson, 2007; Gilmore et al. 2011). Operating at the interface of culture and commerce, advertising agencies can be seen to have a powerful ideological role in promoting consumption as a lifestyle and in framing and normalising all kinds of behaviours. This is not to suggest that we are helpless against the power of advertising – far from it. Indeed, the very fact that advertising sometimes seems to have such power is a tribute to the cleverness of advertising professionals in creating so many iconic campaigns.

Advertising is often the target of criticism because of its putative influence over behaviour and cultural values. But on the other hand, advertising uses culture as its material – it takes what is already out there and combines it with images of consumption. So the question of whether advertising causes certain things or merely reflects them becomes a circular one because of its role as cultural intermediary, mediating between brands and taking language, behaviour, values and trends from everyday culture and transforming them into messages of consumption. Advertising may sometimes magnify or even distort social practices, behaviour and values that are already out there, but whether it deserves the bad press it sometimes gets is open to argument.

SNAPSHOT 4.1

Integration and WCRS

Many advertising agencies preach integration without necessarily incorporating it into their working methods. Leading agency WCRS of London boast a staff roster that includes 34 creatives, 41 digital specialists plus 9 social media specialists, 29 account managers, 6 analysts and 11 strategists (which probably means 17 account planners) and no less than 27 'delivery managers'. These are, presumably, not van drivers but probably people who were once were called 'traffic' and now more often go under the term project management. The agency's website[1] states that 41% of its work in 2012 involved integrated advertising and digital communications. Ad agencies in general are reinventing themselves by bringing in new discipline specialists that formerly might have been outsourced. WCRS recently merged a number of different businesses, including a digital agency. Digital agencies boomed in the 1990s but most have either become service departments, building and servicing websites, or they have been bought up because they found it difficult to make money as a free-standing business. Ad agencies have the strategic and management expertise, and they need to bring digital communication into the centre of brand communication planning.

Advertising language and discourse

Part of the fascination of advertising and promotion for practitioners is that it entails solving problems of communication when the main basis of communication, language, is continually adapting to express new kinds of experience and to accommodate new influences. The English language is especially popular in advertising the world over, probably because of its flexibility and global familiarity as the language of business. Of course, advertising's use of imagery and music makes it a richer device of communication than language alone. Indeed, as we have noted, part of advertising's uniqueness as a discourse form derives from its capacity to combine language with music, pictures and substance or medium (Cook, 2001). But language itself carries meaning within its context: there is a medium of transmission (written or aural) and meanings are nuanced through the combination of language with tone, gesture and other aspects of context. Advertising and promotion offer forms of communication that not only set language in any social context with which we are familiar, but invent new contexts through novel combinations of imagery, words and music. The possibilities for novelty in advertising communication seem limitless.

Advertising can be seen as a form of discourse since it is an identifiable form of communication that can be described. As a discourse, advertising is defined by its conventional narrative forms, but these do evolve and adapt to new media. As we have noted, advertising and communication agencies produce cultural texts that portray consumption by drawing on social practices and symbols extant in the wider, non-consumption culture. For example, at the most simple level, a promotion that pictures people riding on a public bus cannot communicate anything unless viewers of the ad are familiar with the cultural practice of riding on a public bus. Riding on a bus is not merely an act: it is a cultural practice because it is subject to agreed rules that are seldom stated. There are conventional ways of paying one's fare and of inter-acting (or not) with the driver, ways of taking one's seat (or not taking one and standing up), ways of disembarking at the correct stop, even ways of speaking to fellow passengers or to the driver. If one tries to take a bus ride in a strange country with an unfamiliar language the importance of these conventions becomes all too apparent and one can look, and feel, socially inept because one does not know them. As Goffman (1959, 1979) has underlined, there is a quality of performance to social interaction of which we tend not to be consciously aware, except when we are in a situation where we do not know the social conventions. It is part of advertisers' job to act as informal applied sociologists to reveal and understand these social conventions, in order to communicate with consumers using a cultural idiom that consumers will recognise and respond to.

The role of cultural knowledge in interpreting advertising

Advertisements, then, presuppose the consumer's cultural knowledge of local social practices (Thompson et al., 1994) so it is essential for the creators of advertising to share or understand the social milieu of the consumers so that the ads they create will be invested with social significance for the viewer (Bakhtin, 1989; Brown et al., 1999; Hackley, 2002, citing Scott, 1994a and 1994b; Iser, 1978). In portraying everyday activities in rather dramatically enhanced and sometimes in glamorised ways, advertising and promotion reveal us to ourselves. The ordinary things we do are portrayed in film and photography, from taking a shower to buying a coffee. No doubt advertising's use of high-quality cinematography and print techniques and elaborate sets, together with its prominence in public spaces, make our everyday activities portrayed in this way seem dramatically compelling and loaded with significance. Taking a shave with a *Gillette* wet razor (see Colour Section, photo 5), for example, is portrayed in advertising as a symbolic statement of social status and material aspiration, and a gender performance that confers a powerful (symbolic) sexual attraction on the (male) shaver.

Underlying all advertising communication is the implicit message that it is consumption, and not merely its portrayal in advertising, that can make our experience of life more fulfilling. For this communication to work there has to be a shared cultural vocabulary between the makers and consumers of advertising. Advertising and promotional agencies operate at this cultural interface, continually reprocessing cultural meanings to create this communication between brand marketing organisations and consumers. Advertising is, of course, a formidable commercial tool as well as a form of popular communication art. Mass advertising can be a powerful marketing blunderbuss, browbeating consumers into compliance by conditioning through repetition. As we saw in Chapter 3, it also has the flexibility to support many kinds of marketing and business objectives with tailored specificity. It can reflect and magnify social changes and is an important cultural influence. The ways in which advertising and promotion are produced and consumed are constantly changing, reflecting rapid and far-reaching innovations in technology, media and the organisation of agencies. A useful account of advertising practice, then, must be able to accommodate some of this complexity.

SNAPSHOT 4.2

Los Angeles – the world's 'creative capital' and 'content epicentre'?

Los Angeles is well known the world over as the location of Hollywood and the globally recognised American movie industry. It is also a key centre for advertising and in the convergence era the two, entertainment and advertising, are merging, as the skills demanded by each also converge. For some, Los Angeles has become the 'creative capital' of the world.[2] There is a revolving door for movie-makers, actors, musicians and writers between advertising and the

(Continued)

(Continued)

movie and music worlds. Once, these different worlds were separated by a perception that advertising was low culture, and movie making was art. Not any more. They have morphed into a seamless source of cultural production that produces content that is entertaining, promotional and profoundly intertextual. Advertising agencies' role is changing accordingly, and leading practitioners aver that this role is becoming broader as agencies have to move away from being 'media fillers' and toward becoming content creators[3] for brands from a multidisciplinary and multi-media perspective. This does not mean that the traditional agency roles and working practices are redundant, but it does mean that they have to evolve in the convergence era.

The advertising agency in evolution

This chapter will use the traditional, full-service agency as its point of departure for describing the craft skills and working processes of the advertising and promotion business. However, as we have noted, clients are demanding integrated solutions and advertising agencies are coming under increased competition from other specialists such as brand, strategy and communication consultants, media agencies and direct mail and direct marketing agencies. The portrayal of advertising executives in popular culture has contributed to the enigmatic and slightly sinister image of the advertising profession (see Packard, 1957; also Deuze, 2007; Hackley, 2007; Hackley and Kover, 2007). From *Mr Blandings Builds His Dream House* to *How to Get Ahead in Advertising* and, of course, *Mad Men*, advertising in movies and TV shows is the domain of the mendacious, avaricious, driven, superficial, brilliant, and often alcoholic, maverick. In reality, there is less alcohol and less money, but probably just as much angst. It is perhaps fair to say that advertising does not enjoy the same kind of professional prestige as, say, medicine or architecture, or perhaps even politics. Yet there is also a certain glamour attached to working in advertising and promotion, even though the heyday of the *Mad Men*[4] of Madison Avenue is long gone. Competition for graduate trainee or creative positions in agencies remains intense because careers in the area are so prized.

Advertising people are sometimes caricatured in popular entertainment because it is difficult to categorise and its professional activities are not widely understood. It occupies an industrial sector of its own; it is a service but it is also more than that, it is almost, but not quite, a branch of entertainment. It is a business, but then again, not exactly like other businesses. It is part of the creative industries, but quite unlike a theatre company or publishing house. The task of managing the different skills, sensibilities and temperaments that have to work together to produce good advertising has always been somewhat fraught, and it isn't getting any easier.

The integration of marketing communications has been a recurring theme for consultants and academics in the last decade and a half, but the industry of advertising and promotion has been slow to move on from its traditional demarcations, but as we will see below, many are beginning to try to evolve in response to the demands and priorities of the convergence era. As well as advertising agencies and their traditional emphasis on above-the-line mass media, there are agencies that specialise in below-the-line sales promotions, word-of-mouth and viral marketing communications, direct and database marketing, and also public relations, consumer and market research, industrial or business-to-business advertising, new product development, sponsorship, merchandising, strategic brand planning (including those dedicated solely to new brand names), corporate communications and internal marketing, internet-based promotion and interactive communications, media buying and strategy, and so on.

The full-service advertising agency is becoming something of a rarity, but those that remain offer services to clients that may include any or all of the above activities. Their primary expertise lies in advertising, but their strategic perspective covers, in principle, any communications discipline, and they may buy in specialist talent in other marketing communications areas for help in executing an integrated, through-the-line campaign. In fact, agencies have reported increased requests from clients for communications solutions across media channels rather than only advertising, so they have responded by developing a more laterally integrated way of thinking about client problems. Many have acquired in-house expertise in other disciplines such as direct marketing, digital and PR, and they incorporate these into their offer alongside their core advertising expertise.

Early advertising agency practice

The activities of advertising agencies can be better understood in the context of their historical evolution. Advertising agencies emerged as space-brokers, simply buying advertising space in the press on behalf of clients. Gradually, they extended their activities to provide more services to clients and to add value to their business. So they provided artists to draw up the ads for clients as an improvement on text alone. They acquired expertise in typography and print technology, graphic art and photography. With the development of broadcast media, some agencies developed expertise in media planning, scriptwriting and radio production and, later, film production. Many agencies found that because of their location they attracted certain types of business such as retail advertising in the local press or sales promotion. In these cases, many regional agencies developed as specialists in particular categories of work, serving mainly local clients.

Advertising is a fast-moving field but few of its techniques are entirely new. Examples of advertising have been noted since the origin of writing itself. In fact, writing may have developed to facilitate marketing (Brown and Jensen-Schau, 2008). Classified advertising has existed since the advent of print technology and newspapers. It is a common mistake to suppose that, because early advertising was limited to the printed word, it was merely informative rather than persuasive. Detailed research has shown that this is not the case (Harbor, 2007; McFall, 2004). It is another mistake to suppose that techniques such as product placement and branding are modern inventions. For example, British pottery entrepreneurs were keen to get their pottery dinner sets into royal portraits in the Victorian era, and they made use of techniques of segmentation and targeting (Quickenden and Kover, 2007). In another example, a British entrepreneur of the 1800s, Thomas Holloway, pioneered the use of advertising and branding to sell his patented medical remedies. Holloway was said to have employed outdoor posters as far away as China to advertise his health tonics. Holloway was ahead of his time in other promotional techniques too. He managed to get references to his brands inserted into the script of some of the popular plays of the time. He is even said to have asked Charles Dickens to insert a reference to a Holloway brand into his classic novel *Dombey and Son*. Dickens declined. Holloway made a fortune and used it in philanthropic activities. Among them was the building he financed that is now a college of the University of London, called Royal Holloway.

Advertising agencies as strategic marketing experts

The scope of activities ad agencies became involved with, and the expertise their staff developed in a variety of disciplines and markets, gave them yet another dimension. Their skills in artwork and typesetting became useful to media owners since they were able to produce advertisements of a quality that visually enhanced the publication. In addition to skills of art, design and copywriting, agencies developed expertise in strategy and brand planning. Advertising agencies had to understand consumers in varied markets, and they also had to understand the businesses of their many clients. On top of that, they grew to understand media markets. They understood marketing in a way that was free of the practical constraints that limited the thinking of manufacturing organisations. They had a special understanding of the powerful role communication could play in exciting the interest of consumers, and they knew which kind of consumer read which publication. They had, therefore, a special vantage-point from which to offer strategic advice to clients on general business strategy, product development, brand planning and brand communication, possible new markets to enter, market segmentation issues and so on.

So, advertising agencies began to offer strategic advice to their clients as well as simply designing and placing advertisements. By so doing they were able to add value to their offer. The insights acquired in advertising are valued – many advertising agency account planners and strategists move 'client side' in their career to manage the brand planning process from inside the client organisation. It should be noted, though, that advertising agencies are not regarded as strategic partners by all clients in all regions of the world. Many clients, especially bigger ones, prefer to treat ad agencies as service providers who are required to deliver creative ideas, not consulting advice or research (Broadbent, 2009).

Advertising agencies and media

The media strategy and planning tasks are discussed in greater depth in Chapter 6. Here we need to note a few initial points. Contemporary advertising agencies supply strategic communication ideas and sometimes production skills. They also normally possess media expertise and have a voice in deciding how ads will be targeted at selected consumers through particular media channels. Some ad agencies will handle media buying for a client, but media planning is increasingly handled at arm's length from the ad agency by specialist media agencies. Media buying originally formed part of full-service ad agencies' remit but many media departments were eventually sold off to become free-standing specialist businesses divorced from creative services.

In many countries, media-buying services are provided by a limited number of companies because of lateral mergers and high concentration in the media industry. It can be convenient for media owners to sell advertising space to a small number of buyers rather than to thousands of individual clients. However, lateral mergers between communications groups mean that advertisers can be faced with monopoly suppliers in particular media and this places them in a poor bargaining position. For example, in the UK, licences to provide regional television or radio services are sold on a strictly limited basis so that local advertisers often have only one company to buy from. This, advertisers argue, maintains an artificially high cost for certain kinds of advertising medium.

Some media agencies, not content with being the back-room players in the advertising world, are broadening their remit under convergence and adding creative services, to encroach on ad agencies' business. Like advertising agencies, media agencies boast a wide range of expertise, for example, in consumer research, strategic analysis, and brand planning. Convergence demands an understanding of different media channels and media agencies are, of course, well placed to exploit their deep knowledge of consumers and media. The advertising agencies are not usually overjoyed to find that they are pitching against a media agency for advertising business.

The leading agency brands

Given the scope, public profile and economic importance of what advertising agencies do, it is perhaps paradoxical that the names of most agencies are virtually unknown to those outside marketing or communications fields. Ad agencies do not generally advertise themselves. A few of the world's top agency brands[5] do have a high-profile presence in corporate life (see Table 4.1) but most are not nearly as well known among the general public as their client brands. This is partly because client organisations prefer the consuming public to be unaware of the talented intermediaries producing the creative executions that add lustre to the brand. It would be a little like the backing singers getting as much publicity as the star. Agencies have had to learn to be discreet about their abilities: successful advertising must always be about the client, not about the agency. Agency success lies in bringing success to clients. Another reason for their shadowy character in commercial life is that they operate in what is essentially a business-to-business environment where much work is gained through word-of-mouth, relationships and reputation among a small community.

Dentsu dominates Japanese advertising but has been increasing its influence in the West through acquisitions. *Y&R* includes digital and direct marketing agency *Wunderman* and is a subsidiary of *WPP*. *McCann Erickson* is reported (in *Adbrands*[6]) to be the first advertising agency to move into other marketing communication disciplines and today includes customer relationship management (CRM), public relations (PR), sales promotion and branding businesses. *DDB*

Table 4.1   Top agency networks by estimated worldwide revenues, 2012

1. Dentsu
2. Young and Rubicam (Y&R)
3. McCann Worldgroup
4. DDB
5. Ogilvy
6. BBDO
7. TBWA
8. Publicis
9. Hakuhodo
10. Havas Worldwide
11. JWT
12. Leo Burnett

Source: www.adbrands.net/top_advertising_agencies_index.htm accessed 15.2.2014 was founded by the legendary ad man Bill Bernbach and is a subsidiary of media conglomerate Omnicom, while *Ogilvy & Mather* was also founded by an advertising icon, David Ogilvy. *BBDO* generates more revenue that any other agency in the world's biggest advertising market, the USA, and since 2005 the *BBDO* agency network has won more creative awards than any other. It includes the top UK agency *AMV BBDO*.

Types of advertising agency

Worldwide agency networks, such as *BBDO*, *McCann Erickson*, *Leo Burnett* or *Saatchi & Saatchi*, often have local offices in many different countries. One dynamic behind the evolution of the international agency networks was the need for global conglomerates to manage campaigns in many different countries for each of their individual brands, hence the development of multination agency networks. In many cases, they have acquired other agency businesses offering specialisms in other promotional disciplines. A second category of agency consists of smaller networks, usually based on distinctive strengths in creative work. These might have just a few offices worldwide. Examples include *Bartle Bogle Hegarty*, *Wieden & Kennedy* and *M&C Saatchi*. The third category is the most typical; these are individual agencies that might be owned by a larger group but operate independently. Some are large and offer a full agency service, while others are more specialist 'creative boutiques' with distinctive creative skills, often in a particular medium such as digital or television.

The global communication holding groups generate very big business. For example, the London-based *WPP* advertising and marketing group posted revenues of $13.6 billion for 2008, and $15.6 billion in 2012.[7] Holding groups such as these own many individual agency brands, reflecting the increased industry concentration through mergers and acquisitions. *WPP* owns such agency networks as *Ogilvy and Mather Worldwide*, *JWT*, *Y&R* and *Grey*. *Omnicom* owns *BBDO*, *DDB* and *TBWA*. Some agencies create reputations for creativity, usually based on the creative awards they win[8] (see Table 4.2).

The one commodity advertising agencies feel that they own, above all other marketing and media disciplines, is creativity. Ad agencies are nothing if not their ideas, and their creative craft is what sets them apart. Even though they operate in a somewhat closed culture, agencies do have some interest in self-promotion. If they can enhance their reputation in the industry they are more likely to be invited to pitch for new business. To this end, some agencies try to build a reputation in the communication and marketing industry by entering case histories of their work to try to win industry awards (and publishing them in bound volumes), publicising their history and their successes in

Table 4.2 World's top ten agency networks (2012) by creative awards (points)[a]

1.	BBDO (including Proximity)	3,349
2.	Ogilvy (including OgilvyOne, Ogilvy Action)	2,837
3.	Leo Burnett	2,104
4.	DDB (including Rapp)	1,868
5.	Y&R (including Wunderman)	1,762
6.	TBWA (including Tequila)	1,055
7.	JWT	8858
8.	Saatchi & Saatchi	707
9.	Publicis	688
10.	Euro (including Havas)	670

[a] The 2012 rankings are based on 4,459 campaigns or pieces of creative work that won awards at 39 shows around the world.

Source: www.adweek.com/news/advertising-branding/bbdo-again-tops-big-won-awards-tally-146645 accessed 15.2.2014

coffee-table books and producing copies of their ads. Many agencies adopt particular creative techniques or advertising development styles and promote their expertise to differentiate their brand to clients. Frequent social events for awards, campaign launches, annual reviews and so on are an essential part of the networking that is integral to the industry. Advertising is a small community and awards shows and other events create a sense of specialness and exclusivity that is important to the industry in order to offset the lack of wider recognition for advertising expertise and accomplishment. This tendency for advertising professionals to award each other prizes seems important, sociologically, to the industry and it also reflects a self-referential insularity. It is especially important for the creatives. Creatives want their ads to win creative awards, sometimes, it is rumoured, even more than they want their ads to sell product. Creative awards burnish not only creatives' reputations but that of their agency, and are highly prized.

SNAPSHOT 4.3

Advertising careers

The influence of convergence can be seen on the recruitment pages of some leading advertising agency groups. Ogilvy UK,[9] for example, offers careers in advertising and digital, relationship marketing, business-to-business marketing, direct marketing, public relations, retail, experiential and sales promotion, internal communications and social media, media planning and buying, branding, design and production services. Agency groups have evolved through successive mergers bringing formerly outsourced services in-house, and some even bring them under the same roof, and in some cases into the same room. For example, Kaper,[10] an integrated digital and PR agency, have experts in digital, social media, creative and research working together in their enormous London office. Agencies want to solve communications problems with creative thinking so their people need a diverse set of skills and knowledge. As a consequence there isn't a definitive background for an ideal advertising person, they have a wide range of educational backgrounds – a degree is usually essential, but it doesn't necessarily matter in what specialist subject. The key requirements are to be passionate about advertising and have great analytical, communication and inter-personal skills.

Advertising agencies and the pitch process

Advertising and promotion agencies are slightly mysterious places. They have great (and often under-recognised) importance in capitalist economies. They produce work that is often striking and resonant, and they attract some of the brightest and best-educated people to work in them. Yet, explaining exactly how this work results from the hive of activity that is an advertising agency is not an easy task. The advertising world remains an enigmatic one in spite of its importance to the economy.

Marketing and advertising text books and research are remarkably vague about exactly how advertising is created, and even committed and highly skilled advertising professionals themselves are not quite sure how precisely to explain their work. Like much human organisation, the fact that it turns out to be productive can be hard to explain given the messiness, the conflict and the confusion surrounding it. This is more true of advertising than most fields, given the collision of creativity and business that has to be reconciled for advertising to be produced. The enigmatic character of ad agencies means that a descriptive account of roles and working procedures may appear glib. A list of the components of a TV set in no way serves as an account of what it produces. Nevertheless, this chapter outlines these roles and processes while acknowledging that there is much flexibility and indeterminacy in the processes. What is more, as we assert many times in this book, the business of advertising and promotion is in a flux as media convergence throws all the old certainties into question and agencies are experimenting with new forms of organisation and process management in response. Advertising is a creative industry. The superficially chaotic character of agency life may be seen as a reflection of the high intellects and professionalism of advertising folk. Some clients take a different view and regard communications agencies as poorly managed, un-businesslike places that need close direction and cannot be trusted to be prudent with clients' money.

The account that follows is organised broadly around the sequence of activities that agencies must undertake in the course of acquiring and executing client business. The first step, therefore, will be to look at the nature of the agency as a business brand and how this might influence its 'pitches' for business.

Advertising is a very substantial business that punches well above its weight in terms of its contribution to the economy in relation to the size of the sector by number of employees. The American Association of Advertising Agencies (AAAA)[11] has claimed that there are more than 20,000 advertising agencies in the USA generating, according to some estimates, something like $5 trillion of economic activity per year.[12] The UK has perhaps some 700 advertising agencies, but the figure is difficult to establish because so many different kinds of agency are now coming into the advertising scene, as disciplines formerly regarded as non-advertising promotion such as direct mail, sponsorship, public relations (PR) and mobile are subsumed into an integrated advertising and promotion industry. UK advertising spend, the amount spent on advertising by clients, is estimated at almost £19 billion in 2014, driven mainly by large increases in adspend on TV and internet.[13]

The traditional way for ad agencies to get business has been to 'pitch' for new accounts. One of the UK trade associations for advertising, the IPA, has listed the elements of the pitch process,[14] adapted in Table 4.3.

Table 4.3 The pitch process

1. Client brief
2. Identification of potential agencies
3. Gathering credentials
4. Shortlisting agencies
5. Chemistry meetings
6. Pitch briefing sessions
7. Tissue sessions
8. Negotiations
9. Pitch day
10. Field testing
11. Decision and meetings

Source: www.thegoodpitch.com/alternatives accessed 17.2.2014

Table 4.3 illustrates how time-consuming and labour-intensive the pitch process can be for both client and agency. The ten stages listed could develop into many more with iterative meetings possible from each stage. Three months would be a typical timescale for this process, but it could be longer. The eleventh stage is the decision. The client will have to arrange further meetings to inform the agencies of their decision. In this discussion we will focus mainly on the actual pitch conducted on pitch day. The stages of the process include 'chemistry' meetings, at which the client and the agencies will meet to decide if they can establish the 'chemistry' or rapport for a good working relationship, and 'tissue' meetings, which are for establishing whether or not the agency's thinking to date coheres with the client's vision for the campaign. The client will brief the agencies on the pitch nearer the pitch day, and, once the agencies have pitched their ideas, the client will take some time to field-test those ideas in order to decide which are best.

The process of pitching may be preceded by an invited credentials presentation in which selected agencies will try to persuade the client that they are a credible and professional organisation. Track records of successful accounts are important here, as are the reputations of the star personnel. If the agency is already a leading brand then so much the better. The client no doubt has an advertising department and public relations office of its own and needs to be reassured that the agency can add specialist expertise that it cannot provide for itself.

For establishing credentials, agencies have begun to add more and more content to their websites and often contribute to industry blogs. The agency website is a shop window and blogs can also be important in generating comment and presence in the industry. Such presence might lead to an invitation to pitch for business. The client issues a client brief to the agencies it deems worthy to pitch for the business. The client brief contains the background information the client feels is essential to the task, such as the brand name and the category of the product, the company, the desired market and segmentation strategy, the price, the distribution channel and, most importantly, the budget. The selected agencies take the brief, decide how they might solve the client's problem and present their ideas.

SNAPSHOT 4.4

The client brief

The client brief is an important document that sets out what the client wants the agency to do. A written brief facilitates communication and helps each party understand the requirements of the other. The UK Advertising Association suggests that a client brief should include: situation analysis (expressed as 'Where are we now?'); objectives ('Where do we want to be?'); and marketing and communications strategy ('How do we get there?'). Other essential topics include consumer segmentation and targeting ('Who do we need to talk to?'); effectiveness measurement ('How will we know when we've arrived?') and practical issues. The entire project should be managed with clear lines of communication and individual accountability, and not left as an informal, ad hoc or implicit arrangement. Following these principles reduces the risk that the client–agency relationship may become unsatisfactory or unsuccessful.

The pitch itself is a piece of theatre. As with all presentations, it should be well-prepared, convincing, succinct and it should have impact. The ad agency team must come through it appearing to have a deep grasp of the client and their needs, and the level of competence to execute the tasks with creative flair, within budget and on time. Pitching for business is an everyday activity for most advertising agencies. The impact of the presentation is everything; appearances are important and presentational poise and social skills are to the fore. The agency will be judged partly on the creative flair of its ideas, as well as on the strategic planning and professionalism of the pitch. It is the responsibility of account managers and account planners to make sure their pitch presentation is highly professional so that the creative work and strategic thinking are seen in the best light by the client. From the 1960s on, it became common for the creatives to be excluded from the pitch, and from all direct contact with the client, but this convention is increasingly dispensed with today. Creatives are expected to be professional in their dealing with clients, and clients want to have close relationships with the people who will actually be creating the campaign.

If the client does not like the work, the account person who presented it may be accused by creative staff of not trying hard enough or of failing to do justice to the quality of the work. In some cases agencies may toil for two or three weeks on a pitch only to see the business given to another agency. Even worse, it is not unknown for ideas to be stolen, and used without attributing their source. The agency may charge the client for the work they put into the pitch but ultimately will do this work in hope of winning the business rather than with any realistic expectation of a profit from the pitch itself. Exceptionally, an agency might refuse to divulge creative ideas in a pitch, on the grounds that these could be stolen, and in any case, it is a little premature for an agency to pitch creative ideas based only on a client brief. Agency BBH are known for taking this stance. They feel that their reputation should be enough to show the client that they will come up with striking and commercially resonant creative ideas, if they are given the business.

The key elements of the pitch can often be the intangible ones. It is especially important for the client to feel confidence in the agency personnel, and if the agency team can strike a rapport (the aforementioned 'chemistry') with the client team, it can be a basis for trust. The best advertising tends to result from the best client–agency relationships. The agency account team and the client team will have to spend a lot of time together in meetings, so the relationship side of things is very important. The chemistry meeting is an opportunity for each team to appraise each other.

Effective pitches must give the client a strong sense that their wishes and priorities are being listened to with close attention.[15] The agency team has to get and keep the client team's attention instantly, so presentation skills are at a premium. This does not necessarily mean a flamboyant visual show with super-dooper PowerPoint slides. It can come down to the personal styles of the presenters. They have to have confidence in order to make the client team feel confident in them, without appearing to be over-confident. They also have to sing from same hymn sheet. If agency staff talk across each other or appear not to understand or agree with each other's positions, it can look very bad to the client.

The outcome of the pitch might occasionally be that a new or a small agency gets the business rather than the huge multinational agency group. The nature of the brief will influence the kind of agency that is chosen. Some clients want a full strategic communications service, in which case a larger full-service agency is more likely to be chosen. Other clients may be more interested in getting help with specific activities such as creative, production or media strategy and so may choose a smaller agency. A client who, for example, wishes to advertise a brand launch across international boundaries may have more confidence in an agency group that is already operating internationally. The rise of the big communication conglomerates has been driven by the need for major multinationals to manage campaigns in scores of different countries.

The client–agency relationship

Advertising agency professional bodies emphasise the importance of the client–agency relationship. Industry professionals argue that the most effective work results from strong relationships and clear lines of communication between the client and the agency (see, e.g., West and Paliwoda, 1996). Continuity in these relationships gives each the time to understand the other and the business. Agencies claim that a foundation of success is longevity and mutual trust in client relationships, and would prefer reliable clients and repeat business to 'promiscuous' clients. Agencies post news of their campaigns on their websites to publicise their success with prominent clients and to encourage new ones.

The client is effectively the invisible member of the account team. The client's wishes and aims are represented in the client brief. As we noted in Chapter 3, communication and marketing are different things, and client briefs can often require a lot of work by the agency because the client may not have a very clear rationale for communication. This can be a cause of tension in the relationship. It is up to the agencies to research the client brief in order to understand fully the nature of the client's business, markets and brands. Client briefs can come couched in marketing jargon that communication professionals find obscure and misleading. Marketing directors tend to compartmentalise marketing management functions. This leads to elements like pricing strategy, product design, distribution and promotion being considered separately without reference to each other. But advertising professionals have the benefit of a more dispassionate perspective on the marketing process and they recognise that the elements of marketing management and strategy are interdependent. Brand name, price, product design, packaging and distribution outlet all have relevance for the brand communications. Advertising that is able to portray a coherent brand strategy that makes sense to the right consumers has a far greater chance of success than advertising that is trying to use creativity to make up for an ill-conceived marketing strategy. If the account manager (known as the 'voice of the client' in the agency) can act as a consulting partner to a client and gain in-depth knowledge of the marketing function, this will help the agency devise a coherent and successful campaign.

It is axiomatic that agencies traditionally regarded mass media advertising as the answer to every marketing problem. If a client is dismayed at falling sales and allocates a large advertising budget to address the problem, the agency should really concede that advertising may not be the answer to the client's problem – it may be that, say, poor customer service, flawed distribution or poor product design are the cause of the client's problems. Account managers understandably feel under pressure not to turn business away but if a campaign cannot succeed because it addresses the wrong problem then it is wise to advise the client rather than risk the ignominy of a failed campaign. But clients have to be handled sensitively. Some will not accept that they have misunderstood the nature of their own business and will not be protected from their folly. Agencies today are expected to be 'media neutral' in their approach to clients' communication strategies. In other words, they are expected to find and solve the right problem regardless of what the solution might be. Since advertising moved away from the commission system of payment and began to incorporate more elements of non-advertising expertise in their agency groups, media neutrality has become more achievable, and less costly, for them.

The decision to allocate an advertising budget and appoint an agency is a highly political one for client organisations. Client relations are always a sensitive area for agencies and demand astute management skills from account managers. The senior board-level account director will be responsible, along with other agency heads, for deciding whether to accept a client brief. There may be reasons for declining it at the client brief stage, if, for example, the agency's research reveals that communication is not the client's problem. More plausibly, the agency will need to decide if a new client will fit with existing clients. Agencies need to try to ensure that they are not open to conflicts of interest when, say, representing two clients who compete in the same market. Agencies will also have to decide if a client's business fits with their agency brand for ethical reasons. If the pitch goes well, then the agency will be awarded the client's advertising business, called 'the account'.

Account team roles and responsibilities

Work in advertising, media and marketing services agencies is normally organised through account teams. These are the vortex of the advertising development process. The account team roles reflect different yet often overlapping areas of responsibility. The major account team roles are those of account management (also called client services), account planning, the analysis and strategy part, and creative. In addition, there are ancillary roles. These include media planning and buying, discussed in more detail in Chapter 6. Another essential ancillary role is traffic controller, more commonly called production or project management today. Their responsibility is to allocate work, monitor progress and ensure that tasks are co-ordinated to deadline. The traffic controller also ensures that there is a paper trail showing the continuous progress of all the component parts of development. If, for example, the production of a TV ad requires a script to be finished, artwork to be completed and a research brief to be fulfilled before the production company can be given the go-ahead, it will be the traffic controller's job to monitor progress and chase up the staff responsible in order to meet deadlines.

Other staff may be engaged in creative production in artwork, digital, print or TV/video production. They are required because creative teams are there for the ideas and creative logic they can supply; they do not necessarily have production skills. Staff with expertise in graphic art and computer-aided art production, animation and animatronics, website or mobile app design and other production activities can be very useful for agencies to have in-house because they can make the creative ideas happen.

The account manager

If an agency is appointed by a client then the account manager (sometimes called 'account executive' or 'account director', or simply 'account man' regardless of gender) will be the client's first point of contact in the agency. The account manager is essentially the business manager for the accounts held by that account team. Reporting to the client services director, he or she is responsible for liaison between the client and the other account team members to ensure that the campaign is planned, developed and produced on time, on brief and on budget. The account manager is often regarded as the business person or, less respectfully, as 'the suit' (Hackley, 2000, 2003f). He or she has to manage the various personalities and tasks to ensure that the work generates revenue for the agency. Consequently, he or she requires skills in relationship management, project management, planning and co-ordination. Account managers will normally have a good working knowledge of the whole advertising development process. The account manager is normally closer to the client than any other person in the agency. In most agencies he or she will have primary responsibility for client liaison and may speak to the client daily.

In some agencies it is common for the account person to be the only contact point between agency and client. The account manager is consequently regarded as the voice of the client in the agency since he or she acquires a strong sense of what the client wants and will accept. This can present conflicts of interest when the creative staff want the account manager to argue strongly in favour of a creative execution that the client may not want to accept. Account managers will sometimes admit that there are occasions when they do not fight as strongly for their creatives' idea as they might, simply because they know that it is not what the client wants. The specific tasks account managers undertake during the creative development of advertising vary from agency to agency, and from account to account. In many cases they will take the lead in interpreting the initial client brief and developing and presenting the pitch for business. Once the account is won they will convene the various planning and progress meetings to discuss and agree strategy. Either alone or with the account planner they will discuss, research and write the creative brief. In many agencies account managers, rather than account planners, commission consumer and advertising research and interpret the findings at various points in the creative advertising development process. The account manager ultimately holds the responsibility of ensuring that an account is, firstly, won and then retained for as long as possible. Along with the account planner (see below), the account manager will often have responsibility for measuring the effectiveness of the campaign against the objectives that were set for it.

SNAPSHOT 4.5

Implicit theory in advertising account teams

Advertising is a practical business, but as noted in Chapter 2, theory has a role, even if its role is often implicit. Kover (1995) found that creative staff hold differing implicit theories of communication while Hackley (2003d) found that account team members work to differing implicit models of the consumer. Agency working practices entail lengthy meetings and considerable communication. These two research studies illustrated how difficult it can be for agencies to articulate all the implicit assumptions that guide professional communications practice. The three main account team roles of account management, creative and planning often approach marketing communications problems from intellectually incompatible perspectives. While this is a strength of the team approach it is also a source of conflict because the differing perspectives are not well understood.

Account planning

Traditionally, advertising and promotional agencies have been organised hierarchically, with the account manager leading the account team. Research was once conducted behind the scenes by a specialist researcher who serviced the account manager. Strategy and planning were conceived mainly by the account manager. However, some advertising professionals saw this as a problem since research insights were not necessarily integrated into the creative advertising development process, and the account manager was not necessarily the best person to commission and analyse research. A new discipline called account planning was invented. This discipline, in principle, gave the account planner equal status with the account manager.

The account planning role was initiated in the 1960s in London at JWT (by Stephen King) and at *BMP* (now DDB London) (by Stanley Pollitt) and adapted in the USA by New York agency Chiat Day (Feldwick, 2007; Pickton and Crosier, 2003; Steel, 1998). The name 'account planning', a misnomer really, was conceived at a JWT awayday and stuck. The account planner was charged with generating consumer insights through research and with ensuring that these insights were integrated into every stage of the creative advertising development process (discussed in Chapter 5). The account planner, therefore, had to be the intellectual in the agency, the 'boffin' (Hackley, 2000) who was at ease with all types of social research, and who was able to articulate these techniques and their findings with clarity. Good account planners often have a wide range of analytical, linguistic and advocacy skills that enable them to articulate the strategic thinking for brands that contributes to the longer-term management and development of the brand vision.

The role was conceived also as a buffer between creative and account management, resolving or deflecting tension and aiding creativity. It would therefore be a politically important role because it would moderate the tension between creative and account management by offering an authoritative voice based on evidence-driven research (Feldwick, 2007). Originally conceived as the 'voice of the consumer' within the agency (Pollitt, 1979), the account planner's role has broadened with the rise of brand marketing. He or she is now often seen as the brand custodian charged with ensuring that the brand's core values and personality are maintained through all associated marketing communications. The planning discipline has also broadened across new areas such as digital and direct marketing, media, and communications and PR. Planners have always had to be robust though, in making their case, and that hasn't changed, since not all agencies fully support the concept of the planner. Some agencies are almost evangelical about the account planning ethos and the benefits it brings to the agency. Others in the industry are sceptical about the claims made for account planning and ask whether it really constitutes a distinct discipline, or just, as cynics say, a great way to get new business. These agencies use job titles of 'strategist' or 'analyst' instead of account planner. The account planners have a professional body, the Account Planning Group (APG),[16] which tries to address confusion about the discipline by offering training courses, case studies and awards.

Difficulties of the account planning role

There have been three persistent problems facing the account planning discipline, which proves unfortunate when, in the words of one account planner, they see their own role as 'helping creatives and making the work better'. One problem is the hostility of many creative staff towards research (Hackley and Kover, 2007). When the researcher was a lowly backroom person, there was less threat, but when research is a responsibility of the account planner, it has management status. The account planner is a soft target for the angst of creative staff who feel that judging their work against research findings misses the point of what makes advertising appeal to consumers (Kover, 1996).

Secondly, not only do account planners find themselves at odds with creative staff, they may also be at odds with account managers who feel that their status is undermined. Account planners do many of the tasks that were formerly the sole responsibility of the account manager, such as deciding what research to conduct, liaising with the client and writing the creative brief. In agencies implementing the account planning philosophy there often results a three-way power struggle as creatives and account management, comfortable in their mutual contempt, find common ground in their hatred of account planners.

As if these problems were not enough, thirdly, account planners have a credibility problem in the industry as a whole. Just as those agencies that espouse the account planning ethos are convinced of its positive value, those that are not, argue their point of view with vigour. Account planners can be vulnerable to the charge that they cannot easily answer the question of what craft skills they bring to the advertising development process. Many are expert researchers with substantial educational attainments. Others are not, but have found their way into the post through a facility with words and ideas, and a sense of curiosity about people. While creative staff have creative skills, and account management have business skills, account planners are sometimes unfairly seen to have no particular skills that justify their status and power on account teams. Because of these difficulties, account planners require skills of tact and sensitivity in order simply to do their job. As researchers, they require sensitivity to consumers' attitudes, predispositions and preferences, and an ability to work these out from carefully gathered qualitative and quantitative research data.

Digital planners

Some agencies (see Chapter 4 Case Study below) have introduced a new role, digital planner, as part of their effort to instil digital thinking into account team practice. The digital planner has two main roles. One is to understand digital platforms and contribute ideas to the integration effort right from the client brief, rather than as a service function. This means that the implications for digital can be understood immediately any creative idea is put forward, instead of weeks later. Their second role is to educate internal and external colleagues (especially clients) about what is or is not possible on digital.

The truth is, digital platforms are changing so quickly that digital specialists' technical expertise has a time limit. Even they can get left behind, but they have the advantage that they can still baffle colleagues with their technical knowledge. Their status as planner also means that the technical details need not be important, if they understand the broad principles and can apply those to strategic thinking. Some industry bloggers have even suggested that account planning could become redundant in an age of social media, unless the discipline is informed by an understanding of digital and social media.[17] The digital planner, then, apart from just being a fancy new frill for some agencies to boast about, might even move into the centre ground of account planning.

Creative teams

The advertising creative person is a topic of myth and legend. In the *Mad Men* era of the 1960s, creative individuals could emerge, win big reputations and become feted like rock stars, and paid like them too. These individuals could be childish, temperamental, self-indulgent, capricious, frequently late or absent, and it would all be tolerated as long as they kept coming up with ideas the client loved. No longer. Today, creative professionals in advertising have to be team players, they have to be well-organised, and in many agencies they even have to attend business meetings. They are, though, no less important to the agency.

Advertising agencies produce and sell ideas. The quality of their creative output is the benchmark of their standing as an agency. The creative team is responsible for this output, and in many agencies the creative work is organised into teams of two people. There may be one creative person who specialises in words (copywriting, scriptwriting, music jingles) and another who deals in images, and undertakes, for example, visualisations of story boards for TV ads, press ad layouts, poster design, typography and so on. Sometimes, these roles are referred to respectively as 'art director' and 'copywriter'. In US agencies it has been traditional for the term 'copywriter' to be used to refer to the originator of any creative input, the assumption being that a copywriter without visualisation (that is, drawing) skills would simply instruct a designer or production artist to put his or her ideas into visual form. Quite often, the two members in a creative team have interchangeable skills. In some cases, creatives prefer to work alone (McLeod et al., 2009). The creative professionals (the 'creatives') typically swim to a different current than other employees. They draw their cultural influences from art, aesthetics and popular culture. Their business is to know what movies people are watching, what cars they're driving, what they're talking about, thinking about and wearing. As a generalisation, though, it is becoming more widely recognised that advertising is a collaborative process, and creatives are part of a team all of whom have to have a strong sense of the cultural zeitgeist.

SNAPSHOT 4.6

Creative stars and agency culture

Creative professionals in advertising need to have a big ego. It is a career that demands considerable personal drive and confidence. However, where a creative becomes so successful that he or she (most commonly it is a he) comes to dominate the agency with their personality, it can destabilise the working process and undermine the objective-driven creative advertising development process. Creatives live and die by peer recognition, marked by the awards they win (Hackley and Kover, 2007), but clients are more interested in their marketing objectives than in creative awards. In some creative-dominated agencies, clients' briefs may go straight to the creative star without any initial planning or research taking place. This can be fruitful when the creative person's intuition about the market and its consumers results in an effective creative execution. However, it is a high-risk approach since there is no clearly researched basis for creative work and no carefully thought-through strategy. In such a situation, clear criteria for assessing campaign effectiveness might also be disregarded, to the potential detriment of the clients' interests. The creative brief and the layers of account management and planning which buffer the creative from the client are intended to militate the risks of wayward creativity.

Life as an agency creative

Becoming a creative is very difficult indeed. Young creatives often study specialised courses then work as interns for little or no pay just to gain the experience they need. There are more talented and passionate creatives than there are jobs, unfortunately. In many agencies, creative teams operate at arm's length from account management. They often occupy their own sub-cultural space in the agency (Hackley, 2000: Gilmore et al. 2011). Creative staff often feel disempowered by the advertising development process since the worth of their ideas is judged by other, non-creative people (Kover and Goldberg, 1995).

However, creatives who win awards for their work can quickly acquire a star reputation that brings them (and their agency) considerable prestige. In some cases, star creatives can come to dominate an agency.

Creative staff might not be brought into the process until the initial market and consumer research and strategic planning have taken place. They are then presented with a brief and asked to offer creative executions that satisfy the requirements of the brief. This brief is an important document that should inspire creative staff and excite them about the creative possibilities for an account, while also providing them with parameters to work within which are derived from the research and strategic thinking that have gone into developing the strategy for advertising. This should ensure that the creative execution will support the desired marketing objectives of the client (Kelly et al., 2005). When creative work has been approved internally by the agency team (usually by the internal director of creativity) it is presented to the client by the account manager. If the client likes it and agrees that it fulfils the criteria set out in the brief, then the work will be produced and offered for public consumption.

Creative staff enjoy a privileged existence within agencies. They must have the discipline to produce ideas to a deadline, starting with a blank piece of paper. While younger creative staff are often very good on ideas, the task of the creative professional requires both experience and resilience, the former of which is necessary in order to know what will work as an execution in different media. Creative work requires strong craft skills aligned to a knowledge of different media and their properties, along with an intuitive sense of the excitement that consumption generates. Creative staff have to be resilient because, in the words of one experienced creative interviewed by the author, 'of every ten ideas, only one will get made'. Creative staff must accept that the great majority of the ideas they come up with will be rejected as unsuitable for a huge variety of reasons. The creative brief in particular is supposed to discipline the creative work so that it serves the clients' marketing objectives rather than the fetid imagination of the award-hungry creative. In most cases, clients would wish advertising to be based on a more transparent footing, with a business-like approach to planning and accountability.

Chapter summary

This chapter set the culture and working practices of advertising agencies in a wider context by outlining their evolution from space brokers into full-service providers of advertising, research and strategy. It explored the role of agencies as cultural intermediaries, operating in the interface between culture and commerce. The chapter also touched on the current state of the industry with its many kinds of agency and layered agency networks. It went on to discuss the main roles, responsibilities and processes typically entailed in creative advertising development and mentioned some of the key difficulties and controversies. The following chapter will develop more detail on the creative advertising development process, planning and strategy.

■ Review Questions

1. **List the main functional roles in a typical full-service advertising agency. How does each of these roles contribute to the creation of an advertising campaign?**

2. **Form account team groups, one person each taking the role of creative, account manager and account planner. Draft an outline communications plan for the launch of a new brand of long-grain rice. Then each account team should compose a pitch for the business based on their initial ideas. The pitches should cover the likely target market, the major marketing issues, the possible media plan and creative ideas.**

3. **List, explain and discuss some of the major problems of management and control in advertising agencies. How have agencies tried to resolve these problems?**

4. **Research five major advertising agency websites. To what extent, and how, does each bring out the theme of integration?**

CASE STUDY

Leo Burnett London – Creativity and integration

Leo Burnett is one of the world's most famous advertising agencies, with multiple creative awards since its beginnings in Chicago in 1935. Today it is a worldwide agency group with offices in 102 countries.[18] One of the authors [C.H.] was kindly invited to spend a week in Leo Burnett London[19] talking to account team people in late 2011.[20] Leo Burnett London is an integrated agency that incorporates several disciplines as separate but connected businesses, under the same roof. In addition to Leo Burnett London, a full-service advertising agency with extensive creative production facilities in-house, these include Holler,[21] a planning and engagement group, *ARC*, a brand activation specialist, and Atelier,[22] which focuses on fashion and luxury branding.

In 2011 Leo Burnett London had introduced an innovation into their account team role. The role of digital planner was incorporated into the heart of account teams. This was unusual at the time and represented one element of the industry's attempts to deal with media integration by placing it at the heart of their thinking. The digital planner had a difficult task. Not only were they expected to keep up with the rapid developments in digital media production, but they also had the responsibility of explaining the implications of these developments to colleagues and also to clients. The presence of the digital planner in the team from the initial client brief meant that every idea mooted in strategy meetings could be looked at from a digital perspective. This is important because activation and engagement are now seen as inherent elements of advertising strategy, and digital media are central to the way this works. For example, a broadcast ad might be shared on social media and added to with iterative storylines on video clips. These might include something, say an app or a game, that drives interested consumers to the brand website, where they might also find opportunities to engage further by signing up to updates or trials. Digital media demand different creative craft skills to other media, so digital specialists are needed to tell other account team colleagues what creative execution will, or won't work on digital, and how or why.

The agency places a high priority on creativity, but there seems to be an understanding that creativity must have a context. In a convergent media environment, creativity is collaborative, and, as the agency claims, 'a good idea can come from anywhere', which means that it is not only the creatives who can be creative. This attitude could be intimidating to some creatives, who need the credit for creative work because that is all that is in their portfolio. The creatives at Leo Burnett enjoyed working on some of the world's biggest accounts and seemed to be entirely comfortable with the collaborative nature of work. In other agencies there are many stories of account planners and account managers who came up with the key creative idea in a meeting, but the credit was given to the creatives. These stories usually come from account planners and managers, who claim to be content with their role as creative 'midwives'.[23]

In every organisation there are tensions beneath the public view about who gets credit for what and who is listened to. In Leo Burnett London, like every other major ad agency the author has spent time in, one very distinctive feature is the social sensitivity and poise of employees. Cup-throwing tantrums were once regarded as part of everyday life in advertising agencies. Today's advertising professionals are no less passionate about the work than their predecessors, but they also place a priority on skills of emotional intelligence and social sensitivity to facilitative collaborative working.

Case Questions

1. If 'a good idea can come from anywhere', is creativity in advertising now dead?

2. How might it help an account team to have a digital specialist in every meeting? Could there be downsides to this extension of the account team?

3. A lot of people would like to work in advertising, but few get the chance. What kinds of skill and quality do you feel are needed?

4. Every ad agency claims to be (a) creative and (b) integrated. How might clients distinguish between the claims and the reality?

Useful journal articles

(These Sage articles can be accessed on the book website)

Brian Moeran (2009) 'The organization of creativity in Japanese advertising production', *Human Relations*, 62 (7): 963–85.
Mats Alvesson (1998) 'Gender relations and identity at work: a case study of masculinities and femininities in an advertising agency', *Human Relations*, 51: 969–1005.

Manto Gotsi, Constantine Andriopoulos, Marianne W. Lewis and Amy E. Ingram (2010) 'Managing creatives: paradoxical approaches to identity regulation', *Human Relations*, 63 (6): 781–805.

Peter Svensson (2007) 'Producing marketing: towards a social-phenomenology of marketing work', *Marketing Theory*, 7 (3): 271–90.

Charlotte McLeod, Stephanie O'Donohoe and Barbara Townley (2009) 'The elephant in the room? Class and creative careers in British advertising agencies', *Human Relations*, 62 (7): 1011–039.

John Sinclair (2009) 'The advertising industry in Latin America: a comparative study', *International Communication Gazette*, 71 (8): 713–33.

■ ■ Further Reading ■

Ardley, B.C. and Quinn, L. (2014) 'Practitioner accounts and knowledge production: an analysis of three marketing discourses', *Marketing Theory*, 14 (1): 97–118 (first published November 20, 2013).

Deuze, M. (2007) *Media Work*. Cambridge: Polity Press.

Hackley, C. and Kover, A. (2007) 'The trouble with creatives: negotiating creative identity in advertising agencies', *International Journal of Advertising*, 26 (1): 63–78.

Hackley, C. and Tiwsakul, R.A. (2011) 'Advertising management and professional identity in the digital age', in Mark Deuze (ed.), *Managing Media Work*. London: Sage. pp. 209–16.

Jones, J.P. (1999) *The Advertising Business*. Thousand Oaks, CA: Sage.

Packard, V. (1957) *The Hidden Persuaders*. New York: McKay.

Pollitt, S. (1979) 'How I started account planning in agencies', *Campaign*, 20 April: 29–30.

Steel, J. (1998) *Truth, Lies and Advertising: The Art of Account Planning*. New York: John Wiley & Sons.

Notes

1. www.wcrs.com/us/ accessed 12.2.2014
2. www.forbes.com/sites/jenniferrooney/2013/08/14/mad-men-of-la-heres-whats-different-about-the-socal-advertising-world/ accessed 15.2.2014
3. www.forbes.com/sites/jenniferrooney/2013/08/14/mad-men-of-la-heres-whats-different-about-the-socal-advertising-world/2/ accessed 15.2.2014
4. www.imdb.com/title/tt0804503/ accessed 15.2.2014
5. www.adbrands.net/top_advertising_agencies_index.htm accessed 15.2.2014
6. www.adbrands.net accessed 15.2.2014
7. www.adweek.com/news/advertising-branding/wpp-revenue-grew-nearly-4-percent-last-year-147627 accessed 15.2.2014

8. www.adweek.com/news/advertising-branding/bbdo-again-tops-big-won-awards-tally-146645 accessed 15.2.2014

9. www.ogilvy.co.uk/who-we-are/ accessed 15.2.2014

10. www.kaper.uk.com/our-work/ accessed 15.2.2014

11. www.aaaa.org/Pages/default.aspx accessed 16.2.2014

12. www.credos.org.uk/write/Images/The%20contribution%20of%20advertising%20to%20the%20UK%20economy%20311011.pdf accessed 16.2.2014

13. www.adassoc.org.uk/write/Documents/AAWarcH12013.pdf accessed 16.2.204

14. www.thegoodpitch.com/alternatives accessed 17.2.2014

15. www.theguardian.com/media-network/2013/apr/05/four-tips-pitching-client-advertising accessed 16.2.2014

16. www.apg.org.uk/?page_id=269 accessed 17.3.2014

17. www.imediaconnection.com/content/25322.imc accessed 16.2.2014

18. www.leoburnett.com/ accessed 17.2.2014

19. www.leoburnett.co.uk/about-us/ accessed 17.2.2014

20. For this kind invitation I thank Ayesha Datoo, my former student at Royal Holloway University of London, who was at the time an account handler at Leo's. At the time of writing (February 2014) Ayesha is an Account Director at Grey, London. I'm also grateful to everyone at Leo's who very kindly took the time to talk into my digital recorder.

21. http://holler.co.uk/ accessed 17.2.2014

22. www.atelier-lb.com/ accessed 17.2.2014

23. Hackley, C. (2003) 'From consumer insight to advertising strategy: the account planner's integrative role in creative advertising development', *Marketing Intelligence and Planning*, 21 (7): 446-52.

5 Strategy and Creativity

Chapter outline

Chapter 4 introduced the key roles and activities in advertising agencies, and Chapter 5 goes into the creative advertising development process in greater detail. The chapter begins by outlining the steps in the process. It then moves on to strategy development for advertising and integrated marketing communication (IMC) before addressing the creative process. Finally, issues of evaluation will be touched upon before being dealt with in greater detail in Chapter 10.

Key chapter content

- The creative advertising development process
- Developing communication and advertising strategy
- Strategy and IMC planning
- Creative development
- Campaign evaluation

The creative advertising development process

The creative advertising development process in any major agency entails a set of broadly defined tasks that are listed in Table 5.1. Each could be sub-divided into smaller tasks, but for the present we will focus on the broad commonalities of the process. There is, firstly, strategy development. Once the agency has won the work and allocated it to a team, the team must come up with a great campaign. The place to begin is the fist step in the planning process. They will need to analyse the client brief carefully and do any additional research or information gathering that may be necessary to have a full understanding of all the issues at stake. The agency team must understand the brand, its history, its markets, its competitors and its consumers: they must understand the client, and most important of all, they must understand the problem or problems the client wishes to solve with communication.

Table 5.1 Basic stages in the creative advertising development process

1. Developing the advertising strategy
2. Developing the media strategy
3. Developing the creative ideas
4. Pre-testing creative executions
5. Creative production
6. Campaign execution
7. Campaign evaluation

Once the strategy is devised, informed by the careful analysis, the team will be clear about the precise purpose the campaign must accomplish. The strategy will be distilled into one or more objectives. The task of making sure that the team's thinking feeds into the client's marketing strategy is not complete at this stage – that is, an ongoing task, normally the responsibility of the account planner. The planner must ensure at every stage of the creative advertising development process that the client's needs, crystallised in the communication strategy, remain at the centre of the campaign. At this stage, media strategy is a consideration, but for the purposes of exposition this is dealt with in Chapter 6. The issue for many agencies is that media buying will be outsourced to a specialist media agency who will have their own thoughts on media strategy. There can be conflict here. In many cases, media strategy and planning are considered in as much detail early in the process as is necessary for the purpose of developing communication strategy and advertising strategy. This becomes more complex, of course, in integrated campaigns, as discussed below.

The account planner and account manager will then write the creative brief. This document is a key part of the process since it sets out in writing what the campaign must achieve, to whom it must speak, and any other necessary inclusions. The client and agency directors of creativity and client services must all sign off on the creative brief, so it is a very important document for all concerned. It provides a record of what exactly was agreed should the creative development stray from the brief, or should the client later get cold feet about the strategy.

The creative team will take the creative brief and try to develop some good ideas. This is where the magic is supposed to happen. Some issues around creativity in advertising are discussed later in this chapter. The advertising strategy has to be expressed in a way that reflects all the considerations of the creative brief, including target audience, brand positioning and any mandatory inclusions. The creative team might have scope to do something expansive in a big television commercial (TVC) if the budget allows, but more typically there will be clear guidelines as to medium and budget to work to. Within all these constraints, the creatives have to produce good ideas to a (very) short deadline. Advertising creativity, then, may be like artistic creativity in many ways, but it is constrained by many practical and commercial considerations. Hence, advertising creativity demands craft skills and experience.

Draft creative executions will be tested as they develop, until there are ideas that all agree can be moved into pre-production, mocked up and pre-tested in 'link' tests or in another form of consumer 'copy' testing. If the ideas pass those tests, then the ads will go into final production, media planning and buying, before being pre-tested once more before launch. Once the media plan is decided in detail and the campaign is launched, there will be continuous monitoring to evaluate effectiveness against the objectives listed in the strategy. The evaluation of the success or otherwise of the campaign against the objectives that were set for it should then feed back into the strategy development process for monitoring and/or reappraisal.

The creative advertising development process differs in detail in each advertising agency. While these differences are important, it is also true that every agency around the world does broadly similar things in broadly similar ways (Hackley and Tiwsakul, 2008). The differences in management processes between agencies are normally marked by differences of emphasis and tone rather than by more fundamental issues. Ad agencies generate ideas to help clients achieve their objectives through communication. To put this in a long-winded way, ad agencies analyse clients' brands and assess their marketing and communication activities, and then they devise creative communication strategies that aim to help clients achieve their marketing objectives. These strategies might focus on broadcast or print advertising, but, depending on the client, the brief and the agency, could include any element of the communication mix, including, for example, activation or sales promotion, engagement or social media, mobile, public relations or native advertising. Where agencies differ is in their history, their personnel, the emphasis of their process management, and on the particular mix of skills they can access. What follows is a necessarily general but representative outline of the major elements of the process of developing an advertisement.

Developing communication and advertising strategy

To have a strategy means to have a purpose. It has become conventional in management and business studies to use war analogies for business policy, hence the talk is of strategy rather than purpose. Strategy is distinguished from tactics by timescale and resources – a tactical plan would normally be shorter term and demand fewer resources than a strategic plan. A strategic plan would often have major implications for the long term, and demand major resources. An integrated marketing communications (IMC) plan might be strategic or tactical, or it might include elements of each.

Essentially, a strategic plan asks, and answers three questions:

1. Where are we now?
2. Where do we want to be?
3. How do we get there?

For an advertising campaign, the starting point could be an analysis of the brand, the market, the client's marketing plan, the client's objectives and the consumer behaviours and lifestyles. This (sometimes cast as a SWOT analysis for internal Strengths and Weaknesses, external Opportunities and Threats) gives the team a background of good information to contextualise the subsequent discussions. The client will have some idea of where they want to be, cast in terms of marketing objectives (say, a 3% increase in market share within three years) and the client and agency will have to resolve the marketing objectives into communication objectives. These will then be expressed as a communication strategy, sometimes refined into an advertising strategy (discussed below).

The strategy might be expressed as a goal or objective, as in this example from a marketing website:[1] 'Convince marketing communication managers that *AdCracker* CD will help them create more effective advertising, faster, and that now is the best time to buy'. There might be subsidiary objectives, as in this example: ' Achieve 50% brand recognition with target audience as defined by the ability to (A) recognise our logo, (B) describe at least one of our products, (C) associate equivalent products when prompted for brand characteristics; achieve a 2% response rate and sales of $500 per 10 direct mail packages within 30 days; achieve a lifetime value of $1500 on each customer within five years'. These objectives are very specific – unusually so. Nonetheless, the more specific strategic objectives are, the more effectively they can be measured. In this example, the campaign is a sales oriented one – in many brand positioning or corporate campaigns it would be very difficult to pin down strategic objectives realistically to such a level of specificity.

The next part of the process is about answering the question 'how do we get there?' This is where the creativity comes in – the creative team have to devise a way of conceiving and communicating the required message that resonates with the target consumers and motivates them to engage with, and respond to, the campaign. Before looking into this process in greater detail, some details of day-to-day agency life need to be noted first. Specifically, just how does strategy get made? The answer, is through meetings. This is a far from trivial point. It is easy to forget that advertising emerges through language and material objects (briefs, research reports etc.) in human interaction (Alvesson, 1998; Kelly et al., 2005; Moeran, 1996; Svensson, 2007). The way that particular ideas evolve and emerge can assume a dynamic all of their own once human interaction and organisational politics take effect. The values of an advertising agency can often be implicit (Hackley, 2000) and these implicit norms and values can be a guiding rationale for the development of advertising that is as important as the explicit, concrete materials of market analysis reports, consumer discussion group videos, theatre tests and so on.

Meetings, meetings, meetings …

In most ad agencies, campaign planning is conducted through lengthy meetings. From the initial meetings (sometimes called 'plans board' meetings) through to strategy development meetings, views will be heard from all major parties, including the client, creative and board-level account management. These meetings are at the heart of advertising development; promotional campaigns evolve through a process of debate and argument. Although creative work can sometimes be the inspiration of one individual, in an important sense, creative development is a joint effort because of the way ideas develop and reach a certain point through intense discussion. What this means for employees is that ad agencies value people who are socially poised, emotionally intelligent, articulate and also tough – there is a Darwinian attitude to ideas, and egos need to be self-controlled.

This discussion, which sometimes can seem endless, is given direction by the use of documents. In all agencies there are written documents that perform several functions. They provide a template for practice and thereby act as a tool of management control. Life in agencies is chaotic enough; without pro forma documents the chaos would be total. Documents provide a paper trail of accountability and a basis for contractual agreement. Client and agency have a permanent record of what, exactly, was agreed. Documents also act as stimulus tools for directing thinking along predetermined lines. They are handrails for advertising development.

An important semantic note is that ad agencies use the terms analyst, strategist and planner to label the people responsible for developing strategy. The role of planner (as described in Chapter 4) is devoted not only to commissioning and analysing research, but also to integrating the findings into strategy development and, ultimately, writing the creative brief. In some agencies there is a separation of analysis and planning, while in others the analysis is arm's length from the development of the creative brief. For our purposes, we will not distinguish here between planning and strategy – the former is conceived as a broad term referring to the efforts that go into developing the latter. This slightly different from the use of the terms in media, where media strategy is logically prior to, and conceptually superordinate to, media planning, which is more of an operational function.

The communication strategy

There has to be a clear marketing rationale, a purpose, for advertising and communication. Many commentators recommend beginning the process with a SWOT analysis, analysing the internal strengths and weaknesses and external opportunities and threats to the brand. However, other process models simply list 'research' at this stage, since the process model is less important than the outcome, which should be that the agency understands the client brand, its history, its markets and its consumers thoroughly. In many cases this stage can take two to three weeks as the agency team tries to really get under the skin of the brand, the client, the market and the precise problem or issue the client wants to address. The team will use secondary research, drawing on existing sources such as market reports and published consumer research data, and sometimes they will also engage in some primary data generation through small-scale consumer group discussions, just to gain additional insights into the consumer attitudes and behaviours around the brand. The important thing is that the strategy discussions are informed by an astute and comprehensive collective understanding of all the relevant issues.

In many agencies, there is a hierarchy – the communication strategy is conceived as a more abstract and generalised concept into which the advertising strategy will feed. The communication should be expressed in terms 'your mum would understand' as one planner expressed it (Hackley, 2000). A communication objective might be, say, to re-position the brand to a new market segment, while the advertising strategy might be to persuade this new segment to change their consuming behaviour. However, the distinction between the communication objective and the advertising strategy may be merely semantic in some cases – the two clearly overlap. The main case for having both is that a communication objective actively links the purpose of the advertising to the client's marketing strategy in a more general way. Fundamentally, an advertising strategy (as part of the communication strategy) disciplines the account team to think of an advertisement not just in terms of their own personal response to it but in terms of the behavioural or attitudinal outcomes it is designed to achieve. Advertising has to do something for the client's brand. The strategy expresses just what it is that advertising and promotion should do for the brand in order to support the client's marketing objectives.

The communication strategy must include an objective, or objectives. The objective will enable the success or failure of the campaign to be evaluated. The objective will be accompanied by a guiding idea, a sense of who the target audience will be, and a budget.[2] It should also include ideas on media. In the integrated marketing communications environment, it is incumbent on agencies to have an idea of which media they plan to use, and why, right from the beginning of the process.

The notion of communication strategy has been used by many advertising agencies, but not by all. It is becoming more important in the convergence era, as agencies strive for media neutrality and seek to devise communication solutions of which advertising may be a part, but in concert with other media[3] in IMC or 'through-the-line' campaigns.

The advertising strategy

The strategy document, as with all the other documents in the advertising development process, normally poses a series of questions that the account team members, assisted by other interested parties such as the client, are required to address. These usually include:

- What does the client expect the campaign to achieve? (For example, an increased market share, raised brand profile, changed brand identity.)
- To whom is the advertisement to speak? That is, who is the desired target audience? (For example, motorcar drivers between 25 and 69 years of age using ACORN or other segmentation systems.)
- What is the key consumer or market insight that gives consumers a reason to believe the claim made in the advertisement? (For example, that the brand advertised is more reliable/inexpensive/exciting than rival brands.)
- What is the desired reaction the campaign must produce in consumers? (For example, in terms of beliefs, memory, attitudes to the brand and purchase behaviour.)

Photo 1: *BMW* U.O.U The Chapter 1 Case study (page 29) describes *Jaguar's* content marketing initiative, a short chase movie featuring their new sports model. The expensively produced entertainment action feature as promotion was pioneered in the car business by *BMW* with its series of films beginning with the 2001 movie *The Hire* starring Madonna and Clive Owen, and directed by Guy Ritchie. BMW continue to use advertising alongside content marketing, such as this print ad. In English the I.O.U. is phonetically a promise to pay a debt – the ad suggests that you owe yourself a new *BMW 6* Series as a reward for your success.

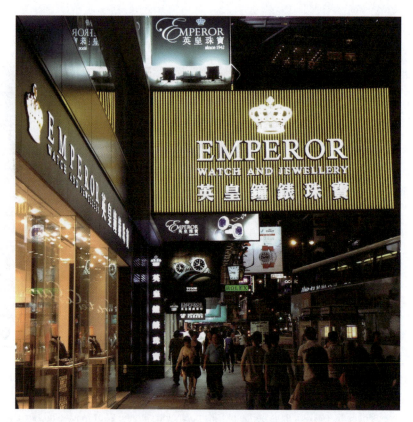

Photo 2: Kowloon street advertising   This street scene from Canton Road, Kowloon in Hong Kong features prominent signage for a local brand. Street advertising, collectively called Out Of Home or OOH promotion (see page 175), includes store signage, promotions on street furniture, billboards and poster sites, vehicular advertising and huge plasma screens, as seen in Times Square, New York, Piccadilly Circus, London, or the Las Vegas Strip. It can have a powerful commercial effect in setting the tone for an environment of consumption. It can also be considered as visual pollution – in Sao Paulo, Brazil, street advertising was banned, so fed up had citizens become with ubiquitous advertising hoardings.

Photo 3: *Strand* cigarettes – You're Never Alone   (See Snapshot 2.1, page 36)
The TV ads for *Strand* cigarettes were so popular with the public that the background instrumental, *The Lonely Man Theme,* became a UK chart hit. But the cigarettes didn't sell and the brand was subsequently withdrawn. This print version of the TV ad from 1960 lacked an appealing strategy – cigarettes are smoked for social reasons, not as a substitute for social interaction. Consumers were not given a compelling reason to buy the brand. The creativity was good, but the strategy was a failure.

Photo 4: *Guinness – Bring It to Life* Polysemic advertisements (See Snapshot 2.4, page 52) have more than one possible meaning. They can be seen as 'open texts' that consumers must actively read and interpret. *Guinness* has a long tradition of making ads that are beautiful and diverting and do not have an explicit sales message as such. Through this approach a local Irish beer with an acquired taste has acquired a global brand presence. 'Bring It to Life' intertextually references the corresponding TV ad. It also points to the history of *Guinness* ads, for those familiar with them. It has a vaguely uplifting tone in common with many other *Guinness* ads, and carries no suggestion of the qualities of the drink.

Photo 5: *Gillette* **– Good Mornings Begin with a** *Gillette*   *Gillette* advertising (see pages 53 and 97) has a long tradition of promoting the lifestyle benefits to men of the razor. In this 1958 poster by British designer Tom Eckersley, the brand is implicated in a lifestyle that includes a beautiful woman who is grateful her man's chin is smooth. Later *Gillette* campaigns have become famous for the slogan 'The Best a Man Can Get', complete with picture montages of handsome men shaving, alongside scenes of pretty ladies, babies, jet planes and sports cars. The brand pushes the boundaries of how many blades can be squeezed onto one handle, for the ostensibly more rational purchaser.

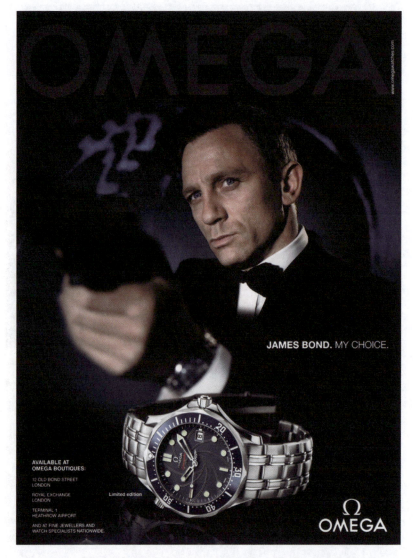

Photo 6: *Omega* and James Bond   Watch brand *Omega* (See page 53) exploited product placement deals in Bond movies by featuring Bond-like scenes in print and TV ads. Bond actor Daniel Craig strikes a typical pose in this print ad, intertextually evoking the movie. Wrist watches featured prominently in Fleming's novels and Bond wore *Rolex* in the movies until 1995. In Craig's 2006 debut as Bond in *Casino Royale* a clunky script reference to *Omega* was greeted with mockery by film buffs, but fans were undeterred. The Bond movie franchise has become almost a full feature product advertisement for multiple brands.

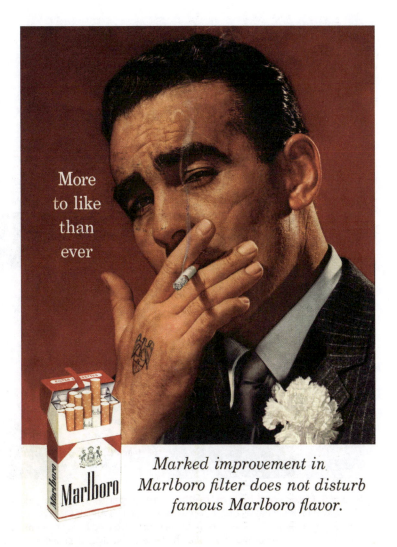

More
to like
than
ever

Marked improvement in
Marlboro filter does not disturb
famous Marlboro flavor.

Photo 7: Tattooed *Marlboro* Man   This 1955 print ad formed part of the famous 'Tattooed Man' campaign. Marlboro was known as a women's cigarette and manufacturers Philip Morris needed to widen the appeal to men. Chicago agency Leo Burnett came up with the *Marlboro* Man concept, of which the most successful was the cowboy. They also used images of general working men, cattle ranchers, and sailors, to promote a macho disdain for health warnings and to make the filtered cigarette seem less effeminate. The macho message, of course, is entirely implicit and visual (see Chapter 2 case study).

Photo 8: David Beckham modelling *Armani* pants   As a midfielder and wide player for Manchester United, Real Madrid and Los Angeles Galaxy, David Beckham (see page 139) was known for his impressive long balls and bent free kicks. His fame grew beyond sport when he began modelling. Beckham has had commercial contracts with *Sainsbury's, Adidas, Breitling, Armani, H&M, Samsung, Diet Coke* and many more. His name and image can help brands reach new markets because he is recognised around the world.

Photo 9: RAH in the Tokyo *Hello Kitty* store Store design can be an important aspect of Out Of Home (OOH) advertising (see page 175), vividly reflecting the brand and its values and making up part of the urban environment. This image from a *Hello Kitty* store in Omotesando Hills, Tokyo, shows one of the authors, RAH, looking excited about all the branded merchandise. *Hello Kitty* first appeared on a coin purse in 1974, the creation of the Sanrio gift company in Japan. Since then, in many variations *Hello Kitty* has become an iconic image adorning gifts and novelty items across South East Asia, and beyond.

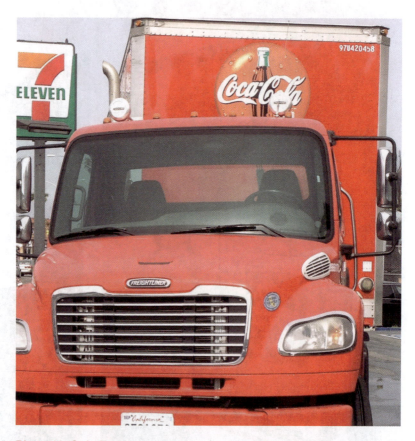

Photo 10: *Coke* Truck   As a form of urban advertising (see Chapter 6) vehicular advertising can extend the brand into the wider environment. Advertisers can buy space on public vehicles, or they can extend their own branding through liveries on their own vehicle. The pictured *Coca Cola* truck has become an iconic presence on American roads and this one, delivering supplies to a 7/11 store in Newport Beach, Southern California, has a striking presence. The truck has been seen by most people in TV advertising many times, so the TV advertising is implicitly referenced when we see the truck in person.

Photo 11: *Açaí* juice packaging   Non-advertising promotion, discussed in Chapter 7, includes the packaging that surrounds the product. The role of packaging is to protect the product in transit, but also to act as a singular promotion wherever it is seen. *Açaí* berry produce, such as the drink photographed, is relatively new in Western marketing, and uses berries familiar in South American countries to create new foodstuffs that are promoted for their taste and healthy properties. The one above was bought in Southern California in early 2014.

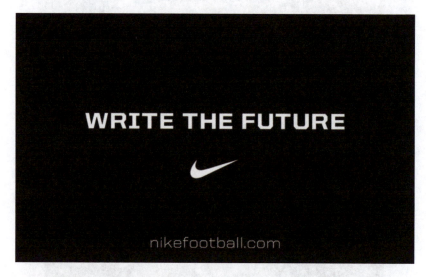

Photo 12: *Nike* **– Write the Future**   The *Nike* Swoosh logo, a ubiquitous sight at major sports events around the world (see page 188) has become one of the most recognisable images in Western culture. Carolyn Davidson, a design student at Portland State University in Oregon, USA, was asked to come up with something as dynamic and economical as the Adidas stripes. She was paid $35 for the Swoosh, and later received $150 worth of company stock. Today, Nike sells some $20 billion worth of shoes and sportswear annually, and Davidson's 500 shares are worth hundreds of thousands of US Dollars.

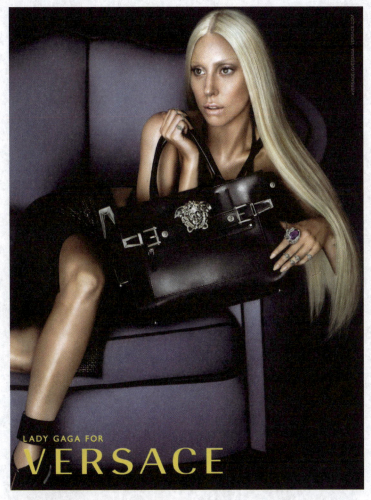

LADY GAGA FOR

VERSACE

Photo 13: Lady Gaga and *Versace* Pop queen Lady Gaga shot a series of ads for *Versace* in 2013 that received modest attention in the media. In April 2014 the raw versions of the ads were 'leaked', before re-touching, with the singer looking pale and apparently without make-up. The leak, if that is what it was, generated a huge surge of internet coverage and amounted to a re-launch of the campaign. Global celebrities make useful endorsers for luxury brands because their appeal reaches beyond Europe and the West into the vast luxury brand markets of Asia and the East (see Chapter 8).

Photo 14: *Calvin Klein,* **Kate Moss and Marky Mark**   British model Kate Moss and American actor Mark Wahlberg (AKA 'Marky Mark') posed for some clothing ads that continued the CK tradition of being sexy in a creepy way, or perhaps creepy in a sexy way. Many in the series have been banned for being too sexually candid or for using models who looked like children. Klein first recruited Moss to star in ads for the CK fragrance 'Obsession', and these were a commercial and critical success. The clothing advertising has been more controversial.

Photo 15: *Wonderbra – Hello Boys*   Czech model Eva Herzigova became world famous as a result of this iconic roadside billboard image that was reported to have stopped traffic when it was launched in the UK in 1994. As Chapter 9 discusses, ethical standards differ around the world and the poster might well have met with complaints at other times or in other countries because of its candid celebration of womens' sexual power (enhanced, of course, by the push-up effect of the bra).

Photo 16: *L'Oreal* and Beyoncé   The *Dove* Campaign for Real Beauty (see Chapter 10 case study) refers to the way that young women are exposed to intensely marketed and unrealistic norms of beauty. Many sectors of the cosmetics market remain unmoved by the Dove CfRB and continue to follow the photoshopped, celebrity-endorsed ideal in advertising, like this sexually charged ad featuring a pouting Beyoncé for super glossy lip shine. The ad features the line 'Because You're Worth It' to reference other *L'Oreal* advertising, and mentions the singer's preference in shade for any fans keen to get the same look. Celebrity advertising accesses the fan base as well as those searching for products, potentially widening the market.

The advertising strategy is seldom expressed in marketing jargon. Agencies usually insist on jargon-free, simple and even monosyllabic expressions for strategy. The rationale for the advertising must be clearly expressed, agreed by all relevant parties, commercially coherent and easily communicable to everyone involved. As communication professionals, advertising people strive for clarity and simplicity in their own internal communications. This clarity does not preclude a certain flakiness: phrases such as 'inject a dose of adrenalin into the brand' or make the brand 'compulsory equipment' are not uncommon. These were, in fact, phrases used in the advertising strategy for one of the most successful campaigns of all, for *Levi's 501* jeans (see below). The value of such phrasing is that it resonates with advertising people who feel that they know just what is meant.

The strategy for advertising will be the measure of the campaign's success or failure. The advertising strategy will form the basis for the creative brief. We should note that just as there may be some overlap between the communication objectives and the advertising strategy, there may also be overlap in the issues noted in the advertising strategy and in the creative brief. This reflects the inter-dependence of the steps in the creative advertising development process.

Media strategy and planning

Media strategy and planning are normally finalised later in the process but it is important that they are considered as factors influencing creativity, especially where campaigns will be integrated across media channels. Creative ideas for advertising creative executions do not happen in a vacuum – as we saw in Chapter 2, the context is important in framing the interpretation of communication. Media issues have moved to the foreground in advertising development with integration and the interactive possibilities of digital media. An additional issue is that media strategy and buying have been pushed out of the agency to media independents (as discussed in Chapter 6). However, broad-brush media and strategy and planning issues can certainly be engaged with by the account team at this stage, taking into consideration the budget, timescale, target group, and advertising and communication strategy and objectives. Creatives will certainly need to know which media channels they have to work within and what kind of media strategy in terms of targeting, timescale and frequency of exposures will be sought.

Some media strategies require very long-term planning – for example, a US company aiming to place a major TVC in a slot during the Super Bowl will need at least a year's lead time for planning, buying and creative production. A campaign based on radio ads, on the other hand, could be planned, designed, created and launched within a month, while some social media campaigns based on reactions to topical events (sometimes called 'newsjacking') have been launched in real time within hours, such as the tweet that made *Oreo* the most talked about brand after the 2013 American Super Bowl (described in Hackley, 2013a).

Creative development

The next step is the development of creative ideas, in order to develop the 'creative execution', what the ad will look/sound like. Once these have been established (discussed in detail below), the creative executions will be pre-tested. That is, they will be subject to audience research to try to predict how they will be received when the campaign is launched. Advertising pre-testing (often called copy-testing) is an area fraught with difficulty. It plays on the insecurities of all concerned. The creatives are insecure about their ideas being blocked on flimsy evidence; the client is insecure because it's their money and they want all the assurance they can find that the campaign is going to be received in the way that they want; account management are insecure because they want the client to feel happy about the campaign, but they also want to back the judgement of their planning and creative team. Copy-testing can be a crude method and many creatives 'hate' it because they feel that it is just a reason not to have their idea made. Copy-testing will be discussed in greater detail in Chapter 10.

Strategy and IMC planning

Communications strategy and advertising strategy are part of the traditional creative advertising development process. They take on a somewhat more nuanced character when applied in an integrated marketing communications (IMC) context. The need to have a strategy that defines the purpose of the communication is not less important in IMC, but perhaps greater. The difference is that the strategy must have the flexibility to be applied through different media channels. Maintaining a strategy coherently in a print campaign with four different creative executions is difficult enough. Maintaining the same strategy through multiple media channels is clearly a more complex task, and the difference is not just quantitative. Consumers consume different media channels in different ways and the strategy has to take this difference into account.

IMC, as previously noted, integrates at the levels of both media and creativity. The integration of media implies a carefully timed and co-ordinated media plan that reinforces the brand values through different channels and hence not only triggers greater recognition amongst the target audience but also extends the audience reach of the campaign. The second level of integration, creativity, is at a more abstract level as the creative themes are iterated through different media in ways that do not, necessarily, simply repeat the same things, but trigger recognition in more subtle ways, perhaps by developing storylines that continue from one medium to another, or more commonly by adapting creative motifs by utilising the qualities and constraints of each medium. For example, a print execution, a TVC and a mobile app would obviously require rather different creative executions. The ways in which the executions are thematically linked would reflect the strategy.

Horizontal, vertical, internal, external integration

There are also other ways to consider levels of integration. These are called horizontal, vertical, internal, external and data integration. Horizontal integration refers to the ways in which different business elements communicate values to consumers and stakeholders. So, for example, the retail outlet, the product design and the corporate livery are all important aspects of the brand, but they would need to be integrated cross-functionally for complete co-ordination to be achieved. Vertical integration refers to the need for communication strategy to be integrated from the brand and product/market level to the business unit and corporate levels. Internal integration refers to the internal marketing communications function and the distribution of the same themes and values to employees for communication to stakeholders. External integration is the level discussed most extensively in this book, and concerns the integration by medium and theme of all the advertising and promotional communications that end users and other stakeholders see. Finally, data integration requires a marketing information system through which data can be shared between functions. This is especially relevant for social media communication strategy and planning, given the importance of data analytics in social media.

Strategic benefits of e-marketing as part of IMC

The benefits of integrating different media in campaign planning are tangible. For example, research by the Internet Advertising Bureau has suggested that when an above-the-line media plan was supplemented by online advertising to 10–15% of budget, the overall campaign benefits (however measured) would show increases of 20–30% (Sharma et al., 2008: xiii). This tendency for integration to leverage disproportionately large benefits has been seen in all media mixes. But what particular qualities do e-marketing approaches bring to IMC campaigns? Firstly, it makes sense to examine what is included in the e-marketing category. E-marketing refers broadly to any marketing through electronic media, especially digital media such as the internet, mobile devices and digital television. Table 5.2 gives some examples of e-marketing techniques. This is the fastest developing area of advertising and promotion since new technology and new applications are emerging very rapidly. The internet, in particular, is the fastest growing advertising medium in terms of reach and share of promotional spend. What is most intriguing about the field, from an advertising point of view, is the rate of convergence between electronic media. Mobile devices combining television and internet will become more and more common, with much improved accessibility and quality in the future. Integration is moving on from being a source of strategic advantage in advertising, to being a default aspect of promotional planning.

Table 5.2 Examples of e-marketing techniques

• Viral marketing by email or video	• Affiliate marketing
• Interactive billboards	• Social networking and buzz marketing
• SMS text messaging	• Search engine marketing
• Microsites and sales promotions	• Interactive product placement
• Podcasting	• Online personal selling
• Advergaming	• Use of online consumer communities
• Branded e-content	• Online advertising, banner, pop-up, embedded video
• Brand blogs	• Search engine optimization (SEO)
• Online direct marketing	• Social media marketing

The meaning of e-marketing is extending all the time. Another old term, viral marketing, has also broadened its meaning beyond email to video, since video sharing websites have become such popular vehicles for viral advertisements. SMS text messaging can make use of location technology to target mobile device carriers when they are in a specific place, such as a particular shopping area. Affiliate marketing refers to co-operative ventures that enable sites to market each other's products or provide direct click-through access to related, affiliated brands. Search engine marketing is the practice of making sure that a particular brand features at the top of category searches by paying search engines and ensuring that search terms are connected with the brand. With online personal selling, a pop-up window connects consumers browsing a site with a live sales person. This can also be done via text, so that the audience communicate with the salesperson (or customer service assistant) via a dialogue box. Online advertising includes banner, classified and click-through ads, while many brands will make use of microsites with brand information, offers and opportunities for consumer engagement such as games, competitions, offers and feedback opportunities.

Advergaming refers to three forms of promotion. One is where a game is placed on a company website for the amusement of consumers, and to encourage them to the site. The second is where a bespoke branded game is created specifically for promotional purposes. For example, both the US and the UK have created online games to increase recruitment by allowing gamers to utilise the kinds of skill and experience (vicariously) the kind of task they would meet with as a recruit. Thirdly, brands buy presence in existing games, sometimes called virtual product placement or in-game advertising. This is a major category of product placement since many games demand realistic urban scenarios, and players want to see actual brands represented in street advertising hoardings and pitch-side banners at sports stadia.

Another method of e-marketing as part of IMC is interactive product placement which makes use of a technology enabling viewers watching TV or video online to click on items in the scene to find out how to buy them.[4] This technology is often deployed on pop videos because they are usually viewed on platforms with cursors that can be run over the desired item. When technological convergence arrives and TV is commonly viewed on screens that also access the internet, interactive product placement could even challenge traditional TV advertising. Search engine optimisation (SEO) refers to the ways in which places can be bought for certain words or brand names on internet search engines so that they come up on the first page of general searches.

In many cases, techniques such as these emerge from more creative ways of understanding how consumers interact with electronic technology. In others, the techniques are technology-driven. For example, computer games have now evolved beyond hand-held devices so that gestures, speech and body movement can involve gamers in a scenario in which they interact with characters. This virtual world clearly has immense possibilities for deepening consumer engagement in promotional communication. On one level we can simply walk through shopping centres and choose products, or we can become characters in the scenarios depicted on screen. So, for example, you could enter a shopping world and have sales people talk to you directly, answering queries you have put to them. Or, you could have three-dimensional games designed around a brand.

These are but a few examples in a crowded and rapidly developing area. Part of their appeal is novelty – they are new, and that has an intrinsic appeal, especially to people intrigued by new technology. There are also significant commercial advantages to be gained from using e-marketing communication. For example:

Cost: an e-marketing campaign can be created at relatively little expense when compared to above-the-line media campaigns.

Reach: e-marketing communications can reach huge volumes of potential consumers globally.

Accountability: there is considerable scope for measuring results from direct response mechanisms in e-marketing through –

Conversion: e-marketing enables customers to make instant purchases, enabling a rate of converting browsers into customers.

Engagement through interactivity: e-marketing makes it possible to engage consumers in dialogue or interaction, for example where brand-based websites offer games, blogs, offers, news and competitions.

Segmentation and database management: it is possible to link the customer database with the company website and achieve personalised, targeted offers based on tracking pervious purchases and inquiries.

Relationship management: since people are accessing the internet via increasingly mobile means it is possible to target and interact with individuals in ways that are tailored to their personal lifestyle.

24/7 service: there is no limit on the opening hours of a website.

Creative scope: e-marketing offers a creative palate for advertisers almost without limit. Different media can be combined and enhanced through display and visual technology, generating powerful possibilities for engaging consumers.

It has always been slightly problematic to separate marketing activities and processes from marketing communication. Some commentators maintain that the two are indistinguishable – marketing *is* communication (Schultz et al., 1993). After all, what is a market but a forum for communication? For example, the brand positioning, the satisfaction of consumer needs, and indeed the purchase, are all predicated on communication, in some sense. E-marketing technology has made the indivisibility of marketing communication all the more evident since it has collapsed sourcing and logistics, order fulfilment and customer service, and promotion, into one entity. The website connects the customer directly with stock control. Of course, behind the scenes there may be many links in the chain. Delivery, for example, is often outsourced to another company, while there may be many stock suppliers, and multi-media advertising and promotion programmes. But the website offers a seamless integration of all these elements from the customer perspective. Not only that, but company websites can generate additional revenue streams taking advantage of the browsing traffic through affiliate marketing programmes or the trade in customer databases for market segmentation and customer profiling.

e-Marketing planning issues

Developing an e-marketing plan entails much the same sequence of steps as for a conventional advertising or marketing communication plan. Firstly, there is a need to devise the strategy, then define the desired or potential target audience. If there are several potential audiences then they should be ranked in order of importance so that media mix decisions can be made on clear commercial considerations. Objective setting is also important. The objectives can be much the same as for any other kind of advertising, such as increasing the market share of an existing brand, positioning or repositioning, brand launch, change attitudes, reach a new market, building sales through the internet, and so on. Once objectives are established the optimum e-marketing mix has to be decided upon. There are numerous techniques from which to choose, depending on the precise objectives, and target groups. Budget setting might be the next stage, given that the objectives and e-marketing mix ought to give an idea about the potential rate of return. In many cases this doesn't happen and the budget is simply a default figure, what is left after essential costs. But this is a short-sighted way of operating since marketing budgets are an investment that will provide a rate of return. True, in marketing the rate of return (often called ROI or return on investment) is notoriously difficult to calculate with precision. But of all marketing media, e-marketing offers the most powerful potential for measuring ROI because of its integration with database management and order fulfilment. The next step in the planning process concerns action, especially tactics. What has to be done to make this plan work? Finally, constant attention to the measurement of results can make it possible to adapt, increase or redirect resources to a particular area where necessary.

Benefits of and barriers to IMC

In practice, as noted in Chapter 3, the differing disciplinary traditions and practices of the various communications disciplines make true integration very difficult for organisations to achieve. It is often more feasible to create a degree of commonality that links the various channels with consistent themes and values while allowing for variation within the overall theme. In other words, organisations achieve limited yet significant control over the way that their brand is portrayed across communication channels by establishing common creative themes, such as logos, scripts, colour schemes or musical links.

The implementation of IMC, then, is limited by, as noted, the different cultures, value systems and craft skills of the different communications disciplines. These can act as 'functional silos' that present barriers to the internal integration of management that IMC demands. In addition to the problems of organisational and disciplinary politics, implementation of IMC is limited by the fact it is a difficult task of management co-ordination. Many organisations may lack the necessary personnel and skills.

The benefits of IMC overall are considered to include enhancing a competitive advantage over those brands that do not take an integrated approach by presenting a clear and coherent brand positioning, by reaching a wider audience, by leveraging social media more effectively, by reinforcing the recognition and increasing the chances of acceptance of the message, and by saving money through efficiencies.

Creative development

The importance of creativity to successful advertising is asserted many times throughout this book. Advertising agencies are ideas factories, they are hubs for cultural production. However, there is a debate within the industry that places creativity and effectiveness in opposition. For some practitioners, this is hard to understand. Surely, they think, advertising that is not creative will not stand out, will not generate interest, and will not inspire consumers to consume anything. Others, though, see creativity as a code word for advertising that ignores the client's marketing objective and, instead, seeks to make something beautiful for its own sake. Many professionals simply deny the validity of the creativity versus effectiveness dichotomy, because they know it is meaningless. Advertising has to be creative to be good.

There's little point in equating creativity with great art – advertising is a creative craft skill. The potential for creativity to be indulged for its own sake, though, worries clients, even though some research studies have shown how important creativity in advertising is to marketing performance.[5] Clients' idea of what creativity means, though, is likely to be quite different from what ad agency professionals mean by it. Even the most down-to-earth of clients would admit that good advertising needs good ideas. Furthermore, they would admit that it needs good ideas that will work well in specific media, and that these ideas have to inspire and motivate the target consumers. And that is advertising creativity, hence there is no contradiction. Where there may be less agreement is how the creativity can be produced. Experienced advertising creatives can indeed come up with ten great ideas before lunch if they have to. But, the demands of IMC and integration today mean that ideas have to go through a lengthy process of iteration as the team discusses how well they fit with the strategy and how well they work within each media channel. All this makes advertising creativity a lengthy and difficult process, that some clients are reluctant to pay for. They don't necessarily see why it should take so long, but they do nevertheless want great advertising.

Advertising appeals

Defining an advertising appeal in terms of one characteristic can seem reductionist, a bit like saying that Shakespeare's play *The Tempest* works through a shock appeal, or that the classic Orson Welles movie *Citizen Kane* was a soap opera. As we saw in Chapter 2, advertising communication can be conceived as a text that has some complexity, including implicit and explicit aspects. The 'appeal' may not be reducible to one dimension. Nor is it meant to be – the creative execution is far more than the basic appeal. Nonetheless, the appeal is a common way of conceiving the basic approach advertising creative executions take to attract the attention of target consumers and to motivate them behaviourally or emotionally. As an analogy, one might think of a pitch for a Hollywood movie screenplay, where the author (or author's agent) has to explain the concept to the producer in one, short sentence. It may be a romcom, an action adventure, a period drama. Similarly, an advertisement might play on a rational appeal, an emotional appeal, humour, shock, fear, guilt, sex … and so on. Advertisements are not high concept – they are ads, and hence the particular appeal taken can be an important part of the creative development that feeds into the strategy. Table 5.3 gives examples of advertising creative appeals.

Table 5.3 Examples of advertising creative appeals

Social-emotional appeals	Personal-emotional appeals	Rational appeals
Social status	Fear	Product knowledge
Peer esteem	Security/safety	Detail and factual comparison
Respect/'face'	Humour	Proprietary information
Embarrassment	Happiness	
Belonging	Self-actualisation	
Acceptance	Joy	
Family values	Nostalgia	
Scarcity	Pity	
	Ambition	
	Sex/sensuous pleasure	
	Music/tag lines	
	Celebrity endorsement	

Emotional appeals

As discussed in Chapter 2, there is an argument that consumption is predominantly emotionally driven, and therefore that most marketing and advertising operate on that level. Emotionality can form the basis for an advertising appeal, there may even be a rational component in the ad as well.

Emotional appeals are sometimes broken down into two categories: personal and social. Personal emotional appeals might be based on, for example, safety or security and fear, love, humour and happiness, joy, nostalgia, sorrow or pity, pride and self-actualisation, ambition or sensuous pleasure. Social emotional appeals, on the other hand, might be based around social status and peer recognition, respect, embarrassment, rejection or belonging, social approval and acceptance.

Fear appeals are often used for selling home security systems, roadside car rescue subscriptions and insurance. The fear is that a terrible fate might befall the viewer if they do not buy the product. We all like to have 'peace of mind', and consequently many of us are over-insured, because we are sold on the idea that we can buy insurance to prevent nasty things happening, like burglaries or car breakdowns. Fear appeals are also used in the cosmetics industry to play on our personal insecurities about our looks or our body image. Fear appeals are typically personal but can also be social – for example, some deodorant or bad breath products play on the fear that others may think less of us because we might smell bad. Fear and emotional appeals are linked in direct to consumer (DTC) drug ads on American TV, in which a sick person is shown enjoying playing with their grandchildren because their life has been extended by a particular branded drug. Fear appeals can become shock appeals if they hit hard enough. Shock is considered to be more effective in getting attention than in generating sales, and it tends to be used more in charities advertising and marketing than in consumer brand marketing.

Humour appeals are very popular as a way to engage consumers' attention and to help us to like the brand. Many of us resent boring advertisements and after we've seen one we just want that 30 seconds of our life back. A humour appeal can help us to forgive the TV station for inflicting that interruption to our entertainment on us. For some clients, humour can seem a creative risk if the ad is so funny it overpowers the reason for consumers to buy the brand. Humour in advertising should not, therefore, be used for its own sake, but should be used when it links in with the advertising strategy.

It is well known that sex sells, and sex appeal has been used in many different ways to sell everything from cars to perfume, from clothes to ice cream, and from soft furnishings to confectionery. Everyone notices a pretty girl, and the less she's wearing, the more she's noticed. As with the humour appeal, this approach to advertising can be risky because the brand is forgotten, or possibly because sexuality and nudity in advertising may be off-putting or offensive to some consumers. For advertisers, it sometimes pays to offend some consumers with sexuality, because it generates controversy and media discussion as people lodge complaints about the ad. Fashion brands like *CK*, *FCUK* and perfume brands like *Yves St Laurent Opium* and *Marc Jacobs* have all made good strategic use of offending some people with their advertising. Sexuality in advertising is subject to very different regulations in different parts of the world, so it is a consideration in international campaigns.

There have been some reactions to the ways in which sexuality is portrayed that had implications for brands. For example, Unilever's *Dove* brand in the UK created a market-leading positioning by mobilising consumer resentment toward conventional cosmetics advertising with its heavily Photoshopped, size zero models. *Dove* has been positioned towards 'real' women, reflecting the reaction of some groups against the standards of female beauty and sex appeal set by the fashion and cosmetics industries (see Chapter 10 Case Study).

An advertising appeal can also be based on music, in the sense that a very catchy tag-line or melody associated with the branding can be powerful as an aid to recall. In the USA, for example, TV advertising is generally known for its creativity, but there is great pressure for it to be effective. One TV ad for insurance has used a simple but very popular sung tagline 'Like a good neighbour, *State Farm* is there'. Scarcity appeals are a timeless marketing technique, as when Amazon declares under a book 'only two left!' Other common scarcity appeals can be tied to sales promotional tools such as limited time to purchase or limited time money-off offers to motivate the consumer to take immediate action.

Celebrity endorsement qualifies as a form of appeal since it is so common, and the precise nature of the appeal is seldom interrogated. Having a celebrity in an ad serves a targeting purpose, since the celebrity's fan base are likely to notice the ad. It also guarantees a degree of social media buzz, since celebrities' every activity is often reported and commented upon in fan forums, including their sponsorship activities. There is often an assumption that fans will be interested in following the celebrity's espoused preferences and will, therefore, buy the product. There have been theories mooted arguing that there must be coherence between the values of the brand and those associated with the celebrity's public persona, their celebrity brand (called the match-up hypothesis). However, celebrity association is increasingly used to create new markets for brands because of their crossover appeal – David Beckham (see Colour Section, photo 8), for instance, enables brands to access new markets and cross international boundaries because of the international span of his fan base, regardless of whether he is promoting underpants, sports shoes, or prestige watches. As an appeal, using a celebrity can be creatively lazy, and carries the risk of alienating potential consumers who are not fans. There have been studies suggesting that celebrity endorsement is often not effective as an advertising appeal.[6]

The emphasis of an ad might be on rational appeals for complex and/or high-involvement products and service, for example, financial services products or business-to-business services. A 'high involvement' product or service is one that the consumer takes some time and trouble over deciding to buy, as in a house, a car, a medical insurance plan or a pension scheme. Typically, rational appeals in advertising are combined with emotional elements.

If the type of appeal forms part of the strategy it will be incorporated into the creative brief and the creative team will need to find a way to express it through a telling creative execution.

The creative brief

One of the key tasks of the account planner and account management is to write the creative brief. As noted earlier, creatives stereotypically don't like briefs, and some claim to throw them all in the office bin. More realistically, experienced creatives rely on the brief to make their work better by giving it the essential context without which it would be meaningless. It is, of course, important that the brief is written well and factually correct. The brief must inspire creatives: a brief that makes the job seem tedious, routine and functional is unlikely to inspire great advertising. For example, traditionally, creatives 'hate' prices briefs; a brief with the strategy focused on the brand's price advantage is often seen as un-creative. In one case, though – a 1990s campaign for Volkswagen cars – the team found a way to make the prices brief seem interesting. Volkswagen has a long and much-lauded tradition of highly creative advertising since Bill Bernbach and DDB[7] started the creative revolution in advertising with their iconic *VW* campaigns.[8] The agency (BMP DDB London) wanted their creatives to do something creative with a strategy that required consumers to believe that *VW*s were less expensive than they thought they were. Qualitative research had suggested that consumers mistakenly thought *VW*s were more expensive than other cars in their class. The campaign addressed this in fun ways that won many awards for effectiveness and creativity over the following decade, with ads like 'Tennis', 'Guard' and 'Lamppost'.[9]

Each agency has its own pro forma documents for strategy and creative briefs. Of these, the creative brief is very important because it is agreed between the client's representative (often the marketing or advertising director) and the agency account management and planning team. Once it is agreed and signed by client and agency it is given to the creative team as the basis for the creative execution. It must be clear, carefully thought through and motivating. Each agency has slightly different conventions for the brief, though the aims are similar. Like strategy documents, the creative brief poses questions that the account team are required to answer. In many agencies the account planner will research and write the creative brief in consultation with the client and account management.

The creative brief would normally begin with some background, a short paragraph stating the scenario to be addressed – brand, market positioning, the context for advertising – such as in this example from a model creative brief[10] from website *Adcracker*: 'This is a test campaign to a selection of Citibank customers. We want them to try Citibank's new "CitiClick" which is available as a mobile app for all operating platforms, from iPhone to Android. This smart app makes online purchases easier and more secure – and we've got a $1 pizza offer to get them started.' This passage is simple, clear and direct, and sets the context for the brief. The subsequent questions in the typical creative brief would be something like those in Table 5.4:

Table 5.4 Questions in the creative brief

1. Why advertise?
2. Who is the audience?
3. What must this communication do?
4. What must the advertising say?
5. Why must the audience believe it?
6. What else will help creative development?
7. What is the tone of the advertising to be?
8. What practical considerations are there (e.g. schedule, mandatory inclusions)?

Question no. 1 in the creative brief, 'Why advertise?', invites the account planner and account manager to express the rationale for advertising, drawing on the strategy document. Without a clear reason for advertising, there is little chance of a successful campaign. There must be an opportunity for communication to accomplish an outcome that will support and enhance the brand's marketing strategy. In the Citibank example, they state that the reason for advertising is that 'We want people to download the free app and use it within 10 days to buy the special offer, a $1 family size pizza from Papa John's'. This is a clear statement of intent and it gives the creative team a strong steer as to exactly what the ad is required to do.

Question no. 2 asks for the target audience to be carefully defined. In the Citibank example the response is 'This campaign will be aimed exclusively at existing Citibank customers in three test markets: Sacramento, Houston and Washington, DC. The primary target will be segments of our customer database: male and female, 20–35 years old, with at least one Citibank credit card. The target will be approximately 70% married, with combined household incomes of $85k on average. The audience is comfortable with new technology, and quick to test new smart phone apps that save their time. They make multiple purchases monthly.' In this example the target audience is conveniently bracketed and not difficult to define. It is an affluent target audience with household income almost double the US median. In more abstract brand campaigns this can be a much more nuanced task, but equally crucial to the success of the brief. The creative team needs to have a very clear idea of the kind of people they need to speak to.

Question no. 3, 'What must this communication do?' asks what the outcome of the advertising should be for the consumer. This is often couched in terms of consumer attitudinal or behavioural change. It must be a very simple and clear statement of what the ad must achieve. It is slightly different from question no. 1 because it focuses on the outcome (for example, to make people feel more positive about the brand) as opposed to the reason for advertising (for example, sales are suffering because people feel less positive about this brand than they did five years ago). In the *Adcracker* Citibank example, the response to this question is 'Citibank will simplify and speed up all of your online purchases, while providing increased security'. From the point of view of the creative team, the outcome might be prosaic and straightforward, but that doesn't mean that they should be prosaic and straightforward about getting consumers to that conclusion. In our list, this question is subdivided into two: question no. 4 refers to the bottom-line message of the ad that the client wishes the consumer to get from exposure to the ad. This is sometimes called the 'proposition' or the 'take-out' (for example, this brand is the leader in its class). In the Citibank example, the answer could be something like 'Citibank value my custom and want to make life easier for me with this app'.

Advertising makes many claims, and can support many different kinds of marketing objective (as we saw in Chapter 3). Good advertising gives consumers a reason to believe the claims. Question no. 5 asks the account team to provide evidence to support the claim, a reason to believe. The reason can be emotional or rational, or both. For example, many motorcar ads try to reassure the consumer that the brand is mechanically reliable and technologically advanced. In the case of German car brands this is not too difficult because in many countries German engineering and technology have an excellent reputation. This attitude can be symbolised economically in TV or print ads, with visual images of working engine parts or a cutaway image of an engine interior. The consumer, primed with cultural knowledge about the quality of German motor engineering, understands the inference implicitly. In our example, the response is given that the consumer should believe the ad because 'it's free, from Citibank, your trusted partner – it's backed with 100% fraud protection guarantee – it has earned rave reviews from real users (with quotes supplied in the ad) – and it is easy to access in seconds via the customer's online account'. The ad, then, has to offer some reason why consumers should believe the claims, and in this example they have several pieces of evidence.

Questions no. 6, 'What else will help creative development', and 7 'What is the tone of the advertising to be?' broadly refer to the way that brand values are reflected in the creative and production values of the ad. In the Citibank example, there is an 'insight' that claims: 'People don't like to put their credit card details and shipping details in over and over again when making online purchases. But they also don't like feeling their credit card information is vulnerable to theft. This app is the solution.' This claim might draw on some research carried out in the planning stage. It does, though, contain a hostage to fortune. The software development had better be right, because if the app did prove vulnerable to fraud, the campaign would be completely undermined. Not all creative briefs include a note about the 'tone' of the ad. In some, for example the iconic 1980s 'Laundrette' ad for *Levi's 501* mentioned earlier, the response to this question was, 'Heroic, but period'. Tone can refer to stylistic aspects of advertising production, including the set, music and narrative, and cinematography. The tone of the ad carries implied values for the brand.

Finally, in terms of practical considerations (question no. 8), there is often a schedule detailing deadlines for initial creative sketches, the creative review meeting and more advanced production of creative ideas, e.g. with colour and/ or sound, for internal and then external (to the client) creative and media presentations, and finally deadlines for finished art work and creative production. There may also be mandatory inclusions that the creatives must take on board. For example, for many years it was mandatory that *BMW* ads featured no human beings; the focus was to be on the engineering and the aesthetics of the car. The *Levi's 501* ad mentioned above had a requirement that there be no words but lots of close-ups of the rivets on the jeans. The ad was to be shown in many countries, so language had to be absent. Some ads have contact telephone numbers as mandatory inclusions, website addresses, particular straplines and so on.

The creative execution

The creative execution refers to the particular way the creative team address the creative brief, considering all the required elements of strategy, target audience, tone, required content and media. The creative execution, in a nutshell, is how the creatives make a great ad out of a particular kind of appeal. It might come in the form of a script for a radio or TVC, a screenplay for a piece of branded content, a striking piece of photography for a print ad, a piece of animation, a memorable jingle, strapline, slogan or logo, a design for an inter-active billboard, a cheap retail flyer, an expensively produced cinema ad, it could be a comedy script, a piece of emotionally tense drama, a one-line gag that captures the public imagination that puts the brand in everyone's consciousness, or any number of other kinds of creative execution. The tone of the ad is often captured in the incidental elements, such as the quality of acting or the production standards.

There is no single best way of producing creative work, every creative has his or her own particular style of working. Typically, the creative team would firstly generate a list of ideas, usually expressed in sketches, roughs, hand-written notes. They would then develop these by interrogating them against the creative brief. They would narrow the ideas down to a smaller number and discuss the implications of each, how they would work on different media, the costs, the time they would take to produce. Subsequent meetings to discuss outline creative executions would involve more members of the account team, and perhaps the director of creativity (DOC) and/or director of planning (DOP). There would be a further stage of development in which ideas would be developed in a more advanced way, making use of production artists to visualise the ideas more completely. There might be a need for research to test the ideas on a panel of consumers, before making decisions on which ideas to present to the client. If the client likes none of the ideas presented to them, the creatives will go back to work. If the client gives final approval on an idea, then it will go into full production.

The enigma of creativity

How creatives create is one of the abiding mysteries of advertising. As McCloud (2009) showed in her research with creatives (also see Hackley and Kover, 2007), they tend to be passionate about their work and they see it as something that is important. They are not salespeople, analysts or account managers since they see the problem from a different place, drawing on their own value judgements that are informed by their love of popular art, comic books, graphic design, literature and everyday consumer culture. The fact that they come to communication problems from a space that is not solely sales-driven is what gives them their creativity, but some clients find it unsettling to think that their bottom line is in the hands of a comic book enthusiast or aspiring novelist. The account management and account planning functions are both, essentially, organisational devices to manage (and to discipline) creativity. The tension between the two cultures of art and commerce (to adapt C.P. Snow's famous axiom[11]) lies at the heart of the fascination of advertising, giving rise both to its conflicts and also to its occasionally astonishing outcomes. The UK Institute for Practitioners in Advertising (IPA) has tried to address some clients' misunderstandings around creativity by commissioning a 400-plus case study programme of research that shows how creativity and advertising effectiveness can be shown to be linked.[12]

It seems self-evident to laypeople that creativity is what makes advertising good, but many clients still view creativity in particular, and advertising in general, with suspicion. The creative execution fills the space between analysis and outcome. Some commentators argue that Bill Bernbach's famous use of self-deprecation in his early *VW* ads was not creativity but brilliant strategy.[13] There may have been a brilliant strategy, but it was expressed by a brilliant and, at the time, daring, creative execution that ran counter to the grain of conventional advertising wisdom at the time. Unfortunately for advertising professionals, there are a lot of marketing consultants and managers who couldn't recognise creativity if it fell on their head.

Depending on the media mix employed, the creative team will have, in principle, a multiplicity of ways in which to encode the message. In practice, of course, a great deal of advertising is not very creative, and much use is made of cliché, stereotypes and outright plagiarism. Not a few award-winning campaigns began life as a YouTube clip uploaded by an amateur, or at least they look as if they did. Then again, a great deal of advertising is not very good, and as in most fields, excellence is rare and difficult.

Creativity can run in cycles, with particular narrative forms or production techniques coming into vogue for a while before being replaced by another. Some creative teams make a career out of one type of ad, or exploit their friendship with a movie star to get some celebrity input. Some ads, though, stand out, and some agencies, and some creative professionals, consistently make ads that stand out. The thing that makes these ads stand out is called creativity, for want of a better word. There is an art in crafting something that is engaging, perhaps amusing, but that also knits with the advertising strategy and resonates with the target audience. Whether the ad made is another great *Guinness* ad, a *Nike* epic, or a corny but catchy execution for a local car dealer, there can be an integrity to the work that is best expressed as creativity.

Advertising creatives have to survive in an exceptionally highly pressured professional environment. They bring varied temperaments, backgrounds, motivations and working methods to their tasks, but most are genuinely passionate about wanting to make great work. It would be hard for them to survive in the business if they were not. Just what, though, should be judged as great work is a point of endless debate. *Budweiser*'s legendary 'Whaaasup' campaign, mentioned earlier, won many awards and was lauded as a hugely notable campaign, but was it great creativity? Great art it certainly was not, but someone had the idea that the idiomatic expression being used by many young American men could be used to link the beer brand with its target audience, and that took a kind of thinking that might be termed creative.

There are many definitions and theories of creativity but one fact emerged strongly from the psychology research in human expertise. This is, that creativity has a context. Ad agencies sometimes set creativity exercises for graduates competing for their graduate trainee posts like 'how many uses can you think of for a brick?' or 'think of an advertisement for lard'. 'Diagonal thinking'[14], lateral thinking or creative problem solving exercises are all very well but without a context for creativity, a creative output it is unlikely to resonate with relevant groups (Hackley and Kitchen, 1997). One of the truisms about creativity is that it is a social accomplishment: it is nothing unless it is recognised as such by others. It takes experience, craft skills and a social presence in a particular milieu, in other words, a network, to have creative output recognised, in any field. This is why creatives in advertising value industry awards from their peers so much.

The best advertising creatives tend not to complain about having to work to a brief – they realise the creative brief is there to make their work better, and if their work lacks any connection to the strategy they are unlikely to win awards. There are always exceptions, examples of advertising creativity that breaks the rules and still works. These, though, are rare, and usually result from a bond of trust between client and agency (or more specifically, between ad agency account team and client brand team). In such cases, the brief can be deliberately broad, leaving the creatives scope to do something that might be seen as risky. When this works well, the results can be highly satisfactory to all parties involved. Such situations of trust are becoming more and more difficult to find though, as commercial pressures swarm into every area of the marketing communication business and measurable return on investment (ROI) becomes clients' abiding priority.

Campaign evaluation

Once ads have been produced and the campaign has been launched in selected media, it is important for the campaign's effectiveness to be ascertained. This task is a perennial problem in the advertising industry (Cook and Kover, 1998) because of the difficulty of conclusively linking the advertising cause with the purchase effect. It is important, though, because clients want the agencies to be accountable for the success or failure of a campaign. Clients need to know their return on investment (ROI) on advertising and media spend, and they need criteria to judge agency performance. For their part, agencies need to know what works and what doesn't, and they need to have feedback on their performance in order to monitor and improve their working methods, and to improve their credibility with clients. Winning creative awards is important, but if the agency is not winning effectiveness awards as well then potential clients will draw their own conclusions. In this section campaign evaluation will be outlined in brief, and the research methods used in the process will be discussed in greater detail in Chapter 10. Some methods of campaign evaluation are summarised in Table 5.5.

Clients need to be reassured that campaigns are effective in meeting their objectives if they are to continue to pay for advertising. As noted earlier, even though TV advertising is holding up pretty well, in general, client adspend is shifting away from advertising and toward digital because of the perception that digital gives a better ROI. Digital media can be subject to complex and

Table 5.5 Methods of campaign evaluation

- Pre- and post-launch street surveys for brand recall/prompted recall
- Social media data analytics for brand engagement (e.g. clicks, page views)
- Sales data/enquiries/conversion rate analysis
- Media content analysis
- Mid-campaign audience/reader surveys
- Surveys of intermediate attitudes, e.g. intention to purchase, brand preference
- Calculation of advertising ROI by ratio of revenue to advertising and media costs
- Market share analysis
- Focus groups
- Case studies

precise analytics so that the value of every unit of adspend can easily be calculated, and that is very attractive to brand clients in comparison to the leap of faith they have to take with advertising. Advertising, though, has proved more enduring than many commentators predicted because there is still a need for a big, mass media ad to drive traffic toward digital engagement. As TV and print audiences/readerships continue to shrink, though, there is an increasing impetus toward digital media.

Ad agencies and professional bodies have done a lot of work in developing evidence bases for advertising effectiveness, but the conventional wisdom is still that a large proportion of advertising spend is unproductive. Evaluation of advertising is, nonetheless, an essential component of the process. Evaluation techniques can only be as successful, though, as the strategy allows. If a campaign had a poorly conceived strategy, leading to confused or vague objectives, there is no method that could ascertain its effectiveness. Adding to the complexity, campaign evaluation is always contingent on market conditions as well as on campaign objectives. For example, if sales fall after a campaign, the client will not be happy, but it would be important for the agency to consider seasonal or competitive factors before declaring the campaign a failure. If every supplier's sales fell during the same time period, but the agency's client's sales fell less, then the campaign could be regarded as a qualified success in bolstering sales and increasing market share in a falling market.

Many agencies try to reduce the risk of failure and quantify the risk by carrying out extensive pre-launch testing. When a creative execution has been signed off by the client, it is often subject to one final phase of pre-launch testing before campaign launch. This is often called 'copy-testing' and is sometimes done through 'link' tests, computerised platforms that allow panels of consumers to access to ads remotely and offer assessments on them through an online questionnaire. If the results of the link test are satisfactory to the client, the campaign will be launched and evaluation will continue throughout the campaign via, for example, recall tests, prompted recall tests and street surveys.

One UK campaign was commissioned by a health charity to get more people to go to their doctor to be tested for diabetes. A survey established that most people didn't know the typical symptoms of diabetes. The poster campaign was launched in the London Underground, and a subsequent survey established that the percentage of people who recognised the symptoms of diabetes had risen significantly. In that example, the objectives of the campaign were clear and easily measured in the medium term. Many ads with a simple appeal can be evaluated in this way, either through street surveys or by email or internet surveys, although without face-to-face questioning it is more difficult to ascertain the respondent's credibility. Ads with a clear sales objective can, of course, be evaluated by looking at sales figures at the time of the campaign, but there is often a difficulty of a time lag both in the available figures, and in the sales effect.

Many campaigns are evaluated through intermediate effects, effects short of sales, such as measures of brand recall, of ad recall, measures of attitude to the brand, and measures of 'purchase intention', in which people are asked if they plan to buy the brand in the future. 'Self-reports' as these forms of research are called can be very imprecise, but they form part of the battery of evidence that ad agencies compile to evaluate the success or otherwise of their campaigns.

Chapter summary

This chapter has reviewed strategy and creativity in advertising. The chapter outlined the entire creative advertising development process before discussing the development of communication strategy and advertising strategy, and then discussed implications of IMC. It then focused on the creative brief and the development of the creative execution. Chapter 6 will discuss the rapidly evolving media environment for advertising, and the implications of convergence for media planning and strategy.

 ■ **Review Questions**

1. **What is the difference between the creative execution and the advertising appeal, and how are they reconciled in the creative brief?**

2. **Is there a tension between creativity and effectiveness in advertising? How might this be resolved?**

3. **Devise an advertising strategy for a new-to-market brand of high fashion wear targeted at women aged 18–25 and branded 'Ms Dynamic'.**

4. **Describe the creative advertising development process and explain the key issues and difficulties at each stage in the process.**

5. **Why is strategy important for advertising campaigns?**

Top ten global communications trends, 2014, by WPP[15]

WPP is the world's biggest marketing communications holding company, and includes business dealing in advertising, media, market research, public relations, branding, corporate identity, direct, digital and relationship marketing. The agency networks owned by WPP include Ogilvy & Mather, JWT and Y&R. WPP's 'Reading Room' web pages offer comment and analysis on advertising and related issues. One story has an employee of one of WPPs ad agencies venturing thoughts on the top ten communications trends for 2014. They read as if the author has a gun pointed to their head while they were writing it, but are fun to pick at for what they imply for the future organisation of advertising and promotional practice.

The first trend listed is a continuing shift of internet traffic to mobile. This, like most of the ten, is not really a trend at all but a current fact that is clearly accelerating. Mobile internet access is likely to surpass desktop internet access this year. This, a central pillar of convergence, has major implications for advertisers and many agencies are trying hard to upgrade their knowledge of digital mobile applications and software in order to be in position to leverage the rapid growth in mobile advertising spend. This trend is connected to a second, which is personalisation. Mobile devices are highly personalised and they take an intimate role in the user's life. They are ideal vehicles for personalised advertising. What the WPP comment does not say is that, currently, the algorithms used by social networking sites to mine user data in order to segment and target personal advertising is crude, and often mis-directs inappropriate offers. The industry either has to solve this problem or abandon the pursuit of individualisation. Advertisers need to learn that there is no way to be relevant when the user simply does not want to see advertising. When one mentions a holiday destination in a private message on Facebook, then a sponsored item for that destination appears in one's newsfeed, it's disturbing, not ingratiating. The way around this problem, of course, lies in the use of branded content and 'native' advertising (promotion that looks like entertainment or editorial) because these categories of promotion are things the user might actually want to see and share.

The WPP author states that social media constitute a third major trend, not surprisingly, and maintains that a fourth is 'brand journalism'. This topic connects with the aforementioned branded content and native advertising, since journalists have the craft skills to write stories that consumers like to read. The author claims that brand journalism 'isn't content marketing or sponsored content'. Which it isn't – as journalism sheds jobs, more trained journalists are finding work blogging for brands, frequently on topics unconnected to the brand, but good writing acts as good PR for the brands and retains website traffic. All of which means, of course, that brand journalism is exactly like content marketing and sponsored content. Indeed, some newspapers, such as the British national *The Guardian*, are explicitly involving journalists in the creation of sponsored native content.[16]

The fifth trend refers to the difficulty social media present to PR, in the sense that negative communication about a client can spread so quickly it is very difficult to respond to it adequately. The author suggests that a solution lies in transparency and honesty in brand communications, important because consumers have access through social media to so many sources of information, they are likely to discover the truth sooner or later. A seventh trend concerns evidence and results measurement for PR, utilising the kinds of analytic tools pioneered by YouTube and Facebook. Using these tools to generate consumer insights beyond simple measurement of retweets, shares, views and likes will be a major challenge.

(Continued)

(Continued)

The eighth trend revisits an old saw, namely that, in marketing, image is everything, and a picture is more powerful than a 1,000 words, a truism borne out by the huge popularity of *Instagram*, *Pinterest* and *Tumblr*. Viral videos, infographics and other visualisations will continue to be of great importance in advertising and social media. A ninth trend the WPP author claims is that corporations will have to have a clearly communicated sense of purpose so that the world knows what they stand for. This connects with the interest in PR crisis recovery management, and the need to be able to tell a convincing story based on track record. However, the need to have a strong and clearly expressed sense of purpose has been a mainstay of strategic management for many decades. Finally, the author notes the 'generational' shift to integration of PR, marketing and advertising. Above- and below-the-line demarcations are becoming redundant and this shift will continue to gather pace.

As someone said, it isn't easy to make predictions, especially about the future. The WPP piece does, though, underline the key issues facing advertising and promotional communication in the convergence era. The survival of agencies depends on their ability to organise their work to address these issues.

Case Questions

1. The ten 'trends' are not so much future events as current ones that will continue. Can you think of any others that will impact on the way ad agencies organise their work?

2. In the light of the trends outlined above, how might account teams change their way of working in the future? How might these changes help ad agencies win and retain business?

3. If adspend continues its shift to digital, how might this affect the creative advertising development process?

Useful journal articles

(These Sage articles can be accessed on the book website)

Anne M. Cronin (2004) 'Currencies of commercial exchange: advertising agencies and the promotional imperative', *Journal of Consumer Culture*, 4 (3): 339–60.

Michael Serazio and Wanda Szarek (2012) 'The art of producing consumers: a critical textual analysis of post-communist Polish advertising', *European Journal of Cultural Studies*, 15 (6): 753–68.

Rowan Wilken and John Sinclair (2009) '"Waiting for the kiss of life": mobile media and advertising', *Convergence: The International Journal of Research into New Media Technologies*, 15 (4): 427–45.

Marsha D. Loda, William Norman and Kenneth F. Backman (2007) 'Advertising and publicity: suggested new applications for tourism marketers', *Journal of Travel Research*, 45 (3): 259–65.

Suruchi Sood, Corrinne Shefner-Rogers and Joanna Skinner (2014) 'Health communication campaigns in developing countries', *Journal of Creative Communications*, 9 (1): 67-84.

■ ■ Further reading ■

Branchik, B.J. and Chowdhury, T.G. (2013) 'Self-oriented masculinity: advertisements and the changing culture of the male market', *Journal of Macromarketing*, 33 (2): 160–71 (first published November 4, 2012).

Hackley, C. (2003) 'Account planning: current agency perspectives on an advertising enigma', *Journal of Advertising Research*, 43 (2): 235–46.

Hackley, C. (2003) 'From consumer insight to advertising strategy: the account planner's integrative role in creative advertising development' *Marketing Intelligence and Planning*, 21 (7): 446–52.

Hackley, C. (2003) 'How divergent beliefs cause account team conflict', *International Journal of Advertising*, 22 (3): 313–32 (reprinted in Chris Hackley (ed.) (2009) *Advertising*, Vol. 1 *Advertising Management*. London: Sage. pp 1–17.)

Hackley, A.R. and Hackley, C. (2013) 'Television product placement strategy in Thailand and the UK', *Asian Journal of Business Research*, 3 (1): 97–110.

Loo, B.K. and Hackley, C. (2013) 'Internationalisation strategy of iconic Malaysian high fashion brands', *Qualitative Market Research: An International Journal*, 16 (4): 406–20.

Tomas Ariztia (2013) 'Unpacking insight: how consumers are qualified by advertising agencies', *Journal of Consumer Culture*, doi: 1469540513493204 (first published June 25, 2013).

Richard Mocarski and Andrew C. Billings (2014) 'Manufacturing a Messiah: How Nike and LeBron James co-constructed the legend of King James', *Communication & Sport*, 2 (1): 3–23 (first published March 11, 2013).

Notes

1. www.adcracker.com/plan/Advertising_Plan.htm accessed 20.2.2014
2. www.thegoodpitch.com/wp-content/uploads/2011/09/CommunicationsStrategy Guide.pdf accessed 17.2.2014
3. www.thegoodpitch.com/wp-content/uploads/2011/09/CommunicationsStrategyGuide. pdf accessed 17.2.2014

4. http://new.clikthrough.com/website/ accessed 22.2.2014

5. www.forbes.com/sites/avaseave/2013/11/30/what-is-creativity-in-advertising-and-when-does-it-lead-to-market-performance/ accessed 17.2.2014

6. www.brandchannel.com/images/papers/522_2011-01_celebrity_marketing_myth.pdf accessed 25.2.2014

7. www.ddb.com/BillBernbachSaid/why_bernbach_matters/revolutionary-work/ accessed 20.2.2014

8. www.greatvwads.com/ accessed 20.2.2014

9. www.advertolog.com/brands/volkswagen,media-adverts,year-1998,products-volkswagen-polo/ accessed 20.2.2014

10. www.adcracker.com/brief/Sample_Creative_Brief.htm accessed 18.2.2014

11. www.age-of-the-sage.org/scientist/snow_two_cultures.html accessed 20.2.2014

12. www.thinkbox.tv/server/show/nav.1372 accessed 20.2.2014

13. www.forbes.com/2007/05/17/jack-trout-marketing-oped-cx_jt_0518trout.html accessed 23.2.2014

14. www.DiagonalThinking.co.uk/ accessed 20.2.2014

15. www.wpp.com/wpp/marketing/publicrelations/10-global-communication-trends-2014/ accessed 17.2.2014

16. www.adweek.com/news/press/guardians-unusual-take-native-ads-155715 accessed 17.2.2014

6 Promotional Media in the Digital Age

Chapter outline

The media infrastructure for advertising and promotion has changed radically over the last twenty years and continues to do so. Convergence is changing the way marketing communications professionals approach their tasks, as advertising now sits at the apex of an integrated media environment. McLuhan's (1964) dictum that the medium is the message is truer then ever, and media strategy has become a multi-channel discipline. This chapter discusses the implications of convergence for media strategy and planning, using the traditional methods as a point of departure.

Key chapter content

- **The media planning task**
- **Media planning terms and concepts**
- **Media strategy**
- **The media mix – channel characteristics**

The media planning task

Think about media channels and media vehicles – which media channels do you access regularly? TV? Or mainly the internet through your mobile? Do you ever buy a print newspaper? A magazine? How about listening to the radio in your car, and do you notice the roadside billboards? So, how would a brand target you through the media you engage with? Into which market segments could you be classified? The job of the media planner is to know this kind of information, and also to know how much it costs to buy the media space to reach people like you.

Advertising media consist of 'any means by which sales messages can be conveyed' to audiences (Jefkins, 2000: 74). Communication is mediated (that is, carried on a medium) when there is some intervening vehicle between the source and the receiver, such as a newspaper, mobile device or billboard site. Advertising messages can be carried on radio waves, static outdoor billboards, paper and ink, ceramic mugs and ballpoint pens, dynamic outdoor sites such as motor vehicles and public transport; even air balloons and loud hailers can carry promotional messages. Media strategy refers to the decisions around media channel, media vehicle, media exposure timing and style in combination with creative execution. Media strategy occupies a more abstract level than media planning, which tends to be focused on the operational task of planning the exposure of the creative execution to the target audience.

SNAPSHOT 6.1

Top twelve worldwide media planning and media buying agencies[1]

1. Starcom Mediavest
2. OMD
3. Zenith Optimedia
4. Mindshare
5. Mediacom
6. Carat
7. MEC Global
8. Havas Media
9. UM Interpublic
10. Initiative
11. PhD
12. Maxus

Source: www.adbrands.com

'Interruption' and 'engagement' advertising media

Media planning and buying today is dominated by media independents, specialist agencies many of which have their origins as in-house ad agency departments (see Snapshot 6.1). The demands of media planning and buying have grown more complex with the proliferation of new media channels and media vehicles. As Dawson (2009) points out, 'Integration is now so much the norm that the term itself seems almost obsolete, with "new" and "old" media rapidly blurring into a single communications armory … Interruption and engagement channels are complementary tools rather than "old" pitted against "new" media' (p. 28). 'Interruption' refers to advertising that interrupts the audience's enjoyment of media entertainment, such as where the TV shows are broken into segments so that ads can be shown in the commercial breaks. In order to get around the problem of audiences not viewing ads placed in advertising spots (say, by recording shows and fast-forwarding through the ads), advertisers can use methods that weave the promotion seamlessly into the audience media engagement, such as by placing branded products in the set of TV shows, using native advertising on digital media brands, or buying 'idents' and other forms of sponsorship that show the ad after the TV show titles to reduce the chance of viewers avoiding them.

What this means is that now it is incumbent on media planners to think not only in terms of advertising exposure but also in terms of brand contact 'touchpoints', that is, all the points across all media at which the consumer has contact with the brand. Brand contact is any planned and unplanned form of exposure to and interaction with a product or service. Television commercials, radio ads or internet banners are planned forms of brand contact. Word-of-mouth (WOM) or social media mentions can be part of a plan, but the outcome is less certain.

'Bought' and 'earned' media

Further complicating the already complex media planning task is the distinction between bought and earned media. The advantage of bought media, acquired by buying a pre-set advertising 'spot' to be aired at a particular time, on a particular day, and on a particular channel, is that there is certainty about when the ad will be broadcast and some degree of certainty about the numbers of the target group who will see it. The advantage of earned media, such as a piece of branded video content that is shared millions of times on social media, is that it can be far more cost-effective and more engaging than bought media spots. The disadvantage of earned media is that content cannot be made to go viral at the whim of the agency. Earned media space depends on the users liking something enough to share with friends, and what people like can be very quirky.

Exceptionally, the content might be shared on such a huge scale that journalists want to write and blog about it, further leveraging the amount of media space earned. This kind of earned space is what public relations (PR), social media marketing and activation agencies hope to achieve, but even with extensive media contacts and a big budget, no agency can earn media on demand. Earned media is often reactive and supplementary to the bought media strategy. Media planning, then, focuses mainly on the craft of and science of planning bought media, but with one eye on the possibilities of leveraging the bought media through PR and social media. The main stages of media planning are summarised in Table 6.1.

Table 6.1   The main stages in media planning

1. Set media strategy and objectives (with reference to advertising/communication strategy)
2. Define target audience
3. Select media channels
4. Schedule media exposures (the media plan)
5. Buy the media space
6. Assess the media effectiveness

Media planning and buying

The media strategy, planning and buying tasks are of key importance in advertising. Media, as they say, is where most of the money goes. The costs of producing broadcast advertising may be very high indeed but the cost of buying mass media time and space to show the ad is usually much higher. The high cost of mass media exposure means that getting the media mix right is every bit as important to the success of a promotional campaign as getting the creativity right. However, according to commentators such as Manning (2009) and Binet (2009), many advertising agencies remain relatively poor at accurately calculating the return on investment of advertising spend on digital media. There is much science in media planning, since there are many data sources detailing consumer media viewing/reading/listening habits, but it also remains something of an art.

The basic media planning task (see Figure 6.1) is to achieve optimum levels of exposure for the campaign, utilising the most cost-effective and appropriate combinations of medium possible. The media planner negotiates the price and buys the space on which the advertisements will be shown, whether TV or radio airtime, out of home (OOH) sites, billboards, print ads in press publications, click-through or banner ads on internet sites, sponsored tweets or whatever.

Outline Media

Plan Product Launch

Oct - Jan

	2010			2011
	OCT	NOV	DEC	JAN
TV				
PRINT				
ONLINE				
RADIO				
IN-GAME				
YOUTUBE				
POP				
SUBARU.CA				
SM.SEEDING				

Figure 6.1 Example of a media plan graphic

The media planner seeks to expose the creative execution(s) to a relevant audience defined by segmentation criteria such as age, sex, demographic, socio-economic or lifestyle/psychographic characteristics. They try to achieve the greatest possible reach and penetration. Reach refers to the proportion of the target audience reached by an exposure. Penetration refers to the accumulated reach over time, including repeated exposures. Timing is important, since the advertisements must be exposed at times when they will achieve the highest impact. Media planners will schedule advertisements according to the campaign objectives, perhaps in a short burst of intensive exposure (called 'blitz'), or alternatively in a stepped exposure of, say, one week on, one week off, over several months (called 'pulsing'). Issues of seasonality of demand also need to be considered. The cost-effectiveness of the exposure is often assessed by the cost-per-thousand (CPT) of the target audience reached.

Media planning terms and concepts

In an era of integrated marketing communications the terms above-the-line and below-the-line are heard less often in the industry than was once the case. Their rationale, which was based on the largely outdated commission model for agency remuneration, is now redundant as most agencies now charge by labour hour. Nonetheless, the terms still have resonance. Above-the-line refers to mass media advertising, television, cinema, press and commercial radio. Once, ad agencies were paid through the commission they gained from buying spot advertising on these media. Below-the-line refers to everything else, from direct mail and database marketing, sponsorship, product placement and celebrity endorsement to sales promotion and merchandising. The term 'through-the-line' refers to media planning, which deploys both mass advertising media and non-advertising promotion in an integrated campaign.

Another term that has become popular in media planning for advertising is media-neutral planning. Media-neutral planning refers to the way the agency agenda has been broadened from advertising to a far broader treatment of the media mix. In the past, advertising agencies were notorious for their attitude that mass media advertising was the default solution for any client's communication problem. Today, with a non-commission billing system predominant, there is less need for agencies to push advertising as a solution as opposed to other forms of promotional communication. There is also much more pressure from clients for ad agencies to provide integrated communication solutions. The media-neutral planning attitude holds that the solution to the client's communication problem might lie in any medium, or in any combination of media, even if none of these include mass media advertising.

SNAPSHOT 6.2

Media planning and media buying[2]

Mediacom, one of the world's biggest media agencies, states that their media planning process is underpinned by their advanced research techniques and sophisticated analysis, all informed by their experience in helping clients to find, reach and engage their actual and potential customers. They then work with advertising agencies to identify the media channels that these consumers use most, in order to negotiate and buy the required media space. Global media agencies buy a lot of media, so they have a strong position for negotiating prices with TV channel owners, cinema chains, radio stations, magazine publishers, or website owners.

The GRP

Other important concepts in media planning include the cost per gross rating point (GRP), which is a measure of the proportion of households who are exposed to the advertisement. GRP can be calculated by multiplying reach times frequency, for example, 100,000 people are potentially exposed to 10 ads and 50,000 people see the ads an average of 5.4 times 50,000/100,000 x 5.4 = 50 x 5.4 = 270 GRPs.

Reach and frequency

Reach refers to unique audience members, while GRP refers to the accumulated figure as a result of repeated airings of the ad. Frequency refers to the number of opportunities a member of the audience has to see the ad (see Figure 6.2). These concepts can be used in setting media objectives. For example, a campaign might be planned to reach 75% of the target audience.

There are different views about the usefulness of repeat exposures. Some commentators feel that many repeated exposures can serve a purpose, while others feel that there is little point to any beyond the first exposure. However, as always, it depends on the nature of the communication problem being addressed, the market, competitive context and target audience characteristics, all of which influence the advertising and the media objectives.

Figure 6.2   Reach, frequency, penetration and audience share

Media platforms and vehicles

Other important terms in media planning and strategy include media 'platform', which normally refers to a channel format, such as the internet or mobile digital communication. A media vehicle is a specific media brand, a newspaper, TV show, radio show, internet channel, magazine etc. Each media vehicle is a brand in its own right, and has a carefully researched audience profile that is used to sell their advertising to brand clients. For example, the TV show *The X Factor* is a media brand that enjoys multiple revenue streams, not from the advertising, although this is lucrative revenue for the broadcasting TV channel, but for other things such as phone voting and music downloads and live show ticket sales from the website (Hackley et al., 2012). The information a media brand holds on its audience is carried on a 'rate card',[3] and this is the information upon which advertisers may base their decision on whether or not to use the media vehicle.

Audience fragmentation

Audience 'fragmentation' refers to the reduction in audience/readership/viewers for media vehicles during the past decade as audiences are now fragmented across hundreds more media vehicles, especially digital media. For example, the top TV shows in the UK now attract around 10–12 million viewers, when thirty years ago the figure for the top shows would be nearer 30 million. A similar pattern can be seen all over the world in all media – consumers' media consumption patterns have changed since we now have many more media channels from which to choose.

SNAPSHOT 6.3

Media budgets shifting away from advertising

In a story in trade magazine *Advertising Age*,[4] *Coca-Cola*'s CEO responded to investors worried at the brand's loss of sales by explaining they would find $1 billion to fund additional media spend and brand building by 2016. A 'multifaceted' strategy is planned that will engage more directly with consumers and respond to concerns about obesity and health. In the last quarter of 2013 *Coca-Cola*'s income was reported to have fallen by more than 8% on the same period in 2012, to $1.71 billion on a fall in sales of 3%. Sales in North America fell by 1%.

There is no suggestion that the shift in media spend is linked to *Coca-Cola*'s controversial Super Bowl TVC in early 2014, in which 'America the Beautiful' was sung in different languages. The ad generated complaints from conservatives.[5] Food multinational *Mondelēz*, makers of *Oreo* and *Trident*, have been candid in announcing that digital and mobile will grow from a quarter of the company's advertising budget to half by 2016, reflecting a loss of faith in traditional advertising to deliver sales. *Mondelēz*'s North American President is reported[6] saying that digital generates twice the ROI as traditional spot advertising. *Mondelēz* may have been influenced by the success of their *Oreo* brand on digital. They claim that *Oreo* is the no.1 food brand on Facebook, with 35 million fans, and a tweet from *Oreo* was the most talked about ad in Super Bowl 2013. These two examples are illustrative of a wider shift in media spend toward engagement media and against the interruptive media of traditional broadcast spot advertising.

Cost efficiency of media

The media planning task tends to be quantitatively driven by the cost-per-thousand (CPT) or cost-per-gross rating point (CPGRP) and number of exposures, as noted above, but it is a mistake to suppose that it is just all about procurement. Judgement is required to decide which combination of media (known as the media mix) will provide the maximum impact for a given advertisement. Questions such as 'What are the viewing/reading/listening habits of the target audience'? and 'How might they be reached and engaged with'? have to be answered. Also, 'What interval frequency of advertising exposure will best support the campaign objectives?' 'Can the campaign creative executions be integrated across differing media so that consumers' view of the brand is reinforced from a number of sources?' A significant constraint, of course, is the budget. This might constrain attempts to shout as loud as competitors, leading to a declining share of voice. 'Share of voice' is an important consideration in media effectiveness. This refers to the share of the total audience for that medium at that time. It can also be measured longitudinally, over a period of time.

Media agencies

The advertising case studies on the website of one of the world's biggest media agencies, *Zenith Optimedia* (ranked no. 3 in the top twelve, see Snapshot 6.1),[7] illustrate integration well. Zenith focus on creating engagement by leveraging social media, but the seamless links between advertising, digital and activation are well illustrated by these cases, which include *BA* and the London 2012 Olympics and *Toyota*'s branded content media campaign. As noted earlier, the media buying scene today is dominated by media independents, agencies that specialise in media planning, scheduling and buying. In a sense, the evolution of advertising agencies has turned full circle, since advertising agencies began as media brokers before developing in-house functions of copywriting, art-work, strategy and research to become full-service agencies. Over time, media planning and also market and media research have been farmed out to become independent agencies. Many advertising agencies that formerly bought media through their own in-house operations now buy their media space through independent media brokers.

Lateral mergers and takeovers have increased industrial concentration in the media industry over the last decade, resulting in fewer sellers and fewer buyers. This means that media costs have been driven up, and advertisers usually have to go through the big media buyers to get the best economies of scale. The rise of the independents has partly been a response to the increasing media buying costs, as well as to technological advances including digital media. The rise in the cost of advertising media, partly resulting from the monopoly position of many regional media owners, has not been well received by agencies. Media buyers therefore needed more buying power to generate economies of buying scale. As a consequence there has been increased industrial concentration among media buyers parallel with that among media owners. Media planning decisions should be uppermost at every stage of the creative advertising devel-opment process, the increased complexity of market conditions for media planning and buying necessitates specialist agencies with the expertise and buying power to perform this function effectively.

Global adspend by medium

The move toward integration is reflected in global adspend trends. Expenditure on TV advertising continues to show growth, and is predicted to be 34% of the total in 2016, but internet is catching up fast. Print media show a continuing decline, with outdoor stable and internet advertising rising fast. Internet advertising accounted for 20.6% of total global adspend in 2013, according to reports,[8] but this is predicted to rise to 26.6% by 2016, with most of the growth within this category driven by a rapid rise in mobile advertising expenditure. Mobile currently takes a small proportion of the total, under 3%, but it is predicted to increase by 50% a year, reaching an estimated 7.7% of total global adspend by 2016. Previously, increases in internet adspend tended to reflect parallel reductions in print spend, but the new figures show how television and social media are intimately linked as advertisers seek to engage consumers and drive social media buzz from TVC platforms. Consequently, internet, and especially mobile, are now independently driving total global adspend growth.[9]

Within internet advertising, banner and display advertising spend is being challenged by 'programmatic' advertising such as data-driven direct promotions on social media, mobile and video advertising. Click-through rates on website banner ads can be low, and advertisers want to use the interactive and multi-media potential of the internet to make advertising more engaging and relevant for consumers. Hybrid forms of advertising, such as native or brand blogging, are, anecdotally, rising fast but the truth is hard to quantify.

Out of home (OOH) advertising continues to grow but at a varied pace, depending on the country. OOH consists of billboards, street furniture, vehicular advertising and alternative media. Billboards are the largest sector and these are being enhanced with digital displays and even inter-active technologies that can personalise a response to individuals using movement-detecting or even face-recognition technology. OOH comprised about 7% of global adspend in 2012.

Media vehicle proliferation

Global trends in adspend are not only shifting because of a change in the priorities of brand advertisers. Integration is also being driven by changes in media consumption patterns. In particular, the reduction in media production costs because of digital technology has resulted in many new media brands coming onto the market, in the form of digital TV channels and radio stations, specialist print publications, new media brand launches such as *Huffington Post*, and of course countless new blogs and brand websites. As a result, global media audiences are fragmenting across many new media vehicles because they have so many more opportunities to access news, comment and entertainment than ever before, especially online but also through new print media vehicles such as free newspapers.

There are more media vehicles than ever before, but each is competing for a small share of audience as audiences fragment across the spectrum of the media mix.

For media planners, the implication of this trend to audience fragmentation is that targeting to specialist interest groups is easier and more precise, but it requires more media vehicles and a wider media mix to achieve the required audience reach.

Conventional wisdom about the strategic importance of a particular medium and also about targeting, audience segmentation and cost-effectiveness are being challenged. Media strategy and advertising strategy increasingly have to be understood as two dimensions of the same thing. Most importantly, account people and media planners can no longer easily categorise their target audience by external indicators like social class, age, income or sex. Instead, they have to think in terms of the lifestyle choices of brand consumption communities and the implications of these choices for media planning.

Media strategy

The term media planning is sometimes used to refer to the entire task of devising media strategy, choosing and buying media, and sometimes it is used more narrowly to refer to the process of media buying and scheduling only. Media strategy uses audience research to ascertain how best to teach the required target consumers in the right way. The media strategy would also consider the communication and the advertising strategies, the creative execution, and of course, the budget. The primary requirement of media strategy is to use relevant information to show that the target audience will be reached in the appropriate time frame and at the appropriate times of day, with the highest possible impact and lowest possible CPT.

The two key components of an effective media strategy are, firstly, accurate knowledge about media audiences, and secondly, a sound advertising strategy. If the advertising strategy is based on an accurate understanding of who the relevant consumers are and the creative execution has assimilated a coherent strategy, then all the media strategy has to do is to deliver the required number of those target consumers. The accurate knowledge about media audiences that is needed is not confined only to who is watching/reading/listening to which media channel. It is also necessary to know how consumers consume media, and why.

For example, how do working mothers in the South-East of the UK research holidays? What newspapers do teachers read? How many Baby Boomers listen to the radio for two hours per day? Which medium do consumers trust the most for factual information? Which media vehicle do farmers in Ohio use the most for their information and entertainment? Much of this kind of information is available to media planners from syndicated research companies such as Global

TGI[10] and Nielson Media Research.[11] For example, Americans now own an average of four mobile devices and spend an average of 60 hours a week consuming content, according to Nielson.[12] Eighty-four per cent of American smartphone owners say they use the device as a second screen for watching TV, very often in order to deepen their engagement with what they are watching by looking up cast members or plot lines on the internet, or discussing the show on Twitter. Mobile devices like smartphones and tablets are driving the uptake of social media. TGI generates its continuous panel data from many regions around the world, so media planners can access the information they need for international campaigns as well as domestic campaigns.

The media strategy could be expressed quantitatively, for example, 'Reach 1.5 million ABC1 25–55-year-olds across the UK'. In this case the ABC1 refers to socio-economic groups, discussed below, but there are many other ways of classifying target groups, many of which are described below. The important issue for advertisers is that the creative execution they think will resonate with their desired audience segment will reach that very segment. This may seem obvious, but as this chapter has noted, the media infrastructure is increasingly complex for advertisers and it is by no means a simple matter to define and to reach large audiences.

SNAPSHOT 6.4

TV ad revenue driven by audience figures

It was reported that British broadcaster Piers Morgan's CNN show *Piers Morgan Live* was cancelled in March 2014 because of poor ratings. It was reported that the prime time evening show was gaining as few as 270,000 viewers, and only 50,000 of these were the group advertisers want to pay to reach, the 25s–54s. In a country of 300 million people, US TV shows are doing exceptionally well if they reach 20 million viewers. The top ten list for February 2014 has NBC's Sochi Winter Olympics coverage taking the top seven positions, with up to 23 million viewers.[13] News or current affairs based programming struggles to reach high viewing figures. Morgan's rival shows on Fox and MSNBC were reported to be reaching up to 1 million viewers. All the major TV channels in the USA are commercial, so viewing figures are reflected in advertising revenue. In contrast, in the UK, the world's biggest public service broadcaster, the BBC, carries no advertising. The market for UK TV advertising is served mainly by ITV, a group of regional channels, and Channel 4, a commercial broadcaster with a public service remit. The top TV show on UK TV in autumn 2013 was a dancing competition, *Strictly Come Dancing*, but since this was shown on the BBC advertisers could not buy advertising around it. Its main rival, ITV's *The X Factor*, averaged around 10 million viewers, making it one of ITV's top shows for generating advertising revenue. The American *X Factor* show, in contrast, slumped to around 3 million viewers in its 2013 series and was cut from the schedule in early 2014. American TV is regarded as a particularly competitive advertising market and new TV shows are cut from the schedule in mid-series if the figures are not stacking up.

Targeting and audience segmentation

It is worth mentioning a little more about targeting and segmentation, given their importance to media strategy. The increase in the number of media channels and vehicles, and the consequent fragmentation of media audiences, means that target groups of consumers are both easier and more difficult to reach. They are easier to reach in the sense that audiences have fragmented into narrow interest groups that are served by thousands of special-interest magazines and TV channels. If an advertiser wants to reach, say, trout fishermen, sports-car enthusiasts or TV soap opera fans, there are specialist publications and TV shows that are ideal vehicles for targeting such narrowly defined audiences. But consumer groups are also more difficult to reach because agencies have great difficulty in categorising audiences into target groups that are sufficiently large to be viable for general advertisers. Being able to target trout fishermen is useful if you are selling fishing tackle, but not for general fmcg (fast moving consumer goods) sales that require varied target groups. While trout fishermen probably have other consumer interests too, media vehicles that cater for one hobby are of limited use to most advertisers.

Each commercial medium that is funded by advertising has a research-based reader/listener/viewer profile which provides an idea of the typical person who consumes their medium. This information (held on a 'rate card') is important for selling advertising space or time to advertisers who need to know the age, sex, income and economic behaviour of the typical consumer. It is not difficult for media owners to construct this kind of profile. Never before have there existed more data sets on consumer habits, behaviour and attitudes. Electronic communications and transactions mean that it is possible to construct and cross-reference massive databases of consumer information. The difficulty brand organisations have is how best to use all these data to focus on the key characteristics of their typical consumer.

SNAPSHOT 6.5

The UK national daily press circulations[14]

The UK has a population of about 64 million, with high literacy rates and relatively high disposable income in the seventh richest economy in the world. Newspaper readership, though declining, remains relatively high compared to many other countries. The Audit Bureau of Circulation (ABC) reported that *The Sun* was the most popular UK newspaper in mid-2013, with just over 2.2 million daily sales. The *Daily Mail* followed, with 1.7 million, and the *Daily Mirror* sold about 1 million copies per day. The market is thus dominated by a mixture of showbusiness

(Continued)

(Continued)

gossip, celebrity scandal and populist political posturing. The *Daily Mail's* website, *MailOnline*, is the most popular and profitable newspaper website in the world. Long-form, analytical journalism trails a long way behind and most national dailies are making huge losses. The right-leaning *Daily Telegraph* sells around half a million copies a day with *The Times* at about 400,000 and the business specialist daily *The Financial Times* at a quarter of a million. Print newspaper sales in general are facing long-term sales decline, along with declining advertising revenue. All print publications rely on ABC auditing so that advertisers will trust their circulation figures. The advertising market is dominated by the *Sun* and *Daily Mail* since these deliver the mass of C1C2D readers (see Snapshot 6.3) under 50 years of age, who are in the market for mass selling consumer goods. Newspaper reader profiles differ in terms of age, education level, political orientation, income and geography. *The Times*, for instance, sells more copies in the South of England than in the North, while *The Guardian* is a favourite with teachers and Labour Party voters. Precise costs for newspaper advertising depend on the timing and other circumstances, but can run to between £30,000 and £50,000 for a full colour page in a national UK newspaper.

International media planning

Campaigns that cross international boundaries present more planning and scheduling problems for the media planner, in addition to the creative problems of cross-national advertising (see Chapter 8). The media infrastructure varies enormously region by region and country by country, as do media consumption patterns, literacy rates and disposable income, and this variation accounts for major differences in the character of advertising and promotion in different national and international contexts. The media mix for national and international campaigns may need to be very different.

In general, in the developed North there is a complex communications infrastructure that reaches most of the population through thousands of press publications, radio and TV shows and other media, and there is almost comprehensive access to internet services and mobile phone networks. In the developing South there is a far less well-developed communications infrastructure, and also lower levels of TV and mobile phone ownership, internet access and adult literacy. This is not to say that there are not still vast potential markets of many millions of people, but audiences are, in general, more difficult to reach where the communications infrastructure is less developed. However, in spite of such variation, the global reach of digital communication is having a striking effect on the tone, type and cost structures of advertising in all its forms, not to mention its effect on audience reach.

The international media agency networks have an advantage in that they are able to administrate the media buying for global campaigns through their various international offices. The media plans for different countries, and also the creative executions, may be different of necessity, although there will be crossover from cable and satellite TV channels and websites that cross international borders.

Demographic segmentation and consumer heterogeneity

The problem for advertisers is that although they may need to reach large numbers of consumers in order for advertising expenditure to be recovered in increased sales, the media consumption behaviour of these large groups is often heterogeneous. Specialist media, then, facilitate more closely specified targeting than mass media, but they tend to serve audience numbers that are much lower than those formerly served by mass market media. The mass media channels of TV, radio and press were once easy access routes to large, relatively homogeneous, audience groups. Today, mass audiences display far more heterogeneity in their consumption patterns and behaviour than they used to. Increased income levels and social and geographical mobility in many countries mean that a person's social status no longer reliably indicates his or her consumption behaviour or lifestyle.

Socio-economic classifications

Demographic and social changes have rendered the old socio-economic groups of A, B, C1, C2, D and E increasingly redundant (see Figure 6.3). Created by the British Civil Service in 1951, the classification of socio-economic groups (SEGS) was extensively revised in 1961, and has been adjusted for various purposes since then. The aim was to create a classification of social class by employment as a basis for social policy analysis. But the original SEG, still extensively used in marketing and media research, carries a number of dated assumptions. For instance, no longer can household members easily be classified and their consumer behaviour predicted on the basis of the occupation of the (male) 'head' of the household. In Western developed economies rising rates of divorce, increasing numbers of females involved in the professions, greater social mobility and increases in the number of single-person households have changed the composition of media audiences. In the past, it was more likely that a person's social status, education level and employment would be the same as their father's, hence the profile of the father was a more reliable indicator of the status of the rest of the family.

A	Higher managerial, administrative and professional (3% of the UK population)
B	Intermediate managerial, administrative and professional (20.4%)
C1	Supervisory or clerical and junior managerial, admin (27.2%)
C2	Skilled manual (21.8%)
D	Semi-skilled and unskilled manual (17.4%)
E	State pensioners, casual workers or unemployed (10.2%)

Figure 6.3 UK socio–economic groups

Another problem of SEG for marketing analysis is that classification of manual or non-manual occupation no longer necessarily indicates income levels in Western developed economies. Many non-manual workers earn less than skilled manual workers. Plumbers or builders might earn more than teachers or junior civil servants, and they may be just as likely to take holidays abroad and drive an expensive car. In spite of their shortcomings, SEGs are still commonly used to classify newspaper readers (*Daily Telegraph* A,B; *The Sun* C1C2DE) as a shorthand for helping advertisers target their brands.

Alternative segmentation approaches

There have been some attempts to improve on SEGs for media segmentation and targeting. For example, one attempt has involved commissioning research to delve into consumer lifestyles and behaviour in order to form proprietary classification systems that claim to capture the intangibles that evade systems based on demographic data alone. One example coming out of Madison Avenue in the 1980s was the Values and Lifestyles classification (VALS), another was termed psychographics. These systems used coined terms to classify consumers according to a claimed insight or set of insights about their lifestyle. For example, two lifestyle segments that entered the popular lexicon in the UK in the 1980s were Yuppies (Young, Upwardly Mobile Professionals), and Dinkies (Dual Income, No Kids). There were many other irreverent, acronymic soubriquets. The agencies' objective was to persuade clients that in spite of the breakdown of traditional mass audience characteristics, they still understood the motivations and behaviour of discrete consumer groups. They could, therefore, claim that they had proprietary knowledge and insight that enabled them to reach exactly the kinds of consumer their clients wished to reach.

There have been periodic marketing buzzes around other consumer segments, such as Baby Boomers (born between 1945 and 1964), Generation X, Millennials (also known as Generation Y) and Generation Z. There are no precise definitions for these terms and they are used very loosely to label anyone born between 1980 and the early 2000s. Conventional media wisdom holds that the Baby Boomers have the income, the pensions and own their houses, while the subsequent generations no longer read print newspapers, watch much less TV, and define their identities through consumer lifestyles rather than through their social class and geographical origin.

Brand communities

Another way to categorise consumers is through their consumption, as a brand community (Muniz and O'Guinn, 2001; Parsons and Maclaran, 2009) or even as a tribe (Cova et al., 2007). The implication of conceiving a consumer group as a community is that there is shared experience that can be exploited through engagement. Brand communities thus fit well with the convergence era in which consumer activism and interaction with brands is facilitated through social media. Academic studies of brand communities have highlighted that the bonds that bind the group can be moral and ritualistic as well as simply consumption-based. To be part of a brand community is to be a member of a sub-cultural group with its own cultural idiom. To *Harley Davidson* owners, *Manchester United* fans, *VW Camper* owners, surfers, snowboarders, die-hard WWF fans and many more, the way they choose to spend their leisure time and money is far more important to them than merely being a purchase decision. The community can be radically heterogeneous but their shared bond is deeply felt. Engaging with these communities in a way that they see as authentic can be highly beneficial for brands.

Increasingly, it is becoming commonplace for brands to refer to their customers as a community, even where there is little basis for regarding it as a sub-cultural group. For many consumers, a fondness for a particular brand may be something they are happy to deepen with various forms of engagement through mobile and social media or other means, but it falls short of an obsession or a lifestyle.

The media mix – channel characteristics

Sales promotion, TV advertising, press, SMS text messaging, direct mail, radio, outdoor billboards, vehicular advertising, point-of-sale promotion and merchandising, cinema advertising, direct mail and direct response marketing, product placement and sponsorship, trade conference and exhibition stands, public relations, internet and interactive TV, social media, email and content marketing, even product packaging and non-mediated channels such as personal selling and word-of-mouth campaigns can all be understood broadly as advertising via different channels. As we have seen, these channels are increasingly used in combination in integrated or 'through-the-line' campaigns. Media planners and creatives alike need an understanding of channel characteristics in order to fully grasp how consumers will engage with different media channels, and thereby to understand how they might react to different forms of communication strategy on different channels.

The choice of media channel is often based on criteria such as the following:

- Coverage of the target audience
- The type of engagement
- The communication context that the medium provides for the brand
- The cost in relation to the promotional budget

These issues have to be considered in the light of specific campaign objectives. For example, a campaign to support a new brand launch demands a different kind of engagement with the consumer, and possibly a different medium, from a campaign requiring a direct response from consumers. A new brand launch needs to spread the word about the brand and link it with the values that reflect the brand's competitive positioning, so for a major FMCG product a mass media channel such as TV would probably form a necessary part of the campaign. Alternatively, a bank launching a new mortgage might place less emphasis on TV and more on targeting their existing consumers with rational appeals through email and social media.

Consumers engage with media channels in different ways. For example, TV viewing is good for conveying big images and simple ideas, but viewers are not paying detailed attention to it, so detail can be lost. Newspapers are regarded as better for conveying detail, say, for financial services products, since readers often give newspaper articles their undivided close attention. As another example, a radio listener may be preoccupied with other tasks and may use radio as a form of minor distraction. A cinema audience may be supposed to pay greater attention to pre-show ads than, say, a TV audience. So, media channels are often considered by professionals to have particular strengths and weaknesses. (see examples in Figure 6.4).

Television

In spite of a decade of predictions of its demise, TV advertising remains the most visible and prestigious form of advertising and the most convenient way to reach an audience of millions. It is especially valuable as a real-time medium – popular sports events are the last media platform delivering real-time audiences of millions (see the Chapter 6 case below). Many viewers record scheduled programming to watch later and skip through the ads. Many others watch DVDs of their favourite shows and don't bother with broadcast

Medium	Strengths	Weaknesses
TV	Dramatic audio-visual impact Large audience reach in real time Can demonstrate products Prestige	High production cost Low attention Short exposure Long lead time
Newspapers	Source credibility Immediacy Regular exposure	Cost can be high Short exposure Uneven audience reach
Magazines	Special interest targeting Long life in household	Lower circulations High cost
Radio	Regular, repeated exposure Lifestyle targeting Immediacy, low cost	Low attention Low prestige Short-lived
Out of home (OOH)	Prominent in busy settings High local visibility Repeated exposure for commuters Creative possibilities (electronic, 3D)	High cost Geographically limited
Internet	Engagement Direct response Measurability for ROI	24/7 exposure and monitoring Sensitivity to PR Difficult to build traffic
Direct mail	Personal communication Tailored message Sales trigger	Resistance Database currency Low response rates
Mobile	Immediacy, intimacy Individual targeting	Software issues Consumer resistance
POS and merchandising	Sales trigger Persuasiveness	Limited reach (in-store) Low coverage
Sales promotion	Sales generator Local impact	Low reach Short-term benefit
Exhibitions	Source credibility B2B capability	High cost per event Time- and labour-intensive

Figure 6.4 Media channels: strengths and weaknesses for advertising

shows at all. Translating TV show viewing figures directly to the spot advertising for pricing has always been a dubious principle, but today it is more questionable than ever because of viewers' changing habits and more flexible scheduling and on-demand programming.

TV is expensive, at least for national, peak-time spots. Figures of up to $4 million for a 30 second spot have been reported for the most expensive advertising on American TV, during the Super Bowl American football final. Depending on time of day, regional coverage and the viewing figures of the TV show, the figure can come down a lot.

TV has such a dramatic impact that it will often dominate a room, demanding attention even if the people present are not particularly interested. Appearing on TV bestows prestige on a brand that ripples outward to impress not only consumers but also employees, suppliers and other stakeholders such as shareholders. A TV ad sends a message about the aspirations of the brand and places it in juxtaposition with the most prestigious brands. TV is the media vehicle that most powerfully reflects and projects audience aspirations and fantasies. It is therefore the perfect medium for portraying brands as accessories to these aspirations. In addition to TV channels, there are over 1,500 independent production companies making TV programmes. Most of the new stations are commercial, funded by advertising and sponsorship revenues. Audience fragmentation into consumer communities and lifestyle groupings has made selected audiences more accessible through lifestyle and special-interest TV channels. Millions round the world now have access to satellite TV channels that cross international borders, widening exposure to potential new markets.

TV has extraordinary dramatic power to convey values and to communicate norms across cultures, where the ways TV is consumed show striking similarity. TV is viewed in a relaxed mood, often in the home and in the company of other people. It can be a social occasion as well as a leisure pursuit and a source of relaxation. TV gives advertisers intimate access to domestic settings. What is of interest to advertisers is that TV's assimilation into social settings means that people are suggestible when they are watching. TV advertising reaches those who are looking for entertainment, information and ideas about new ways of living and consuming.

TV, then, retains its importance in the media mix because of its potential to create huge dramatic impact for the brand and to drive large audiences to social media. The creative possibilities are vast for televisual portrayals of the brand in lifestyle settings. The global reach and prestige of TV advertising, then, still surpasses that of any other medium. For many brand clients, though, TV advertising is problematic because ROI is difficult to calculate precisely.

Get it right and it can create a powerful sales impetus for brands. Get it wrong and a lot of money disappears very quickly. As noted above, production costs for a modest TV ad are often a mere tenth of the cost of airing the ad a few times at prime time. Such ads can take many months from storyboard to airtime exposure. They last only a few seconds, although today the lifecycle of TV ads is extended indefinitely through video sharing websites and compilation TV shows of the best, strangest or funniest ads.

The attentiveness of viewers to TV ads has been problematic for clients. Some studies have suggested that viewers don't really watch the ads. Whether this is a problem for clients depends on whether they feel that conscious attention is necessary for the ad to be effective, or whether they feel that TV ads feature at some level in viewers' unconscious even if they are not paying explicit attention to them (Heath and Feldwick, 2008). For brand clients, a TV campaign represents something of a leap of faith. The potential benefits are great but unpredictable, and difficult or impossible to quantify.

Print publications

Classified and display advertising in print publications is a declining sector of advertising, and many print publications are struggling to find a business model to replace the loss of advertising revenue. Circulations are falling and advertisers are increasingly tempted by the flexibility, reach and ROI of digital media. Adspend on print publications remains substantial, but some predictions suggest that total spend on all digital media will surpass spend on newspaper and magazine advertising by 2015.[15]

There are many kinds of print publication, including national and local daily newspapers, local free-of-charge newspapers, local and national general-interest magazines and special-interest magazines. Digital technology has made it cheaper and easier to launch new print publications. Conventional media wisdom holds that newspaper and magazine readers may be more critically engaged and more attentive than TV viewers when consuming advertising. Classified and display in newspapers and magazines might, therefore, be well-advised to use more rational content and offer greater product detail, while TV advertising should rely on the simple message with a big impact.

Press, especially daily newspaper advertising, has a quality of immediacy that TV does not. That is, press advertising can respond to current events in a lead time of days, whereas TV advertising requires months or even years of production and planning. This topicality can be leveraged further with 'native' advertising, sponsored content that looks like editorial. Newspapers can be useful vehicles for targeting. The readers of particular newspapers, while heterogeneous in their consumer behaviour, often share particular demographic characteristics of age, social status and income. Regional and free newspapers offer opportunities for advertisers to reach local consumers within the context of local news and events. This too is an opportunity to present the brand in a setting that makes it more accessible for potential consumers. In many regions of the world reading the newspaper is a symbolic social ritual, engaged in daily, often at the same time every day, perhaps in the same place, in the same company and accompanied by the same refreshments. Newspapers consumed as intimate parts of social normality are powerful vehicles for promoting other types of consumption, since the context of the advertisement implies that the products and services portrayed are also a normal everyday part of the social fabric.

Radio

The Radio Advertising Bureau (RAB) of America states that radio is a 'social medium that sparks brand conversation', and also claims that 'heavy' radio listeners who listen for more than two hours per day (as many people would in their car on their commute to and from work) generate 329 billion word-of-mouth impressions annually, more than heavy TV, print media or internet users.[16]

In recent years radio has acquired greater credibility among advertisers for its reach and impact, and has even been used as the main medium for new brand awareness campaigns in countries where radio can give national coverage. Radio can also be highly focused for local campaigns. Radio has the quality of immediacy, since radio ads can be produced in a few hours and broadcast that very day. Unlike TV or print media, radio is seen as a medium that occupies the periphery of people's attention. It is often background music in workplaces, motorcars or households, and listeners are generally doing other things while the radio plays. However, with the radio on for long periods of time there is plenty of opportunity for a listener to hear and recognise a given ad.

Furthermore, radio may play an intimate part in listeners' lives if they forge a relationship with a particular show or announcer that they listen to at the same time each day. Most consumers listen to the radio at some time during the week, so the medium has extensive reach to many kinds of consumer segment. Another advantage is that the relatively low cost to advertisers gives scope for many iterations of a creative execution. For example, in a *Capital One* radio campaign is the USA, the brand used 135 vignettes of local life across 15 USA radio markets.[17]

Outdoor or out of home (OOH) advertising

Outdoor advertising has a long and distinguished history but is being transformed by new technology. Traditional billboards can yield considerable influence, and in the UK, one in particular is widely regarded as the most successful billboard advertisement of all time. It was produced by Saatchi & Saatchi for the UK Conservative Party's 1980 election bid. The poster featured a queue of people, snaking from a sign saying 'Employment Office'. On the top in huge capital letters were the words 'LABOUR ISN'T WORKING'.[18] In the bottom right corner, in smaller letters, were added the words 'Britain's better off with the Conservatives'. The reader is left to infer the intended meaning by drawing on his or her cultural knowledge. In order to 'get' the ad, the reader has to understand the pun on 'working', which refers both to a general failure of Labour policies, and a literal lengthening of queues of unemployed people outside employment offices. The reader would need to know that people queued up in employment offices to see the clerk, and they would have to infer that Labour policies had caused the queue to lengthen. In fact, the poster apparently failed to elicit much voter attention until the Labour Party discovered that the people photographed in the poster were not unemployed, but were Conservative party activists. This deceit (these were innocent days in British political advertising) was mentioned by Labour in Parliament with the intention of discrediting the Conservatives. The ploy backfired, the poster became famous and was credited with winning the 1980 election for the Conservatives and Margaret Thatcher. [19]

New technology has permitted many developments on the static poster or 36-sheet billboard. Some appear to move as the viewer goes by in a car, sites with digital LCD displays, sites that are three-dimensional with large items (sometimes motorcars) stuck on to the site for added effect, and laser-beam projected promotional images on the sides of large buildings. OOH advertising includes adverts on street furniture like postboxes, bench seats, lamp posts and bus shelters, ads on moving vehicles especially taxis and buses, and of course street billboards and shop signage (see Colour Section, photos 2, 9 and 10). There are more than 80,000[20] static poster sites in the UK, most near or in large centres of population, especially by roads with large traffic volume, and about a third of these are digital billboards that can carry moving images and show many different ads in a loop. Digital OOH is a rapidly growing sector of advertising and the possibilities for OOH to feature personalisation and other aspects of internet advertising are increasing as the technology develops.

There are also numerous non-static, outdoor advertising sites. For example, many vehicles such as London taxis and public bus companies sell their advertising space. There are companies specialising in providing advertising space on air balloons or airships for exposure at large, open-air public events or simply in the sky above towns and cities. Digital outdoor has taken off in a big way with video outdoor sites showing a range of ads in strategic sites (see Snapshot 6.6).

SNAPSHOT 6.6

Static, mobile and digital OOH advertising

Outdoor promotion specialists (such as *CBS Outdoor*) offer packages that include (in the UK) advertising on trams, tube trains and buses: according to the Target Group Index (TGI), 29 million people in the UK see an ad on a bus each week. Entire buses can be painted (wrapped) with the advertisement to maximise impact. Lenticular designs allow advertisers to use moving images, making a 3D effect on bus sides. Bus advertising can be used regionally to coincide with TV campaigns. The London Underground is a fertile site for outdoor advertising since commuters using the underground are predominantly young (49% are between 15 and 34 years old) and in the ABC1 socio-economic category. Outdoor specialists offer custom paint and design services to convert virtually any visible object in the urban environment into an advertising medium. Digital OOH is making new techniques possible. For example, research showed that purchases of Stella Artois cider brand *Cidre* rose in line with the ambient temperature. OOH outfit Posterscope created 120 digital screens linked with site-specific weather data so that content was triggered when the temperature rose above a certain threshold.[21] The science fiction scenario of billboards and posters that recognise consumers personally is also being realised through face recognition technology.[22] Some poster sites on Tokyo shopping districts use holographic technology to position a sales assistant to welcome shoppers into the store. The holograph reacts to customer body movements and gestures.

Car drivers are supposed to be focusing only on the road, but roadside billboards are difficult not to notice. In some urban areas in some countries the skyline is pitted with billboards as high as tower blocks, such as on Sunset Boulevard in Hollywood. In the UK, many farmers have sites for mobile billboards in their fields if they are adjacent to motorways. OOH agencies can make fine calculations on the footfall or traffic volume on busy roads and they use these data to price static OOH sites. In general, national coverage is difficult to achieve and targeted audiences cannot always be well defined, but outdoor advertising can be a powerful medium for local awareness and sales promotion.

Internet

The internet is still seen as a communication channel category but it has developed many branches that are sometimes treated as separate categories for media planning. Mobile, social media, websites, email or SMS campaigns can use video or textual content and can be transmitted through broadcast for mobile or programmed targeting. 'Digital' is a technology rather than a medium, but it is often used to refer to all digital advertising technology including internet, mobile and OOH digital sites. Digital also covers TV and radio (for example, for internet-only TV and radio channels) and even print, since many print publications have a branded website carrying print stories but also facilitating reader comment and links with archived stories. E-marketing is another category sometimes used (as in this book) because it is conveniently broad, but it covers all the above plus email and SMS marketing, and these in turn can be accessed on mobile. Indeed, mobile is becoming the most important category simply because the technology is developing to permit most internet functions to be accessed on mobile devices. With the penetration of mobile devices, especially smartphones, approaching that of TV, many promotional techniques covered under the categories internet, e-marketing and digital can be accessed through mobile. Hence, we have a convergent media environment in which most channels can, in principle, be connected and accessed on one device.

The possibilities internet advertising holds for audience reach, target group segmentation, personalisation, inter-activity, consumer engagement, retail interface functions, order reconciliation, integration of and inter-connection with mass media, customer service and CRM are discussed with examples throughout this book. Programmed advertising that responds through algorithms to target consumers based on their browsing or buying or demographic or social profile has boomed and is helping to push internet into rapid growth as a channel category. Social media marketing has become a sub-discipline in its own right, although it is strictly not a channel, but a wide variety of techniques that use the internet as a channel. Because of their importance, this chapter will conclude with some points about mobile as a sub-channel category of the internet, focusing mainly on smartphones.

Mobile advertising

Mobile devices such as mobile phones, notebooks and iPads, as well as laptops and other devices with mobile connectivity such as in-car satnavs and iPods, are the central space in which media convergence is taking place. According to Sharma et al. (2008: 47), the first mobile advertising was created in Japan in 2001 when the country's largest mobile operator and the advertising agency Dentsu formed the first advertising agency specialising in mobile, calling it D2C. New developments in mobile gaming soon followed. Internet advertising in general is the fastest-growing category of advertising spend, and mobile is the fastest-growing sub-category of internet advertising.

At the time of writing, the *Samsung Galaxy S5* smartphone is being launched at the mobile World Congress and, appropriately enough, with a piece of native advertising/editorial in the British *Daily Telegraph* that includes an embedded video clip.[23] Amongst many technological advancements, including an advanced camera, large touchscreen and fingerprint screening to facilitate rapid mobile financial transactions, the phone doubles as a fitness monitor with heartbeat measurement. It has the capacity for twelve hours of video watching or ten hours of web browsing before recharging, making it an ideal vehicle for personalised advertising, engagement promotion and branded content. Smartphones are taking over from desktops and notebooks as advertising media and are driving rapid growth in online video advertising.[24]

Mobile phones are, of course, highly personal devices: people feel that their choice of phone is a statement, and the device occupies an intimate part of their lives. It is often on for 24/7 and never leaves the arm's reach of the user. It contains masses of personal data, memos, contacts, photographs, saved web pages, movies and music. Some apps can access this personal information to facilitate personalised advertising and promotion, although many users are not comfortable with this level of access on privacy grounds. Mobile phones are also fashion accessories, as well as highly practical devices. They can be used to get us home when we are lost, if we use the satellite navigation and GPS facility. A parent who gives a mobile to a child knows that they can always find them, provided the phone is switched on, and advertisers too can always find us if we have the GPS location service switched on. Smartphones can be used for pleasure, for work and for business, and through social media they have been credited with facilitating popular revolutions, as well as being implicated in crime. Smartphones can be used to access your bank account, to switch the lights on and off or to lock the front door in your home, to locate a restaurant, to play games (branded, of course), to show you the way home … and the number of functions is multiplying.

In sum, mobile digital communication is driving convergence and creating countless new scenarios for advertising and promotion. Some of these are fraught with ethical problems, especially privacy. They also hold out enormous potential for improving quality of life, and advertising techniques are evolving to become integrated into this new, always internet-connected, way of living.

Chapter summary

This chapter has reviewed current issues in media strategy, planning and buying for advertising. The media environment is evolving rapidly under convergence and the media planning and buying functions are becoming more complex. The chapter outlined the media infrastructure for advertising and discussed the characteristics and qualities of the media mix for advertising and promotion. It described the tasks and terminology of advertising media planning and outlined the ongoing changes that are taking place in the global media infrastructure.

■ Review Questions

1. Devise an IMC media plan to support the launch of a new model of motor car. The creative executions include a 20 second TV ad, national daily press ads and direct-mail shots to current owners of cars in that class. How would you plan your targeting? Which media vehicles might you use? Explain the timings of exposure. What are the main problems and difficulties of this task?

2. Discuss the axiom 'The medium is the message'. What does it imply? Offer examples to support your suggestions.

3. Discuss ways in which media impact might be reconciled with segmentation and targeting issues. Is there an economic trade-off between impact and targeting?

4. What are the key characteristics of mobile phones and how might these be useful to advertisers?

5. Imagine that you are part of an account team devising a campaign for the launch of a new chocolate snack called 'Sleek'. It is to be positioned to a largely female market as a sensuous indulgence. What suggestions would you have for media planning?

CASE STUDY

The American Super Bowl: real-time audience reach – at a price

TV advertising has continued to grow its volume of global adspend, in spite of predictions that it was outdated as an advertising medium. However, the signs are that its rate of growth is slowing and more adspend is beginning to migrate to digital and engagement media (see Snapshot 6.3). At the same time, more digital TVs are being produced, so media channels are converging in a pincer movement as more TVs acquire internet connectivity, and more mobile devices acquire the software to play broadcast TV as well as video. One reason why TV has held up so well is because it is the only medium that can give advertisers access to large audiences in real time. A great deal of TV is now watched on demand, on DVD box sets, or recorded for viewing later. Only live sports coverage offers real-time audiences and this is why sports sponsorship has boomed. An advertising hoarding around the perimeter of a sports field used to be viewed only by the spectators physically present at the game. Now, with global coverage on TV and internet, the audience reach for pitch-side advertising is potentially huge, and many of these viewers are watching live.

The importance of a live audience to advertisers is shown by the hype around the Super Bowl, the American football final held early each year.[25] On Sunday February 2, 2014 the MetLife Stadium in East Rutherford, New Jersey, hosted the Seattle Seahawks versus the Denver Broncos. American football matches last about an hour, but TV coverage is stretched to four or five hours with TV ad breaks. American audiences are used to this, but the owners of the game, the NFL, want to grow their revenue overseas.

(Continued)

(Continued)

The NFL is the richest sporting franchise in the world. According to a report in *USA Today*, it generates around $10 billion in annual revenue, the largest portion being earned through their monopoly position exploiting TV viewing rights in the USA. The NFL is bent on expansion and part of the plan to double revenue is to export the sport to London. Three NFL games planned for London for 2014 quickly sold out.

The NFL know that sport is the last TV platform that can deliver mass audiences for advertisers in real time. Live viewing figures for TV shows have crashed with the advent of view-on-demand, streaming and recording, and of course the internet. Only sport is still watched live in huge numbers, and the Super Bowl claims to deliver 100,000,000 American viewers, about 1 in 2 American households.

American TV channels, advertisers and the NFL all have a vested interest in boosting the hype over Super Bowl ads. The channels are reported to charge up to $4,000,000 for a 30 second TV slot during the Super Bowl. They have to, to get the money back they paid the NFL to show the game. The advertisers use the spectacle as an informal competition in which they step outside the typical hard-sell American TV ad script to try harder to charm audiences with a little creativity.

All this is designed to generate all-important social media shares. In the 2013 Super Bowl, to the ad agencies' dismay, the most talked about ad was a tweet by biscuit makers *Oreo* that was shared 14,000 times in a few hours.[26]

Of course, these figures make the Super Bowl look like a school sports day compared to the one billion worldwide audience the BBC reached for the 2012 London Olympics, but then the BBC can't show advertising, so only the Olympic sponsors could benefit. The NFL want to internationalise, and no doubt they are envious of the worldwide audience British Premiership soccer (or football, to Brits) reaches. The NFL can imagine the riches if Asian sportsfans started to care about American football. Or indeed if anyone did, in addition to Americans.

The quintessentially American character of American football is both part of its appeal and a limit to its worldwide marketing reach. One very American feature that will be difficult to translate overseas is the frequency of cutting to ad breaks during the action. In the UK, even commercial channels are only allowed to show up to 7 minutes of ads per hour. The NFL has the problem of how to earn the kind of advertising revenue they do in the USA without piling on the ad breaks. American viewers may not be thrilled about the amount of advertising foisted on them but they're used to it. In the UK, the BBC, the world's biggest public service broadcaster, carries no advertising yet airs many of the top UK sporting occasions, giving fans an entirely ad-free experience. The NFL know their game has appeal in the UK. They have to think of ways to monetise it in a very different media infrastructure to that in the USA.

Case Questions

1. Why is a live audience platform so valuable for advertisers?

2. What reasons can you give for sport turning out to be the last big live audience platform for broadcast media?

3. List five ways sports coverage might translate into consumer engagement via social media.

4. In what ways might the NFL's media business model have to be adapted for it to succeed commercially in the UK?

Useful journal articles

(These Sage articles can be accessed on the book website)

Justin Walden (2012) 'Global advertising, attitudes and audiences', *New Media & Society*, 14 (5): 886-8.

Chris Hackley, Stephen Brown and Rungpaka Amy Hackley (2012) 'The *X-Factor* enigma: Simon Cowell and the marketization of existential liminality', *Marketing Theory*, 12 (4): 451–69.

Alex Bevan (2013) 'Nostalgia for pre-digital media in *Mad Men*', *Television & New Media*, 14 (6): 546–59 (first published August 14, 2012).

Michaela Dewe, Jane Ogden and Adrian Coyle (2013) 'The cigarette box as an advertising vehicle in the United Kingdom: a case for plain packaging', *Journal of Health Psychology*, doi: 1359105313504236 (first published October 22, 2013).

Jiang Wu, Bin Hu and Yu Zhang (2013) 'Maximizing the performance of advertisements diffusion: a simulation study of the dynamics of viral advertising in social networks', *SIMULATION*, 89 (8): 921–34.

■ ■ Further reading ■

Chalaby, J.K. (2008) 'Advertising in the global age: transnational campaigns and pan-European television channels', *Global Media and Communication*, 2008 4 (2): 139–56.

Croft, R. (1999) 'Audience and environment: measurement and media', in P.J. Kitchen (ed.), *Marketing Communications: Principles and Practice*. London: Thomson Learning. pp. 111–34.

Katz, H. (2006) *The Media Handbook: A Complete Guide to Advertising Media Selection, Planning, Research and Buying*. Mahwah, NJ: Lawrence Erlbaum Associates.

Kawashima, N. (2006) 'Media advertising agencies, media and consumer market: the changing quality of TV advertising in Japan', *Culture & Society*, 28: 393–410.

Kelley, L.D. and Jugenheimer, D.W. (2008) *Advertising Media Planning: A Brand Management Approach*, 2nd edn. Armonk, NY: M.E. Sharpe.

Ridout, Travis N. and Smith, Glen R. (2008) 'Free advertising: how the media amplify campaign messages', *Political Research Quarterly*, 61: 598–608.

Notes

1. www.adbrands.net/top_media_agencies.htm accessed 21.2.2014
2. www.mediacom.com/en/what-we-do/media-planning-and-buying.aspx accessed 21.2.2014
3. http://i.telegraph.co.uk/multimedia/archive/01863/Digital_Media_Pack_1863797a.pdf accessed 18.2.2014

4. http://adage.com/article/news/coca-cola-boosts-marketing-spend-demand-slows/291747/ accessed 22.2.2014

5. www.nydailynews.com/entertainment/tv-movies/coca-cola-super-bowl-ad-angers-conservatives-article-1.1600849 accessed 22.2.2014

6. http://adage.com/article/digital/mondelez-plans-big-digital-ad-spend-jump/291753/ accessed 22.2.2014

7. www.zenithoptimedia.com/case-studies/ accessed 19.2.2014

8. www.ft.com/cms/s/0/c02669da-5ec3-11e3-8621-00144feabdc0.html#axzz2u4zarlpJ accessed 22.2.2014

9. www.adexchanger.com/agencies/2014-forecasts-global-ad-dollars-surge-driven-by-mobile-social/ accessed 22.2.2014

10. http://globaltgi.kantarmedia.com/ accessed 24.2.2014

11. http://globaltgi.kantarmedia.com/ accessed 24.2.2014

12. www.nielsen.com/us/en/newswire/2014/whats-empowering-the-new-digital-consumer.html accessed 24.2.2014

13. www.nielsen.com/us/en/top10s.html accessed 24.2.2014

14. www.pressgazette.co.uk/july-abcs-most-national-newspapers-see-month-month-circulation-boost-royal-baby-month accessed 22.2.2014

15. http://online.wsj.com/news/articles/SB10001424052702303330204579246003193822532 accessed 24.2.2014

16. www.rab.com/ accessed 24.2.2014

17. www.rab.com/public/ncs/pdfs/Capital%20One.pdf accessed 24.2.2014

18. www.citizenarcane.com/index.php/archives/2005/04/18/labour-isnt-working/ accessed 4.3.2014

19. For the *BBC News* account of the story see http://news.bbc.co.uk/1/hi/uk/1222326.stm accessed 4.3.2013.

20. www.cityam.com/article/1391399919/digital-advertising-street-why-posters-are-no-longer-static accessed 25.2.2014

21. www.cityam.com/article/1391399919/digital-advertising-street-why-posters-are-no-longer-static accessed 24.2.2014

22. www.businessinsider.com/advertisers-using-facial-recognition-technology-2013-5?op=1 accessed 24.2.2014

23. www.telegraph.co.uk/technology/news/10659758/Mobile-World-Congress-2014-Samsung-launch-Galaxy-S5-and-Gear-Fit-smart-band.html accessed 25.2.2014

24. www.usatoday.com/story/tech/columnist/shinal/2014/03/02/online-video-advertising-prices-new-tech-economy-john-shinal-usa-today/5870323/ accessed 4.3.2014

25. http://america.aljazeera.com/articles/2014/1/31/a-football-game-withoutcommercial-snotonthissideoftheatlantic.html accessed 25.2.2014

26. I discuss this case in detail in Hackley, C. (2013) *Marketing in Context*, London, Sage.

7 Non-Advertising Promotion

Chapter outline

Advertising is often conceived narrowly as a 30 second television commercial (TVC) or radio ad, or a classified or display print ad, with other promotional techniques grouped together as 'below-the-line'. A major theme of this book is that categories of promotional communication are becoming less easy to distinguish under media convergence, but there is, nonetheless, a need for classification, however provisional it may be. Non-advertising promotion is a term used to describe the many techniques that do not conform to traditional definitions of advertising. This chapter reviews a number of the most popular techniques of promotional communication that do not usually fall under the category of traditional advertising, and sets these within the broader context of integration.

Key chapter content

- Non-advertising promotion in IMC
- Sponsorship
- Product placement
- Public relations
- Other elements of non-advertising promotion

Non-advertising promotion in IMC

One of the main themes of this book is that advertising is evolving new forms in concert with developments in digital communications and the thrust for integrated communications planning. These new forms challenge traditional classifications of the promotional mix. As a general category, non-advertising promotion has assumed greater importance in the media mix in the last ten years. Brand clients want to see the brand values portrayed across several platforms simultaneously as part of 'through-the-line' or integrated marketing communication (IMC) campaigns, and many non-advertising promotional techniques are being absorbed into advertising agency practice as part of the move towards IMC. Non-advertising promotional techniques such as direct mail, events management, public relations (PR), product placement, branded content, sponsorship, native advertising, digital and direct response are being assimilated into and around traditional mass media advertising campaigns. Spot advertising on television, classified or display ads in print media, outdoor/out of home advertising, commercial radio and cinema advertising spots before the main feature, all remain poplar with advertisers. But alongside these traditional methods non-advertising approaches, especially digital, are taking an increasing proportion of promotional budgets. Table 7.1 gives some examples of non-advertising promotion.

What, precisely, is advertising as opposed to non-advertising promotion, or non-traditional advertising, can be difficult to define given the rise in hybrid promotional methods. For example, product placement, the practice of putting branded items in shot as scene props, combines elements of advertising, public relations (PR), celebrity endorsement and sponsorship (Balasubramanian et al., 2006[1]). As another example, content marketing can include videos made as advertisements but circulated virally on earned media space, while traditional advertising can include a direct response element. All these forms of promotion confound easy categorisation. A further

Table 7.1   Examples of non-advertising promotion

- Direct mail/direct response
- Conferences and exhibitions
- Pop-up shops and events
- Public relations
- Product placement
- Branded content
- Sponsorship
- Native advertising
- Ambient
- Sales promotion
- Merchandising and POS

difficulty is the question of when a form of promotional communication should be classified according its medium, as in direct mail, or by its genre category, as in branded content. Classification in marketing is invariably provisional, and always tends to be challenged by the next innovation. Because of this definitional difficulty, it is easier to define non-advertising promotion by what it is not, than by what it is. It can be seen as any promotional communication that does not clearly fit into a definition of traditional mass media, above-the-line promotion.

SNAPSHOT 7.1

Epic Split – branded video content going viral

2013 saw a number of content marketing videos go viral, creating a lot of goodwill and profile for the brands that paid for them. One was called 'Epic Split'. Movie star Jeanne-Claude Van Damme is known for his karate skills, although at over 50 years of age he could be forgiven for spending more time with his slippers and a crossword puzzle. In spite of his age he did the splits with one foot on each of two *Volvo* trucks as they reversed along a highway. The viral video[2] has been seen some 100 million times on YouTube and other video sharing websites, making it the third most successful viral video of 2013, according to a newspaper report, after *Dove* 'Real Beauty Sketches', a series of videos that together accumulated more than 135 million views in about six months, and *Turkish Airlines*'s 'selfie shootout',[3] at 130 million views. Commercial content that goes viral cannot be guaranteed, but the most popular branded virals have serious resources and strategy behind them. Some virals made cheaply can also capture the public imagination and become hits. The key is to create compelling content, then devise a well-conceived media plan to push the video out to a receptive audience. After that, it all depends on the public.

The examples of content marketing in Snapshot 7.1 defy easy categorisation. Should they be classified as sponsorship, since the brand has sponsored the making of a piece of entertainment? Are they advertisements, admittedly not sales-oriented but of the brand-building variety, that are simply using digital 'earned' media space instead of traditional 'bought' advertising spots? Could they be seen as public relations, since they are designed to generate publicity, or even as product placement, since the brand is visible in the movie as a scene prop but otherwise not mentioned? They are treated as 'content marketing', since they are created as entertainment that is free to access, but they are clearly branded and intended to be promotional in their effect. They count as non-advertising promotion since they were produced mainly for video sharing websites and not for traditional advertising spots. In addition, they do not conform to the advertising genre category since they do not actively promote the brand, although it has to be said that many spot advertisements are equally as tacit in their appeal.

In 'Epic Split', Van Damme is not scripted to say 'buy *Volvo* trucks', and if he did, it is doubtful that his fanbase is focused in the truck-buying business. The video is clearly demonstrating not only the actor's prodigious flexibility but the precision steering of the trucks, yet there is no apparent targeting strategy here – the video was made to be shared by anyone in order to generate publicity. In an indirect way, the makers intend that the video will contribute to the prestige and profile of the *Volvo* brand, which is better known amongst most consumers for cars rather than trucks. Hence, while the video satisifies some of the genre conventions for a TVC, it is also a piece of entertainment that is strategised not as advertising, but as publicity.

Some clients would be very wary of this kind of marketing since they may not be able to see a direct link between exposures and sales. Nonetheless, it cannot be denied that, as publicity, viral videos like 'Epic Split' have been astonishingly successful in their own way since they have reached global audiences far in excess of the numbers they could reach with a traditional advertising exposure, and at a fraction of the cost. When successful, viral videos can be seen to be far better value than traditional advertising, at least in terms of the number of pairs of 'eyeballs' that see them. Whether or not they represent good value in terms of sales ROI is another question.

Non-advertising promotion, then, can be a difficult area to classify, but it is of such importance in IMC that it cannot be treated as entirely separate from advertising. As we note, it can be defined by exception, as promotional communication that is not a traditional TVC, newspaper or magazine print ad, OOH billboard or radio ad. However, as we have seen in these examples, medium-based definitions fail to capture some of the changes in the way the concept of advertising is being challenged in hybrid promotional forms. One of the most striking changes in non-advertising promotion in recent years has been the rise in importance and variety of sponsorship.

Sponsorship

Sponsorship is essentially a mutually beneficial business arrangement with defined outcomes between two or more parties (Cornwell, 2014; Fill, 2002, 2009; Head, 1981). A sponsor makes a contribution in cash or kind – which may or may not include service and expertise – and expects a return in publicity. Sponsorship was originally seen as a part of public relations since it offers a support medium to mainstream advertising and is not necessarily as explicit as advertising. In recent years the value of sponsorship has come to be understood as less a matter of exposure than an opportunity to activate consumers through social media and/or on-the-ground events and experiences. Television sponsorship has a high profile and it has been common in the USA from the beginning of the television era in the 1950s.

Sponsorship expenditure has grown at 4–5% between 2010 and 2014, and amounts to well over $50 billion.[4] In the USA, 70% of total sponsorship spend goes on sports-related sponsorship, with 10% on entertainment sponsorship, and the rest on arts, causes and festivals.[5] This proportion is reflected globally, with sports sponsorship dominating the spend. The growth in sponsorship spend has slowed since its breakneck pace of growth between 1980 and 2005, but it is still growing.

Sponsorship grew so quickly for several reasons. In some cases, brand marketing organisations have been forced to move to sponsorship by factors beyond their control. For example, some governments legislated against mass media tobacco and alcohol advertising, forcing brand owners in these industries to seek other promotional methods. For example, after the UK government banned cigarette advertising on TV in 1965, huge tobacco advertising budgets began to shift into sports sponsorship and OOH advertising. Another factor pushing advertisers toward sponsorship is the increase in cost of mass media advertising relative to other channels. Still another factor has been the growth of affluence which, for the fortunate, has seen increasing leisure time for sport and TV viewing. Consequently, TV programme makers naturally looked to new spectator events that could provide cheap TV. As we saw in the Super Bowl case study in the previous chapter, many sports events now receive blanket media coverage and constitute a highly attractive promotional vehicle (Amis et al., 1999; Cornwell, 2014; Meenaghan, 1991; Meenaghan and Shipley, 1999).

For example, in the UK, entrepreneurial sports agents have introduced sponsors to unlikely spectator sports such as snooker and darts as their popularity and media profile has grown. In the 1980s, snooker became, for the first time, a televised sport in the UK. A minority sport became a global television phenomenon because of the charisma and publicity-generating acumen of stars such as Alex 'Hurricane' Higgins. Cigarette and alcohol companies realised that the sport needed funds for promotion and prize money, and they faced increasing controls on their mainstream advertising. Sponsorship of televised sports offered a new way of getting their brand into mainstream media. Sports sponsorship offered the perfect alignment of need and opportunity. Sport has assumed even greater importance for brands since media audiences fragmented and live TV viewing fell. Live televised sports events now offer the most important real-time audience platform that brands can access.

The Barclays Premier League

The *Barclay's (English) Premier League*, the top-tier of English soccer (football), is watched by a cumulative global audience of 4.7 billion people according to consultants Brandwatch,[6] so sponsors from around the world, including brands from China, Thailand, the USA, the United Arab Emirates, South Korea and South Africa,[7] were encouraged to spend a record £166 million on shirt sponsorships in the 2013/14 season. This figure doesn't include Manchester United's £19 million a year deal for their training kit. North London club Arsenal was reported to receive £30 million a year from *Fly Emirates* for shirt sponsorship, while Liverpool received £20 million from *Standard Chartered* bank, and Chelsea £18 million from *Samsung*. A big rise is anticipated in 2014/15 when Manchester United's £50 million deal with *Chevrolet* kicks off. Clubs make additional sums from pitch-side advertising hoardings. Many Premiership grounds have LCD technology on their hoardings so that they can show specific ads when the play goes to a particular area of the ground, followed by the camera. They also earn revenue from sponsors of matchballs, stands, hospitality boxes, and anything else that a brand logo can be printed upon. Finally, TV rights revenue is reported to be £1 billion a year to Premiership clubs. TV channels now use live sport to drive cable and satellite subscription sales and to ramp up audiences to make their spot advertising more attractive to brands. Not all sponsors are convinced of the value for money. It has been reported that *Barclays* is reviewing its £40 million a year sponsorship deal with the Premiership since the bank is in no need of profile in the UK.[8] Other leagues, such as the German *Bundesliga*, are beginning to get wider international coverage and might emerge as rivals to the Premiership.

Sponsorship of sport has become the top sponsorship category over the past three decades. *Nike*, the world's biggest sportswear brand, followed the trail blazed by *Adidas* (see Chapter 8 Case Study) into sports sponsorship. Phil Knight, *Nike*'s co-founder, persuaded the US middle distance athlete Steve Prefontaine to wear his running shoes. Since then *Nike* has targeted countless sports personalities who gain international fame so that each post-performance TV or press interview is accompanied by an image of the hero of the hour wearing the ubiquitous *Nike* 'Swoosh' on his or her clothing or cap. *Nike*'s current deals are reported to include Christiano Ronaldo, Kobe Bryant, Kevin Durant, Maria Sharapova, Roger Federer, LeBron James, Derek Jeter, Rory McIlroy, Raphael Nadal, Tiger Woods and Michael Jordan, who has been sponsored by *Nike* for some thirty years.[9] This is celebrity endorsement, but the endorsement is largely implicit, making it sponsorship. The suggestive sub-textual power of sponsorship is telling; no explicit celebrity statement is required. The unspoken message is that *Nike* is cool by association, because it is the choice of winners. Sponsorship taps into the sub-text of mediated communication by juxtaposing brands with images of success, objects of desire and mythical heroes and heroines. The message is covert and all the more powerful for its subtlety.

TV show sponsorship

Sponsorship of TV shows, once common (originating in 1950s American TV with the original 'soap operas' sponsored by soap manufacturers such as P&G and Lever Brothers) has made a comeback in the last decade, although the format differs. In the UK, a brand may sponsor a TV show and place a short film, called an 'ident', after the titles but just before the action begins. The sponsorship deal allows the sponsor to identify with a particular show more closely than it could by buying spot advertising in the commercial break. In addition, the ident means that it is more difficult for viewers to fast-forward recordings to avoid seeing it. Alternatively, the sponsorship deal might simply entail briefly being announced as the sponsor of the show, and being listed as such on the website. For example, sponsors of shows on the UK commercial Channel 4 include *Fosters*, the Australian lager brand (comedy shows); *Honda* (documentaries); *Rimmel* (fashion); *Dubai Holdings* (horse racing); *Anadin* (Deal Or No Deal); *Kia Carens* (The Simpsons); *Old Jamaican Ginger Beer* (Man v. Food); *Halfords Autocentre* (motoring shows) and many more.[10]

In some countries, such as the USA, commercial TV channels allow advertisers to broadcast 'paid programming' which is effectively an extended advertisement constructed as a quasi entertainment, sometimes with a studio audience cheering wildly while an actor demonstrates the product. This kind of 'advertorial' is not permitted on UK TV, but is common on commercial TV in Thailand. Sponsors of UK TV shows are not permitted to show their own products in the same show, but they can purchase advertising around which the show is wrapped. On Thai TV, and on TV in the USA, sponsored shows often use the sponsor's brand in scenes throughout the show.

Sponsorship of the Arts and good causes

Sponsors also make use of the arts. A brand name seen in association with a book award, health organisation or theatre production creates goodwill that may resonate with the target group of consumers and pass for community involvement or Corporate Social Responsibility (CSR). Prestigious promotion can also have a positive influence on the perceptions of other interested groups such as shareholders, local government authorities or the press. Arts sponsorship provides funds for traditionally under-funded arts organisations and so there are social benefits that can generate general goodwill towards the brand organisation (Chong, 2009). Gaining publicity for the sponsorship among a wider audience may depend heavily on whether the sponsored organisation can gain media coverage.

Sponsorship links between commercial and non-profit or charitable companies are based on a mutual benefit: goodwill and publicity for the commercial organisation, revenue for the charity, so they are highly sensitive to negative publicity. For nine years *Nike* sponsored cyclist Lance Armstrong's *Livestrong* cancer charity but the deal ended when Armstrong admitted taking performance-enhancing drugs.[11] Sponsorship relationships are evaluated closely for the advantages they bring to the sponsor. As the fortunes of the sponsored sports star or sports club wax and wane, the sponsors make business decisions that will benefit their brand. As noted in Snapshot 7.2, the English Premiership is a huge commercial success, but its sponsor *Barclays* is reported to be wondering whether the cost of renewing the deal in 2015 will outweigh the benefits.

Sponsorship evaluation

Sponsorship is an intuitively appealing communications technique because of the potentially high profile it can generate through public relations and press coverage, the targeted audiences it can reach and the positive connotations it can generate around the brand. Its traditional drawback has been that it is a promotional technique the precise effectiveness of which is far from easy to measure. However, it is increasingly seen as a technique that should be used in tandem with digital and experiential forms of activation.

As with advertising, sponsorship evaluation can make use of measures of brand recall, awareness, liking and purchase intention before, during and after a sponsorship arrangement. Sales and inquiry patterns are, of course, also carefully tracked. But, like advertising, the precise ROI of sponsorship is difficult to calculate. Conventional wisdom around sponsorship today is that its value will not be maximised unless its publicity is leveraged with social media buzz, experiential events and consumer engagement.

It is possible for sponsors to gather evidence that can, with careful interpretation, provide insights into the impact of a campaign or a relationship. Measures of audience viewing habits and purchasing behaviour deriving from panel data provide some data-driven insights into the effects of sponsorship. Its effectiveness is invariably contingent on the objectives that were conceived for it. Measures of awareness may be irrelevant in comparison with the way that the meaning of the brand is reinforced and consumers are reassured through the sponsored link. The outcome can only be conclusively assessed in terms of long-term brand market share, share price, sales revenue and profitability.

Sponsorship, like advertising, works to normalise a set of contrived brand values by juxtaposing the sponsoring brand with a separate brand in another field, for example where the *Emirates* airline engages in sponsorship with Arsenal football club. In this case, a brand that had been relatively unheard of in the UK became a household name, juxtaposed with a quintessentially British brand. This presumably supported the airline's internationalisation strategy. This kind of exposure can be seen to be extremely powerful, since it operates at the sub-textual level of suggestion and renders the sponsor's brand a taken-for-granted part of consumer cultural life. The benefits of sponsorship in such cases might be measured in terms of attitude scales or recall/promoted recall tests.

Product placement

Product placement refers to branded items being placed in the scene or mentioned in the script of movies or TV shows. Product placement is also common in pop songs, novels, radio broadcasts, computer games and stage plays (Lehu, 2007). In movies, in particular, it has become common for brands to feature as part of a commercial arrangement, generating a contribution to production costs or free scene props for the movie production company, and getting valuable exposure in a glamorous setting for the brand. For example, *General Motors* (GM) provided scores of cars for the movie *Transformers: Revenge of the Fallen* and the sequels, *Dark of the Moon* and *Age of Extinction*. GM did not charge a fee for the cars but enjoyed huge sales of the *Camaro* model as a result of its role in the movie. Chinese brands such as *Lenovo* and *Shuhua Milk* also bought placements in *Transformers*.[12] *Superman: Man of Steel* was reported to have earned more than £110 million from product placement deals, more than 75% of the movie's production costs.[13] Product placement is also common in TV (Tiwsakul et al., 2005), although regulations controlling it are tighter than in movies. For example, placements for alcohol, cigarettes and unhealthy foods, and placements targeted at children, are regulated more strictly in most countries for TV than for movies (Hackley et al., 2008).

Product placement can take various forms (d'Astous and Seguin, 1999). Placements can be visual, scripted, peripheral or in tight focus, position on the screen can be varied (and rated and costed differently): brands can be used actively in the scene, or simply passively present as screen props, sometimes described as integrated or non-integrated placements. Musical scores can constitute brand placements where particular artists or musical tracks receive valuable exposure in advertisements. For example, the Dandy Warhols gained valuable exposure by licensing their music for ads. More established artists like Lenny Kravitz have used ads to pre-launch a new single, bypassing the radio playlist route to get exposure to millions for nothing. Variations on product placement are sometimes called brand placement, entertainment marketing (in the sense that brands are inserted into entertainment vehicles) or embedded marketing. In spite of the revenue that can be earned by TV channels and programme makers for brands placed in their shows, it is estimated that only 2 in 5 brands seen on TV have been paid for in the USA, and a lower proportion in the UK (Hackley and Hackley née Tiwsakul, 2012). One reason for this is that the pace and volume of TV programme making simply outpaces the ability of marketers to arrange contracts for every brand exposure. Producers, prop managers and set designers need branded items as scene props, and they often need them quickly when they are working to tight production schedules.

Many brands are not worried about how their products are seen in entertainment, they value the exposure regardless of the context. Consequently they are happy for their goods to be used as scene props. In some countries, such as Thailand, product placement contracts on TV can be very closely specified, with the brand dictating exactly how the brand will be used, seen or spoken about in the show (Hackley and Hackley, 2013). In some other countries, such as the UK, brands are not permitted to influence editorial, while in the USA, for example, brands can dictate content if they buy entire programmes as 'paid for programming'. In the UK, all paid-for placements on commercial TV were banned by the regulator, Ofcom, until February 2011. As a result, there is a thriving industry in free prop supply, whereby product placement occurs through agencies supplying scene props on demand to programme makers. The agencies earn a retainer from the brand suppliers, and they use sophisticated content analysis methods to track and rate the exposure of their clients' brands.

Since 2011, a small paid-for product placement market has emerged in the UK alongside the free prop supply market (Hackley and Hackley née Tiwsakul, 2012). To date, this market has not grown as rapidly as the industry hoped because of the tight restrictions placed on paid-for placements by Ofcom, but it has apparently provided a boost to the UK TV free prop supply market which seems to be booming.[14] The non-commercial BBC dominates the UK TV scene, with a 30% audience share across its six channels, and it produces about 27,000 hours per year of new domestic programming. That means a lot of scenes that need cars, clothes, breakfast cereals, fully stocked supermarket shelves, street furniture, mobile phones and other scene props. The BBC is not allowed to sell product placements, so it has to rely on the free prop agencies. As a result of these market dynamics, opportunities for paid-for placements on UK TV are somewhat limited.

Product placement pros and cons

There are a number of advantages to product placement as a promotional technique. One is that, as with sponsorship, the link between the entertainment vehicle and the placed brand is implicit rather than explicit. This means that the consumer is left to read the association in the entertainment text. Leaving the consumer to complete the gestalt, as it were, can be powerfully persuasive. What is more, product and brand placement offers brand organisations a way of circumventing consumer resistance to or cynicism towards, conventional 'interruptive' advertising.

The hybrid status of product placement (Balasubramanian, 1994) as a form of promotion that combines advertising, celebrity endorsement, sponsorship and PR gives it great flexibility as a tool for generating brand awareness, demonstrating product features, and creating brand positioning in the context of highly aspirational and attractive settings. Product placement can be exceptional value for brands in comparison to traditional spot advertising. The brand owner pays once for a placement but there may be multiple re-runs, DVD sales and internet clips, not to mention the leverage to be gained if a movie or TV show becomes a big hit winning huge audiences. Added value can be gained if the brand owner leverages the appearance in the entertainment vehicle with additional advertising and digital engagement activities, as beer brand *Heineken* did in their deal with the James Bond movies, *Quantum of Solace* and *Skyfall*. On the other hand, the brand owner paying for the placement takes the risk that the movie might bomb, making the brand placement poor value for money. Generally, while costs of placements vary widely, they compare favourably with the costs of producing a TV advertisement and paying for airtime.

The dilemma for brands is that placements that are not paid for, called serendipitous placements, can be as useful as those that are. For example, brand partners in James Bond movies have included *Heineken*, *Omega*, *Audi*, *Sony* and *Adidas*, who paid heavily for the privilege, but *Macallan* Scotch whisky was scripted in *Skyfall* at no declared cost to the manufacturer, and achieved exposure valued at over $7 million worldwide according to one marketing analytics company.[15] Brands can be very useful for scriptwriters and directors to develop characterisation, and Bond is known for his discernment and fine taste in alcohol. Declaring a fondness for a 50-year-old brand of Scotch whisky is a way to signal that aspect of Bond's character, and the brand merely had to give their permission. Brands are important to entertainment makers, since consumers of movies, video games and TV soaps want to see verisimilitude in scenes, they want the entertainment to look realistic in terms of the urban settings and consumer lifestyles of characters, so there is a huge latent demand for brands that are interested in the exposure.

Some brands worry about the precise context of the exposure, and occasionally veto movie scenes. For example, a case of product 'displacement' was reported in the 2008 movie *Slumdog Millionaire*, when director Danny Boyle claimed that *Coca-Cola* and *Mercedes* asked for their brand logos to be obscured after they had seen the rushes and didn't like their brands being seen in the context of Indian slums and gangsters.[16] The movie turned out to be a huge hit. Editorial control can be a sticking point for some brand placement deals.

Music and brands

Music is very important in marketing. It makes advertising and promotion more fun, it gives dramatic force to the visuals, it aids brand recall, and, in the case of licensed popular music used in ads, it pre-segments the audience by making the people who like that track turn their heads to notice the ad when they hear the music. Today, jingles are regarded as corny, and music licensing is the most common method used. Musicians once felt chary about working with brands. It wasn't considered cool. Not any more. Many rock musicians are happy to have their music featured in an ad.[19] Not only that, but brands have found that sponsoring and supporting popular music is a way of reaching young audiences in a subtle but high profile way. The benefit has sometimes been reciprocal – a new track licensed for an advertisement is gaining exposure for the artist or for the single release, so the music is in effect 'placed' in the advertisement.

Companies such as *BMG* can license classics from artists from Iggy Pop and Frank Sinatra to Christina Aguilera and Coldplay to provide a musical hook to a broadcast advertisement. The track guarantees the attention of a particular audience segment. The advertiser who wants to use an original track to give the ad extra impact has to buy rights to both the CD master and to the published sheet music, which are often owned by different music-licensing houses. They have to get the agreement of the original artists as well. In some cases the stars as well as their music become vehicles to gain the attention of the desired target audience: 1960s American rock icon Iggy Pop featured, in person, in a series of 2009 advertisements for an insurance company. A few years ago that would have been considered the definition of un-cool, but today the artistic barriers between marketing and advertising, and entertainment, seem to have dissolved.

In fact, established performing artists are falling over themselves to win contracts with brands, as celebrity spokespeople, as 'creative directors', or simply as actors featuring in the brand's ads. Sometimes, the endorsement itself appears to be reciprocal, such as where celebrities are appointed to quasi-official positions as creative directors for major brands. Fashion designer Marc Jacobs moved into a successful perfume line before being appointed as creative director by *Diet Coke*,[20] Stella McCartney was given a similar title to design athletes' outfits for *Team GB* and *Adidas*[21] and none other than Lady Gaga took a (no doubt 9–5 with lunch vouchers) post as creative director for *Polaroid*.[22] These show appointments might be nominal, but they represent a mutual accommodation between the creative ego of the artist and the commercial imperative of the brand. The artist and the brand (Schroeder, 2005) now work on the same plane, using the same media materials.

Intertextuality and embedded marketing

Embedded marketing in general, including product placement, music licensing and all forms of entertainment marketing, makes use of intertextuality (see Chapter 2).

When differing media draw on shared symbols and reference points they can instantly convey particular values in association with a brand, as the Bond movie did when they had Bond declare his love of *Macallan* Scotch. Bond may be a murderer, but he's a cultivated murderer. We listen to music for our own entertainment, if we hear the same track in an entertainment vehicle this provides a bridge between the world of entertainment and our personal cultural experience. Intertextuality, in effect, is what makes advertising and promotion meaningful as cultural products.

Music, in particular, is a deeply personal choice, bound up with our sense of identity (Shankar, 2000). It can reach out with an emotional hook to segmented audiences. Indeed, embedding popular cultural references within advertising and promotion, and embedding brands within popular cultural media, represents the logical development of the 'the entertainment economy' (Wolf, 1999), and perhaps of the 'culture industry' (Horkheimer and Adorno, [1944] 2002). Of course, marketing is not all about entertainment; it is also about innovation, materials sourcing, design, organisation, manufacture, logistics and more. But important features of marketing are converging in the entertainment and communications areas. In post-industrial economies, increased affluence and leisure opportunities have created a huge demand for entertainment. Sports coverage on TV now extends to the internet and mobile, while movies, music and news, information and retail shopping can all be accessed digitally, driving the demand for mobile devices. The absence of an explicit sales message in much embedded marketing communication does not impair the promotional effect: humans are interpreting creatures, we seek to impose meaning and coherence by making sense of our experience. We actively make the connections between brands and values that are left implicit in embedded marketing initiatives. Convergence is driving the marketing wedge ever deeper into consumer cultural life. Whether this is a force for ideological domination, or a force for postmodern liberation (Firat and Venkatesh, 1995), is a matter of debate.

SNAPSHOT 7.4

PR, viral, content marketing, or newsjacking?

The difficulty of categorising non-advertising promotion in the convergence era was illustrated by one initiative from tampon brand *Bodyform*. A Facebook post attributed to aspiring author 'Richard'[23] (who wanted to plug his book) lamented that watching *Bodyform* advertising over the years led him to believe that, once a month, his female friends would be the most terrific fun, taking him bike riding, skiing, mountain climbing or horse riding and enjoying life with a verve he would hardly be able to match. The reality, he claimed, was sadly different, reminding him more of a scene from the horror movie *The Exorcist*, in which the main female character gets a little bad tempered, and he blamed the advertising for creating this altogether misleading impression. The post went viral and earned 40,000 likes in a day. Just four days later, *Bodyform* had a witty video response on YouTube with an actress in the role of *Bodyform* CEO explaining the true nature of periods to Richard. The video had earned over 3.7 million views[24] at the time of writing. SCR, manufacturers of *Bodyform*, and their ad agency, Carat, picked up on Richard's Facebook joke and ran with it, supported by astute PR. Much admiring press comment followed, adding to the buzz.[25] Essentially, this rapid response initiative was a piece of PR, since it generated huge buzz and many column inches of mostly admiring press comment. Getting almost 4 million views of a 1 minute 45 seconds TV ad could cost several million in production, even before the TV spots were paid for. A video for YouTube normally costs tens of thousands, or less. Consider that viewers actively sought out the video to watch it and share it with friends, as opposed to half-listening to it during a TV ad break, and you have the essence of branded content: active consumer engagement. The scriptwriting was astute: the YouTube video parodied sanitary promotion, but it also invoked *Bodyform*'s tradition of advertising in an admiring way that dovetailed nicely with the brand history. The tone of this social media exchange was, perhaps, rather British – the humour of the video seemed offbeat and a little weird or vulgar to some. This unique marketing initiative was founded on an acute sensitivity to the particular context in which the exchange would be received.

Public relations

The Institute of Public Relations (IPR), the main professional body for the discipline in the UK, defines public relations as 'the way organisations, companies and individuals communicate with the public and media'. The IPR's website goes on to state that 'A PR specialist communicates with the target audience directly or indirectly through media with an aim to create and maintain a positive image and create a strong relationship with the audience. Examples include press releases, newsletters, public appearances, etc. as well as utilisation of the world wide web'.[26] The Public Relations Society of America (PRSA)[27] emphasises PR's task of helping an organisation to interact, communicate with and win the co-operation of its public.

PR is a function where the aim is to create goodwill towards the brand or the corporation, to deflect criticism, or to foster a generally positive view of the corporation or brand among stakeholders and the general public. It encompasses the dark art of 'spinning', much used and criticised in politics. 'Spinning' means putting a positive interpretation on information or news that might be interpreted negatively.

At the turn of the century, public relations (PR) was very important in selling big business to America. Historian Roland Marchand (1998) showed in his historical studies of corporate America how big business had to manufacture a sense of legitimacy. Ordinary American citizens saw the growth of the big corporations like *GM* and *AT&T* as threats to Main Street America. Small operators were being put out of business by these new Leviathans and questions were even being asked at Presidential level about the threat they posed to the American way of life. They had to present a human face to the public and used PR techniques, including well-publicised corporate philanthropy, sponsorship of good causes, educational programmes for workers and for consumers, advertising and direct mail to humanise the corporations. It worked. Today, Corporate Communications has evolved as a distinct sub-discipline involving PR for big corporations, as opposed to PR for brands, individuals or other kinds of organisation. For many years, PR operated in the shadows, little understood and somewhat separated from marketing and advertising. Today, under integration, PR has been brought within the marketing and advertising toolbox.

Edward Bernays is often credited with inventing PR. Bernays, Sigmund Freud's nephew, was a wartime propagandist for the USA who coined the term 'public relations' because he felt that the term 'propaganda' was too closely associated with war. Bernays believed that the best way to influence public opinion was through news media, and one of his early successes illustrated his method well. Charged with a brief to persuade more American women to take up cigarette smoking, Bernays realised that he had to undermine the severe social stigma that surrounded female smoking in the USA at that time. Women could even be arrested for public smoking. He commissioned a psychoanalyst (not his uncle) to explain that cigarettes were symbolic phalluses, and if women were persuaded to smoke, they would have the feeling of male power.

Bernays saw an opportunity at the New York Easter Parade of 1929, which he knew would be heavily covered by press and TV reporters. He hired a group of debutantes to join the parade. At a given signal, they would take out *Lucky Strike* cigarettes from their garters, and light up. This shocking sight was sure to attract the attention of the camera crews and journalists. Bernays told the women to say they were demanding their rights by lighting up 'torches of freedom'. He thought this term would evince an emotional response because of the metaphoric visual link with the Statue of Liberty. The newsreels duly presented the sight of smoking debutantes as a spontaneous protest on behalf of women's rights to self-determination. The incident was credited with breaking the taboo against female cigarette smoking in public, and the practice was both normalised and valorised. It was normalised because women of high social standing were seen to do it without shame, and it was valorised through the association with feminine freedom and the values of America. Bernays enjoyed similar success with many other corporate clients.

PR practitioners generally keep lines of communication open between their client or organisation and their stakeholders and respond to enquiries and questions clearly and in the light of the client organisation's agenda. They also actively try to influence public opinion through the media by, for example, issuing press releases of stories they would like to be published as editorial. They also engage in dialogue with journalists and influential people and organisations. Most organisations like to tell 'good news' stories as often and as loudly as possible. PR specialists (often former journalists) solicit stories, write them up as press releases and use their journalist contacts to get coverage for them.

Other elements of non-advertising promotion

Direct mail

Direct mail (incorporating many forms of database marketing) continues to be popular for its accountability and cost. The attraction of direct mail advertising over broadcast media is that each mailshot can be directed at a named person who may have a personal interest in the products or services being offered. Of course, email marketing, SMS messaging and algorithm-driven social media advertising also offer digital versions of the same method. As any householder knows, the belief of advertisers that direct mail is good value is highly suspect; much of it ends up unread in the waste bin, and a lot is misdirected because the customer databases driving direct mail campaigns are notoriously difficult to compile and maintain accurately. Databases have to be 'cleaned' regularly otherwise they date rapidly as addresses and phone numbers change for an increasingly mobile population.

The volume of mail in developed countries is reducing as fewer people write letters and use email or SMS instead. Accordingly, direct mail agencies are expanding their remit to reflect the trends of convergence. The UK-based Institute of Direct Marketing (IDM), for example, changed its name to the Institute of Direct and Digital Marketing (IDDM)[28] to reflect the shift towards digitisation, anticipating a time when paper-based marketing might be displaced to an even greater degree by digital forms of direct and database-driven marketing.

Sales promotion, ambient marketing, POS and merchandising

Sales promotion refers to a vast range of novelty items that can carry promotional messages or a visual representation of the brand. Often these items, such as coffee mugs, pens, bags, T-shirts or other things, are given away, so the element of goodwill is bound up with the brand when they are used by a consumer.

Sales promotion also refers to in-store promotions such as two-for-the-price-of-one, temporary price discounts, free gifts, redeemable coupons, competitions or money back for returning so many bottle-tops or labels (the latter technique is called the self-liquidating premium). Conventional marketing wisdom holds that the major strength of sales promotions is that they can persuade people to try the brand. It can also be argued that some brands use perpetual sales promotions to encourage repeat purchase and brand loyalty. For example, *McDonald's* hamburgers regularly have a promotional offer of free toys with children's meals, usually thematically tied in with a movie release. Long-term sales promotion encourages not just trial but long-term, repeat purchase.

SNAPSHOT 7.5

Ambush marketing at the London 2012 Olympics

Ambush marketing loosely refers to incidents that are designed to earn publicity for a brand when they didn't pay for it. In one notorious example at the 2010 World Cup in South Africa, a Dutch beer brand block-booked 36 seats in the stand and at a given signal women paid by the company all stood up, wearing the colours of the brand. The incident gained a lot of publicity, along with a lawsuit.[29] *Beats by Dre*, the headsets brand associated with rap artist Dr Dre, contributed to the distinguished history of ambush marketing[30] at London 2012 Olympics. The organising committee, called LOGOC, had made clear their intention to block ambush marketers. Brands including

(Continued)

McDonald's, *Coca-Cola*, *BMW*, *Samsung*, *Omega* and *P&G* were paying up to a reported £65 million each to be top-tier sponsors while supplying products and services too. LOGOC wanted to protect these investments while also staying within the rules of Olympic broadcaster the BBC, which is the biggest non-commercial public service broadcaster in the world and does not carry paid advertising or promotion. LOGOC was, however, outmanoeuvred by *Beats*, who noticed that the Olympic swimmers liked to wear headsets to block out the noise until the starting pistol fired. The swimmers were given free *Beats by Dre* headsets, and then wore them as they entered the swimming venue in front of a worldwide TV audience of 1 billion. Top category, 5* product placement ensued, closely followed by thousands of column inches of trade press comment, most of it admiring. This exposure fitted the youthful, rebellious positioning of the brand perfectly, and the association with cool, young, multinational athletes resonated with the *Beats* target audience. The stunt was probably premeditated – *Beats* had reportedly performed a similar ambush at the 2008 Beijing Olympics by giving headsets to American basketball star LeBron James who passed them out to other team members.

Some sales promotional techniques converge with customer relationship management (CRM) approaches in that they seek to reward, and thereby encourage, brand loyalty. Airlines and credit cards try to reward repeated use with air-miles for free travel and points or cashback. Credit card companies and mortgage providers often offer good rates to new customers for loan servicing in countries where only short-term loans and mortgages are offered. In the UK, for example, most new mortgage offers are for 2, 3 or 5 years, while in the USA it is common for house buyers to be offered 20- or 30-year fixed rate mortgages. Many credit card customers now switch suppliers readily to take advantage of short-term promotional interest or balance transfer rates.

Some retailers have abandoned the conventional wisdom of sales promotion inducing trial and have opted instead for continuous sales promotion to solicit bargain-conscious consumers. In Europe, *Aldi* and *Netto* supermarket brands are just two that are positioned as cheap, no-frills providers. There has been a huge growth in the UK in £1 shops and similar, continuous sales promotion retail positioning. In the airline market there has been a rapid growth in low-cost air travel, with firms such as *easyJet* and *Ryanair*, and many hotel chains have developed low-cost, no-frills rooms, such as the French chain *Formula 1* and the *Holiday Inn Express* chain of budget hotels. Sales promotion, of course, implies a tactical manoeuvre which is short-term, while low-cost as a marketing strategy is a rather different approach. Nevertheless, low-cost marketing strategies simply extend the logic of sales promotion, because many cost-conscious consumers are not brand-loyal as such but shop around for bargains all the time.

Ambient marketing (Shankar and Horton, 1999), the insertion of brands into the consumer's experiential environment, comes in many forms and can cross into other categories such as outdoor, packaging, sales promotion or direct mail. The key element is how the promotional message has been inserted into the consumer's environment. For example, ambient promotion has a longstanding, in-store tradition in retailing: supermarkets pipe the smell of baking bread into the shop to create a relaxed and pleasing ambience that is conducive to uncritical purchasing. Retailers play lift-music that relaxes shoppers so that they put more goods into their basket than they really came in for. Ambient promotion has become a taken-for-granted aspect of the urban shopping scene. We now expect to see brand promotions, advertisements and logos everywhere, including theatre programmes and car parking tickets, on steps and walls in underground train stations, on petrol pumps, on street furniture, beer mats, and even on dogs' coats, cars (that are 'wrapped' with ads in exchange for a fee) and baseball caps. In recent years brands have become so cool that it is now common to see people wearing clothing with the brand name prominent, effectively turning themselves into a mobile advertising hoarding for the brand. Brands are now common sights in urban settings (see Colour Section, photos 9 and 10), on OOH displays or being worn as clothes or accessories by commuters and shoppers.

Celebrity marketing

Sponsorship of celebrity sportspeople is well established as a marketing ploy. Sometimes they actively wear the brand as part of the deal, and at other times they merely promote it. Beyond sports marketing, the use of celebrities has moved beyond the traditional model in which a celebrity, famous for achievement in some other field, is chosen for the way their personal brand fits ('matches up') with the sponsor's brand, and then acts out scripted ads in which he or she claims to be a keen user (see, for example, Erdogan, 1999; Hackley and Hackley, 2014; McCracken, 1989). The convergence of media channels through the digitisation of communication has connected market segments and provided a powerful space for leveraging brand equity (Powell, 2013). Conventional wisdom in branding holds that extending brand strategies across new markets and new audiences carries risks (Aaker, 2004), principally the risk of confusing consumers by diluting the brand positioning, but these risks seem to be at least partly ameliorated through the connection with celebrities such as David Beckham (see Colour Section, photo 8), whose fanbase cuts across nationalities and socio-demographic groups, allowing his sponsors to reach new markets with their brands. Beckham has had commercial contracts with *Sainsbury's, Adidas, Breitling, Armani, H&M, Samsung, Diet Coke*[31] and many more, and, according to Steve Martin, Chief Executive of M&C Saatchi Sport & Entertainment,[32] his retirement from football will increase his earning potential to upwards of £15–20 million a year.

In new model celebrity marketing, the celebrity is sometimes given a nominal but official position with the brand. This hints at a strategic relationship that, if believed, is deeper than a typically insincere 'endorsement'. Some, though, seem to have a stronger fit than others. For example, Katy Perry's deal with makers of *The Sims*, *Electronic Arts*, might seem more meaningful as a partnership than others, such as Madonna's with *Diageo*.[33] The artist and the brand (Schroeder, 2005) now work on the same place, using the same media materials.

In some other cases, the brand appoints a relative unknown, because the publicity generated will not only give the brand exposure but will make the appointee more famous, hence increasing the brand exposure again.[34] For example, in 2010, *L'Oréal* appointed a relatively unknown actress as brand spokesperson.[35] In still other cases, unknowns can become celebrities in their own right, and then they can earn sponsorship deals. Some performers have used YouTube as a platform to generate exposure, earning major press coverage, recording contracts[36] and TV appearances, while some bloggers are now regarded as celebrities within their milieu, whether that be fashion, film criticism, or travel writing.[37]

SNAPSHOT 7.6

Japanese girls use their bodies as billboards

According to news reports, some 4,000 young Japanese women have been making an income of up to $100 a day by renting their thighs for 8 hours a day to advertisers and posting photos of themselves online.[38] Non-advertising promotion on the human body has also included brand tattooing and 'sandwich' boards.

Native advertising/content marketing

Native advertising is a rapidly growing category of promotion for media brands – for example, news and entertainment media brand *Huffington Post* announced a 47% increase in revenue from native advertising in 2013.[39] Native advertising is regarded by some as just another angle on content marketing or branded content. Content marketing, as discussed at the beginning of the chapter, is the art of creating entertaining media content in the form of news stories, videos, photographs or anything else that might interest media users and can be shared. The content may be informative, entertaining, surprising, shocking or intriguing, but the motive is always the same – to subtly promote a brand's internet presence. Native advertising is a category of content marketing that focuses on digital content, and especially on media brands.

Native is somewhat similar to old style print advertorial, a bought section of a newspaper that looks like editorial, unless the eagle-eyed reader notices the word 'advertisement feature' in tiny letters by the headline. Proponents argue that native advertising entails a wider variety of techniques, although the fact that content is paid for should always be clear to the reader. Sponsors want the source credibility of news media but they don't want to buy their display or classified advertising, so native advertising has been mooted by media owners as the saviour of journalism since it apparently offers a new business model to replace the collapsing advertising model for newspapers. It has been adopted by some serious organs of record, such as the UK *Guardian* and the *New York Times*[40] as well as by the newer showbusiness and sensation-driven media brands. Native advertising raises questions of media and marketing ethics. When marketing techniques are not necessarily immediately apparent for what they really are, it raises questions about ideological influence (Hackley et al., 2008). This has been called implicit or 'masked' marketing. The ethical question is to what extent should consumers be credited with sophistication about such marketing techniques.

Trade conferences and exhibitions

According to one estimate,[41] $24 billion is spent annually on exhibiting in the USA. Many of these are trade exhibitions for business-to-business promotion but some also include consumers, such as trade exhibitions for motor vehicles, higher education, home furnishings and leisure crafts. The bigger exhibitions charge an entry fee to the public and attract many thousands of visitors to the manufacturers' exhibition stands. Exhibitions can generate a massive throughput of actual and potential consumers while also acting as a presence in the market in general. The advantage of trade exhibitions is that audiences are pre-segmented, and they come direct to the manufacturers. The disadvantages are cost, time and effort, and manufacturers are situated in a hall with all their major rivals. A well-attended conference and a well-organised stall can, however, generate considerable business.

Point of sale and merchandising

Merchandising is normally a term used in a broad sense to refer to the whole retail setting for purchase, including the way the product is displayed and promoted in the retail store. POS is sales promotion that takes place at the point of sale, by the checkout. POS promotion might entail a sales person offering free samples, or a cardboard model of the product featuring prominently on display to put the brand foremost in consumers' minds at the point of sale. The term can also be used more broadly to refer to any in-store promotion such as liquid crystal TV screens placed in-store showing continuous ads for a brand sold there, or other promotional structures such as 'tubes' – printed with promotional images of brands – which customers have to walk through.

Advertising and promotion at the POS are intended to create a persuasive ambience in the space where the consumer makes a decision and hands over the cash. POS should give a cutting edge to the broader merchandising activities that are common in retail marketing. In the small TCN shops (tobacco, confectionery, newspapers) that are common in much of the UK and Europe, brand marketers know that the position their branded item occupies is crucial to its sales performance – the 'golden arc' consists of an arm's length radiating from the cashier's position on each side. This is where leading brands of tobacco and confectionery prefer to be located in the shop for easy viewing and access. In larger retail stores brand marketers know that the volume of shelf space occupied is a powerful generator of sales and they will use all the bargaining power they can to get retail managers to devote as much of this volume as possible to their brand.

Chapter summary

This chapter has reviewed a number of non-advertising promotional techniques. The difficulties of definition under convergence have been noted, and many examples cited to illustrate some of the ways in which categories of the promotion mix are being split into hybrid forms. Some, like product placement, combine elements of celebrity endorsement, sponsorship, advertising and PR. Others seem to be a digital revision of traditional analogue methods, like native advertising as a digital development of advertorial. Still others, such as content marketing, seem to be contingent for their effect on a combination of genre and medium. Overall, the category non-advertising promotion is becoming more important to advertisers since it is taking an increasing proportion of promotional budgets.

 ■ **Review Questions** ■

1. Record an evening's TV viewing on commercial channels. Watch the play-back and list the number of sponsorship and product placement events. What do the results tell you about the changing practices of sponsorship and brand placement on broadcast entertainment? What impact do you feel such events have in comparison with conventional TV advertising? Has the character of TV advertising changed to reflect the growth in sponsorship and its variants?

2. How can sponsorship of TV shows generate tangible benefits for brand organisations?

3. Imagine that you are the public relations officer of a soccer club, a university or a retail organisation. Think of six ways in which you could draw on other communications disciplines to promote a positive public perception of your organisation.

4. Find five examples of native advertising. Explain how they benefit sponsors, and discuss what ethical issues they might raise for journalism.

━━━━━━ **CASE STUDY** ━━━━━━

The selfie that 'broke Twitter'[42]

The 2014 Hollywood Academy Awards, the 'Oscars', were sponsored by the world's biggest handset business, *Samsung*.[43] Host Ellen DeGeneres used a *Samsung Galaxy Note 3* smartphone to take a selfie of herself, Bradley Cooper and Meryl Streep. When Kevin Spacey, Julia Roberts, Brad Pitt, Angelina Jolie and Lupita N'Yongo also managed to squeeze into the pic, along with N'Yongo's brother, DeGeneres tweeted it, and the re-tweets caused Twitter to briefly crash. DeGeneres announced that the image 'broke Twitter'. By the next evening, CNN reported that the selfie had been re-tweeted more than 3 million times, making it the world's biggest viral selfie, and achieving more than triple the shares of a selfie taken by US President Barack Obama. During the coverage *Samsung* products featured in something like 5 minutes

(Continued)

of screen time, along with advertisements in the commercial breaks. The selfie, no doubt a planned piece of spontaneity, leveraged this sponsorship through viral social media shares into peak time, global mass media news coverage, trade press and comment.[44] The 2014 Oscars shown live on ABC gained its biggest American TV audience in ten years, some 43 million, with probably many millions more watching around the world. According to research specialists Nielson,[45] the 3 hour telecast was tweeted about 11.2 million times by 2.8 million people. In this case, sponsorship was combined with advertising, brand placement, celebrity endorsement, content marketing and PR, and achieved a highly leveraged combination of bought and earned media pace.

The Oscars selfie is a good example of how elements of the promotional mix no longer operate independently. Sponsorship was undertaken of a televised event that was certain to achieve a large live TV audience (the event was also streamed live on the internet) and global coverage in news and entertainment media. It was leveraged through in-coverage placing of the sponsor's brands, allowable under US TV sponsorship rules, and the coverage was wrapped around bought spot advertising. The selfie tweet achieved news coverage in its own right and huge earned media space as the most shared selfie ever. Other media stories even piggy-backed on the selfie story, giving it even more earned mentions, with reports that some stars tried to push their way into the selfie group and failed, and that DeGeneres used an *iPhone* to take another selfie backstage. The incident illustrates that, under convergence, integration is an integral part of the dynamic of advertising and promotion.

Case Questions

1. **How might you categorise the 2014 Oscars selfie tweet as a form of promotional communication?**

2. **In what ways might viral content benefit brands? Are there risks?**

3. **What are the advantages and disadvantages of earned media space over bought media space for brands?**

4. **In what other ways might sponsorship deals be leveraged through social media? Give five examples.**

Useful journal articles

(These Sage articles can be accessed on the book website)

Anne M. Cronin (2011) 'Researching urban space, reflecting on advertising: a photo essay', *Space and Culture*, 14 (4): 356–66.

Karen Smith (2006) 'Rhetorical figures and the translation of advertising headlines', *Language and Literature*, 15 (2): 159–82.

Andrew McStay (2013) 'I consent: an analysis of the Cookie Directive and its implications for UK behavioral advertising', *New Media & Society*, 15 (4): 596–611 (first published September 30, 2012).

Joanne Morreale (2014) 'From homemade to store bought: *Annoying Orange* and the professionalization of YouTube', *Journal of Consumer Culture*, 14 (1): 113–28 (first published October 15, 2013).

Iben Bredahl Jessen and Nicolai Jørgensgaard Graakjær (2013) 'Cross-media communication in advertising: exploring multimodal connections between television commercials and websites', *Visual Communication*, 12 (4): 437–58.

■ ■ Further reading ■

Bernhardt, J.M., Alber, J. and Gold, R.S. (2014) 'A social media primer for professionals: digital dos and don'ts', *Health Promotion Practice*, 15 (2): 168–172.

Eckhardt, G.M. and Bradshaw, A. (2014) 'The erasure of antagonisms between popular music and advertising', *Marketing Theory*, doi: 1470593114521452 (first published February 12, 2014).

Fan Yang (2014) 'China's 'fake' Apple store: branded space, intellectual property and the global culture industry', *Theory, Culture & Society*, doi: 0263276413504971 (first published March 17, 2014).

Hackley, C. (2003) 'IMC and Hollywood – what brand managers need to know', *Admap*, November: 44–7.

Hackley, C. and Hackley née Tiwsakul, R.A. (2012) 'Unpaid product placement: the elephant in the room in the UK's new paid-for product placement market', *International Journal of Advertising*, 31(4): 703–18.

Lehu, J-M. and Bressoud, E. (2009) 'Recall of brand placement in movies: interactions between prominence and plot connection in real conditions of exposure', *Recherche et Applications en Marketing (English Edition)*, 24 (1): 7–26.

Taylor, C.R. and Weih Chang (1995) 'The history of outdoor advertising regulation in the United States', *Journal of Macromarketing*, 15: 47–59.

Tiwsakul, R., Hackley, C. and Szmigin, I. (2005) 'Explicit, non-integrated product placement in British television programmes', *International Journal of Advertising*, 24 (1): 95–111.

Notes

1. http://class.classmatandread.net/pp1/out-2.pdf accessed 28.2.2014
2. www.youtube.com/watch?v=M7FIvfx5J10 accessed 25.2.2014
3. www.theguardian.com/technology/2014/feb/26/secret-to-viral-video-marketing accessed 25.2.2014
4. www.sponsorship.com/iegsr/2014/01/07/Sponsorship-Spending-Growth-Slows-In-North-America.aspx#.UxAK4yifPao accessed 26.2.2014

5. www.sponsorship.com/iegsr/2014/01/07/Sponsorship-Spending-Growth-Slows-In-North-America.aspx#.UxAK4yifPao accessed 26.2.2014

6. www.brandwatch.com/wp-content/uploads/2013/05/Brandwatch-Barclays-Premier-League-Report-May-2013.pdf accessed 26.2.2014

7. http://blogs.independent.co.uk/2013/08/26/premier-league-shirt-sponsors-pour-record-166m-into-top-flight-bank-accounts-with-arsenal-seeing-the-biggest-rise/ accessed 26.2.2014

8. www.telegraph.co.uk/finance/newsbysector/banksandfinance/10597404/Barclays-considering-exit-from-Premier-League-sponsorship-deal.html accessed 26.2.2014

9. www.tsmplug.com/richlist/nike-highest-paid-endorsement-deals/ accessed 26.2.2014

10. www.channel4sales.com/advertising/sponsorship/current_sponsors accessed 28.2.2014

11. http://articles.chicagotribune.com/2013-05-28/business/chi-nike-livestrong-20130528_1_texas-based-livestrong-lance-armstrong-livestrong-spokeswoman accessed 26.2.2014

12. http://articles.latimes.com/2012/sep/11/entertainment/la-et-ct-chinese-pay-for-product-placement-in-hollywood-movies-20120910 accessed 28.2.2014

13. www.mirror.co.uk/lifestyle/going-out/film/superman-film-man-steel-rakes-1947071 accessed 1.3.2014

14. http://newmediagroup.co.uk/uk-product-placement---nmg-product-placement's-market-predictions-201314/ accessed 3.3.2014

15. www.brandchannel.com/home/post/2012/12/20/James-Bond-Skyfall-Heineken-Macallan-122012.aspx accessed 1.3.2014

16. http://adage.com/article/madisonvine-news/coke-mercedes-avoid-gritty-film-cameos-slumdog/132301/ accessed 1.3.2014

17. http://newmediagroup.co.uk/nmg-oscar-success-philomena/ accessed 1.3.2014

18. http://brandsandfilms.com/2011/09/product-placement-in-pictures-the-smurfs/ accessed 1.3.2014

19. www.usatoday.com/story/money/business/2014/01/17/pepsi-grammy-super-bowl-halftime/4529529/ accessed 1.3.2014

20. www.findingoutabout.com/marc-jacobs-unveils-his-diet-coke-can-designs-after-being-appointed-new-creative-director/ accessed 20.1.2014

21. http://styleclone.com/17342/stella-mccartney-appointed-creative-director-for-team-gb-and-adidas/ accessed 20.1.2014

22. www.brandchannel.com/home/post/2013/02/08/Celebrity-Creative-Directors-020813.aspx accessed 18.1.2014

23. www.facebook.com/Bodyform/posts/10151186887359324 accessed 23.02.2013

24. *Bodyform*'s video response is here www.youtube.com/watch?v=Bpy75q2DDow accessed 23.02.2013

25. Including this piece in the UK *Daily Mail* www.dailymail.co.uk/femail/article-2218920/Bodyform-viral-spoof-YouTube-video-Response-Richard-Neills-Facebook-rant-period-adverts.html accessed 23.02.2013

26. www.ipr.org.uk/ accessed 1.3.2014

27. www.prsa.org/ accessed 1.3.2014

28. www.theidm.com/ accessed 3.3.2014

29. www.marketingmagazine.co.uk/article/1010807/fifa-cracks-down-world-cup-ambush-marketing-stunt accessed 3.3.2014

30. www.businessinsider.com/best-ambush-marketing-campaigns-2012-6?op=1 accessed 3.3.2014

31. www.therichest.com/sports/david-beckham-earns-37-million-from-commercial-contracts-alone/ accessed 20.1.2014

32. www1.skysports.com/football/news/12040/8718003/Brand-Beckham accessed 19.1.2014

33. http://chrisreed.brandrepublic.com/2012/02/13/madonna-v%E2%80%99s-katy-perry-sponsorship-v%E2%80%99s-brand-partnership/ accessed 17.1.2014
34. www.news.com.au/entertainment/celebrity/jessica-gomes-replaces-miranda-kerr-as-david-jones-ambassador/story-fn9076o9-1226603425211 accessed 16.1.2014
35. http://brandvisibility.org/branding/hello-world/ accessed 16.1.2014
36. Maria Aragon is one of numerous singers who have used YouTube as platform to gain a recording contract www.ctvnews.ca/youtube-sensation-maria-aragon-inks-recording-contract-1.674417 accessed 19.1.2014
37. 'Blogger Gains National Recognition for Travel Writing: Curacao Chronicle' www.curacaochronicle.com/tourism/local-blogger-gains-national-recognition-for-travel-blog-writes-about-curacao/ accessed 19.1.2014
38. www.dailymail.co.uk/news/article-2375732/Japanese-women-paid-adverts-THIGHS-catch-attention-men.html accessed 4.3.2014
39. www.businesswire.com/news/home/20131216005482/en/Huffington-Post-Announces-Record-Year-Audience-Growth#.UxVfGSifPao accessed 3.3.2014
40. www.theguardian.com/media/media-blog/2014/jan/05/native-advertising-paywall-transparency accessed 3.3.2014
41. www.tsnn.com/news-blogs/ceir-releases-new-version-how-exhibit-dollar-spent-report accessed 3.3.2014
42. www.reuters.com/article/2014/03/03/us-oscars-selfie-idUSBREA220C320140303 accessed 3.3.2014
43. http://adage.com/article/media/samsung-breaks-samsung-campaign-oscars/291938/ accessed 3.3.2014
44. www.engadget.com/2014/03/02/samsung-galaxy-s5-oscars-selfies/ accessed 3.3.2014
45. www.latimes.com/entertainment/envelope/cotown/la-et-ct-oscars-ratings-ellen-degeneres-20140303,0,6631180.story#axzz2uxfDdxy6 accessed 3.3.2014

8 International Advertising

Chapter outline

Brand marketing is now conducted in an international space that crosses national and cultural boundaries. Standardising brand marketing communication across the globe is attractive to organisations because of the potential savings and control over the brand image. However, communicating one message to different national cultures raises many difficulties. This chapter discusses some of the managerial opportunities and problems of promoting brands internationally, and explores some of the wider implications of the globalisation of the marketing environment.

Key chapter content

- Advertising and the global economy
- Cross-cultural communication
- Standardisation or localisation of advertising and promotion?
- Cultural tensions around global brand advertising
- Advertising management in non-domestic economies

Advertising and the global economy

Advertising expenditure is closely liked to growth in economic activity, and the generation of jobs and wealth. It is seen as a reflection and also a driver of Gross Domestic Product (GDP)[1] growth. Rising expenditure on advertising is seen as a healthy sign of a growing economy, and the opposite is also true – when advertising expenditure contracts, the general economic picture is probably poor. The causal relationship between advertising and GDP growth is difficult to establish one way or the other, but it has been shown that digital advertising, in particular, contributes to company performance.[2] Advertising and economic growth can be said to be two sides of the same coin – they are intimately interconnected. One cannot happen without the other. The International Advertising Association (IAA) emphasises the choices advertising makes possible in its 'Case for Advertising' campaign, launched in early 2014.[3] These include widening choices of product and service and making consumers aware of these choices; creating more choices in employment by creating jobs; creating more choices in news and entertainment media by creating revenue to fund those media; and helping to generate revenue for entertainment, the arts and sport.[4]

Advertising is fundamental to the global economy. At the time of writing, global advertising expenditure is projected to rise by more than 5% a year until 2017 by consultants McKinsey and Zenith Optimedia,[5] while digital advertising is predicted to show double-digit annual percentage growth over the same period. According to some estimates, digital growth will be led by mobile, which is forecast to be worth $42 billion globally by 2017.[6] Worldwide advertising spend in total is estimated at just over $500 billion.[7] Television, cinema, out of home (OOH) and radio advertising also show modest growth, but advertising expenditure (known as adspend) on print newspapers and magazines is predicted to continue its relative decline. Digital media extend the reach of businesses across the world and advertising is an essential part of business growth. The global penetration of digital media is increasing as an increasing proportion of the world's population acquires access to internet-enabled smartphones and other devices. It is estimated that some 20% of the world's population owns a PC, and 22–30%[8] own a smartphone.[9] This degree of penetration is making new global markets more easily accessible through digital media.

Advertising's global scope is extended by the shift in the proportion of adspend toward digital media. This includes purely digital formats such as *Google Adwords*,[10] sponsored content on social media such as Twitter and advertising on Facebook,[11] or native advertising on internet media brands, but it also extends to film, audio and print ads conveyed on digital media channels. For example, *Dove*'s 'Real Beauty Sketches',[12] a viral YouTube ad with more than 160 million views (discussed in Chapter 10) was uploaded to forty-five YouTube channels in twenty-five different languages. The videos were not differentiated for national audiences, just the commentary, reflecting the need to maximise the reach of the video across *Dove*'s international markets. The global audience reach of the internet, especially via mobile, has changed the terms of the debate around international advertising from 'what can work with international audiences' to 'what must work with international audiences'. There is more need than ever before for advertising and promotion agencies to deploy their communication craft skills in ways that translate across cultural, ethnic and linguistic boundaries – indeed, internationalisation, like integration, is becoming a default position for promotional communication. Advertising and promotion will be viewed across the world via mobile, PC and internet cable TV, even if it was not conceived specifically to achieve a global reach. Social media sharing of popular marketing content tends to span the globe-marketing news quickly becomes global.

The topic of international advertising remains fraught with potential difficulties of interpretation and complexities of media planning. There is still a need in traditional mass media for above-the-line executions that will be designed, or at least conceived, by a group in one country, to be consumed by audiences in other countries. The need for cross-national mentalities in advertising remains. In addition to the difficulties presented by differences of cultural and linguistic communication codes, ethical standards and regulations, media agencies have to negotiate radically different media environments in different counties. So, in a sense, the problems of international advertising are not fundamentally different in the convergence era – they are simply extended through all levels of integration because of the reach of digital media.

Why advertise across borders?

Global marketing entails risk, but there remain sound and pressing reasons why brand marketing organisations want to operate on a global scale. In fact, as noted above, given the increase in global access to cable television and the internet via mobile, it can be difficult for brands to remain local. A website, for example, is intrinsically a global presence, at least in the sense that it can, in principle, be accessed by anyone, anywhere. Information and advertising cross cultural boundaries, increase consumer choices and raise consumers' lifestyle expectations. The scenes of affluence portrayed in brand advertising or in movies viewed around the world on satellite TV or the internet have a powerful effect. This helps to stimulate latent demand for brands and in so doing helps to wear away cultural and political resistance to controls on the movement of labour, goods, services and capital. This creates potential foreign markets for domestic producers. When domestic demand reaches a point of slow growth because of increased competition or saturated local demand, foreign markets offer a means of continued organic growth. In addition, domestic competition drives up labour costs and foreign countries seeking inward investment can offer global brand corporations cheaper labour and production costs, adding momentum to the cycle of globalisation.

SNAPSHOT 8.1

National stereotypes in promotion

In Europe, there are stereotypical beliefs that the best policemen are British, the best chefs French, the best mechanics German, the best lovers Italian and the best organisers the Swiss. As the old joke goes, 'Hell is where the police are German, the chefs are British, the mechanics French, the lovers Swiss and it is all organised by the Italians'. Such stereotypes can be exploited in promotions that humorously draw attention to them while also using them to illustrate a serious point. A long series of advertisements for HSBC and have humorously drawn attention to ways in which cultural differences of non-verbal communication can cause embarrassment, offence or misunderstanding, through misread gestures, body language or behaviour. One ad looks at the Chinese tradition of adults presenting envelopes of money to children on special occasions,[13] while another contrasts American and Japanese work rituals for business meetings.[14] Other campaigns have made humorous use of national stereotypes. One that is especially popular with creatives is the German reputation for being passionate about precision engineering, exploited in a series of ads for *VW* and *BMW* cars. One particularly popular one aired during the American Super Bowl showed engineers growing wings every time a *VW* clocked up 100,000 miles, and generated multiple millions of social media shares and views.[15] In another twist on the theme of national stereotypes, a *Heineken* TV ad makes fun of British tourists who expect Jamaican locals to conform to a steel-drum-playing, reggae-loving stereotype.[16]

The impetus for global marketing may often derive from competitive activity. If brand X is active in a particular foreign market, then brand Y will want to be there too in case it loses ground against the competition by not having a presence in that market. Another factor in the globalisation of markets is the relative ease of technology transfer. National boundaries no longer hinder the transfer of production capability to low-wage economies. The competitive need for international expansion, the ease of access to new consumer markets and low-wage labour markets, and the cross-cultural communication driving an ideology of brand consumption are, taken together, important drivers of the globalisation of corporate activity. So, while global markets are far from homogeneous (see Levitt, 1983) there are considerable opportunities for international brand marketing activity given the relative ease of capital transfer and cross-border transportation, the internationalisation of financial payments, and the latent demand for many brands created by the international reach of, and increasing access to, cable television, movies and the internet.

Problems and pitfalls of internationalisation

Marketing in non-domestic markets presents a number of managerial problems that may be less acute when dealing with domestic markets alone. For example, the marketing and communications infrastructure may differ widely between regions. In advanced economies well-developed road, rail and air transport links, the presence of wholesale distribution facilities and easy access to local retail or other sales outlets facilitate marketing by domestic or non-domestic firms. In less developed economies the absence of a well-established communications and marketing infrastructure may present real challenges. Logistics can be a problem: while densely populated cities may have good communication links, vast numbers of people live in areas with poor communications and few retail outlets. Rates of literacy and access to TV, internet and telephones differ widely from region to region. Factors such as these clearly have major implications for the design of marketing initiatives.

In addition to practical and managerial problems of marketing internationally there is the self-evident difficulty of communication across linguistic, cultural and ethnic boundaries. Advertising and promotion agencies deal in culturally specific linguistic and social practices and this local knowledge is indispensible to coherent and resonant promotional communication. Advertising agency management is subject to much the same kinds of cultural variation as advertising itself. A great many international agencies are organised along similar operational lines with account management, account planning or research, creative and media roles in account teams. There are, nevertheless, differences in management approach that reflect broader cultural differences (Hackley, 2003a; Hackley and Tiwsakul, 2008; West, 1993). For example, the Thai advertising industry has evolved under Western influence (Punyapiroje et al., 2002), it has also developed a distinctive style reflecting the particular cultural mores and traditions of Thailand. Thai agencies tend to have local management, creative and planning functions, within Westernised corporate structures, reflecting the distinctive media infrastructure, demographic and the unique communication culture of Thailand. To plan global campaigns effectively it is necessary to make use of detailed local knowledge of the advertising and consumer cultural environment (Hackley and Hackley, 2013).

A further managerial difficulty of advertising internationally is the fact that codes of advertising practice, media law and consumer marketing regulation can differ greatly from country to country. As noted in Chapter 9, in France, for example, no alcohol advertising is permitted. In Italy, the use of children as models in advertising is restricted, while in some countries such as Greece it is forbidden to advertise children's toys on television before 9pm. In the UK, advertising cigarettes in mass media is forbidden. The differences in international advertising regulation present a further problem for standardisation in international advertising campaigns.

There are many differences in the cultural practices of international business that will influence how advertising and marketing are managed regionally. For example, the difficulty of getting distribution agreements for Western brands in Japanese markets is legendary. This is at least partly because the Asian tradition of building mutually advantageous business relationships carefully over long periods of time (within a culture of Guanxi, in China, and similar relationship-orientation elsewhere in Asia) is difficult for the Western business mentality, which is based on instant rapport, agreements of convenience and instrumental relationships. A further difficulty is that the language and dialect used in neighbouring regions may have nuances that can only be understood by local people, creating highly locally specific trading and communicating conditions within a single national border.

SNAPSHOT 8.2

The international appeal of the BMW MINI

The 2013 'Not Normal'[17] ads[18] for *BMW MINI*, from California agency Butler Shine, Stern & Partners, continued the quirky but cool brand positioning that has proved so successful since the re-launch of *MINI* in 2001. BMW now sells more *MINI*s in the big-car dominated USA, over 60,000 per year, than it does in the UK. BMC (British Motor Corporation), formed from the merger of the UK car brands Austin and Morris, launched the Mini in 1959. The car, then owned by Rover, ceased production in the UK in October 2000 after over 5 million had been manufactured. The revolutionary front-wheel drive design of Sir Alec Issigonis created a car with great appeal, but sales were falling sharply by the late 1950s. BMW bought the brand in 2001 and Frank Stephenson redesigned the car, keeping the sense of fun and style but producing a vehicle that is contemporary in style and performance. The promotions for the new *MINI* brand positioned it as a pan-global small car and exploited its quirkiness. Traditional Mini advertising made much use of TV,[19] but the new *MINI* has largely exploited experiential, content, OOH and digital advertising, and also sponsorship of TV shows, brand placement in movies (especially the re-make of *The Italian Job*), numerous publicity stunts, and extensive PR coverage. The *MINI* has been a resounding commercial and critical success across the world. Its international success reflects a conscious effort on the part of BMW to position the car internationally rather than over-exploiting its British heritage. Many new consumers of the *MINI* are unaware that it is an icon of 1960s Britain. This connotation of the car, while arguably an important part of its appeal, was downplayed in the marketing communications for the new *BMW MINI* in favour of a more powerful global appeal.

Communicating and doing business may be very difficult for foreigners who do not have a deep knowledge of local culture, language and business practices. Systems of business regulation and attitudes to communication can differ widely from culture to culture. For example, what is acceptable in advertising in one country may not be allowed in another. In Muslim countries, for example, the portrayal of females in advertising must adhere to the public standards of dress and conduct expected, while portraying sexuality and nudity in advertising is often regulated more liberally in Scandinavia in Northern Europe than in the USA or the UK. Specific rules about advertising of particular goods can differ as well. For example, in Sweden no TV advertising directed at children under 12 is permitted. Marketing internationally encounters numerous differences in regulation, infrastructure and consumer culture.

To some extent, the advance of digital communication has ameliorated some of these management problems, since communications with a global reach through social media and other digital formats can be managed locally. For example, the *Dove* campaign 'Real Beauty Sketches' (mentioned above) was created by a Brazilian agency and achieved global impact. The management challenges of localisation are perhaps more intense with regard to 'old' media, but are still relevant to non-advertising promotion and digital.

Cross-cultural communication

Advertising is inherently a cultural product. The managerial problems of advertising internationally cannot be reduced simply to a matter of accurate translation of the message, and neither can they be addressed by recourse to crude stereotypes like 'power-distance' (MacSweeney, 2002). Different people interpret advertising communication through quite different systems of value and symbolism that are both cultural, and sub-cultural. Advertising is a curious case in communication because it is at once a universal symbolic language, and a personal appeal. In a general sense, all advertising communicates exactly the same message. It tries to persuade us to buy stuff. Advertising represents a global value system, the value system of capitalism and the consumer lifestyle, from a predominantly Western perspective representing the historical economic dominance of the West. Advertising holds a unique place in contemporary discourse, it permeates global culture (Lash and Lury, 2007), carrying consumer ideology in forms that are framed within local cultural meaning systems. Advertising executions for global brands that cross cultural borders have to achieve a balancing act, so that the sense of the brand is preserved in a persuasive way but articulated through local cultural communication codes.

Global brands' international advertising, then, must achieve two levels of communication. On the one hand, the ad must be instantly recognisable through some commonality of theme that transcends local communication codes. On the other hand, it must also say something in the local idiom, in order to resonate with local consumers. For example, one *McDonald's* advertisement in Thailand used the same 'I'm Lovin' It' slogan used all over the world but the artist recited a rap song in Thai language. In a Japanese TV ad, the iconic clown Ronald McDonald was played by a Caucasian woman.[20] *McDonald's* advertising is localised in many different countries, but it is also always recognisable as *McDonald's* by anyone from any culture, through the use of the colour scheme, the arches, the strapline, the jingle or the clown. The flexibility of brand symbolism offers scope for adjusting the international market positioning. For example, German sportswear brand *Adidas* was better known for its association with soccer and track and field athletics in Europe for many years but moved into rugby with the help of a joint sponsorship deal with national team the All Blacks in rugby-mad New Zealand (see Chapter 8 Case Study).

Exacerbating the problem of cross-cultural communication, people will take different meanings from a promotional communication even if they happen to have the same cultural background. Where cultural backgrounds differ, there is even more scope for consumers to take different meanings from the same advertisement. The elements of cultural background that might influence interpretation include ethnicity, language, locality, religion, family, sub-culture, peer group, education and any other influences that have featured in individuals' environment. Of course, as we have noted in Chapter 2, many advertisements are designed to be relatively 'open' texts that can be interpreted in many different ways. The key issue for advertising in the convergence era is to create a sense of cultural resonance around the brand, perhaps generating enough interest amongst consumers for them to want to share the ad and talk about it on social media. The fact that different consumers will bring different interpretations to an ad is not, then, fatal to a campaign's success. This stands in contrast to the sales-directed logic of AIDA (Attention–Interest–Desire–Action) (described in Chapter 2), but nonetheless reflects a truism about advertising that pre-dates the convergence era: that is, an ad that is talked about is a good ad, regardless of whether it is hard sell or soft sell.

Saying that there is a positive value to open advertising texts, though, should not be misconstrued to imply that attention is everything and meaning is nothing. The kinds of discussion around a piece of promotional content are important and they can be cued through artfully designed creative executions. It is important for advertisers to understand the ways in which meanings are cued in different cultures of communication in order to create constructive conversations around brand stories.

It may seem self-evident to draw attention to differences in cultural and meaning systems and the challenges these present for advertisers. Nevertheless, it is important to understand that all of us can fall into conventional, culturally bound ways of seeing the world which can impede our understanding of otherness. In our everyday communication we constantly interpret visual and linguistic signs whose meanings, as we easily forget, are highly specific to our own idiom, culture and sub-culture. International advertising offers examples of cultural differences in communication that can consistently surprise because local cultures of communication are so easy to stereotype or to take for granted.

SNAPSHOT 8.3

Mattel finds Barbie doesn't translate in the Chinese market

One of the most famous toys in America, the iconic *Barbie* doll, failed to gain purchase in the Chinese market in spite of a huge investment. In 2011, Mattel closed its $30 million 'House of Barbie' (Wang, 2012)[21] flagship store in Shanghai, China, just two years after it had opened. The store was spread across six floors and featured a fashion runway, Barbie bar and design studio. It held the world's largest collection of 875 *Barbie* dolls, displayed on a spiral staircase.[22] China is often considered as a challenging market by many toy companies because of the education-focused Chinese culture. Chinese parents see toys as a waste of time. 'Tiger moms' in China would rather have their daughters reading books than accessorising *Barbie* dolls. Peter Broegger, Mattel's Asia Pacific Senior Vice President, in an interview with the *Wall Street Journal* was quoted saying 'Joy and learning are like oil and water in China'. Learning and education are serious business for Chinese parents, and not to be confused with toys and play.

Mattel tried to localise its products and advertising strategy. For example, Mattel's *Fisher Price* toys are labelled 'Play IQ', rather than 'Joy of Learning', as they are advertised in Western markets (Burkitt, 2013)[23]. The company changed its emphasis on fashion and lifestyle to incorporating learning as a part of Barbie's life. Mattel launched a *Violin Soloist Barbie* to appeal to the Chinese culture of learning and persuaded the Chinese government to encourage more play time in school by asking China's Ministry of Education and Ministry of Culture to present research on the educational and developmental benefits of play (Miller, 2013)[24]. However, the Barbie store seemed ill-fated since it was built without a real attempt to popularise the *Barbie* concept in China. It may also have been hindered by the lack of an ethnic range of dolls. *Barbie* is strongly associated with an American ideal of female beauty and glamour, and rivals such as *American Girl* (Diamond et al., 2009) play up the association with national identity, while also adapting more ethnic variations into the dolls. The *Barbie* concept may be just too American, and perhaps too dated, to translate into Chinese markets.

Non-verbal communication

The use of national stereotypes in advertising is common (see Snapshot 8.1) often as a lazy source of humour to ingratiate the brand with those for whom the stereotype resonates. It is deeply misleading to overstate the notion of national characteristics (see McSweeney, 2002) but, nonetheless, there are cultural conventions of communication that are of great importance in advertising development. As a useful exemplar of the quirkiness of communication practices it may be instructive to look briefly at a few aspects of non-verbal communication. It is axiomatic that 95% of face-to-face communication is non-verbalised or implicit in gesture, tone, intonation, 'body language' and facial expression. This is also true of advertising, as Chapter 2 notes. There are implicit, non-verbal aspects of communication encoded into visual advertising that provide important context for the decoding of meaning. Non-verbal communication is an integral feature of many visual promotions, and this element of communication can be highly sensitive. This is not just an issue for consumer interpretation of advertising. Advances in technology are resulting in outdoor advertising that can recognise and respond to face and gesture, as in examples in Tokyo and also Sydney, Australia.[25] Street billboards can be constructed to recognise whether the person approaching is a male or female, and a tailored message is provided. Other street displays react to the gestures of the viewer.

As Cook (2001) points out, communication always has a context that informs the meaning of a message. Viewing ads in the company of people from countries and cultures other than one's own can be a salutary reminder of this truism. A university class of international students asked to explain a particular ad will usually illustrate this vividly with widely diverging interpretations. They are all viewing the ad from a different cultural frame of reference. Advertising is a social text, as we have seen, that has to be learned, and there is much local cultural knowledge that is necessary in order to interpret an ad plausibly. Advertisers therefore need to be especially sensitive to the uses of gestures in a TV commercial script or press ad, in case meanings are construed that are not consistent with the brand values. The international marketing world is awash with stories of brand names, packaging designs or ads that failed because they were interpreted to mean something inappropriate or outrageous in some regions. This generally happens because the brand planners did not think outside their own cultural frame of reference. This is a communications lesson that even domestic advertisers and marketers must learn. It is a fundamental precept of brand planning that the cultural beliefs and practices of the target consumers should be thoroughly understood by creative teams and brand planners. If this level of understanding is achieved, it may be possible to design communications that resonate with meaning for the intended target audience.

Standardisation or localisation of advertising and promotion?

An important question facing brand organisations is to what degree they ought to try to standardise their advertising throughout the world. We have already seen that the meaning of advertising narratives is often unstable and open to a variety of interpretations, even within relatively homogeneous consumer communities. How much more difficult must it be to maintain brand coherence through communications that cross international boundaries? As we have noted, the rise of digital communication technology, liberalisation of regulation in many media, financial and product markets and increase in foreign travel for the rising middle classes have created a ready audience for global brands. As brand organisations compete to exploit this tendency by internationalising their brands they face the decision of how best to do this in a way that maximises effectiveness and minimises costs.

The management problem of whether to standardise or localise arose partly because the issue was initially represented as a dichotomy in the 1980s as world markets began to open up. A famous article in the *Harvard Business Review* (Levitt, 1983) expressed this oversimplification on the basis that heterogeneous cultures around the globe appeared to be converging in attitudes, aspirations and consumer lifestyles, tastes and beliefs. The logic of the argument was simple. If you can see *Nike* trainers and *McDonald's* hamburger joints in practically every capital city in the world then is this not evidence that consumers the world over are essentially the same in their needs and wants? Or, as an alternative interpretation, could it be that global consumer wants were converging under the umbrella of Western style consumerism?

The suggestion that the aspirations and values of differing cultures have united under the ethos of consumerism seems far-fetched more than thirty years after Levitt wrote his article. The values of economic neo-liberalism have swept across the world in some respects (Hackley, 2009b) but there remain powerful and often strident voices articulating alternative visions of capitalism, along with anti-capitalist ideologies since the 2008 financial collapse of the Western banking system. Consumption has become a prime site of contested ideologies around environmentalism and sustainability, consumer rights, gender and economic inequality. For many commentators, economic globalisation is predicated on a need for relentless consumption-driven economic growth that is unsustainable environmentally and socially.

At the very least, we can say that the standardisation thesis understated the robustness and uniqueness of local cultural values and the heterogeneity of global consumers, not to mention the tensions inherent in global capitalism. It remains true that most major global brands are Western in origin, but it is also true that the most successful have mastered a pan-global marketing orientation that assimilates international cultural communication codes, while increasing numbers of non-Western brands are becoming influential in the West (Loo and Hackley, 2013, and see Snapshot 8.4).

In sum, when discussing international advertising campaign planning, it is important to specify just what might converge in differing cultures and what cannot. Indeed, the notion of converging cultures makes little sense since cultures are defined by enduring and powerful differences. In important regards, what is of a particular culture can only be understood in terms of its difference from other cultures. But in the smaller world of advertising it is still worth posing the question to what extent is standardisation feasible because of the evident commonalities between cultures that make global consumer brands possible. One might also view this from a critical perspective in terms of the power of marketing to transcend, or perhaps to suppress, cultural difference. This latter viewpoint is the one that most attracts anti-brand and anti-marketing voices which argue that marketing in particular and economic neo-liberalism in general tend to obliterate local culture. Yet, consumption appears to be a site in which both globalisation and diversity seem represented. Indeed, the allure of cultural difference, the mystique of other-ness, seems to be part of the dynamic that gives domestic brands appeal for global consumers.

The business case for standardisation of international advertising

One of the reasons why the arguments for standardisation of international marketing gained credence among the academic and consulting circles of management was the force of the business case. The appeal of standardised international marketing lies in economy and control. As regards cost, it is expensive for a brand organisation to appoint a local advertising agency to create bespoke campaigns for the same brand in each country. Production and media costs increase with the number of different national campaigns that are needed. Creating just one ad to show all over the world, co-ordinated by one advertising and one global media agency, means saving a lot of expense in production and advertising development costs.

Cost minimisation is one issue, control over the way the brand is represented is another. Control results from keeping creative executions under central command rather than having to co-ordinate the work of local agencies, so that brand values and the brand personality are portrayed in exactly the desired way in every region. International brand organisations take a great deal of time and trouble to develop the ideas of their brand's values and personality, and to plan how these values might be portrayed in advertising and promotion. Giving control of advertising away to an agency in another country is seen as a risk for major brand organisations. Local agencies will invariably employ a culturally specific interpretation of the brand values, which may not necessarily be the interpretation that the brand organisation conceived of in its strategic planning. The risk of diluting the brand identity and/or confusing consumers is seen as a major one to be guarded against for fear of damaging long-term brand equity.

In practice, the question of whether to standardise or localise advertising and promotion is not a straight choice between alternatives but a question of nuance. Most international organisations reach an accommodation between the need for localised communications strategies driven by culture-specific knowledge, and a need for control over costs and creative executions.

'Glocalisation' in international advertising

Most international brand marketing organisations have found that neither localisation nor global standardisation entirely serves their purpose. What they require instead is a policy that reconciles the need for consistency of presentation of the brand in all communications across the world on the one hand, and the need for advertising to resonate with culturally specific consumer groups on the other. To achieve the specificity required, the brand values and personality have to be portrayed in terms of local language, priorities and practices. The broader marketing mix activities, in addition to the advertising, have to reflect local realities and practices.

The term 'glocalisation' refers to the local adaptation of globally oriented marketing. Global brand marketing organisations often seek to impose control over the presentation of their brand at a certain level, allowing local marketing agencies some licence to portray the brand in ways that will cohere with local cultural meaning systems. So, for example, the brand logo and colour scheme might be mandatory inclusions specified in the creative brief, as appears to be the case in *McDonald's* advertising, mentioned above, and perhaps the strapline, jingle and music, even if the creative execution in other respects is generated by the agency to fit with local consumer interpretive frames. There are many ways this could be done. As we have seen, in some *McDonald's* print ads in China, the context of the imagery is distinctively Chinese, with Chinese customers in a restaurant or a Chinese sports star pictured, while the image of a burger and the arches is universal.

A glocalisation policy in international advertising is often pragmatically the best course. Local agencies can place the brand in an appropriate localised context while preserving key aspects of a global brand personality. The flexibility of this approach in advertising reflects the extent to which brand symbolism can be semiotically extended. Consider the economy of brand signs such as the *Nike* 'Swoosh', *McDonald's* arches, *Apple's* forbidden fruit logo, and logos for *Google, BMW, Adidas, Pepsi, Coca-Cola, Virgin, Polo, Shell*[27] and many more (see Colour Section, photos 1, 4, 10 and 12). These signs offer instant recognition, but are also relatively open texts in the sense that readers can associate them with a flexible range of stories and meanings. The brands can take on and exploit those stories they wish to, while rejecting those that they don't. Many advertising texts develop a story element and only acknowledge the brand with a logo placed in a discreet location in the visual image. This says both less and more, in the sense that rhetorical understatement can signify confidence that the brand and its values will be widely recognised without the need for overelaboration. A powerful logo facilitates brand storytelling over a wide range of media formats.

Standardising international advertising

A relatively small number of brands have been able to standardise advertising cross-culturally if their ad agency can find a common denominator of meaning that transcends cultures. They have to exploit this common meaning by devising ingenious creative executions, but no communications solution is effective indefinitely and brands must remain connected to the ebb and flow of consumer cultures if they are to retain vitality and relevance in the marketplace.

One can argue that many globally recognised brands represent something that does not cross cultures at all, but, rather, transcends culture in some way. Iconic brands (see Holt, 2002) can be understood in this way. For example *Coca-Cola, Mercedes–Benz* and *BMW* all proudly represent their national origins but also succeed in spanning the globe in spite of their distinctive national history (but see Snapshot 8.5).

SNAPSHOT 8.5

Advertising and national identity

The *Coca-Cola* brand has long been associated with its origin in the USA. It represents something distinctively American and its cultural resonance has been exploited in 125 years of *Coca-Cola* advertising campaigns.[28] During the Second World War the brand realised that American servicemen stationed abroad were pining for *Coke* because it reminded them of home, and they also gave it away to win the hearts and minds of local people. Free consignments of *Coca-Cola* were sent out to military service personnel overseas to exploit this cultural resonance. According to Holt and Cameron (2010), this may be one reason why *Coca-Cola* is an iconic brand and *Pepsi* is not. For *Coca-Cola*, advertising campaigns such as the legendary 1970s ad 'I'd Like to Buy the World a *Coke*'[29] have helped maintain the brand's iconic status, showing the brand as a symbol of America and also as a worldwide symbol of friendship. However, while iconic brands can help to resolve ideological dilemmas (Holt, 2002) such as the tension around nationhood and identity, they can also expose those tensions. A *Coke* ad aired during the American Super Bowl in 2014[30] celebrated America's multi-ethnic population and showed people of many ethnicities singing 'America the Beautiful' in different languages. The ad caused a storm on social media, with many supporters lauding its multicultural theme, but many others claiming that it did not reflect their idea of a predominantly white, English-speaking America.

Many global brands are American in origin because the USA has been the world's foremost economic power during the era of branding. Of the world's top ten brands by value noted in Chapter 3, only two are not American – *Toyota* and *Samsung*.[31] This is because of 'soft' cultural influence as well as because of manufacturing, marketing and innovation. The worldwide popularity of Hollywood movies and TV shows has popularised American culture, making its brands commonplace anywhere American movies can be seen. In the Western economic boom of the 1950s, US products gained a reputation for representing luxury, affluence and high-quality production standards. American provenance is no longer a guarantee of prestige, and economic times have changed, Asian economies are advancing at speed and Asian brands are slowly gaining a global foothold beyond their strong bases in car manufacturing, electronics and fashion (Loo and Hackley, 2013).

Cultural tensions around global brand advertising

Foreignness can be a marketing virtue. Country-of-origin effects can bestow a halo of prestige on brands emanating from particular countries. For example, German motorcar design and engineering, Japanese electronics, Swiss watches,

Russian vodka, French food and wine, Italian fashion, Colombian coffee, Indian tea, Belgian beer and holidays in Thailand are all thought to have special qualities. In many Asian consumer markets brands with a European connotation are often thought to have special glamour or prestige, while Asian brands of beer and fashion are making inroads alongside the traditional strengths of Asian brands in manufacturing and electronics.

It is very human to feel desire for the unattainable or the unfamiliar, the allure of the 'other'. No doubt there is something of human nature in the country-of-origin effect.

National or regional reputations, myths and symbols that resonate with consumer aspirations are powerful drivers of consumption. This can be a strong lever for advertising and marketing internationally. And, as we have seen, there can be an adverse effect for brand marketing corporations if they happen to be closely associated with a country that acquires negative press coverage and receives international disapproval for whatever reason.

Not everyone welcomes the globalisation of brands. In many countries, there is a sense that brands from other countries represent an ideological challenge to traditional values and lifestyles. In many South-East Asian countries, for example, Western brands are loved by younger generations, but older generations regard extravagant consumption with suspicion. When *Walt Disney* wanted to set up *Paris Disneyland*, and *McDonald's* were planning to set up in France, there were popular movements and protests against the imposition of American brands on French culture. The *McDonald's* ethos of fast and simple food is anathema to French cuisine, but the restaurants remain popular in France as elsewhere. *McDonald's* has also attracted criticism for the effect of its supply chain practices on agriculture. In the USA, the brand has created a supply chain establishment that has apparently changed the structure and culture of the farming and cattle processing industries (Schlosser, 2002). French farmers have been worried that the same thing might happen in France. The protests against the *Walt Disney* theme parks seemed to be more focused on the resistance to the imposition of American popular culture in the land of *Asterix the Gaul*.

SNAPSHOT 8.6

De Beers Gem Diamonds' standardised campaign

One interesting example of a creatively standardised campaign was that of *De Beers Gem Diamonds*. De Beers is a South African diamond producing and cutting organisation. In 1996, in response to competition from West African diamonds and new technology that enabled a

(Continued)

brand logo to be stamped on a diamond, De Beers commissioned JWT to create a campaign that would make *De Beers* known as a prestige diamond brand in a largely unbranded gem market. JWT's consumer research found that one common factor linked the meaning of diamonds across all cultures – diamonds meant love.[32] This theme was adapted into the differing diamond-giving practices in different countries in creative executions designed to resonate with local consumers.[33] The giving of diamonds to convey love was celebrated in national contexts of Continental Europe, the Middle East and the UK. The campaign, filmed in black and white and called 'Shadows', used a (then) new cinematic technique that enabled diamonds to stand out on a TV screen. The ads were made in the same studio and same style, and the script and music were adapted to reflect different diamond-giving ritual in regional variations. For example, the UK version featured a large stone on a wedding ring, a Spanish version featured an anniversary ring and a Middle Eastern version featured extravagant diamond necklaces and tiaras. Significant sales increases were reported and the campaign was reputed to have helped change the cultural meaning of diamonds by encouraging their use in cultures not traditionally predisposed to diamond-giving. In Japan, for example, it was said that there was no word for diamond before the 1960s but the term 'diamondo' became widely understood after the *De Beers* campaign.

Global brands can also hold a powerful sense of liberation for citizens who want access to the brands of the world. For example, for much of the twentieth century it was unthinkable that an American brand would have a state-approved presence in Russia, but in 1990 what was then the world's biggest *McDonald's* restaurant opened on Pushkinsklaya Square in Moscow. Customers queued for 6 hours to taste the first American fast food served in Russia.[34] As Russia has opened up to the world in the post-Soviet era its taste for Western brands is reflected in a demand for luxury marques like German, Swedish, Italian and Japanese cars, French fragrances and fashion, and Swiss watches.[35] Brand globalisation has seeped across borders in spite of the animosities, alliances and human tragedies of the Second World War less than half a century before *McDonald's* opened in Moscow. As Snapshot 8.5 shows, national identity can be a powerful force in branding, and the *Coca-Cola* ad that caused such a media storm for its alleged 'un-American' style illustrated the sensitivities than can sometimes obtain around brands and nations. However, in many cases, it seems that brands have more power to unite than national flags.

The resistance to what is sometimes seen as the cultural imperialism of brands is not always in an Eastern–Western direction. In the 1970s electronics industries from Japan and Taiwan began to undercut indigenous British and European electronics brands, whilst in the 1980s Asian car brands began to appear in the giant US car market. In both cases there was some resentment and some anti-brand activism, although that soon faded away as consumers solved the ideological problem by choosing the best, and the best value, products. Now, there seems to be no resistance at all to Asian brands in the West – indeed, an Asian provenance is regarded as a major positive for brands in many sectors, including food, electronics, beers and cars. Some brands make a virtue of their national origin – for example, American clothes brand *American Apparel* trumpet the fact that their clothes are made in Los Angeles, California, rather than being made in low labour cost countries like Bangladesh and India. Their 2014 ad called 'Made In Bangladesh'[36] featured a Bangladesh-born employee posing topless in a sideswipe at other clothes companies that outsource their manufacturing.

Global supply chains make brands vulnerable to bad press. Brands including *Apple* and *Nike* have received criticism because of the labour practices in low wage countries where they manufacture their goods, while budget clothing brand *Primark* was heavily criticised when a Bangladesh factory where its clothes were made collapsed in 2013, killing more than 1,100 low paid workers.[37] Western brands can make huge profits by manufacturing in Asia. Since the 1980s, many European jobs have effectively been exported to Asia because of the lack of strong unionisation, low labour costs and high skill levels. Ethically, this presents a dilemma. On the one hand, when a global brand comes to Asia bringing thousands of manufacturing jobs, local wages and conditions will improve. On the other, the gap between local pay and conditions and those that obtain in the West is stark. Even global brands that have the will to do so find it difficult to police labour practices and quality control down the supply chain. Resistance to globalisation often rests on issues such as discriminatory or unfair labour practices, and the unsustainable use of raw materials and environmental damage. In a social media age, negative coverage can quickly gain purchase and credence.

From the brands' point of view, global brands make excellent copy for media editors, and hostile stories make even better copy. It is right that global brand corporations should be subject to close scrutiny regarding their social and environmental responsibility. But there can be little doubt that global brands sometimes become symbolic weapons in media circulation and political contests. The activities and consequences of global brand corporations operating in local cultures is an important area of debate and investigation. It is the global profile itself that makes the corporation both more powerful and more vulnerable to criticism. Our concern here is not with the wider issue of the corporate social responsibility (CSR) and ethics of big corporations. Nevertheless, the general values of the organisation will influence the perceived values of their brands. Global brand corporations have certain resources and media, especially advertising, under their direct control. They have influence rather than control over others, through PR. Global corporations are acutely aware of the importance of public perception. Consumer movements that turn attention away from consumption of the brand and towards the activities of the producer can be powerful influences on corporate behaviour. Given the sensitivities over the activities of (mainly Western) brand corporations, communications assume great importance in managing or responding to consumer and activist attitudes and expectations.

Advertising management in non-domestic economies

Management of advertising in non-domestic economies presents many challenges then, including the establishment and management of staff, the design of creative executions and media strategy. But it is an effort worth making. Liberalisation of currency controls and capital transfer, increases on global travel, rising middle classes, growth in disposable income and the rise of digital and cable technology have made the world, for brands at least, into a kind of global village (McLuhan, 1964) in which our senses have become extended through electronic media so that we can experience far-away events and objects as if they are at hand. The internet, above all, has made brands accessible internationally and sparked global demand. Even where an economy is developing, this does not mean that there are not large and sophisticated consumer markets in the urban centres. Indeed, the rising middle classes of the high growth economies in South and South-East Asia and South America are providing the fastest growth areas for many global brands.

South and South-East Asian markets for advertising

Asian 'Tiger' economies such as China, South Korea, Taiwan, Thailand, Japan, along with Indonesia, Malaysia and South Asian nations such as India and Pakistan and Bangladesh, all represent important advertising and consumer growth markets for certain brands. Many of the world's most valuable 100 luxury brands[38] are seeing record growth driven by sales in Asian markets (Chada and Husband, 2006). *Louis Vuitton* tops the list of global luxury brands (see Table 8.1), worth $27 billion. But growth is not only in luxury brands. In China, for example, the top five foreign brands are *KFC*, *Pampers*, *Colgate*, *Olay* and *Crest*[39]. According to a report by *Kantar Media*, the Chinese market for Western brands is complex and difficult but holds huge potential. Western brands need a deep knowledge of consumers in different regions of Chinese markets to succeed. The practical difficulties and cultural sensitivities, though, cannot be overlooked. In developing countries, the cultural juxtaposition of Western-influenced consumer advertising and local cultural and economic norms can seem particularly discordant. This demands sensitive handling and detailed local engagement.

Table 8.1   Top global luxury brands, 2013

1. Louis Vuitton
2. Hermès
3. Gucci
4. Prada
5. Rolex
6. Chanel
7. Cartier
8. Burberry
9. Fendi
10. Coach

Source: www.uk.kantar.com/business/brands/brandz-top-10-most-valuable-global-luxury-brands-2013/ accessed 19.3.2014

In Malaysia, for example, the advertising market is reflecting global trends in that traditional media still represent the largest part of adspend but the digital advertising sector is growing.[40] Advertising standards in Malaysia are very high with advanced production and creativity, as shown in the showcase of the AAAA.[41] In Malaysia, many magazine ads seem to locate Western consumer values in an Islamic cultural context. Malaysia is a culturally complex country, with three main ethnic groups, Indian, Chinese and Malay. Each has a separate language and many differing traditions, but there is also a great deal of commonality. There are also groups of Thais, Filipinos, Taiwanese and Indonesians. Advertising in such a context has to be distinctively Asian and must conform to local sensitivities. There has been some resentment in Malaysia when global brands use advertising produced for Western markets but dubbed into local language. This is always clearly evident and a lazy way for international brands to advertise overseas, but it usually results in mockery. Approval for ads is often given directly by government officials. There are detailed codes of practice for the advertising of different products and services.

SNAPSHOT 8.7

Muslim values in Western-style advertising in Malaysia

A Bahasa fashion magazine has many examples of 'glocal' advertising portraying Western products with Western values but in a creative execution that is adapted to be acceptable to Muslim readers. One product, Johnson's *pH5.5* cooling body wash, is intended for use in the shower. However, it would not be allowed to show a photograph of a female in the shower, so the ad shows a woman with naked shoulders in a sensuous pose while a graphic, water-like abstract design fills the background. The model's hair is fixed in place so that she might even be wearing

(Continued)

(Continued)

a headscarf. The ad's suggestion of a female in the shower is clear, but the advertisers can claim that it does not show a naked female. Other Malaysian print ads portray females in a way that offers a compromise between the traditional values of home-making and husband-nurturing and the less traditional values of female independence. One ad for a 'Pewani' savings account offered by Bank Islam (in a daily newspaper) promotes a savings account for women with the strapline 'Nurturing success for today's women'. The visual shows a woman in a traditional head-scarf with her husband and children and promotes the idea of the account as a gift to her family. Presumably, the ad has become necessary because more Muslim women in Malaysia are going out to earn money independently from their husbands.

The art of adhering to advertising codes and regulations literally while going beyond them is symbolically a mark of advertising under advanced capitalism. Ads such as the Johnson's ad described above illustrate the ideological force of advertising, which promotes the values of consumption while subtly negotiating, or circumventing, other cultural values. Clearly, capitalism and the ideology of consumption tend to exist in a state of tension with religious and traditional values in Western countries as well as Eastern ones. Advertising persists in spite of this tension partly because it is seen as trivial and benign. It is also the case that the imperative for wealth creation means that advertising is usually seen as a lesser evil than poverty.

Thailand, for example, is a developing country with concentrations of urban wealth contrasting with much rural poverty. Unilever's *Dove* brand of personal care products, sells small sachets of its products to rural consumers who cannot afford the full pack sizes, reflecting the need for Western brands to adapt to the uneven distribution of wealth in Asian markets. In urban areas, though, the Thai economy, consumer culture and media infrastructure are sophisticated, with a highly international outlook. Thailand is a country with a long tradition of valuing Western products as a symbol of social status (Tirakhunkovit, 1980) but Western-style commercialism is not pursued at the expense of Thai cultural values. Some ads are distinctively Thai, such as one for *Sylvania* light bulbs that plays humorously on the Thai belief in ghosts and spirits.[42] Many others, though, reflect the cosmopolitanism of Thai consumer culture. An ad for Japanese snack food *Bun Bun* carries Thai-language subtitles, while a Japanese green tea brand runs a charming TVC in Thai.[43] Other brands such as *Lays* seaweed-flavour crisps, *Pote* snack food and *Giffarine* facial cream (a local brand) combine Japanese and Thai influences in their advertising. Thais are also very interested in international brands such as *L'Oréal*, *McDonald's* (the 'I'm Lovin' It' jingle is sung in Thai) and *Scott* toilet tissue (showing the same ad as in the UK). *Sony*, *Samsung* and *Orange* all create Thai advertising executions. Chinese culture influences Thai TV ads for *Choice* soup mix, *Mistine* powder for oily skin and *Pond*'s facial foam. The leading Thai brand of cooling powder, *St Luke's Prickly Heat*, was established by a British entrepreneur.

Thai advertising has been known for being racially insensitive, although this is gradually dying out and occasional controversies, for example in 2013 over a *Dunkin' Donuts* ad that featured a white woman in black make-up,[44] are regarded as lapses. In contrast, a great deal of Thai advertising is very heart-warming, and one 2013 ad called 'Giving Is the Best Communication'[45] for *True Move* mobile was shared many times on social media by viewers who loved its sentiment.

Managing a communications campaign in Thailand demands detailed under-standing of the local media infrastructure (Hackley and Hackley, 2013). The Thai advertising industry is a mixture of locally owned agencies and branches of global communications conglomerates such as Saatchi & Saatchi, JWT, Publicis, Dentsu and many others (Tiwsakul, 2008). It has a significant adspend (Punyapiroje et al., 2002) and production standards are as high as in any devel-oped country, as are standards of creativity.[46] Advertising content tends to be soft-sell and replete with scenes of humour, fun, sensuousness and love,[47] reflecting the easy-going and creative character of Thai consumers (Supharp, 1993). Typical advertising is often very visual, reflecting low literacy rates among the rural population and indicating the subtleties of tone, image and gesture in visual communication to which Asian consumers are attuned. Thai consumers love freedom and novelty and this is reflected in brand-switching behaviour (Sherer, 1995).

(Continued)

15–19 as an influential style-leading group. In the ad, a young man enters a laundrette, takes his clothes off down to his boxer shorts and washes them in a machine, then puts them back on. The astonished reactions of the other customers are nicely contrasted by his laconic style.

The stunning success of the 'American hero' style of *Levi's* ads lasted for a decade until the allure of American provenance faded. The jeans market as a whole eventually lost sales and fragmented into niches, each with a somewhat younger profile and different style values. The *Levi's 501* campaign was right for its time and its values seemed to transcend the cultural particularities of the countries in which it was shown. But by the early 1990s the cultural meaning of denim jeans had changed. For young people who had never heard of Brando and Dean and never saw movies like *Rebel Without a Cause* the American hero ad style meant nothing. Jeans simply meant comfort and informality. They no longer represented rebellion or any distinctively adolescent virtue: how could they when your Dad was wearing them?

Japan is a very different economic, religious and ethnic proposition for brand advertising from Malaysia or Thailand. It has a technologically and aesthetically sophisticated consumer culture and high if quirky[49] creative standards in advertising.[50]

Advanced as Japan is in terms of economic development and consumer culture, advertisers still have to use symbolism to suggest meanings that they hope will prove persuasive to consumers. Indeed, symbolism, particularly erotic symbolism in advertising, seems to be a mark of the state of development of the consumer markets it serves and reflects.

In one pair of examples (in Tanaka, 1994: 46–51) two ads for a miniature TV set were shown, each of which appeared in the risqué publication *Fookasu* in 1985. In one, the TV set was pictured in a scene with two girls and a man in a sensuous setting. The innuendo is supported by the advertising copy which claims that the satisfaction of curiosity is the key to mankind's development. It goes on 'Can't do this, can't do that … there are many things forbidden in this world. What's the point of living unless we can at least watch what we want to when we want to …' The other ad shows the TV in a scene with two girls embracing over a piano. Sexuality is generally not a subject of public discourse in Asian countries. The magazine or ad agency could easily deflect accusations that they were promoting either in a literal sense. But, as we saw in Chapter 2, much of the power of advertising lies in its ability to suggest meanings that are not accessible unless read by the audience, thus imputing the meaning to audience interpretation rather than to the artifice of the advertiser. The ads were in tune with the risqué editorial tone of the publication in which they appeared. They allowed a mundane item to be portrayed in a way that made it seem, perhaps, far more interesting to some readers.

While these ads are not typical of Japanese advertising as a whole,[51] they do illustrate how advertising can be devised that undermines, or at least evades, local cultural taboos and norms. Consumption can therefore be made to appear an act of symbolic self-realisation that reinforces individual identity because it (symbolically) transgresses social conventions. This individualistic dimension of consumption is often taken for granted in the West, but in the more collective social culture of the East such implicit individualism may promote and also reflect far-reaching cultural change.

Chapter summary

This chapter has reviewed issues of international advertising, focusing mainly on the managerial perspective. The discussion revolved around the dichotomy of standardised versus localised advertising, taking in issues such as differing local advertising regulations and codes of marketing practice, differences in language and culture, and resistance and protest towards brand 'imperialism'. Another issue touched upon was the cultural role of advertising as a carrier of (Western) consumer ideology, and the tensions this can create where it conflicts with traditional values in particular countries. The chapter concluded with some comments about advertising management in South-East Asia.

■ Review Questions

1. In groups, decide upon a local brand that you feel has potential to be marketed internationally. Decide on the core brand values that may be communicated. Devise an outline advertising strategy with creative themes using integrated media channels. How will you ensure that the brand values are interpreted appropriately? What are the major difficulties of promoting this brand internationally?

2. Choose six print or TV advertisements that promote internationally marketed brands. Discuss the need for globally marketed brands to accommodate cultural differences in their advertising. Use specific examples of cultural differences of behaviour, attitude or social practice to inform your discussion.

3. Try to find examples of advertisements for the same brand in different countries. Compare and contrast the respective ads and try to work out the possible differences in local segmentation and positioning and communication issues.

4. What is glocalisation? In what ways is the concept relevant to advertising internationally? Offer examples to illustrate your points.

5. Try to think of potential international co-branding opportunities. To explore the coherence of the respective brands, you will need to list all the possible connotations of each brand and discuss their various merits both singly and in conjunction with the co-brand. What opportunities do you think might arise from such co-branding initiatives?

CASE STUDY

Adidas develops co-branding promotion with the All Blacks

The German sportswear manufacturer *Adidas* has been well known in Europe for its sports footwear products for many years, and has a long presence in track and field athletics, boxing and football. More recently it has added rugby, general fitness and street style, along with sports accessories and training gear.[52] Erich Stammer, *Adidas* President and CEO, says that *Adidas*'s strategy has moved into 'content' in the sense that they seek to provide everything a sportsperson might need for training and performance. Sponsorship of leading athletes and teams has been part of their strategy since Adidas founder, Bavarian shoemaker Adolf 'Adi' Dassler, supplied track and field athletes with footwear from the 'Dassler Brothers' for the 1928 Olympics. In 1932 Adi Dassler persuaded sprint star Jesse Owens to wear his running shoes in the Berlin Olympics in what is thought to be the first sponsorship of a black athlete. The 1932 Berlin Olympics is regarded as a PR disaster for the Nazi Party because Owens, a black American, won four gold medals, making Adolf Hitler's ideology of Aryan supremacy look absurd. The Dassler Brothers joined the Nazi party a year later and their factory supplied footwear and other equipment to the Wehrmacht.[53] After the war, Adi re-named the company *Adidas* and his older brother, Rudolph, left to found rival sportswear brand *Puma*. In 1949 the distinctive three stripes were added to *Adidas* shoes to strengthen them, and this was adopted as the official logo in 1996.[54] Today, the *Adidas* sponsorship roster includes a long-standing partnership with Lionel Messi in a series of ads in which Messi performs his football magic using *Adidas* kit, as in the 2013 'Speed of Light' ad[55] and the 2014 'Road to the Fifa World Cup' ad.[56] The *Messi* branding is as prominent as the *Adidas* branding in these films.

The partnership that pushed *Adidas* into the New Zealand rugby market is perhaps their most counter-intuitive. In 1999 Adidas won a contract to supply kit to the famous New Zealand All Blacks rugby team. In 2008 they extended the sponsorship deal until 2019.[57] This was always more than a promotional agreement; it was a cross-national, co-branding initiative. The New Zealand Rugby Football Union (NZRFU) is as interested in globalising the *All Blacks* brand as *Adidas* is in globalising the *Adidas* brand.[58] The association of a German sportswear brand and the New Zealand rugby team might seem incongruous on the face of it, and it initially it met with resistance from the New Zealand media. New Zealand people are passionate about the All Blacks and the team represents the national identity in an emotionally powerful way. Many people felt that a local sponsorship deal would have been more appropriate. The incongruence of the respective national cultures (rugby has few followers and little tradition in Germany) seemed overridden in this case by the linked connotations of the respective brands. Saatchi & Saatchi developed creative executions for advertising that played on the reverence New Zealanders feel for All Black players and reflected the proud winning tradition of the team with TVCs like 'Haka'[59] in 1999 and a 2014 clip called 'Alive With Pride'.[60] *Adidas* has continued to expand its markets globally using an innovative promotional mix and in 2011 was voted the top German brand in social media with more than 17 million internet fans and subscribers across the world, engaged in conversation with 25 full-time *Adids* social media employees.[61]

1. Using internet sources, describe how *Adidas*'s advertising strategy has evolved to fit with and support its expansion of its product lines and movement into new geographical and sporting markets.

2. In what ways do sporting goods brands leverage their sponsorship deals through advertising and promotion?

3. Rugby is a minor sport in Germany, the game is a national obsession in New Zealand. The Second World War saw the two countries on opposing sides. How do co-branding deals such as the *All Blacks* and *Adidas* counter cultural incompatibility? Does the success of this partnership say something about the power of brands (and brand stories) to resolve, or perhaps to obliterate, ideological dilemmas?

Useful journal articles

(These Sage articles can be accessed on the book website)

Brook E. Harmon, Christine E. Blake, James F. Thrasher and James R. Hébert (2014) 'An evaluation of diet and physical activity messaging in African American churches', *Health Education & Behavior*, 41 (2): 216–24.

Peter Shields (2014) 'Borders as information flows and transnational networks', *Global Media and Communication*, 10 (1): 3–33.

Ping Shaw and Yue Tan (2014) 'Race and masculinity: a comparison of Asian and Western models in men's lifestyle magazine advertisements', *Journalism & Mass Communication Quarterly*, 91 (1): 118–38.

Kieran Cody and Steve Jackson (2014) 'The contested terrain of alcohol sponsorship of sport in New Zealand', *International Review for the Sociology of Sport*, doi: 1012690214526399 (first published March 19, 2014).

Jillana B. Enteen (2014) 'Transitioning online: cosmetic surgery tourism in Thailand', *Television & New Media*, 15 (3): 238–49 (first published November 14, 2013).

Min Jiang (2014) 'The business and politics of search engines: a comparative study of Baidu and Google's search results of Internet events in China', *New Media & Society*, 16 (2): 212–33 (first published April 22, 2013).

■ ■ Further reading ■

Banister, L. (1997) 'Global brands, local contexts', *Admap*, October: 28–30.

De Mooij, M. (2013) *Global Marketing and Advertising: Understanding Cultural Paradoxes*, 4th edn. London: Sage.

De Pelsmacker, P., Geuens, M. and Van den Bergh, J. (2010) *Marketing Communications: A European Perspective*, 4th edn. London: Financial Times/ Prentice-Hall.

Hsu Jia-Ling (2008) 'Glocalization and English mixing in advertising in Taiwan: its discourse domains, linguistic patterns, cultural constraints, localized creativity, and socio-psychological effects', *Journal of Creative Communications*, 3: 155–83.

Kobayashi, K. (2012) 'Globalization, corporate nationalism and Japanese cultural intermediaries: representation of *bukatsu* through Nike advertising at the global–local nexus', *International Review for the Sociology of Sport*, 47 (6): 724–42 (first published September 12, 2011).

Levitt, T. (1983) 'The globalization of markets', *Harvard Business Review*, April/May: 92–107.

Motion, J., Leitch, S., Brodie, R.J. (2003) 'Equity in corporate co-branding: the case of Adidas and the All Blacks', *European Journal of Marketing*, 37 (7/8): 1080–94.

Tanaka, K. (1994) *Advertising Language: A Pragmatic Approach to Advertisements in Britain and Japan*. London: Routledge.

Turow, J. and McAllister, M.P. (eds) (2009) *The Advertising and Consumer Culture Reader*. London: Routledge.

Usunier, J.-C. (2009) *Marketing Across Cultures*. London: Financial Times/ Prentice-Hall.

White, C., Oliffe, J.L. and Bottorff, J.L. (2012) 'From the physician to the Marlboro man: masculinity, health, and cigarette advertising in America, 1946–1964', *Men and Masculinities*, 15 (5): 526–47.

Notes

1. http://ovalordapublicidade.apan.pt/McKensey_FinalAdvertising_2012.pdf accessed 17.3.2014
2. http://ovalordapublicidade.apan.pt/McKensey_FinalAdvertising_2012.pdf accessed 17.3.2014
3. www.iaaglobal.org/files/Campaign%20for%20Advertising%20launch%20release%20 2%2011%2014-FINAL.pdf accessed 17.3.2014
4. www.iaaglobal.org/YourRightToChoose.aspx accessed 17.3.2014
5. www.reuters.com/article/2013/12/09/us-advertising-spend-idUSBRE9B800420131209 accessed 17.3.2014
6. www.gartner.com/newsroom/id/2653121 accessed 18.3.2014
7. www.reuters.com/article/2013/12/09/us-advertising-spend-idUSBRE9B8004 20131209 accessed 17.3.2014
8. www.wired.com/gadgetlab/2011/11/smartphones-feature-phones/ accessed 17.3.2014
9. www.businessinsider.com/smartphone-and-tablet-penetration-2013-10 accessed 17.3.2014
10. www.google.co.uk/adwords/start/?channel=ha&sourceid=awo&subid=uk-en-ha-aw-skmp0~36361006495&gclid=CJanm4Gqn70CFeXLtAodhwEALQ accessed 17.3.2014

11. www.facebook.com/advertising?campaign_id=214294157440&placement=phrase&creative=29764582712&keyword=advertising&extra_1=39b49a38-28b1-72c9-c216-000065f21b54 accessed 17.3.2014

12. http://realbeautysketches.dove.com/ accessed 17.3.2014

13. www.tellyads.com/show_movie.php?filename=TA14255 accessed 17.3.2014

14. www.youtube.com/watch?v=ALWwK7Vz4gY accessed 17.3.2014

15. www.youtube.com/watch?v=ns-p0BdUB5o accessed 17.3.2014

16. www.youtube.com/watch?v=WmUeeurvXgo accessed 17,3,2014

17. http://adage.com/article/news/bmw-s-mini-fends-rivals-normal-ads/243609/ accessed 17.3.2014

18. www.youtube.com/watch?v=6R_D4V-Ns3Y accessed 17.3.2014

19. www.mirror.co.uk/news/bmw-mini-launch-classic-adverts-2793304 accessed 17.3.2014

20. www.youtube.com/watch?v=_UKLncvGxQ8 accessed 17.3.2014

21. www.forbes.com/sites/helenwang/2012/10/24/why-barbie-stumbled-in-china-and-how-she-could-re-invent-herself/ accessed 6.3.2014

22. www.bbc.co.uk/news/business-12670950 accessed 6.3.2014

23. http://online.wsj.com/news/articles/SB10001424052702304672404579183324082672770 accessed 6.3.2014

24. www.brandchannel.com/home/post/Mattel-Barbie-China-110813.aspx accessed 6.3.2014

25. www.jcdecaux-oneworld.com/2012/05/facial-gesture-recognition-outdoor-adverts/ accessed 17.3.2014

26. www.telegraph.co.uk/finance/newsbysector/retailandconsumer/10070234/Chinese-love-affair-with-Burberry-propels-sales-to-record.html Accessed 18.3.2014

27. http://impressivemagazine.com/2013/07/18/9-stories-behind-famous-brand-names-origins/ accessed 19.3.2014

28. www.youtube.com/watch?v=4f6Y3ns46NI accessed 18.3.2014

29. www.youtube.com/watch?v=dfU17niXOG8 accessed 18.3.2014

30. www.latimes.com/entertainment/tv/showtracker/la-et-st-coca-cola-super-bowl-ad-stirs-controversy-20140203,0,1361331.story#axzz2sbl6JaIo accessed 6.2.2014

31. www.interbrand.com/en/best-global-brands/2013/Best-Global-Brands-2013.aspx accessed 11.2.2014

32. www.youtube.com/watch?v=fH9bHq9Cvsc accessed 19.3.2014

33. www.youtube.com/watch?v=4vXHm8TzLzE accessed 19.3.2014

34. http://bridgetomoscow.com/curious-fact-moscow-mcdonalds accessed 19.3.2014

35. http://luxurysociety.com/articles/2012/05/the-top-50-most-searched-for-luxury-brands-in-russia accessed 19.3.2014

36. www.glamourmagazine.co.uk/news/fashion/2014/03/10/american-apparel-bangladesh-ad-controversy accessed 3 July 2014.

37. www.bbc.com/news/business-24646942 accessed 19.3.2014

38. www.top100luxury.com/en/ accessed 19.3.2014

39. www.uk.kantar.com/business/brands/top-20-foreign-brands-in-china-kfc-tops-list/ accessed 19.3.2014

40. www.skmm.gov.my/skmmgovmy/files/attachments/Ad_Dev_Malaysia.pdf accessed 22.3.2014

41. www.aaaa.org.my/index.php/showcase accessed 22.3.2014

42. www.youtube.com/watch?v=8fgPTN0E6ys accessed 19.3.2014

43. www.youtube.com/watch?v=TgPmaNMReKQ accessed 19.3.2014

44. http://newsfeed.time.com/2013/08/31/dunkin-donuts-ad-causes-uproar-in-thailand/ accessed 22.3.2014

45. www.youtube.com/watch?v=JPOVwKPMG8o accessed 22.3.2014
46. http://thaiadvertising.com/ accessed 23.3.2014
47. http://adsoftheworld.com/taxonomy/country/thailand accessed 23.3.2014
48. www.campaignlive.co.uk/thework/895156/ accessed 23.3.2014
49. http://hight3ch.com/top-20-japanese-commercials/ accessed 19.3.2014
50. http://adsofjapan.com/ accessed 19.3.2014
51. http://adsofjapan.com/ accessed 23.3.2014
52. www.adidas-group.com/en/group/history/ accessed 18.3.2014
53. www.spiegel.de/international/germany/shoes-and-nazi-bazookas-the-prehistory-of-adidas-and-puma-a-611400.html accessed 22.3.2014
54. http://forums.stashedboxes.com/thread/adidas-brand-history/39009/ accessed 22.3.2014
55. www.youtube.com/watch?v=yjjb_Dy7tXg accessed 22.3.2014
56. www.youtube.com/watch?v=6h1uMNUeqx4 accessed 22.3.2014
57. http://news.adidas.com/GB/Latest-News/ALL/adidas-extends-All-Blacks-sponsorship-until-2019/s/cfed5176-9238-45b9-85c4-fd1f864fde1d accessed 18.3.2014
58. http://news.adidas.com/GB/Latest-News/ALL/adidas-extends-All-Blacks-sponsorship-until-2019/s/cfed5176-9238-45b9-85c4-fd1f864fde1d accessed 18.3.2014
59. www.youtube.com/watch?v=JUiGF4TGI9w accessed 18.3.2014
60. www.youtube.com/user/adidasrugbytv accessed 18.3.2014
61. www.theconversationmanager.com/2011/03/29/adidas-most-successful-german-brand-in-social-media/ accessed 18.3.2014

9 Advertising and Promotion – Ethics and Regulation

Chapter outline

Advertising and promotion, as we have seen, occupy a particular cultural space. Promotional messages perform an economic function but they are also part of the free flow of communication and ideas. As such, they can elicit great controversy and disagreement among different audiences. Advertisements can generate a sense of 'giving offence' on a scale and with an intensity that even the most controversial works of art, drama or literature would find hard to match. The chapter outlines some of the major issues of advertising ethics and regulation, and introduces some concepts of moral philosophy that can be of assistance in understanding the ethical dimensions of advertising.

Key chapter content

- Ethical issues in advertising and promotion
- Ethics and controversy over advertising
- International advertising regulation
- Advertising to children
- Applied ethics and advertising regulation

Ethical issues in advertising and promotion

Why should organisations care about ethics? They have ends to achieve, and ethics seem out of place in a competitive environment, don't they? Or so one line of argument goes. Marketing, in particular, is often accused of being an ethics-free zone, and advertising is often seen as the dark heart of marketing (see, for example, Packard, 1957). A chapter on ethics in an advertising text might be seen as tokenistic, or worse, it might be seen as a manual for ticking the ethical communications box in Corporate Social Responsibility (CSR) programmes. If the shareholders, regulators, employees and senior officers of the company, along with the trade press, are all happy, then consumers can look after themselves.

But this mis-characterisation oversimplifies the nature of ethics in management. The purpose of this chapter is not to caricature or to preach, but to try to tease out some of the complexity entailed in considering the ethical status of advertising and promotion. There are many topic areas in marketing that connect to ethics, including consumer protection, environmental protection and sustainability, financial reporting, employment practices and community responsibility. Advertising and promotion agencies of all kinds along with brand marketing organisations need to pay heed to all these and more for reasons both commercial and non-commercial. In this chapter we will focus mainly on the ethical issues that are particular to advertising and promotional communication. The chapter will argue that this is far more complex than a matter of telling truth or untruth. Advertising may be a mass communication but we read it as if it were directed at us individually, and like personal communication, it can be infinitely shaded with subtleties of meaning that do not necessarily accommodate dichotomous, truth-or-falsehood judgement.

What is the meaning of ethics?

Ethics refers to what is right, good or consistent with virtue. A related concept concerns justice, in the sense that we would all like to be treated justly and fairly by the organisations with which we deal. The study of ethics is often concerned with abstract principles, and the study of morals is seen as an applied field that focuses on personal behaviour in specific situations. However, the terms are also linked and sometimes used interchangeably, as in 'applied ethics'. Marketing in general offers a variety of ethical issues for consideration, many of them mobilised through advertising (Hackley et al., 2008). For example, is it right to advertise to children using the same techniques that are used when advertising to adults? Is it right to advertise toys that are not necessarily good for children's development, and which might cost their parents or carers a lot of money? Should advertising be permitted to use imagery and words that

Table 9.1 Unethical advertising practices

- Overselling
- Exploitation of vulnerable groups
- Deception
- Misuse of lists
- Intruding on privacy
- Promoting negative racial, sexual or gender stereotypes
- Promoting prejudice against certain vulnerable groups
- Promoting socially or personally harmful values or behaviours
- Offending public taste
- Exploiting base motives of greed and envy

shock, offend or insult particular groups? Should advertising intrude on such a large number of social spaces such as roadside billboards, posters and even in-school advertising? Indeed, is advertising intrinsically a medium of exaggeration, mendaciousness and illusion? Should it be permitted at all? These and many more questions arise around advertising.

Advertising communications can commit many acts of dubious ethics in their attempts to seduce us into buying. Some are listed in Table 9.1.

Ethical issues in product or service marketing can be relatively clear-cut in the sense that if, say, a car explodes when shunted from the rear because of a rear-mounted petrol tank, this is clearly dangerous manufacturing practice. If a product or service is injurious to health, such as cigarettes or alcohol, again this is subject to public view and can be handled accordingly. We can probably all agree that things that might harm anyone's health are generally bad, even if some may be legal in some countries. The problem with advertising, as we can see straight away, is that ethical judgements in general are predicated on certain values and interests that are not universally agreed upon. People cannot agree on matters of secular civil governance that are, on the face of it, quite concrete and substantial, such as the correct penalties for particular crimes or the right way to fund education. How much more difficult is it to agree on the ethical status of an advertisement, especially since all too often, as we saw in Chapter 2, it is far from easy to agree on exactly what the ad means?

Advertising's publics

For some people, business is business and one should always be sceptical, even cynical, in assessing commercial claims. *Caveat emptor*, or 'buyer beware' is a maxim that could apply here. Another way of putting this is to say don't be a sucker or you deserve to be ripped off. Advertising is just trying to sell us stuff, so perhaps we should not be surprised if it sometimes crosses into hyperbole. After all, we often read press or books and watch TV news reports that we regard as exaggerated, inaccurate, one-sided, misleading or even in bad taste, so why should we expect advertising to be any different? On the other hand, just because someone wants to sell you something can they be excused from any ethical standards? Is making money more important than other values? It is all very well to say that buyers in a marketplace have a responsibility to look out for themselves, but should they not also be protected from unscrupulous or mendacious sellers? Furthermore, advertising is a profoundly symbolic communication form that operates in a grey area characterised by polemic, puffery and implicit, rather than explicit suggestion. It is often very hard to reduce advertising claims to truth or lies. What about *Axe/Lynx* advertising and its claims that the deodorant will make men irresistible to women, or bread advertisements that evoke Victorian values when they are, in fact, made by modern production methods (see Snapshot 9.1)? The question is, to what extent should consumers be regarded as sophisticated readers of advertising?

SNAPSHOT 9.1

Allinson bread and implicit suggestion[1]

The Real Bread Campaign (RBC) is a food lobby group. RBC contacted the author [C.H.] for support in a complaint they made to the UK advertising regulator, the ASA, about an advertisement on the website of breadmaker Allinson. The ad, made up in sepia with Vicorian images, juxtaposed a picture of a pair of hands kneading dough with the line 'Allinson Today'. RBC felt that it misleadingly suggested that the bread was made by Victorian methods, when in fact it is made by modern production methods. The ASA ruled that the complaint was without grounds because consumers would be expected to know that the images were merely part of the branding, and did not literally suggest that human hands were involved in kneading dough as part of the manufacturing process. Advertising regulation tends to hinge on debates about the meaning of ads, which often assumes that they carry distinct meanings, as with legal or scientific material. As we have seen, much advertising carries both ostensive and covert communication used in combination. The precise intended meaning of the ad is left open to interpretation. Cook (2001) uses the example of a British TV ad for Cadbury's *Flake* chocolate bar to illustrate that ads, like any discourse, have connotations that are subtle and personal. The 1960s *Flake* campaign[2] was open to a Freudian interpretation, since it used an amusing though sexually risqué visual metaphor. The consumer who points this out is risking the accusation that they are relating their interpretation, not the reality. As Cook (2001: 51) states, the 'assumption that meaning resides in the text quite independently of group or individual perceptions, is depressingly common in discussions of advertising'. Of course, the fact that certain individuals, perhaps even large numbers of individuals, might read particular connotations into an ad is well understood and used as a stratagem by the advertiser. Their indeterminacy of meaning makes ads a more intriguing and more compelling communication. Ads are frequently accused of using sexual suggestiveness and symbolism; they are able to do this without risk of official censure by locating sexual connotation within the covert dimension of the ad, where its presence cannot be objectively proven.

Further complicating advertising ethics is the fact that advertising serves many disparate interests: consumers, manufacturers, media owners, government agencies, charities, the economy as a whole, employers, employees, and so on and so forth. Consequently, deciding whether an ad is ethically acceptable by agreed standards, or unacceptable, can be a complex matter because of the different interests advertising must serve. An ad might be very effective in generating sales, and that is good for the company, its employees, its shareholders and its suppliers. If it is deemed to be an unethical ad, then consumers will be protected if it is banned, but what of the potential harm to the employees, shareholders and so on? Most shares are held by large financial institutions such as pension funds and insurance companies. These financial institutions manage savings schemes and pension funds and invest in businesses. People depend upon these funds for their retirement, health insurance, savings and so on. Hence, advertising is not simply a matter of greedy companies trying to get our money – it is part of the connected economic system into which we pay, and from which we hope to get employment, pay, a lifestyle and eventually, if we're very lucky, income for our retirement.

Even consumer protection is not a simple issue. Which groups, exactly, deserve protection, and from what or whom? Should citizens be protected from advertisers? Or should advertisers (and the income and employment they generate) be protected from citizens who are too easily offended by communications that were not aimed at them? Are there groups that deserve extra protection, such as children, the elderly, the less educated, the poor?

Ethical issues in advertising are not confined to the matter of economic relationships. Advertising does not merely sell stuff, as we have seen, it is also a form of social communication that can illustrate the social norms and conventional values of its time. Advertising, in the broadest sense, is a historical document detailing changing tastes, fashions, norms and attitudes. It reflects current standards of public taste and decency and modes of public discourse. By implication, from an ethical perspective, we get the advertising we (as in the silent majority) want and deserve. Of course, the 'we' in question is a heterogeneous group with the sharply differing views and values of the communities in which we live. Controversies about advertising, then, can serve a social function as a public forum for revealing fundamental differences between social groups. Advertising also impacts on pressing issues of public policy such as alcohol-related social harm and ill-health, obesity, or lung and heart disease through unhealthy food and smoking, and there are ethical issues around guns, drugs or environmentally damaging products. All can elicit protests from lobby groups promoting a particular cause.

Advertising's economic role

All these potentially problematic issues cannot obscure that fact that advertising exists for a very important reason. It creates wealth, for individuals, for companies and for economies. The regulations surrounding advertising must take account not only of ethical issues but also of the economic functions advertising fulfils. Advertising performs the indispensable economic function for capitalist economies of communicating offers to consumers.

Table 9.2 Economic benefits of advertising

Through advertising, producers are able to:

- Expand their markets, enter new markets, defend market share
- Differentiate offers to target heterogeneous consumer groups
- Take advantage of economies of scale to reduce unit production costs
- Increase revenue, employment, investment funds and returns to shareholders
- Make consumers aware of choices, product qualities and offers
- Compete with other producers, lowering prices and stimulating innovation
- Contribute to GDP growth and aggregate employment

For whole economies, there is a strong correlation between advertising expenditure growth and growth in gross domestic product (GDP).[3] Growth in advertising expenditure reflects general economic confidence and feeds through to increased demand. So, advertising is indispensible to economic growth, wealth and job creation. Without it, competition would be blunted since consumers would not be aware of the rival offers and product features available. Manufacturers could not communicate offers and local monopolies would thrive. Companies would have no incentive to be more efficient or to improve their offer. Advertising is the price we pay for wealth creation. There is an argument that poverty is the greatest evil facing the world and if advertising can help reduce poverty by creating demand, jobs and income then it should not be subject to regulation at all. But for others, advertising is too important not to be regulated since uncontrolled advertising could not only discriminate against minorities and offend public decency, it could also undermine public trust in marketing by making exaggerated or untrue claims.

SNAPSHOT 9.2

Advertising regulation – TV ads for drugs[4]

Advertising regulation differs in different countries depending on local laws. In the USA, for example, direct to consumer (DTC) TV advertising of controlled prescription-only drugs is permitted, when it is not allowed in many other countries, including the UK. TV ads for drugs create a pull-effect when patients ask their doctors about brand named drugs for particular conditions, putting pressure on the medics to supply those drugs, even though the patients typically have no pharmaceutical knowledge. From the drug companies' point of view, why should they be prevented from using advertising for their legal products? TV advertising is also beginning to be seen for drugs that were, until recently, highly illegal. Several states in the USA have legalised marijuana for personal use either for medical use, for personal leisure use, or both. *USA Today*[5] reported that a major cable TV operator, *Comcast*, was to air possibly the world's first TV ads for marijuana, in March 2014. The ads were for a website that matched doctors who prescribed marijuana with prospective customers. The ad was based on the strategy that marijuana users should be reassured that their doctor would offer better quality assurance than an illegal street dealer. The creative execution went something like this:[6] a shady guy in a dark street asks a passer-by 'psss ... do you wanna buy some sushi?' The voiceover says 'You wouldn't buy your sushi from this guy, so why buy your marijuana form him?' The ad goes on to recommend getting marijuana from a real doctor, presumably because doctors know their blow. Anti-legalisation groups expressed disappointment at the ads, which would not be aired in children's programming or before 10pm, while pro-legalisation groups pointed out that the product is now legal. In some states, for example Colorado, the use of marijuana for medical or leisure uses is perfectly legal and retail suppliers are booming, but retail advertising was not permitted at the time of writing, in early 2014.

The expression 'public trust in marketing' might have brought a smile to some readers' lips but the role of trust in economic growth should not be underestimated. At a basic level, we need to believe that if we pay for something, we will receive the product we saw in the advertisement. It helps too if we can feel pretty confident that the things an advertisement says about a product or service are substantially true. Trust, in this sense, is a fundamental requirement of commercial communication and a very underestimated component of Western business practice. The element of trust only becomes apparent when one experiences an economy with very low levels of trust, and the extent to which lack of trust inhibits trade becomes starkly apparent. Advertising is no exception to this rule and it spite of its poor public image, much of it does not tell literal untruths because it would not be in the long-term interests of any advertisers to do so. In the age of social media, bad faith on the part of advertisers is rapidly exposed.

Advertising's ideological role promoting consumption and corporatism

In order to understand our reactions to advertising it is important to appreciate that it has always been a contested area. Four hundred years ago there was public concern at advertising's presence as a form of 'social pollution' (Hackley and Kitchen, 1999) in London streets (McFall, 2004). Even in the USA, advertising was not always welcomed with enthusiasm. In particular, early advertising was associated with the large corporations. The activities of these corporations were met with great suspicion, even open hostility, in the USA at the turn of the century. These corporations needed some help to create the public acceptance of mass marketing and mass retailing that they required. It was to advertising agencies that they turned for that help.

Historian Roland Marchand (1985, 1998) has described how the rise of big business in the USA was facilitated by advertising and communication. At the turn of the twentieth century, there were many mergers and acquisitions in US business. As a result there were fewer, bigger corporations. Many Americans regretted the demise of the local high street store and the rise of vast, 'soulless' corporations. As corporations grew, many feared that they posed a threat to American values and institutions such as the church, the family and the local community. Serious questions were asked at presidential level about the activities of these leviathans and their influence over American cultural life. The entrepreneurs who created great corporations such as *AT&T*, *GM*, *GE*, *Ford Motors* and *US Steel* were acutely aware of the need to legitimise their activities and manufacture a 'soul' for the new corporatism. Over the following decades a profound transformation took place in the public image of corporations.

From being perceived as potential threats to American values, the giant corporations became the very epitome of those values and a legitimate part of American life.

Marchand (1998: 2) points out that this new legitimacy flew in the face of classical economic theory that held that the nature of competitive businesses is that they cannot rise above self-interest or the dictates of the market. As these companies attained extraordinary size and power it became clear that they were no mere slaves to market forces but exercised considerable monopolistic power. Not only did they have to persuade the public of their right to play a part in American life, they also had to create an identity to soften their soulless image. The corporations addressed this pressing problem partly through welfare capitalism and patriarchal initiatives to improve the workforce through education and training. Many corporate PR and advertising campaigns personalised communications to give a human face to the faceless corporation. Anthropomorphism in marketing is by no means confined to corporate communications, but is a mainstay of brand strategy (Brown and Ponsonby-McCabe , 2013).

They also used grand architecture to impress their status and power on the skyline, such as the gothic spectacle of the *Woolworth* building in New York City and the massive factories of manufacturers such as the *Jell-O* company and *Pillsbury's*. Retail emporiums quickly took up the challenge to inspire consumers with the imaginative and evocative use of physical space, for example with John Wanamaker's store in Philadelphia, now occupied by *Macy's*. Paris has possibly the world's first purpose-built department store, *Le Bon Marché*, and the stunning *La Samaritaine*, a blend of art nouveau and art deco, the largest department store in Paris and home of the *LMVH* luxury goods brand. These cathedrals of consumption invited their guests to trade up in social class, by entering the stores, buying the goods and acquiring the symbolic cultural capital to display in their living room, or on their arm. Architecture became a PR tool as the images were reproduced in posters and on company literature. The semiotic force of architecture helped bring lifestyle consumption to the masses. In a sense, the spaces of retail buildings and headquarters were invested with ideology (discussion in Hackley, 2013a). Sociologists have long understood that spaces are not neutral but can be seen as ideologies that inform the way people think and feel.

Corporate advertising, corporate architecture (that often featured in the advertising) and public relations, then, played a significant part in creating a soul for corporate America. Their advertising agencies produced a stream of imagery and copy on postcards, posters, in magazines and press editorial and, later, on radio portraying the corporations in terms of such values as integrity, service to the community, localism, tradition and moral uprightness. This corporate advertising also served a more pragmatic purpose in helping to produce an internal sense of corporate identity (and a sense of collective purpose) for thousands of employees.

In legitimising capitalist corporatism and selling consumption to citizens as a lifestyle, advertising was central to the development of the marketing ideal of consumer orientation. Consumers were taught, through advertising, that manufactured products reflected their discernment and met their requirements. Through responses (or non-responses) to advertising, consumers could play a part in the market mechanism and cast a vote in favour of their own personal consumer vision. Consumers' collective sense of self-interest is fired by the drama of consumption played out in advertising. Clearly, in affluent economies most categories of consumer need are not fundamental and absolute, but derivative and relative. Consumer goods are not created by advertising, but the social status of the attributes of goods is (Leiss et al., 1997: 299). Advertising teaches us that the social status of brand attributes is scarce and carries a premium cost. In this important historical sense, advertising has been central to the development of the idea of consumer marketing. The consumer orientation preached by marketing management textbooks can be seen as a continuation of the ideology promoted by the early American corporations. In spite of the practical limits to consumer orientation in large manufacturing organisations, marketing texts nevertheless deploy the rhetoric of consumer orientation to promote a sense of connection between you, the little consumer, and your friend, the big corporation.

The rhetorical force and apparent popularity of marketing rhetoric (satisfying consumer needs, being customer-focused) might reflect a continuing need for capitalist corporatism to re-assert its legitimacy (Hackley, 2003g) amid a contemporary crisis of confidence in the activities and motives of global business corporations. Advertising's success in setting the preconditions for a consumer society has been striking even while organised resistance to global capitalism is evident in the form of sporadic but numerous consumer protests and boycotts (see, for example, Klein, 2000). Capitalism, though, seems to be infinitely creative in re-inventing itself, and in the convergence economy (Jenkins, 2008) we are seeing yet more manifestations of this astonishing creativity.

Advertising's collective effect

On a wider scale, it can be argued that advertising and other forms of promotional communication collectively create the cultural preconditions that lead to consumers' acceptance of marketing and the consumer society (Wernick, 1991). Of course, marketing communications managers and brand managers are interested only in the efficacy of advertising for their particular brands. However, in order to fully understand advertising's specific effects it is necessary to also appreciate its collective influence. It is a form of communication that, as consumers, we have to learn how to read. There is a level of cultural understanding that is a precondition for interpreting ads. Once we are acculturated to reading advertising texts, experiencing new forms of advertising modifies our understanding of subsequent ads. Advertising and promotion within promotional culture constitute a self-generating system of signs that frames our experience as consumers and places our sense of social identity and economic relations within a consumption-based sign system. By being exposed to different kinds of advertising text over time, consumers are educated to understand advertising in all its complexity and variety, which masks the fact that at one level all advertising promotes the same thing – consumption. The ethical status of advertising and promotion have to be understood in the context of its ideological frame.

Ethics and controversy over advertising

Interest in the ethics of advertising is not new. There are, for example, letters to London magazine *Punch* expressing disquiet over advertising dating back over 200 years ([McFall, 2004). Controversy over the quantity of advertising, over its styles of representation and over the ways in which it seems to wield its influence are not confined to the post-war era. Advertising has, though, grown in volume and now reaches us on many new media technologies.

The subjectivity of ethical judgements means that questions of ethics in advertising are clouded in a fog of contrasting opinions, which are often held very strongly indeed. Particular ads or campaigns occasionally become topics of controversy, that is, they attract widely diverging opinions that are expressed in public forums such as newspapers' letter pages, editorials, TV documentaries and even in political debates.[7] Of course, not all controversy over advertising is based on questions of ethics. But many disagreements emerge from differing ethical standpoints. Often, the media stories are given their narrative hook by strongly held opinions about whether an ad or campaign should or should not be permitted, broaching issues of free speech and censorship in regulation. In many cases, the brands are grateful for this coverage since, even though it is critical, it publicises the brand to a far greater extent than the advertisement alone could have done. There are even compilation articles in the media of the top ten most controversial ad campaigns, in which ads that were regarded as especially offensive gain additional media coverage.[8]

SNAPSHOT 9.3

Courting controversy – Benetton advertising in the 1980s–1990s

Oliviero Toscani, one of Italy's top photographers, was given sole control over *Benetton*'s advertising by Luciano Benetton in the early 1980s. He decided to change the focus of *Benetton* advertising from product to lifestyle. Toscani's work turned *Benetton* from a local clothing company into one of the world's most recognised brands. From 1984 the creative executions increasingly carried Toscani's personal agenda of social injustice[9] into the commercial world. The 1984 campaign featured teenagers of different races together with the slogan 'All the Colors of the World'. The print and billboard campaign was distributed by *JWT* in 14 countries and generated complaints from racists in South Africa and also the USA and the UK.

Toscani, suitably encouraged, continued with the 'United Colors of Benetton' theme for subsequent campaigns. From 1989 *Benetton* took all its advertising production in-house to give it complete independence and control. The ads were consciously provocative to racial sensibilities. They outraged many consumers while continuing to give a massive profile to the *Benetton* brand. One poster, featuring a black woman holding a white baby to her naked breast, generated such protest in the USA that it was withdrawn. For some consumers it evinced an era of slavery. For others, public breast-feeding itself was offensive. The ad also received more praise than any other *Benetton* visual and won awards in five European countries. Other ads continued the theme of racial juxtaposition. One featured a black hand handcuffed to a white

(Continued)

(Continued)

hand. It generated complaints in Britain where it was assumed that the white hand belonged to a police officer. London Transport refused to display the poster. Toscani created a series of iconic images, including copulating horses, a dying AIDS victim, war images, a newborn baby, and a nun and priest kissing, each of which created a PR furore and raised the brand profile even further, until a campaign in 2000 featuring photographs of prisoners condemned to death in American prisons. *Benetton* retailers suffered a backlash, some business relationships were ended (e.g. with *Sears*) and some stores were even vandalised by people sympathetic to the victims of the crimes committed by the prisoners and outraged that the men were featuring as poster models. Toscani left *Benetton* three months later, after eighteen years in charge of their advertising. In 2012 Benetton tried to revise the brand's controversial positioning with a series of ads featuring photo-shopped images of statespeople and religious leaders kissing. Called 'Unhate', the campaign won industry awards[10] although many people were unimpressed and the ads were withdrawn, although the *Unhate Foundation* continued.

Controversy as a public relations tool

In some cases, controversy over advertising is nothing more than a marketing technique that leverages extended public relations coverage by generating media chatter. As Snapshot 9.3 discusses, brands with a youthful and edgy positioning know that if they can succeed in antagonising groups other than their own target market there are likely to be useful side-effects, such as free editorial publicity and a stronger brand identity. The letters pages of national newspapers, weblogs, comment threads and Twitter comments can act as forums for strongly held feelings about advertising campaigns that are perceived as being offensive, dishonest or irresponsible. If there seems to be a rising tide of popular opinion complaining about an ad, editorial comment starts to appear in the form of feature articles and opinion pieces in the press and on 'magazine' TV shows. Pretty soon, the brand is all over the media, earning sales and brand presence because of all the free publicity, and delighting its market segment if they like the idea that their brand is edgy. These campaigns exploit the provisional status of advertising as a 'parasitic' communication form that continually challenges discourse conventions of what advertising ought to look like.

Of course, there are risks too, and some deliberately 'edgy' advertisements result in a negative market reaction for the brand.[11] The way the campaign will be received by different groups has to be finely judged, and the tone of the ad needs to fit with the brand values. In the Chapter 9 case below, the ads for *Cadillac* and *American Apparel*, for example, seem to have been well judged in this respect, in spite of, or rather because of, the irate negative reactions they received on social media.

It should also be remembered that controversy over advertising cuts both ways, and can sometimes be used as a platform by the complainant to gain publicity for their interests. For example, complaints about ads based around ethnicity and national identity can mask sentiments that may be racist in their motivation, thus gaining a platform for their views. This was a suspicion with a proportion of the complaints about *Benetton* ads (see Snapshot 9.3). A more recent parallel example could be the *Coca-Cola* TV ad shown during the 2014 American Super Bowl[12] that generated complaints because it was too multi-racial and not 'American' enough. As it turned out, the *Coca-Cola* ad was deemed to be one of the more successful Super Bowl ads that year,[13] although company profit growth was slow in 2014.

Advertising is vulnerable to public disapproval because it is a soft target. Advertising is highly visible and it is easier to draw simplistic cause and effect relationships between advertising and social ills than to look at the more complex underlying socio-economic issues. To some extent, the considerable media coverage of advertising in the form of magazine articles and talk on chat shows, dedicated websites and compilation TV shows, reflects advertising's status as a part of the media complex. It is unsurprising that advertising is often discussed in the editorial content of the popular press and TV shows, given the symbiotic relationship between advertising and other media such as the press, movies and TV entertainment. This profile gives advertising media oxygen that allows both brands and lobby groups to breathe the intoxicating vapours of publicity.

Advertising controversial products

Some controversies over advertising relate to the nature of the product rather than just to the advertising. Advertising for alcohol, drugs, guns and cigarettes all tends to attract close critical scrutiny because of the intrinsically difficult ethical problems surrounding the marketing of those products. For example, an American gun company used an image of Michaelangelo's 'David' holding an Armalite sniper rifle in one advertisement, much to the annoyance of the Italian government. As well as guns, drugs can be controversial in advertising. In the UK, for example, direct-to-consumer (DTC) advertising of pharmaceutical drugs is not allowed at all, though in the USA and many other countries it is common. On TV in the USA, prescription drugs are often advertised alongside ads for lawyers who will sue the drug companies for you when the drugs go wrong. For example, at the time of writing, TVCs for testosterone are juxtaposed with ads from lawyers looking for cases to launch against drug companies on behalf of men who have had heart attacks or strokes as a result of being prescribed testosterone. In the UK, TV advertising for cigarettes has been banned since the 1960s as evidence of the damage of cigarette smoking to health mounted, but it is allowed in many other countries, while TV advertising for marijuana is allowed in some US states (see Snapshot 9.2). The World Health Organization (WHO) has called for a worldwide ban on all cigarette advertising. In the UK, the medical lobby the BMA (British Medical Association) has called for a ban on all alcohol advertising.

WHO argues that where partial bans on cigarette advertising have been instituted, the benefits in terms of lower smoking rates and reduced lung cancers and other diseases are significant. The problem for health authorities is that cigarette companies simply shift resources to different media when necessary. So, for example, when cigarette advertising was banned on UK TV, cigarette manufacturers shifted resources to sports sponsorship and OOH advertising. Advertising bans in general have a poor record of reducing harm in the medium term, unless accompanied by other legal measures. For example, the 2010 Ofcom ban on advertising foods that are high in fat, salt and sugar (HFSS) during TV programmes made for children on UK TV has had no impact on rising obesity rates. On the other side of the debate, pro-smoking campaigners argue that tobacco companies are promoting a legal pursuit that mature individuals have the right to indulge in without interference from the state. As the box above illustrates, the topic has moved on and now the same debates circulate around marijuana advertising.

Alcohol advertising

In many countries, alcohol advertising is a source of ethical sensitivity. In most predominantly Muslim countries it is forbidden, as is alcohol consumption, while in many other countries there are limits placed on the type and extent of alcohol promotion. Alcohol advertising has become an area of considerable controversy in the UK because of possible links with increases in alcohol-related diseases such as cirrhosis of the liver and connected social harm such as violence, crime and social disorder. The World Health Organization made alcohol advertising control a key priority in its anti-alcohol campaigns (WHO, 1988, in Nelson and Young, 2001). The sexualisation of alcohol advertising and its role in constructions of gender have been linked with increased alcohol consumption among young people and the promotion of a 'binge' drinking mentality (Hackley et al., 2013; Szmigin et al., 2008). The BMA has repeatedly called for an outright ban on alcohol advertising.

Cigarette advertising changed the historical view of femininity and promoted cigarette smoking as a normal social practice of the liberated and independent woman (Williamson, 1978), and alcohol advertising is seen to be playing a similar role in locating alcohol brands as discursive resources for the construction of female (and male) social identity (Griffin et al., 2009, 2012;

Lemle and Mishkind, 1989; Young, 1995). Young people are often thought to be particularly vulnerable to marketing (Calfee and Scherage, 1994) that associates drinking alcohol with social and sexual success. The extent of official disapproval reached such a pitch that the Advertising Standards Authority and the Broadcast Committee of Advertising Practice were forced to re-write the code of practice on alcohol advertising in 2006, to try to ensure that it did not link alcohol with social or sexual success or overtly promote drinking to young people. TV campaigns such as those for rum, vodka and other drinks have attracted complaints that their scenes of wild partying so glamorise alcohol consumption that they may implicitly promote high-risk sexual behaviour in both sexes. The ASA responded to the increased sensitivity around alcohol advertising by banning a number of ads and insisting that the codes of practice are strictly adhered to. The alcohol industry has representation on the ASA committee and lobbies in favour of the industry. The Portman Group[14] is an alcohol industry funded body that manages the alcohol industry responses to public policy concern around alcohol advertising and marketing.

Gender and alcohol

The representation of gender in UK alcohol TV advertising has turned full circle over the last thirty years. In the 1980s, ads for *Hofmeister* lager featured a man in a bear suit who was the centre of an admiring crowd of young men and women. The ads featuring the lager drinker as a cool, streetwise and charismatic male character allowed females only to be the grateful objects of male attention. These ads, created by legendary advertising man John Webster (see Snapshot 9.4) replaced those that portrayed females only as domestic drudges. In later campaigns for *Archer's*, *Lambrini* and other alcoholic drinks targeted at females it is female drinkers who are portrayed as independent, quick-witted and rebellious. The men portrayed are mere accessories. Such advertising would be unthinkable in 1960s Britain. One might argue that these ads represent a step forward in gender representation, placing women on an equal footing with men, at least when it comes to drinking. Others would take a different view, since gender remains something to be constructed, and women still have to negotiate complex norms and expectations. Heavy drinking is merely a different scenario for women, and not necessarily an equalising one (Griffin et al., 2012).

The UK *Hofmeister* beer ads were a turning-point in alcohol advertising, not only because they contributed to a major shift in UK beer drinking habits from dark to light beer. They also used imagery attractive to children to advertise adult products. The bear in the ads was a character that children enjoyed and understood. Previously, a man dressed in a hairy bear suit would only have been seen at a children's entertainment aimed at pre-schoolers. The ads took a cultural sign that denoted kids' entertainment and placed it in an adult context in connection with an adult pastime, beer consumption. While the product was not targeted at children, the advertising had become very attractive and memorable to children. Advertising agencies know very well that advertising for adult products and services that is visually or thematically appealing to children can be extremely useful in getting a brand name into a household, hence many financial services products are advertised on kids channels in UK TV.

SNAPSHOT 9.4

Advertising tone in UK alcohol advertising

A London agency formerly called DDB London held the *Courage* beers account for some twenty-five years. When the account moved elsewhere the agency produced a compilation video that is a revealing document of social history. The tape runs from the 1970s ads with elderly Northern English men enacting scenes of conspiratorial male congeniality in ads for *John Smith's Yorkshire Bitter*. In these ads stereotypes abound, with men portrayed as big children whose main aim in life is to escape the 'nagging' wife so that they can get together with other men to drink beer and giggle. In the 1980s the trend turns to light beers drunk by younger 'Jack the lad' heroes in watershed advertising moments such as John Webster's *Hofmeister* bear ads. Webster created many iconic campaigns of that time and was particularly fond of dressing actors up in bear suits – he also created the *Sugar Puffs* Honey Monster character. Subsequent campaigns for Australian lager brands *Foster's* and *Castlemaine XXXX* featured post-apocalyptic scenes reminiscent of the Mad Max movie genre, self-deprecation and ironic humour. The adolescent appeal of alcohol branding intensified throughout the 1990s and beyond. The young British drinkers who are displaying strikingly increased rates of liver and other alcohol-related disease today are the first generation who were toddlers when alcohol advertising on TV started to use imagery that was visually appealing to pre-school children.

International advertising regulation

It is to be expected that attitudes towards advertising vary in different countries, reflecting differing public standards of propriety and levels of tolerance. Consequently, approaches to advertising regulation differ widely.[15] In some countries there are systems of industry regulation that overlap with legal constraints. In others, advertising is part of a censored broadcasting communication system that is directly overseen by state agencies that have to approve every promotional communication. In many countries there are widely differing standards applied to advertising as regards, for example, the veracity and level of proof required for product claims, the timings and placing of advertising on broadcast and print media, and the portrayals of consumption and language used in advertising content.

SNAPSHOT 9.5

Variability in international advertising codes of practice

Advertising regulation can seem highly inconsistent and even quirky when looked at from a cross-national perspective. At various times, the following regulations have been in force:

- TV advertising for marijuana and Viagra is legal in some American states.
- In some countries of Eastern Europe, alcohol advertising heavily restricted.
- In Sweden, TV advertising for toys targeted at under 12s is banned.
- Tobacco advertising on TV is banned throughout the European Union (EU).
- In Argentina, all advertising was banned on subscription cable-TV channels in January 2004.
- In Austria and Finland the use of children in ads is heavily restricted. Italy banned the use of children in advertising in 2003.
- In many predominantly Muslim nations, women in advertising must be fully clothed and wearing headscarves, and advertising of non-halal food products is not allowed.
- Hungary prohibited the 'use of erotic and sexual elements in advertising for purposes not justified by the object and substance of advertising' and no advertisement 'may be such as to reduce the reputation of the advertising profession or undermine public confidence in the advertising activity'.
- In the UK, alcohol advertisements cannot use actors who appear to be under the age of 18 and they cannot show people drinking quickly; they must sip their drinks.
- In Greece, TV advertising of toys to children is banned between 7 pm and 10 pm.
- An EU directive limits the amount of advertising that can be shown each hour on TV across the EU to under 12 minutes.
- The French advertising regulation body, the Bureau de Vérification de la Publicité (BVP), recommended the withdrawal of a Benetton poster showing a kissing priest and nun in the 1990s. The same poster won an award in the UK.

Regulations such as those in Snapshot 9.5 do tend to change as different lobbies win attention for a particular cause, or as media conditions change. Some of the above regulations may no longer be in force, but new ones may have been substituted. Other issues are governed not by regulation but by conventional practice. For example, UK television advertising tends to be quite conservative as regards nudity or sexual references when compared to advertising in some other European countries such as Sweden, Denmark, France and Germany, but the UK is quite liberal in this respect when compared to advertising on American television (see the Wonderbra ad in the colour section).

Advertising regulation is sometimes covered by general rules of thumb as well as by specific codes of practice for particular product categories. For example, the UK Advertising Standards Authority (ASA), an independent, industry-funded body responsible to the government communications regulator Ofcom, applies a rule that advertising must be 'Legal, Decent, Honest and Truthful', while the Hungarian code of advertising ethics uses the principles 'Lawful, fair and true'. In Australia, the Advertising Standards Bureau[16] has a remit to 'ensure that the general standards of advertising are in line with community values'. The American Association of Advertising Agencies applies its own code of practice that seeks to be a 'constructive force in business' by not producing advertising that makes false claims, is deceptive or offensive.[17]

UK advertising regulation

Advertising agencies and the sellers of advertising space in the UK agree to be bound by the rulings of the ASA,[18] even though there is no legal requirement for them to do so. The ASA is part of Ofcom, the UK media regulator. The ASA applies the codes of advertising practice that are created by the Broadcast Committee of Advertising Practice (BCAP). Its remit covers press and print advertising, email and SMS text message advertising, broadcast advertising and also internet advertising where this originates from an identifiable UK-based source. The ASA rulings may not have the force of law but they do offer a quicker, more flexible and more efficient regulatory system than the law could provide. Media owners and ad agencies agree to be bound by the ASA rulings, so if the ASA decides an ad is to be banned, it will be promptly withdrawn.

Advertising must be careful about claims regarding the efficacy of products or services, offers of prizes or guarantees. Advertisements cannot make factual claims that they cannot prove. For example, one famous pet food ad strapline claimed that '8 out of 10 owners said their cats prefer *Whiskas*', and *British Airways* (BA) ads used the strapline 'The World's Favourite Airline' for many years. After intervention by the ASA the '*Whiskas*' line was qualified to those owners 'who expressed a preference'. If the manufacturer is to continue using that line they must be prepared to set up an experiment which representatives from the ASA can watch to verify the claim. The *BA* claim was mere hyperbole and after some years the ASA eventually ordered the ads to stop making the claim.

Reading ASA judgements, all of which are published on their website,[19] offers a useful insight into how the voluntary regulatory system works. The complaints also reflect current public tastes and trends. What was acceptable in advertising in 1950 or 1960 may not be considered acceptable today, and of course, the reverse would also be true – much advertising today would seem excessively coarse or sexualised to a 1960s audience. Alcohol advertising is a particularly powerful indicator of changing social norms, especially with regard to gender relations. Ads that are taken for granted today might well have provoked heated complaints ten or twenty years ago.

Advertising and children

Advertising and children has become an increasingly problematic issue with many debates around the world as to what the correct regulatory approach should be.[20] The ASA code of practice today forbids alcohol ads that use imagery attractive to children, but much alcohol advertising seems to be designed to do exactly that. As noted above, the use of imagery in adult advertising that a short time ago one would only associate with children's shows has become commonplace. Many ads on UK TV use animated cartoon characters but are ostensibly directed at adults to sell, for example, branded chocolate, tea and gas central heating. This is no accident – childish advertising might appeal to the child in the adult, but it also conscripts children into brand consciousness.

The trend towards infantilism in advertising reflects the relentless pursuit of novelty in advertising but also springs from the increasing awareness of brand marketers that children are very important to advertisers of adult products. Children enjoy advertising, they remember it and they discuss it. The attention of a child brings a brand into the household and it then becomes a brand that is considered in household buying decisions. Not only do children influence the household budget: they learn about and become conscious of brands at a very early age. Widespread access to video games, the internet and mobile phones has enabled many children to become more active consumers (Bassiouni and Hackley, 2014) taking part as agents in their own consumption as well as being agitators 'pestering' parents to buy toys and games. Research has suggested that children under the age of 10 are often unaware that when they are watching TV advertising what they are watching is in fact an offer to buy, but access to the internet night be changing the age at which children become commercially aware.

Advertising industry groups lobby to maintain the freedom of advertisers to target children with responsible advertising (for example, in the USA, the *Children's Advertising Review Unit*[21]). Other groups try to raise awareness of the potentially damaging effects to children of unrestricted advertising. There are now concerns about the effects of advertising for fast food on growing rates of child (and adult) obesity in the UK, USA and increasingly in other countries too. There is evidence that where fast food outlets have become established in Asian countries, obesity among children is becoming an issue there too. In the UK, advertising for foods high in fat, salt and sugar (HFSS) was banned during programming watched by a majority of under-16s. This seems to date to have had a sharp negative effect on commercial television advertising revenues but not on rates of childhood obesity, which continue to rise.

Clearly, the existence of codes of practice and voluntary regulatory regimes does not reassure everyone that the brand marketing and advertising industries are exercising proper social responsibility. Debates about advertising's influence on social issues are invariably clouded in supposition, since there is no proven and direct causal link between advertising and behaviour. Yet, while textbooks have regarded this lack of a causal theory of advertising as a problem, the industry itself has managed very well. In this book there are examples of advertising campaigns for which compelling circumstantial evidence has been gathered showing that they did indeed influence consumer thought and behaviour. Even if this point is accepted, the idea of stricter advertising regulation jars with the freedom of choice that advertising represents. Certain individuals and groups have always been quite favourably disposed towards lifestyles that might be regarded by some as unwise or unhealthy. Advertising presents a smorgasbord of options and consumers have the right to exercise their choices as they see fit. Then again, the ability of consumers, and especially children, to exercise truly individual choice may be sharply circumscribed where there is an acutely asymmetrical power between consumers and brand marketing corporations. For all the marketing textbook rhetoric about consumer sovereignty, consumers clearly do not have multi-million dollar budgets to spread their point of view all over the media.

Applied ethics and advertising regulation

Advertising regulation needs to consider ethics but its role is not purely ethical. Public policy regulation is political and pragmatic, while ethics in its pure sense is the study of value in itself. Advertising regulation is a political process in that it acts under the influence of complex interests. The values that influence advertising policy are not always based on those of ethical good but on a trade-off between the competing interests of consumer lobbies and other interest groups, the rights of citizens not to be gratuitously offended by commercial communication, and the needs commercial and policy bodies have to use advertising to publicise brands and issues of social concern. Regulators exist as much to protect advertisers from the wrath of the public as to protect the public from the excesses of advertisers. Nevertheless, there is an implicit ethical dimension to advertising codes of practice. However obscured advertising regulation may be beneath complex webs of interest, its rationale at some level is to make life better or more acceptable in some way than it would otherwise be without regulation, and this coheres with the Platonic ethical notion of universal 'justice'.

If we are to analyse the role of ethics in advertising regulation we need to have some ethical concepts to work with. Ethics is broadly concerned with asking questions about the best or most correct way to live, but using terms such as 'better' carries implicit value judgements that complicate ethical debates. The study of ethics entails thinking about which particular acts, thoughts or practices are consistent with living a life of virtue according to given standards. For many followers of formal religious systems, living the good life means living in accordance with particular moral precepts and codes of behaviour that have been set down by religious authorities. The great world religions all place great importance on these codes and compliance is considered compulsory. Observation of the codes is therefore a matter invested with both individual as well as collective significance. But secular ethical systems deny the need for prescribed codes of behaviour or belief and aver that reason and experience, not religious authority, are an appropriate basis for all moral decisions. Humanism, for example, denies the need for either the fixed codes of morality or the eschatology (doctrine of last things) and moral judgement, of formal religions.

Moral precepts are, of course, culturally bound and informed by religious traditions. One could make a crude distinction between the Judaeo-Islamic-Christian traditions on the one hand, and the eastern religions such as Hinduism and the versions of Buddhism found in Japan, China and parts of South-East Asia on the other. Both broad groups of religious traditions promote adherence to abstract moral principles such as honesty, compassion, sobriety, piety, non-violence and so on, supplemented by specific rules about clothing, eating and food preparation, sexual conduct and so forth. The cultural, ethnic, national and religious variations in moral codes mean that advertising can be a particularly sensitive area for ethical disagreement. Advertising has to negotiate religious sensibilities in regions where religion is the chief authority. In the West, where secular values predominate, even in countries with strong religious traditions, the religious point of view, while still important, becomes one among many.

Advertising and Western moral philosophy

We might seek some clues as to the ethical status of advertising by looking at the works of ancient and modern philosophers (Hackley and Kitchen, 1999). Advertising is far from new – evidence of promotional communication has been found in the ancient civilisations of Greece and Egypt. Modern advertising has been seen since the development of print media in the West some 400 years ago (although printing itself was first developed in China long before). In general, though, advertising, as an aspect of commerce, escaped the specific attention of ancient philosophers. It is probably fair to say that ancient philosophers would look upon advertising with some considerable disapproval, but we can try to apply some concepts of Western philosophy in a way that might take into account the cultural variability of ethical standards. Advertising could be seen as a part of public communication much as oratory, poetry and plays were in the ancient world. It may be a part of commerce, but advertising is also a part of literature because it entails the creation of public texts and could be viewed in the same light as the street-corner storyteller in that it recounts the myths and legends of its time. Of course on another level it is also analogous to the street hawker, and perhaps sometimes to the bar-room comedian. Advertising in its modern forms panders to popular sensibility, is seen on a wide scale and excites and alters the emotional states and values of those to whom it is directed. The poetry of Homer and the plays of Aeschylus were written to produce a similar effect. In *The Republic* Ancient Greek philosopher Plato specifically mentioned Homer's poetry as a candidate for censorship because of what he saw as its morally degrading influence on young people. There are those today who would take a similarly stringent view of the influence of advertising.

One might infer that Plato would not appreciate advertising, though as a member of the elite social class he had no need to respect the imperatives of commerce. But Aristotle, another famous Greek philosopher, eschewed social engineering in his *Nicomachean Ethics*, written for his son Nicomachus. He seemed to have little paternalistic interest in the improvement of the plebian classes but, rather, adopted the view that individuals should take a balanced approach to personal ethics based on their own predispositions and needs. Aristotle's view of advertising might be liberal, in the sense that advertising would be seen as but one of the challenges individuals must face in the world. By coming to a moderate accommodation with advertising one reaches an ethical standard that is personal to oneself. Aristotle saw the world as a place full of potential deceit, indulgence and temptation that one must learn to live with ethically. He took no account of the need for vulnerable groups to have some degree of protection from the wiles of the powerful.

Another, more contemporary liberal view came from John Stuart Mill, whose book *On Freedom* famously argued that free and unfettered expression and behaviour were necessary prerequisites for a progressive society in which individuals were free to develop according to their needs and imagination, and hence society as a whole progresses through the free and unfettered interplay of the ideas of individuals. Advertising, it is often claimed, is one form of free expression that should not be regulated. But Mill was aware that some popular voices can drown out those of others and he warned against a 'tyranny of the majority'. In other words, free expression that allowed the loudest and most populist voice to dominate public discourse was not consistent with genuine freedom. Perhaps Mill would have regarded advertising as a tyranny of the majority, because it takes the ordinary person's experience of daily life and reflects it back bathed in the warm glow of consumption. The voice of commerce dominates public discourse and makes alternative (not consumption-oriented) ways of thinking, being and behaving difficult to express amid the hectoring insistence of advertising.

Ethical concepts for judging advertisements: deontology, consequentialism and virtue ethics

It can be useful to apply Western ethical concepts to advertising not because they offer solutions to debates and arguments over advertising but because they can clarify the ethical issues that are involved. Without some theoretical concepts, it is impossible to move beyond the subjective views of individuals that particular ads are OK, or are not OK. Deontology, consequentialism and virtue ethics offer us three such useful concepts.

Deontology

The ethical status of an act may be judged according to whether it is regarded as ethically good or bad according to a fixed standard. This often applies to religious systems. For example, if an ad promotes condoms, alcohol, beef or pork, such ads might be deemed unethical by Catholics, Muslims, Hindus and Jews respectively, for whom consumption of these items runs counter to religious teaching. Deontological judgements, then, rely on moral values that are seen as given and absolute. Clearly, deontological judgements on the ethical status of advertisements have limited use where there is a wide divergence of views on what is intrinsically good or bad. One could argue that most or all world religions would agree that communication ought to be truthful and just, and not coarse or vulgar, and hence there may be cases where an advertisement might be judged unethical on deontological grounds by most religious and secular moral systems. The problems arise when different moral systems apply different standards. A key point about deontological ethics for advertising is that it is the act in itself, in this case, the advertisement, that may be deemed ethical or unethical. There is no need to consider the motive or the consequences, or perhaps even the context. Hence, arguments that 'it is just advertising' or 'people don't have to look at ads that offend them' would be no defence. If the ad is wrong, it is wrong. On the other hand, being offended by an ad in itself would also be irrelevant unless the ad also contravened a given moral code.

Consequentialism

Consequentialist approaches judge the consequences of an act and not the act in itself. Good or bad in this case may be concerned with positive or negative social effects. For example, an ad promoting the use of condoms to prevent the transmission of sexual diseases might be unethical on deontological grounds to someone who feels that the public depiction of sexual relations in any context is indecent and therefore wrong. However, if the consequences of the ad were that fewer people became infected with sexually transmitted diseases then the consequences of the ad might be judged to be good, at least from the public health point of view. A consequentialist approach seems to be taken by the UK regulator in allowing public service and charities ads that would not be appropriate if the motive was commercial. Some ads shown in UK TV have been quite upsetting, such as depictions of car crashes to encourage people to drive more carefully or to wear seatbelts, and depictions of child cruelty to encourage viewers to donate money to child protection charities. Shocking people ('shockvertising') can get attention but has a poor record of success on a commercial level. There is no proof that it is more successful for promoting charities or public safety, but it seems to be more justifiable as a tactic to get attention in those contexts.

Utilitarianism, the doctrine that acts should be judged on the criterion of the greatest good for the greatest number, is a consequentialist doctrine. Advertising that has socially good or benign consequences would be deemed permissible when judged according to a consequentialist ethical approach. Of course, we still have the problem that both deontological and consequentialist approaches entail value judgements about what is a bad act in itself or what is a good or a bad consequence for the individual or for society Moreover, some people would argue that advertising as a whole promotes wealth generation and that poverty is the greatest evil for humanity to conquer, therefore all advertising is good on consequentialist grounds. However, most would take issue with giving advertising a free pass on ethics. While it may be good for wealth generation, there are questions to be asked about what prices we are prepared to pay and what compromises we are prepared to consider in order to generate that wealth.

Virtue ethics

Virtue ethics considers the motive of the author of an act. As a general ethical principle, people should be considered as ends not as means. If they are being considered merely as means (to make money) then the ethical status of an act such as an advertisement could be regarded as negative, and wrong. On the other hand, if an act such as an advertisement is well intentioned, then it might be regarded as ethically satisfactory even if it contravened fixed moral standards and resulted in negative consequences for some. Aristotle's 'golden mean' is sometimes regarded as an axiom of virtue ethics since he regarded ethical behaviour as relative to personal circumstances. For example, one might consider a coffee brand's offer to give more money to coffee growers as a well-intentioned act that helped consumers feel morally better about drinking the coffee, even if it might not make a huge difference to the coffee growers.

These three concepts help us to identify what we feel is unethical about an ad, if we feel that an ad is wrong in some way. It is useful to be able to state clearly why an ad is ethically satisfactory, or not. Unfortunately, many intractable questions remain. Take the example of TV advertising for marijuana, discussed earlier in Chapter 9. In whose interests should the ethical status of marijuana advertising be judged? Sale of marijuana earns taxes in the US states where it is legal, and much good can be done with those tax revenues since they can be invested in schools, roads and infrastructure. Marijuana or cannabis advertising could, then, be judged ethically appropriate. It would probably also be supported by consumers who feel that the drug has major health and pain control benefits for people with certain medical conditions. On the other hand, promoting the drug might encourage younger people to try it, and research has suggested that maturing brains can be damaged by marijuana use. Of course, the same can be said of alcohol and cigarettes, and although legal, both are indeed the cause of massive social harm for young and also old people. Will legal marijuana use be the cause of as much social harm as alcohol in twenty years time?

There is, then, a moral compromise to be reached in advertising, as in life in general, between doing what is right, and doing what is best. The kinds of reasoning applied in judgements about advertising combine moral, social and economic arguments. Which will hold sway depends very much on the way that advertising has been constructed, the creative execution. As Chapter 2 pointed out, what is implied but not explicitly stated in advertising can be powerfully suggestive. The implicit dimension of advertising is often the key area for ethical argument, For example, alcohol ads in the UK may not explicitly encourage young people to drink excessively, and they may not explicitly suggest that young people will be more socially successful and confident if they do drink, but do these ads *imply* these things? Advertising regulation often focuses on the explicit, but there is invariably a process of interpretation. Here we get to the nuance and complexity of advertising communication. For an ethical judgement to be made about an ad, a judgement first has to be agreed upon about what the ad means. This ambiguity is the area that advertising often exploits.

Advertising is normally a purely commercial text that links images of health, happiness and success with consumption of marketed brands. Images of social reality are normally confined to news media or government-sponsored campaigns. Oliviero Toscani's *Benetton* advertising (discussed in Snapshot 9.3) created a new form of cultural communication, but one that generated discomfort. Advertising as a whole is a powerfully ideological form of communication (Elliott and Ritson, 1997). It assimilates signs and symbols into a text that promotes consumption above all else. Toscani's work simultaneously revealed and undermined advertising's ideological character and this created a frisson of unease that, perhaps, showed the profound cultural significance of advertising. The tacit agreements and interpretive consensus that surround the public face of advertising were fractured. Ethical judgements applied to advertising were seen in themselves to be based on highly provisional and culturally sensitive notions of value.

Chapter summary

This chapter has explored advertising ethics and discussed its considerable capacity for generating intense controversy. The chapter discussed some regulatory approaches taken in different countries and offered many examples of advertising that has caused offence and generated complaint. Three concepts from Western moral philosophy were offered as principles to apply to advertising in order to clarify the often subjective reasons behind judgements as to the ethical status of particular advertisements.

■ Review Questions

1. How is advertising regulated in the UK? Illustrate how it is applied with examples from the ASA website.

2. Discuss the ethical status, as you see it, of three specific print or TV ads. What ethical concepts might you employ to bring some intellectual clarity to the debate? In your view, do these concepts bring clarity to the debate?

3. Using the ASA website, print off five recent adjudications on ads for which you can obtain printed copies. Ask a group of your peers for their views on the ethical status of each of these ads. Discuss the views expressed and compare them with the ASA adjudications. What do the various opinions reveal about the people who hold them?

4. Is advertising ethical? How can ethical principles be applied fairly with integrity in a diverse, market-driven society? Use practical examples and theoretical concepts to discuss your response to this question.

5. Examine the arguments for and against advertising regulation. What might be the result if advertising were not subject to any regulation at all?

CASE STUDY

Controversial and banned ads[22,23]

Controversial and 'banned' ads are always a topic of interest for what they tell us about the limits of public toleration of advertising, and the branding opportunities that come from testing those limits. 'Banned' is a term sometimes used to generate PR for a viral ad. Video sharing websites carry anthologies of banned ads, many of which are not banned by any regulatory authority at all but created to be 'edgy' viral content. Setting aside the venality of some PR campaigns, advertising does have a nice way of shining a light on cultural tensions around communication and representation. Some cultural tensions exist around what should or should not be advertised. As noted above, different cultural and religious traditions sometimes dictate the answer to this question. Others change over time. For example, Snapshot 9.2 shows that marijuana and prescription-only drugs are advertised on American TV. More commonly, the tension occurs around the content of advertising, rather than around the commodity that is advertised. The archetype for this type of campaign was set by *Benetton* in the 1980s and 1990s (see Snapshot 9.3 above), which used photography more typically seen in news and documentary broadcasting but never in advertising. In effect, the campaign challenged the discourse conventions of advertising. *Benetton* were followed in their controversial advertising campaigns by *FCUK*, *CK* and many other fashion and style brands. All these examples were a huge commercial success for a time, before the novelty faded and the brand positioning became tired.

More recent campaigns included an ad by a UK gambling company exploiting an ongoing murder case which generated the most complaints ever seen by the UK advertising regulator, the ASA, for its tastelessness. [24]. The ad offered odds on the defendant being found not guilty. The brand, *Paddy Power*, has made a successful strategy out of controversial and banned ads, with a ten-year record of profits rising in parallel with outrage.[25] Italian knitwear brand *Benetton* set the standard for this kind of strategy back in the 1990s but *Benetton* also found that there are limits to public tolerance when they misjudged the line, lost business and changed back to a more anodyne brand positioning. *Paddy Power* might have discovered the same line. Giving of offence can work well in generating PR provided the target market is not being offended. Being 'edgy' and controversial can give a brand stronger positioning, as fashion brands *CK*, *FCUK* and *A&F* have demonstrated at various times over the past decade. Cultural theorist and brand commentator Grant McCracken[26] noted that an ad for *Cadillac* that generated much critical comment for its American exceptionalism was a good ad in the sense that being controversial can be a stronger positioning than trying to be inoffensive to everyone as consequently lacking a strong identity.[27] In another example, also mentioned above, US clothing brand *American Apparel* has a record of highly sensual advertising, which, in March 2014, featured a semi-naked employee who originates from Bangladesh, with the strapline 'Made In Bangladesh'. The ad was a side-swipe at other clothing brands that outsource their manufacturing to South Asia. *American Apparel* make their clothes in Los Angeles. The ad made the news media globally,[28] generating huge additional publicity.

Case Questions

1. What are the risks and opportunities of creating a controversial advertising campaign, and how might the risks be assessed and mitigated?

2. How are the discourse conventions of advertising being challenged by digital media?

3. Can the giving of offence for commercial gain ever be justified?

4. What do controversial ad campaigns tell us about culture?

5. Search 'controversial and banned ads' and try to find three examples that could be judged as unsuccessful and ultimately damaging to the brand. In what ways were these campaigns misjudged?

Useful journal articles

(These Sage articles can be accessed on the book website)

Kenneth M. Winneg, Bruce W. Hardy, Jeffrey A. Gottfried, and Kathleen Hall Jamieson (2014) 'Deception in third party advertising in the 2012 Presidential campaign', *American Behavioral Scientist*, 58 (4): 524–35.

Alice Kendrick, Jami A. Fullerton and Yeo Jung Kim (2013) 'Social responsibility in advertising: a marketing communications student perspective', *Journal of Marketing Education*, 35 (2): 141–54.

Agnes Nairn and Pierre Berthon (2005) 'Affecting adolescence: scrutinizing the link between advertising and segmentation', *Business & Society* 44 (3): 318–45.

Jacob Ostberg (2010) 'Thou shalt sport a banana in thy pocket: gendered body size ideals in advertising and popular culture', *Marketing Theory*, 10 (1): 45–73.

Barbara J. Phillips and Edward F. McQuarrie (2011) 'Contesting the social impact of marketing: a re-characterization of women's fashion advertising', *Marketing Theory*, 11 (2): 99–126.

Michael Prieler (2010) 'Othering, racial hierarchies and identity construction in Japanese television advertising', *International Journal of Cultural Studies*, 13 (5): 511–29.

Carly O'Neill, Dick Houtman and Stef Aupers (2014) 'Advertising real beer: authenticity claims beyond truth and falsity', *European Journal of Cultural Studies*, doi: 1367549413515254 (first published February 3, 2014).

■ ■ Further reading ■

Bassiouni, D. and Hackley, C. (2014) 'Generation Z children's adaptation to digital consumer culture: a critical literature: Review', *Journal of Customer Behaviour* (in press).

Cayla, J. and Elson, M. (2012) 'Indian consumer *Kaun Hai*? The class-based grammar of Indian advertising', *Journal of Macromarketing*, 32 (3): 295–308.

Hackley, C., Tiwsakul, A. and Preuss, L. (2008) 'An ethical evaluation of product placement – a deceptive practice?', *Business Ethics – A European Review*, 17 (2): 109–20.

Lirola, M.M. and Chovanec, J. (2012) 'The dream of a perfect body come true: multimodality in cosmetic surgery advertising', *Discourse & Society*, 23 (5): 487–507.

Measham, F. and Østergaard, J. (2009) 'The public face of binge drinking: British and Danish young women, recent trends in alcohol consumption and the European binge drinking debate', *Probation Journal*, 56 (4): 415–34.

Pollay, R.W. (1986) 'The distorted mirror – reflections on the unintended consequences of advertising', *Journal of Marketing*, 50(April): 18–36.

Solow, J.L. (2001) 'Exorcising the ghost of cigarette advertising past: collusion, regulation, and fear advertising', *Journal of Macromarketing*, 21: 135–45.

Szmigin, I., Bengry-Howell, A., Griffin, C., Hackley, C. and Mistral, W. (2011) 'Social marketing, individual responsibility and the "culture of intoxication"', *European Journal of Marketing*, 45 (5): 759–79.

Notes

1. www.campaignlive.co.uk/news/1150466/asa-rejects-real-bread-campaign-claims-allinson-misled-consumers/ accessed 4.3.2014
2. www.youtube.com/watch?v=6mYr90nCFZE accessed 4.3.2014
3. http://ovalordapublicidade.apan.pt/McKensey_FinalAdvertising_2012.pdf accessed 8.3.2014
4. www.bloomberg.com/news/2014-03-04/marijuana-legalization-makes-tv-commercials-funny.html accessed 6.3.2014
5. www.usatoday.com/story/news/nation/2014/03/03/marijuana-medical-legalization-pot-advertisement/5982815/ accessed 4.3.2014
6. www.youtube.com/watch?v=jyzxs33B6FA accessed 6.3.2014
7. www.themost10.com/controversial-print-advertisements/ accessed 4.3.2014
8. www.creativebloq.com/advertising/10-controversial-ad-campaigns-2013-12135346 accessed 4.3.2014
9. www.cnn.com/2010/WORLD/europe/08/13/oliviero.toscani/index.html accessed 9.3.2014
10. www.huffingtonpost.com/2012/06/20/benetton-unhate-campaign-cannes-ad-festival-award_n_1613757.html accessed 9.3.2014
11. www.businessinsurance.org/9-controversial-ads-that-overshadowed-their-product/ accessed 4.3.2014
12. www.usatoday.com/story/news/nation-now/2014/02/03/coca-cola-ad-super-bowl-racism/5177463/ accessed 9.3.2014
13. http://online.wsj.com/article/PR-CO-20140310-905049.html accessed 9.3.2014
14. www.portmangroup.org.uk/ accessed 8.3.2014
15. www.international-television.org/regulation.html accessed 4.3.2014
16. www.adstandards.com.au/ accessed 5.3.2014
17. www.aaaa.org/about/association/Pages/standardsofpractice.aspx accessed 5.3.2014
18. www.asa.org.uk/ accessed 5.3.2014
19. www.asa.org.uk/Rulings/Adjudications.aspx accessed 8.3.2014
20. www.economist.com/news/international/21590489-are-children-fair-game-sophisticated-and-relentless-marketing-techniques-many accessed 7.3.2014
21. www.asrcreviews.org/ accessed 8.3.2014
22. www.mirror.co.uk/tv/tv-news/save-children-advert-10-most-3184308 accessed 4.3.2014

23. www.huffingtonpost.com/tag/controversial-ads accessed 4.3.2014
24. www.theguardian.com/media/2014/mar/05/paddy-power-oscar-pistorius-ad-withdrawn-immediate-effect accessed 6.3.2014
25. www.telegraph.co.uk/finance/newsbysector/retailandconsumer/9506027/Paddy-Powers-10-most-controversial-adverts.html accessed 7.3.2014
26. http://blogs.hbr.org/2014/03/provocative-cadillac-rescuing-the-brand-from-bland/ accessed 7.3.2014
27. www.telegraph.co.uk/finance/newsbysector/retailandconsumer/9506027/Paddy-Powers-10-most-controversial-adverts.html accessed 7.3.2014
28. www.dailymail.co.uk/femail/article-2576055/EXCLUSIVE-I-fully-comfortable-photo-shoot-Meet-topless-Muslim-model-American-Apparels-controversial-new-ad.html accessed 9.3.2014

10 Research in Advertising

Chapter outline

Advertising agencies act as intermediaries between consumers and brand marketing organisations of all kinds. To fulfil this role they need research craft skills to generate actionable insights into markets, consumers and communication. The aims, methods, purpose and relevance of research are all matters for intense debate both within agencies and between agencies and clients. This chapter outlines the main research techniques used in the field and sets this within a discussion of the major debates about the methods and the uses of research in advertising and promotional communication.

Key chapter content

- **Research in advertising: role, issues and origins**
- **Types of advertising research**
- **Uses of advertising research**
- **Research ethics**

Research in advertising: role, issues and origins

It is axiomatic that research is the foundation of effective advertising. Major advertising industry bodies reflect this ethos, for example in the David Ogilvy Awards given by the Advertising Research Foundation (ARF) for the most powerful advertising research and named after an industry pioneer of the role of research in advertising.[1] Effective promotional campaigns of all kinds are based on knowledge of who the target segment is, where they are, what they do, what they're like and how they think and behave. Agencies also need a wider understanding of the market in which the brand operates, the competition and the wider economic conditions.[2] Finally, agencies need methods for pre-testing advertising executions and post-testing campaign effectiveness against agreed objectives.

Advertising is a knowledge business and research is used in advertising, so that the knowledge agencies need is more robust and transparent than mere opinion, hearsay or speculation. Knowledge gained through research should be systematic, coherent and evidence-based, and should be communicable. It should be systematic in the sense that there should be a research framework that raises the knowledge thus generated above the level of mere supposition. It should be coherent in that the framework or method should make sense in terms of the kind of knowledge that is to be generated, and it should be evidence-based in that it should be supported by facts about the world. Finally, it should be communicable because the most important role of social research is not to generate new knowledge but to make existing knowledge public. In advertising, it is not enough to have a penetrating insight giving a hook of reality upon which to hang the fantasy of advertising. That hook of reality that underpins the advertising strategy must be clearly understood by the client team as well as the agency team, so that the reasoning behind the campaign can be articulated, discussed and justified.

SNAPSHOT 10.1

Syndicated panel data and store data

Advertising agencies do not always commission or carry out their own research. They also buy the use of secondary data that are produced by commercial research organisations. Major research companies such as Neilson[3] and TNS Global[4] publish syndicated panel data based on continuous surveys of consumers. Studies may investigate trends in, for example, household brand shopping and usage, TV viewing, radio listening or internet usage. The information contained in these surveys can be useful for advertising professionals to understand the underlying trends and behaviours that are typical in a given product or service category to help brand clients on decisions such as advertising strategy and targeting.

It is important to distinguish panel data from store data. Store data are gathered from retailers and show exactly what customers are buying day-by-day, pack sizes, brands, categories and so on. If the customer has a loyalty card this scanner data can be cross-matched with customer profiles to break down into demographic segments, depending on the detail of the customer profile. Store data can track volume sales in different stores, which can be particularly useful for measuring the effects of regional retail price and sales promotions.

Panel data, in contrast, are based not on store sales but on households. This means that households who sign up to a panel will be giving daily information through diaries or other means on what they buy, who buys it and how frequently. The detailed demographic information means that deeper insights can be generated than from store data. On the other hand, panels are necessarily limited in size and self-selecting, limiting the extent to which the results can be generalised. Panel data analysis focuses on four elements: penetration (the percentage of total households that have bought an item), buying rate (the average amount bought by households over a time period), purchase frequency (the number of an item bought by a household over a year) and purchase size (the amount of an item bought on each buying occasion).

Research in advertising is undertaken to improve the effectiveness of communication by, for example, generating ideas and inspiration for strategy and creativity, for keeping abreast of consumer trends, for filling in gaps in knowledge outside the immediate field of expertise, for enhancing creative development by generating ideas, for testing creative executions, and for monitoring campaign effectiveness. Advertising research includes the use of secondary sources such as panel data and market reports, and also primary research methods such as focus groups, depth interviews, ethnographies and video ethnography, projective studies, discourse analysis and content analysis of internet sources such as chat, comment threads and Twitter trends, observation research, street or online surveys and consumer panel 'link' tests, prompted and unprompted recall tests, ethnographies, eye-tracking and psycho-galvanometer experiments, neuro-psychological MRI scans and other laboratory methods, and many more.

Research in advertising uses broadly the same methods as market research but the conditions under which it is used and the objectives are somewhat different. Typically, research in advertising is pragmatic, time-constrained and a means to an end rather than an end in itself. Consequently, it may not conform to the usual sequence of research in marketing (see Table 10.1).

Research in advertising has to be less formal and more flexible than commissioned market research projects because it has to be undertaken within a condensed timescale and without a formal budget – the client is paying for advertising and promotion, not for insights. If the client wants research, they usually go to a specialist research provider. The agency needs the insights from research, though, to drive the effectiveness of its campaigns. In advertising, the

Table 10.1   The five main stages for research in marketing

1. Defining the research problem
2. Setting research objectives
3. Deciding on research method
4. Collecting data and analysing results
5. Presenting findings

research problem definition and research objectives will often be very broad and exploratory, particularly in the early stages of the advertising development process. The research method will often be a default method given the budget and time constraints – for example, secondary sources such as panel data and discussion/focus groups for initial brand and market research with target consumers. Data collection and analysis will often be done rapidly and informally by the account planner in discussion with the rest of the team – for example, focus groups might be videoed and the videos replayed to the group. The findings, similarly, will not necessarily be formally presented within the account team, but the key insights that underpin the communication strategy may eventually be presented more formally to the client at one of the client meetings.

Another reason why research in advertising can be less formal than traditional market research is that research in advertising agencies is contested and political. The different disciplines involved in making advertising have very different perspectives on what constitutes a valid insight (Hackley, 2008). To make matters even more complex, there is an inherent tension between formal research as part of bureaucratic business processes, and creativity. Advertising and promotion agencies are ideas factories and the ideas can come from anywhere, or indeed, ideas can come out of nowhere, but clients need to see accountability, process and evidence. This tension in advertising as a creative and cultural industry can be productive, and it can also be destructive.

There are widely diverging opinions about the role and methods of research in advertising. In agencies, knowledge, about the market and the consumer, about communication, and about the brand, is a hotly contested area. The winners are the people who get their ideas put into action in a campaign. As we noted in Chapter 4, different agency disciplines often carry quite different implicit assumptions into their work. Advertising agencies are not known as places where a meeting of minds is the daily norm. More often, the relevance and implications of research findings are matters of passionate debate. There is a view among some practitioners that research in advertising is often used in the same way that a drunk uses a lamp-post, for support rather than illumination. Clarity about the aims, purpose and also the limitations of research can help to focus the illumination it can offer.

Research in advertising is important for client–agency relationships because clients are more likely to accept the agency's strategic advice if it is backed up with evidence from research findings. In this chapter we will try to negotiate a route through this complex area to outline the most commonly used research approaches in advertising and promotional communication. We will also examine the key areas of contest and debate around the uses of research in the field.

Origins of advertising research

Advertising research has a long history (see Hackley, 2010, for overview). Advertising agencies established their own research departments as they grew the services they offered to clients, and the distinct fields of audience, attitude, opinion, market, media and consumer research evolved. In time, many advertising agency research departments grew to become independent successful businesses in their own right. Many of today's leading market and consumer research agencies were originally advertising agency research departments. Agencies need to know as much as possible about the client's business, the market sector and the relevant consumers before devising an advertising strategy. The advertising legend David Ogilvy points this out when he refers to the need for advertisers to 'do their homework' (Ogilvy, 1983), in other words, to find out as much about the consumer as they can before trying to devise solutions for the client.

According to Richards et al. (2000: 20), US agency group JWT began to commission research in 1916 to acquire greater understanding of the social and demographic trends and structures that formed consumer groups. Universities were sometimes called upon to add methodological sophistication. For example, the behavioural psychologist John B. Watson was diverted from his university career to become an advertising man for JWT. Behavioural psychology aspired to provide a unified theory of human learning and behaviour. If the behaviourists were right, then ads could be conceived in terms of behavioural control, changing human behaviour through operant conditioning and behavioural reinforcement without the need for the added complication of consumers who think. Many other academic social science research methods from disciplines including cognitive psychology, sociology, anthropology, neuropsychology and literary studies have been adapted for use in advertising. Examples include attitude measurement, ethnography, surveys, MRI scanning and discourse analysis, respectively.

Types of advertising research

'Research showed that' is a phrase often invoked in debates as a rhetorical device intended to end the argument. Research carries great authority to justify courses of action, but the truth about research is that it is based on a lot of opinions. That is not to dismiss its value – indeed, it is essential in advertising, as it is in countless other areas of science, public policy, health and social work, and commerce. But it is important that anyone who uses research understands some underlying principles, because without that understanding it is impossible to make informed judgements about how much weight to give to research findings in strategy decisions.

While this is not the place for a section on philosophy of science, it is worth noting one particular source of tension in advertising research. Creative professionals often feel that formal research fails to capture the essence of consumer experience. As a result, they feel that it measures things that are not relevant. Of course, for creatives, 'research' is just a word used when they're being told their idea is no good (Hackley and Kover, 2007), as in 'research showed that' a panel of consumers didn't like their creative execution. Many feel that their informal and personal engagement with consumer culture, aided by their creative intuition, is enough. They watch the movies, they engage with popular media, they avidly follow consumer cultural trends and they bring their eclectic intellectual and aesthetic interests to bear on their work. The intuitive understanding of top creative people is built on wide and eclectic interests. It is also based on characteristics such as a capacity for hard work, an acute sense of observation, high intelligence, intellectual flexibility and the ability to work under pressure (McKeil, 1985; Ogilvy, 1963; Wilmshurst and Mackay, 1999). Research, for many creatives, represents the bureaucratisation of a cultural and creative industry, it is a means of imposing managerial control (Lears, 1994). Research is necessary for business people to justify broad budget decisions, but many creatives feel that it doesn't necessarily help to improve the work. Indeed, many feel that research acts as an impediment to risk-taking and creativity. They see it as a futile attempt to explain myths with science.

Of course, to many clients, both risk-taking and creativity are anathema, and the idea that they are propagating myth would astound them. They want certainty. For many on the account management and the client-side, research is a tool to keep creatives under control, so that they do work for the client rather than for themselves. A more balanced perspective is that research is necessary but should be treated with care. It can tell creatives things they need to know, such as to whom they need to speak, and it broadens their range by enabling them to communicate with cultural milieu outside their personal experience. Research gives clients something to work with other than blind faith, and it enables them to justify promotional budgets to main board members, shareholders and other stakeholders. For clients, research cannot guarantee success in marketing initiatives, but it does provide a means of managing risk by helping to eliminate really bad work.

The question for advertising agencies, then, is not whether they should use research, but how to use it. This is why it is important that agencies have a good understanding of the details of social scientific methods of data gathering and data interpretation. The following section will not develop detailed methods but, rather, will outline some important principles in research for advertising.

Primary and secondary research

There is an important role for secondary research in advertising. Secondary research entails using information sources that are already published, and there are many to choose from for advertising that deals with market data, continuous consumer panels, opinion surveys, media and audience research and demographic studies, from companies like Nielson, YouGov, WARC, ARF, BRAD (formerly British Rate and Data) and BARB, from government statistical sources, and many others. For example, BARB will tell media planners what shows UK TV viewers are watching, how long they watch, and what audience share each show achieves[5] week-by-week, while Mintel carries market reports, panel surveys and provides competitive intelligence.[6]

Secondary research such as continuous consumer panel data can be expensive. However, it is usually cheaper, and certainly much quicker to access, than commissioning primary research studies. Secondary sources are very useful for building an initial platform of understanding about a brand, its competitive market situation, and general issues of the buying patterns of target consumers.

SNAPSHOT 10.2

Focus group insight informs a VW advertising strategy

Volkswagen has earned fame for the groundbreaking creativity of its advertising since Bill Bernbach's iconic *VW* ads in the 1960s.[7] More recently, its Game Day TVCs aired during TV coverage of the American Super Bowls have been shared millions of times on social media.[8] In a multi award-winning European campaign, focus groups conducted with car consumers by the ad agency BMP DDB revealed two related insights that drove the advertising for the *VW Polo* and *Golf* ranges for two decades. Firstly, the research found that consumers thought they were quite knowledgeable about car prices, but in fact they had very little knowledge about actual pricing structures. Secondly, the research found that consumers had an impression that *VW* cars were more expensive than other cars in their class. In the case of the (then) new *VW* small car range, this was incorrect. However, the perception clearly held advantages, since it carried an implication of superior quality. The creative problem was compounded because consumers in Europe and the UK were resistant to advertising that emphasised a price benefit. Not only that, but creative staff in ad agencies are usually bored by a brief that asked them to

(Continued)

(Continued)

merely say that 'this price is lower than the others' (called 'a prices brief') because of the perception that little creatively interesting can be done with a prices brief. As a solution the agency produced a creative brief that described a need to make ads that were telling but off-beat in their quirky humour. With humour, the campaign could convey the message about price without alienating or boring consumers. The brief resulted in a campaign that ran for over ten years, based on funny ways to tell consumers that they were wrong about *VW* pricing. Awards were won and *VW* increased its market share substantially. The research insight that drove the creative work was derived from qualitative data, interpreted creatively by the agency account planner. A 2014 UK ad for *VW* called 'Shark Cage' has turned the prices brief on its head, not claiming that *VW*s are less expensive than one expects, but pointing out the risks of going for the cheaper alternative.[9]

Primary research studies (see Snapshot 10.2 above) produce new data for specific purposes. They can be useful since they generate proprietary data – no competitors have access to these data, so primary studies can generate a competitive advantage. They are also useful because they can focus on a specific set of questions and a specific sample that are directly relevant for a particular brief. They are, though, time-consuming and they require specialist expertise. Primary studies can be flexible. For example, many advertising agencies use 'focus' or discussion groups as a default method of primary data gathering during creative development, not because they offer generalisable or even robust findings, but because they provide stimulation for ideas. Discussion groups can be organised and executed rapidly using agencies that keep a roster of participants from various demographic groups. The agency can use them either to explore consumption practices amongst a small but representative group, or to get consumer feedback on ideas in development.

Qualitative and quantitative data

Advertising and promotional agencies make use of both quantitative and qualitative data in their research. Quantitative data consist of numbers and can be analysed with statistical methods and broken down into bar charts and line graphs. Qualitative data consist of words, pictures, videos, audio recordings, typed interview transcripts and so on, and therefore cannot easily be analysed statistically (although some forms of content analysis can enable a quantitative analysis of qualitative data sets). In the era of convergence, the rise of digital media is creating a vast new area for numerical analysis given the Big Data sources that now exist for analysing online consumer behaviour.

Qualitative vs quantitative research

One leading London agency has stated in its own literature that the quantitative approach to creative research often 'looks at aggregated data instead of understanding individuals, and judges advertisements against artificial and often irrelevant criteria ... we prefer the flexibility of qualitative research'. This position on advertising research, well established and formalised in the role of the account planner, is not universally shared in the advertising industry. Many agencies prefer quantitative data as the research basis for planning decisions. Qualitative research may involve focus or discussion groups, observation studies or in-depth interviews. Sometimes, qualitative advertising research explicitly draws on anthropology for its theoretical foundation. A major US agency in New York has a 'discovery' team of anthropologists who conduct consumer research studies; it has conducted deprivation studies drawing on anthropological techniques to determine the value and meaning attached to the possession of particular types of consumer goods (Hackley, 2000). Agencies have used techniques of ethnography to give their qualitative research greater theoretically-driven insight and hence, they hope, greater intellectual weight with clients. However, what agencies claim as ethnography tends to be based on studies of weeks or months rather than the years typically required of ethnography (Elliott and Jankel-Elliott, 2002). Some agencies have a relatively informal approach to their qualitative research. They regard qualitative research as 'talking to' consumers (Hackley, 2000) and treat the data of videos, transcripts and audio recordings as stimuli for ideas rather than as empirical evidence to support or reject hypotheses. One major agency in Bangkok, Thailand, assimilates a commonsense understanding of consumers they call 'street smarts' throughout the advertising development process (Hackley and Tiwsakul, 2008). Other agencies will have a more explicit, theoretically informed approach to qualitative data interpretation, but most do not. The research skills and sensitivity to nuances of data of experienced planners are relied upon to a great degree, although the interpretations of qualitative research are often hotly debated in the agency account team.

There can be many advantages to quantitative approaches. For example, advertising effectiveness is sometimes tracked using sales figures in relation to the number of target TV spots that the advertisement hits. Clearly, quantitative measurements such as this are essential in fully understanding the impact of a campaign. Statistical techniques such as multivariate analysis can be useful in separating out possible causal variables that might intervene between an advertisement and consumer purchase. Results from experiments can be collated and cross-tabulated, and survey questionnaire results can be statistically analysed for significance. Of course, much of the initial research into the brand category and competitive situation will draw on numerical data to establish items such as brand usage frequency, consumer segment demographics, competitive structure, relative sales volume of the market and so on.

Quantitative data-gathering approaches include surveys, experiments including biometrics, and many digital measurement tools. There is a tendency to use the term 'qualitative research' as if it refers to a commonsense interpretation of naturally occurring social data such as audio recordings of talk or video recordings of behaviour. However, such approaches are more accurately labelled 'interpretative research' because the interpretation of qualitative data is not self-evident: qualitative data are invariably open to a range of interpretations.

Qualitative data-gathering methods are largely drawn from traditions of anthropology (especially ethnography) and cultural sociology (Hackley, 2003e) and include participant observation, in-depth interviewing and questionnaire surveys, consumer diaries, 'focus' or discussion groups, ethnographies (or more accurately, quasi-ethnographies) and other observational methods. Advertising agencies also make use of psychological research methods, such as projective tests (asking the respondent to interpret an image or to complete an incomplete story) and other psychodynamic approaches, and 'depth' interviews (see Packard, 1957, for a famous critique of the use of depth psychology in advertising). Methods derived from literary interpretation include semiotics and discourse analysis.

Much qualitative research focuses on the meaning of consumption, in the hope of generating a resonant insight that can be incorporated into the creative execution to make the consumer emotionally nod with recognition when they see the ad. It does this by seeking methods to understand the lived experience of the group in question. Studies such as Levy (1959), Sherry (1983, 1987, 1991) and Holbrook (1995) have shown how consumers seek and find meaning in their lives from their consumption experiences in ways that are non-trivial and far-reaching. Consumption is carried out not just to solve practical problems but to indulge fantasies and feelings, and for fun (Holbrook and Hirschman, 1982). Qualitative research methods allow consumers to share reflections on their experience of consumption in a non-judgemental setting. The aim is not to elicit rationalisations, which are all too common in consumer research, but sincere insights into the meanings consumption brings to peoples' lives.

Quantitative data sets give the appearance of scientific objectivity and therefore carry a powerful rhetorical force. Findings from qualitative data-gathering methods can be seen as more dependent on subjective interpretation, and hence lack the same pseudo-scientific resonance on a PowerPoint display. In practice, day-to-day marketing relies heavily on qualitative research for its flexibility, ease of use, and ability to generate insights as well as facts.

Experimental research

Advertising has a long tradition of scientific experimental research. For example, in campaign pre-testing experiments a selected audience might be gathered to watch an advertisement in a theatre. The audience presses buttons on their seat arms to indicate whether they like or dislike particular parts of the ad. The results are presented in graphical and statistical form. In less technologically enhanced conditions the audience may be given questionnaires to fill out after they have watched the ad, to determine how much or how little they liked it and how well they recalled various components.

Research that tests audience reaction to creative executions is often called copy-testing. There are many variations on the technique for copy-testing. For example, the theatre test described above is often executed today through what is called a link test. Consumers on the panel view the ad on computer and give their response via online questionnaire. A further development of the technique involves magnetic resonance imaging (MRI) scanning. Participants are shown an ad, or elements of it, while in an MRI scanner, and their brain response is monitored. This kind of neuro-psychological research method is becoming increasingly popular in marketing because it avoids the problem of the inaccuracy of self-reports by going straight to the consumer's unconscious physiological response. Self–report methods such as questionnaire surveys are notorious for being inaccurate. The source of this inaccuracy is sometimes our inability to accurately assess and articulate our inner emotional states. Inaccuracy also often occurs because of poorly designed questions, or because of the incapacity of survey methods to capture nuance of emotional response. If I like a certain brand, then according to a survey I have to like it somewhere on a Likert scale from 'not at all' to 'very much'. I cannot qualify my answer with contingencies, exceptions or contradictions.

Other examples of experimental research in advertising include using psycho-galvanometer equipment to measure consumers' central nervous system response to stimuli, and heart monitoring. Biometric tests such as these show our emotional responses through our physiological levels of excitement throughout engagement with a stimulus such as an advertisement. It is axiomatic that humans are primarily emotional rather than rational, and biometrics (including neuroscience) have become fashionable because they offer clear and indisputable data. If my heart rate doubles and my hippocampus lights up while I'm viewing an ad, I cannot deny that I was excited by it. It is taken as a measure of emotional engagement.[10] Ultimately, of course, biometrics and neuroscience suffer exactly the same weakness as surveys – they cannot capture the nuance of human meaning-making.

Many creative staff, incidentally, feel that experimental and quasi-experimental copy-testing techniques are based on mistaken assumptions about how audiences engage with advertising and therefore miss the point. Experimental research designs lack ecological validity because they do not accurately replicate the conditions under which consumers typically engage with advertising. As many researchers have pointed out (for example, Ritson and Elliott, 1999) consumers view advertising in social situations, not in experimental viewing booths. Our responses to advertising are similarly socially mediated. Naturalistic experiments try to accommodate the consumer ecology to some extent by attempting to re-create the consumer-advertising environment in the hope of getting more relevant results, for example by setting up a specially created advertisement for consumers to watch in a group. However, even these situations cannot get around the fact that they are contrived experimental conditions. For many account managers and clients, though, experimental designs for copy-testing offer a succinct and measurable means of assessing creative executions before incurring the expense and risk of a full campaign launch.

SNAPSHOT 10.4

Qualitative research informs advertising strategies

There are many examples of products and advertising strategies being developed through qualitative research insights. A successful re-design and re-launch of the (now discontinued) *Huggies* brand of disposable nappies (or diapers) in the 1990s was developed with the aid of ethnographic observation of parents changing their babies in a dedicated room in the ad agency. A Thai ad agency used a technique they called 'street smarts' and observed how consumers used Nestlé *Coffee Mate*, a very popular brand in Thailand, in the social context of coffee shops, so that their creative work was informed by an intimate understanding of how consumers use the product within a social setting. In another example, *Hovis*, a 125-year-old brown-bread brand famous in the UK for its evocative advertising,[11] was suffering declining revenue in the 2000s because of intense downward pressure on price from competition and discounting. Volume was growing but profit declining. DDB London conducted primary research in the form of questionnaire surveys in order to fully understand why brand equity was diminishing. The brand was seen as out-of-date and spontaneous brand awareness was in decline. Qualitative research using projective methods had previously found that people described a '*Hovis* room' as a warm and inviting kitchen. By 2001 participants were describing people standing outside the room looking in: people no longer identified with the traditional, old-fashioned positioning of the brand. The new TVC was drawn in a cartoon style[12] reminiscent of animated TV shows like *The Simpsons* to distance it from the old advertising filmed on the cobbled streets of northern England. The relaunch also used new packaging, PR and a supporting website. The brand increased sales while also raising price. The combination of a radical new advertising approach, new packaging and below-the-line support in the form of PR and a website succeeded in repositioning the brand in a contemporary new light. The brand, refreshed, later reached a compromise positioning with a stunning television ad that crossed a century of the brand's history, positioning it in a way that retained a sense of nostalgia but also reinforced its place as a feature of British life in the contemporary age. By 2014, though, the *Hovis* brand was again in decline. A new brand revival is planned.[13]

Survey research

Survey research has traditionally been a part of advertising research, although its use tends to be confined to wide-scale opinion and attitude surveys. Surveys (as noted above) are often designed with semantic scales such as Likert scales that invite a response on a five-point scale to a question or statement. This enables survey questionnaires to be analysed using statistical tests of significance. Survey results can be analysed and presented in a wide variety of ways according to the needs of the users. They can be foundational to advertising development. If 78% of survey respondents aged 18–30 report that they never buy a paper publication, access all their news and information from the mobile internet and watch less than 2 hours TV a week, then advertisers will need to seek digital campaigns to reach this group. The above 'finding' is invented, but there have been surveys that suggested a movement in this direction, hence the radical shift in promotional budgets from traditional mass media to digital and mobile.

Surveys can be useful for extending findings from qualitative research to larger samples. For example, if a consumer discussion group revealed that people felt that their music buying was more important to them than their daily newspaper purchase, this could then be tested on a wider scale with a questionnaire survey. Surveys offer a flexible data-gathering tool since they can be administered in person, by telephone or online, and sample sizes can be large. However, sampling is problematic. It is difficult to verify the respondent's characteristics (did the CEO really fill out the survey, or the intern?) and response rates tend to be low, making the generation of truly random samples very difficult. Consequently, regardless of the sample size, surveys can lack generalisability of findings.

The survey industry is a big business: political polls, opinion polls and questionnaire-based market research studies are commissioned daily at great cost. Many people want to know what large numbers of the population think about brands and about politics. Survey companies such as Ipsos-Mori carry out numerous opinion surveys on a wide variety of topics connected to politics, policy and commerce.[14] As with all research, questionnaire surveys can only be useful if they are designed well to achieve carefully thought-through objectives. The interpretation of findings can be complex and must be done in full knowledge of the limitations of the method.

study in which security cameras were used to monitor shoppers' in-store browsing behaviour. The research aim was to generate insights that might help improve in-store retail design or merchandising techniques. A sign had been erected at the store entrance warning customers that their behaviour might be filmed for research purposes. On exiting from the store researchers approached the consumers to ask them to explain their behaviour. But the exit interviews proved less than informative. When asked why they lingered for so long at one display, or why they moved from display X to display Y, most consumers had little recollection of their movements and some insisted that they had not behaved in the way described, even when confronted with the film evidence. We are not very good, as consumers, at remembering our behaviour.

There are some famous examples of the flaws of self-report research. The *Sony Walkman*, the first personal music system, is said to have met with adverse market research results, presumably because the consumers questioned could not grasp the concept of walking around with a hi-fi playing in their ears. The company ignored the negative research findings and launched the product, to great success. Truly innovative marketing ideas require creative entrepreneurship and teach consumers new consumption concepts. They are beyond the scope of conventional, market research techniques because consumers have nothing with which they can compare a truly innovative concept.

Ethnography and observation

Advertising agencies like to employ anthropologists, for their skills in observing how people derive meaning from their lived experience. To make great advertising, agencies need to understand consumers from an insider perspective – they have to see the world through the consumers' eyes. Indeed, this reflects the classic marketing concept. Anthropologists understand that for humankind the search for meaning is paramount, and ritual and symbolism are central to meaning-making. Brand communications often imply that owning or displaying the brand can transform the consumer's experience or confer upon them a new identity or social status. This experience of liminality (Hackley et al., 2012), even in forms that are transient and perhaps illusory, is a fundamental need for humans. Anthropological methods can capture elements of consumer experience that translate well to advertising with its ability to confer symbolic significance on objects and practices.

Advertising agencies make considerable use of cut-down versions of research methods derived from anthropology, including ethnography and observation. Ethnographers traditionally spent two years or more living with an indigenous tribe, learning their language and rituals, then they would write a book about the experience. Classic anthropological methods are too time-consuming for the business of advertising, but it does make use of 'quasi-ethnography'

(Elliott and Jankel-Elliott, 2002), that is, small slices of ethnographic participation or observation. Just as cultural sociologists of the 1960s might become members of a biker gang or football hooligans for a time in order to understand and write about the inner motivations of members, so advertising people sometimes try to become a member of a consumer group for a short time in order to experience the world through the eyes of those people and thus generate deep cultural insights that can be translated into advertising and marketing strategies. If that is not possible, they might use ethnographic observation as the next best thing, via video, internet (sometimes called netnography, Kozinets, 2009) or direct observation.

Ethnographic methods can also involve asking consumers to keep diaries or take photographs or video clips of events or situations, for analysis by the agency. The aim is to understand how the consumer makes sense of their subjective experience. Typically, ethnographic studies make use of a variety of data-gathering approaches, including observation, researcher field notes and interviews. The whole data set is then studied carefully for clues as to the symbolic meaning of the participants' actions, talk and behaviours. Ethnographic principles may be applied very loosely in marketing, such as when Toyota established a design centre in Newport Beach, California, to help their development of the *Lexus*. Newport Beach is an area packed with wealthy people driving prestigious cars, so it is a good place to be in order to understand luxury car consumption. Being physically present in a centre in which certain kinds of consumption are heavily concentrated assists in understanding the cultural milieu of those consumers, their motivations and behaviours. As noted earlier, ethnographic observation can be effective when conducted at arm's length, through the careful analysis of field data.

Uses of advertising research

The advertising industry is both similar and different across the world. It is similar in that it does pretty much the same thing everywhere, and in superficially much the same way. It is different in that each agency has an individual style and difference of emphasis which manifests in its working practices and style of work (Hackley and Tiwsakul, 2008). So there is room in a creative industry such as advertising for a range of different approaches. Nonetheless, the role of research has been and continues to be a major one in influencing the kinds of advertising we see.

Different advertising agencies place different degrees of emphasis on applying research at various stages in the creative advertising development process. In this section we will look at both methods and uses of research, since the choice of method is often informed by the purpose for which research is needed.

Among the relatively little published academic research there is on how advertising agencies develop campaigns, Punyapiroje et al. (2002) offer an account of advertising development in Thai advertising agencies and McCracken (1986: 74–6) describes the creative advertising development process in US agencies. Scott's work (1994a: 468) focuses on the ways agency creatives tap into the symbolic consumer consciousness and refers to the 'shared social milieu' upon which advertising professionals depend for the 'learned cultural/textual conventions' (p. 463) that will mobilise meaning in their ads. This is the key to great advertising – consumers have to see a kind of truth in the ad, a cultural nod of recognition. Scott and McCracken both refer to the cultural knowledge underlying advertising interpretation that binds both ad maker and ad watcher in a mutually connected communication. 'Research' is part of the industry's attempt to routinise this effect by reaching out into consumer culture to translate its idiom into commercial signs. Hackley and Kover (2007) discuss the tension within which the creative team have to operate as agencies try to reconcile the informal cultural understanding that informs creativity with the formal cultural understanding, derived through research, that reflects the advertising agency's nature as a bureaucratic organisation. Advertising is constructed mainly through talk and texts, in the form of meetings, debates, arguments, presentations, reports, plans and charts (Kelly et al., 2005; Svensson, 2007), punctuated by material objects such as visuals or video ethnographies. Research is an important resource in this process and it is invoked to give force to the argument, in a kind of discourse power game (Hackley, 2000).

The stages of the creative advertising development process at which research can be useful are listed in Table 10.2

Table 10.2 Research in the creative advertising development process

Stage in the process	Types of research that can be undertaken
Client brief	Secondary research into market, business, brand, competitors
Strategy development	Primary studies into relevant consumer groups
Creative brief	Anthropological and/or focus group studies of target consumers
Creative development	Focus and/or observational consumer studies
Media planning	Media/audience research using published sources
Pre-launch	Copy-testing, attitude scaling with finished creative executions
Post-launch	Tracking studies, awareness studies, sales response tracking

Research in the advertising development process

The creative advertising development process begins with the client brief, which the agency account team needs to investigate thoroughly in order to set the terms of reference for the campaign. Initial research will often be undertaken as soon as the client's brief is received. This will establish basic parameters of knowledge about the brand, its market, its consumers and competitors, and the way that the brand fits in with the client's business. All of this work will inform the communications brief, which is the agency's interpretation of the client brief and forms the basis for the advertising strategy, the statement of the purpose for advertising.

Much of this initial research is likely to rely on secondary data sets, that is, data sets already recorded as part of other studies, such as commercial market reports or syndicated surveys, panel data and household data (see Snapshot 10.1). Key questions to be asked and answered through secondary research at this stage might include what is the brand history and who is the target consumer of this brand? What is the brand marketing strategy and what does the client want to achieve with communication? What are the target consumers like, where do they live, how old are they, what kinds of lifestyle do they live, what is their typical income? How many items do they buy per year, where do the buy them from? There will also be questions about the market, the competitors and their strategies. Brand positioning is relative to competitors – so where is this brand in relation to competitors? Agencies will need to have some knowledge of these issues in order to suitably address the client brief and to develop it into a communications brief. In some cases, agencies may commission some primary research as well at this stage.

Once the client brief is translated into a communications brief, research might be useful in some cases to refine the advertising strategy. The ad needs to connect with consumers and the best way for it to do that is for it to reflect some aspect of the consumers' experience that is important or significant to the target audience. There's little point in an ad trumpeting the virtues of paper towels that are made of six layers if the relevant consumers don't care how many layers of paper there are in their kitchen towels. This is where advertising has to reflect the marketing concept and not the product concept – the appeal must be relevant to the consumer, regardless of what the manufacturer feels is important about the product. Research is the way that advertising and promotion agencies get to understand the consumer milieu from the perspective of the consumer. The advertising strategy must reflect what is important to the consumer.

When the brand and the market are fully understood, and the advertising strategy agreed, the creative brief may need additional research into consumer motivations and behaviours. If the strategy is to make the target consumers believe that a particular fashion brand is essential for style leaders, just what kind of appeal might convince them? What kinds of persuasion are most effective with this group? Aesthetically appealing visuals? Ironic humour? A transgressive, anti-authority positioning? *Diesel*, for example, seems to have used all of these kinds of appeal in their advertising over the past decade, exemplified in their award winning 'Be Stupid' campaign.[15] Very often, studies conducted earlier in the process will be engaged with once again, perhaps with more carefully selected participants, or with more focused questions. For example, discussion groups held at the client brief stage might have established broad truths about the consumer group in terms of their attitudes and motivations, but there may be a need at the creative brief stage to dig deeper and perhaps to tweak the sample of respondents.

SNAPSHOT 10.6

The limits of pre-launch testing

Arthur J. Kover, former editor of the *Journal of Advertising Research* and Emeritus Professor of Marketing at the Fordham University Graduate Business School, New York, kindly offers this vignette on the limits of advertising copy-testing.

'Valentine Appel, a revered figure in advertising research, once claimed that research of finished commercials could do two things well. One was to eliminate advertising that is really bad. The other was to select advertising that is really good. Often, however, really innovative advertising does not test well because it cannot be captured by the rational measures of much advertising research. Given the limitations of advertising research to pre-test commercials, one wonders why it is required. The answer is partly political: advertisers need to gain budget approval from many individuals. They therefore need statistical evidence, even if it merely supports the obvious. The other, related reason is that advertisers are highly risk-averse. Advertising research can provide reassurance. It is close to a truism that much advertising is neither good nor bad, just mediocre. Research can test three executions, for example, and show if one is preferred to the others. The advertising manager has the basis for a decision based on concrete numbers, on science, even though the chosen commercial is not really different from the rejected ones. It makes little difference what he or she selects. Cynical? Yes. Reality? Yes. Advertising testing may not be important for decisions but it is necessary for careers.'

Creative research is a source of tension in advertising, as suggested in Snapshot 10.7. Some agencies prefer the solid-looking nature of quantitative research, although this can lack flexibility of interpretation. Others feel that qualitative research provides that flexibility when ideas are provisional and iterative. Qualitative studies can provide feedback on ideas in development, or stimulation for idea generation, because of their relatively unstructured character. Consumer research participants in discussion groups or during ethnographic observation can come up with original insights that capture some element of the brand, when the research approach allows them that latitude of expression. A rigid approach to creative research might fail to capture whether a creative execution is emotionally engaging, but it might serve to measure consumer attitudes toward an element of the creative content. This might generate a clear steer for the team, but it would not allow for any nuance to come through. Consumer experience is often contingent, provisional and nuanced, rather than black and white. We don't really know for sure if we like or dislike something, but we are open to suggestions. Creative research should facilitate creativity, rather than close it down.

Media buying is usually carried out by external media specialists, and they will often be involved in devising the media strategy, but media strategy and planning will also be considerations in the creative advertising development process since so many creative issues cannot be dealt with in a media vacuum – account teams, and especially creatives, need to know which media channels they can use. Many creative craft skills are media-specific. Media research entails finding out who reads, views, listens to or uses what media channels, when, how and how much. This is often done through specialist suppliers of media research such as BRAD[16] and Kantar Media.[17]

Once the agency team and client are happy with a creative execution they might wish to reassure themselves about the response of target consumers to specific aspects, such as the script (or copy), the action, scene and actors (if it is a TV ad) or the combination of colours and copy for a print ad. Ads may be adjusted or even abandoned altogether because of results from a pre-launch 'copy'-test. Many a creative execution has been abandoned at pre-launch because of the wishes of the client representative, often to the frustration of the account manager. Copy-testing, as discussed above, often takes place through 'link' tests in which a creative execution is shown to a panel of consumers, possibly in a form such as animatronics rather than a finished production, and they respond to an online questionnaire. If the consumers don't like the idea enough, it may be adjusted or even cancelled and the creative team is told to come up with a new idea. Research agency Millward Brown provide 'Link' tests and also a shorter version called Express Link.[18] As mentioned above, some advertisers make use of biometric measures such as neuropsychological scanning to assess the response of consumers to advertising stimuli, although the Link or other online versions of the theatre advertising test can be used on larger samples of participants.

After campaign launch, there is a need to evaluate the effectiveness of the campaign against its objectives, so tracking studies can be undertaken using a combination of research methods. If, for example, the campaign objective was to change attitudes to a brand in a particular location, then a simple street survey before and after launch could measure the extent to which this has been successful, or not. If the campaign was supporting a new product or brand launch, prompted and unprompted recall tests could be used. More complex statistical tests such as multivariate analysis could be deployed for long-term assessment of advertising effects.

Evaluation continues throughout the campaign but the most information is available to make the judgement on its success after the campaign has finished. The agency will need to provide a detailed assessment of how effective it was. Tracking studies are very important for agencies since they constitute a record of the campaign's evolution and its marketing results. They can provide evidence for clients that the campaign accomplished the objectives set for it. Case histories that are written up from successful campaigns provide a learning resource and, if they are submitted to awards competitions, can be useful PR for the agency itself. Most ad agencies carry case histories of their successful campaigns on their websites as advertisements for their skills.

Tension and conflict around research in advertising

Much misunderstanding about research in advertising occurs because it is not one entity but many. As we have seen, research is conducted for a number of different purposes. First, it is what is done to initially investigate a brand's market category, its role in the client's business and the consumer segments that are relevant. Second, it is what account planning staff do to try to generate facts about consumer reality that can give communication a particular resonance with the target group. Third, research is what is often done to draft creative work before the campaign is launched, in an effort to predict the likely consumer response. Fourth, research is the process of trying to track the response of consumers to the campaign. Debates around research method in advertising, then, revolve not only around fundamental questions of research philosophy but also around the usefulness of particular methods in given situations. As Kover (1995) and Hackley (2003c) suggest, advertising agencies comprise professionals with very different intellectual backgrounds and equally different implicit theories of practice. These differences are caused by different assumptions about the nature of advertising and consumers, and they give rise to impassioned debates about what a given research finding implies for a particular campaign.

SNAPSHOT 10.7

Creatives and research

Research is an essential part of the advertising and marketing industries, but creatives feel that it can be damaging to the standards of creativity in advertising. Indeed, many creative professionals in advertising would put it much more strongly than this: many are openly hostile to formal research. They see research as a power tool wielded by those who have little understanding of how or why consumers engage with advertising. The following quote is from a copywriter complaining about research in the New York newsletter of the American Marketing Association: 'Don't tell me that … [your] little questions and statistics can pinpoint the complexity and richness of how people respond to my work' (Kover, 1996: RC9). This quote neatly illustrates the conflicts that can arise when research is conceived as a formalised and method-driven technique that offers definitive findings, while creative see their craft as one of motivating consumers through aesthetically inspiring imagery (Hackley and Kover, 2007).

The debates in advertising practice are reflected in academic research. For example, much research in the field has its basis in the transmission model of communication (deriving from, for example, Schramm's mass communications research, 1948) described in Chapter 2. The linear model of communication conceives of advertising as something that acts on individual consumers in social isolation and this assumption has framed much of the research in the field. Academic researchers (e.g. Mick and Buhl, 1992) have argued that this preoccupation with advertising exposure isolated from its social context risks misconstruing the fundamentally social nature of the interaction between consumers and advertising (but also see Scott, 1994a, for comments on Mick and Buhl, 1992). Consumers usually engage with advertising in a social context and not alone in a viewing booth. Ritson and Elliott (1999, citing Holbrook, 1995: 93; McCracken, 1987: 123, in support) have suggested that advertising cannot properly be understood as if it operates in a social vacuum. Advertising, they argue, is actively consumed, reinterpreted and used for purposes of social positioning and identity formation (Buttle, 1994; O'Donohoe, 1994).

The linear information processing tradition of advertising theory also emphasises conscious and rational information processing. Academic researchers have drawn attention to the symbolic character of advertising communication, suggesting that consumer motivations are not invariably dominated by conscious reasoning. For example, McCracken (1986) has alluded to the deeply symbolic character of consumption and argues that this feature has been marginalised in favour of a rational model of how advertising works. For this researcher cultural meaning has a 'mobile quality' (p. 71) and advertising is an 'instrument of meaning transfer' (p. 74). Mick and Buhl (1992: 314) draw critical attention to the tendency for some advertising research to regard ads as 'relatively fixed stimuli' and consumers as 'solitary subjects, without identities, who react to ads through linear stages or limited persuasion routes, for the principal purpose of judging brands'. Holbrook and O'Shaughnessy (1988: 400) maintain that humans live 'embedded within a shared system of signs based on public language and other symbolic objects'. Advertising can be seen as a major site of signification, taking consumer cultural meanings, placing them in the context of brand marketing and reflecting them back so that consumers can perform cultural practices symbolically through the consumption of marketed brands. The particular signs that carry meaning in a given context for a given consumer community are difficult for brand advertisers to ascertain unless they can understand the world in the same way as the group of interest. For Thompson et al. (1989: 433) 'personal understandings are always situated within a network of culturally-shared knowledge, shared beliefs, ideals and taken-for-granted assumptions about the nature of social life'. The implication is that social research cannot fully appreciate personal understandings without also understanding how they interface with the social context in which they are formed. This squares with the creatives' complaint that copy testing fails to capture the true character of consumers' engagement with advertising, but fails to acknowledge the political role of advertising research in agencies.

Advertising is an area in which art and business collide, often with aesthetically striking and commercially fruitful results. Understandably, there are conflicts resulting from the differing values and mindsets associated with each community.

Research ethics

Given the heightened sensitivity over ethical issues in advertising and marketing in general, it is worth briefly discussing some issues of research ethics that might impact in advertising contexts. Conducting research with consumers involves prying into their and our attitudes and lifestyles. In some cultures, consumers tend to be very open about this and happy to tell a researcher whom they have never met before intimate details of their consumer behaviour. In others, it is much more likely that a cold-calling researcher would be given short shrift. Where consumers are willing to give of their time to discuss aspects of their consumer experience, it is incumbent on the researcher to treat information as highly confidential and to respect the wishes, feelings and wellbeing of the research participant.

The leading professional bodies have their own ethical standards to which they require professionals to adhere. There are, also, various ethical conventions that are widely accepted as good practice, such as confidentiality and respect for the individual's wellbeing. Many psychological experiments that are regarded as 'classic' studies would not be permitted by a university ethics committee today. Research studies should not cross legal or ethical boundaries in any way. Some research studies might wish to use minors (children), in which case detailed procedures of vetting and ethical approval would have to be sought. Research participants in focus groups who are being videoed would need to be reassured that the film would be used only for the precise purpose for which it was being undertaken, and only by officials of the relevant companies involved in the research study. They would also need to be reassured of the integrity and trustworthiness of the researcher.

It is important that participants in advertising research studies take part freely and willingly, and that their rights are explained to them at the very start of the session. The uses to which the research will be put should be clearly explained. They should be assured that they can stop and withdraw from the study at any time, that they do not have to make any responses that they feel uncomfortable making, that their opinions and experiences will be treated with respect, and, most importantly, that their contribution will remain completely confidential.

Chapter summary

Chapter 10 has outlined types and uses of research in advertising. Rather than focusing on the execution of methods, it has discussed some of the conceptual foundations of research and the ways in which these can be put to rhetorical use on advertising agency politics. The chapter outlined some key methodological distinctions in advertising research, including qualitative/quantitative and primary/secondary and it discussed a number of methods. The chapter went on to discuss the role of research in each stage of the creative advertising development process. Finally, some points regarding research ethics were briefly outlined.

■ Review Questions

1. Place yourself in the position of an account planner trying to understand a new brief from a manufacturer of branded disposable nappies (diapers). What sources and kinds of information will be required? What primary research methods could be useful? Explain your choices.

2. Why is research a source of potential conflict in advertising agencies?

3. Pick three print ads and conduct copy-test experiments with an audience. Devise scaled questionnaires to assess the strength of feeling subjects have towards various components of the ad. What issues arise? How useful are the findings?

4. Convene a discussion group to explore the issue of ethics in advertising. Use a selection of ethically controversial ads as stimulus material. Write up the main findings. Now write a brief assessment of the main problems and uses of this research technique.

5. Outline how a new brief for a brand of fruit-flavoured alcoholic drink might be better understood through informal and qualitative research.

CASE STUDY

Consumer insight and the Dove CfRB[19]

The *Dove 'Campaign for Real Beauty'* (*CfRB*) reportedly raised the brand's UK market share by 30% in the first few years following its launch in 2004 (Robinson et al., 2009). The brand wished to improve its consumer engagement and a global research study revealed a key consumer insight – specifically, conventional, aspirational ('*Revlon* don't sell cosmetics, we sell hope'[20]) cosmetics advertising played on women's low self-esteem by making them feel insecure about their appearance. Traditional cosmetics and fashion branding present ideals of beauty that are unattainable, even for the models themselves, since every asymmetry and blemish is photoshopped away. The team had garnered from interviews that some women resented conventional cosmetics advertising because it didn't represent women 'like them'. The team wanted to feed this insight into campaign featuring 'real' (i.e. not photoshopped or

(Continued)

size zero) women. Legend has it that the predominantly male, middle-aged Unilever board resisted this radical move until presented with videos of their own wives and daughters explaining how insecure typical cosmetics ads made them feel about their bodies. The idea was sold, and *Dove CfRB* was born. *Dove* positioned their brand as giving (or to be accurate, selling) women's self-esteem back to them. The theme was expanded across different media platforms with clever PR, tons of media coverage and initiatives including the *Dove* self-esteem website,[21] charitable donations to *Dove*'s Self-Esteem Fund for disadvantaged women, and some striking viral videos, including one called 'Evolution' of a model being photoshopped, made by Ogilvy Toronto[22] (and a follow up called 'Onslaught' focusing on the influence advertising might exert on young girls' self-image). The positioning was controversial, at least for cynics, who pointed out that Unilever also operate a stable of brands that hardly demur from exploiting beauty stereotypes. Unilever's men's deodorant brands *Lynx* and *Axe* are notorious for their ads sexualising women, while the skin whitener *Fair And Lovely* exploits beauty myths about light skin in the African subcontinent and South, as well as South-East, Asia. What is more, *Dove*'s social marketing strategy seems to play out differently in international markets that don't buy into the media criticism of conventional model shoots – for example, *Dove* billboards look very conventionally aspirational in Hong Kong.[23] The *Dove CfRB* campaign insight required an appreciation of the wider context of the issue (beauty myths and the visual representation of women in media), including the way this topic was playing out as a media debate in Western fashion circles. For example, there was much media criticism of 'size zero' fashion models and the role an ideology of super thin-ness was playing in the rise of eating disorders such as anorexia. This issue was expanded further by *Dove* to take in wider cultural issues of female children's psychological development and women's education and social role. This seems to be an example of consumer insight that was generated by sensitively using qualitative interviews in a way that was flexible enough to accommodate contextual insights. The resulting campaign radically challenged the Western discourse of cosmetics advertising. *Dove*'s 2013 viral campaign called 'Thought Before Action' (on YouTube[24]) offered a piece of software that secretly reverted photographs back to their un-photoshopped state. A number of commentators (for example a brand consultancy called Quo Vadis[25]) pointed out that, while female body image is unquestionably manipulated by marketers, *Dove* is not exactly above the fray with its enhanced photography of the products (a bar of used soap never really looked this good), its chemical masking of the way the products really look and smell, and its alleged double-standard in exploiting ideologies of female beauty by claiming to take a stand against them. In spite of criticism, the campaign theme has continued to gather pace over a decade and *Dove*'s multiple award-winning 2013 YouTube campaign 'Real Beauty Sketches' has become the most watched online ad ever, according to Unilever, with 163 million views to date[26] and over a million likes on *Dove*'s Facebook page. The films, made by Ogilvy & Mather Brazil, feature a trained artist sketching women according to their own description, and again according to others' description of them. The sketches drawn from self-description show less attractive women than those from third party description, suggesting that women downplay their own beauty. They could also be an illustration that some nice people are naturally self-deprecating, while being generous in describing the physical appearance of others. Whatever the interpretation, the campaign continues to resonate powerfully with huge audiences.

1. In what ways does the *Dove CfRB* advertising illustrate the advantages of qualitative research insights in creative advertising development?

2. Why has *Dove CfRB* achieved the success that it has?

3. Look at the *Dove CfRB* material available on the internet. Are there any other initiatives you feel *Dove* could deploy to leverage the deep sense of engagement its consumers have with the brand?

4. How might a small, regional cosmetics brand without the resources to fund a global research study generate a powerful insight from its research that could ignite social media and engage new consumers?

Useful journal articles

(These Sage articles can be accessed on the book website)

Marsha D. Loda, Barbara C. Coleman and Kenneth F. Backman (2010) 'Walking in Memphis: testing one DMO's marketing strategy to Millennials', *Journal of Travel Research*, 49 (1): 46–55 (first published May 19, 2009).

Adam E. Barry and Patricia Goodson (2010) 'Use (and misuse) of the responsible drinking message in public health and alcohol advertising: a review', *Health Education & Behavior*, 37 (2): 288–303 (first published August 10, 2009).

Daniel Wentzel, Sven Henkel and Torsten Tomczak (2010) 'Can I live up to that ad? Impact of implicit theories of ability on service employees' responses to advertising', *Journal of Service Research*, 13 (2): 137–52.

Jos Hornikx, Frank van Meurs and Anja de Boer(2010) 'English or a local language in advertising? The appreciation of easy and difficult English slogans in the Netherlands', *Journal of Business Communication*, 47 (2): 169–88.

Chris Miles (2004) 'The prospect and schizogenesis: a Batesonian perspective on the implications of the double-bind in advertising messages', *Marketing Theory*, 4 (4): 267–86.

Robert E. Smith and Xiaojing Yang (2004) 'Toward a general theory of creativity in advertising: examining the role of divergence', *Marketing Theory*, 4 (1–2): 31–58.

■ ■ Further reading ■ ■

Alozie, E.C. (2010) 'Advertising and culture: semiotic analysis of dominant symbols found in Nigerian mass media advertising', *Journal of Creative Communications*, 5 (1): 1–22.

Basadur, M., Gelade, G. and Basadur, T. (2014) 'Creative problem-solving process styles, cognitive work demands, and organizational adaptability', *The Journal of Applied Behavioral Science*, 50 (1): 80–115 (first published December 3, 2013).

Chávez, C.A. (2014) 'Linguistic capital and the currency of Spanish in Hispanic advertising production', *Journal of Communication Inquiry*, 38 (1): 25–43.

De Pelsmacker, P. and Dens, N. (2009) *Advertising Research: Message, Medium and Context*. Antwerp: Garant.

Ehrenberg, A. and Barnard, N. (1997) 'Advertising and product demand', Admap, May: 14–18.

Gidlöf, K., Holmberg, N. and Sandberg, H. (2012) 'The use of eye-tracking and retrospective interviews to study teenagers' exposure to online advertising', *Visual Communication*, 11 (3): 329–45.

Jiang Wu, Bin Hu and Yu Zhang (2013) 'Maximizing the performance of advertisements diffusion: a simulation study of the dynamics of viral advertising in social networks', *SIMULATION*, 89 (8): 921–34.

Jones, J.P. (1990) 'Advertising: strong force or weak force? Two views an ocean apart', *International Journal of Advertising*, 9: 233–46.

Rajabi, M., Dens, N. and De Pelsmacker, P. (2014) 'Attention and memory effects of advertising in an international context', in H. Cheng (ed.), *The Handbook of International Advertising Research*. Oxford: Wiley–Blackwell.

Wells, W.D. (ed.) (1997) *Measuring Advertising Effectiveness*. Hillsdale, NJ: Lawrence Erlbaum Associates.

Notes

1. http://thearf.org/ accessed 15.3.2014
2. www.warc.com/ accessed 15.3.2014
3. www.nielsen.com/content/corporate/uk/en.html accessed 15.3.2014
4. www.tnsglobal.com/ accessed 15.3.2014
5. www.barb.co.uk/viewing/weekly-total-viewing-summary accessed 17.3.2014
6. www.mintel.com/ accessed 16.3.2014
7. www.creativereview.co.uk/cr-blog/2011/august/happy-birthday-bill-bernbach accessed 17.3.2014
8. http://mashable.com/2014/01/28/vw-super-bowl-2014/ accessed 17.3.2014
9. www.youtube.com/user/UKVolkswagen accessed 17.3.2014
10. www.ipsos-mori.com/researchspecialisms/ipsosasi/ourapproach/biometrics.aspx accessed 17.3.2014
11. www.brandrepublic.com/news/1228764/remember-classic-Hovis-TV-ads/?HAYILC=RELATED accessed 16.3.2014
12. www.youtube.com/watch?v=48aHtegMo88 accessed 17.3.2014
13. www.brandrepublic.com/news/1228649/ accessed 17.3.2014
14. www.ipsos-mori.com/ accessed 17.3.2014

15. www.creativeadawards.com/diesel-be-stupid-advertising-campaign/ accessed 17.3.2014
16. www1.bradinsight.com/brad-media-planning accessed 16.3.2014
17. www.kantarmedia.co.uk/ accessed 17.3.2014
18. www.millwardbrown.com/Libraries/MB_Solutions_Downloads/MillwardBrown_LinkExpress.sflb.ashx accessed 17.3.2014
19. http://selfesteem.dove.co.uk/Articles/Written/Our_Mission.aspx?WT.srch=1&gclid=CLXE2J2-mr0CFQKWtAodbRcAyg accessed 17.3.2014
20. This is a comment often attributed to a *Revlon* executive and used in textbooks as an illustration of the way the marketing concept focuses on end-user benefit. Other similar illustrations include the alleged comment of a power tools executive that 'We don't sell drills, we sell holes'.
21. www.dove.co.uk/en/Our-Mission/Self-Esteem-Toolkit-and-Resources/default.aspx accessed 4.3.2013.
22. www.youtube.com/watch?v=iYhCn0jf46U accessed 22.02.2013
23. This comment is based on nothing more scientific than my discussion with students while teaching in Hong Kong, and my observation of the poster advertising for the brand.
24. Dove 'Thought Before Action' viral video www.youtube.com/watch?v=m0JF4QxPpvM accessed 7.3.2013
25. Quo Vadis blog www.qvbrands.com/dove-rant/ accessed 7.3.2013
26. www.thinkwithgoogle.com/case-studies/dove-real-beauty-sketches.html   accessed 17.3.2014

Glossary

Above-the-line, below-the-line, through-the-line   Terms that originate from the UK system of ad agency remuneration (now largely defunct). If a medium generated commission payment to the agency, it was regarded as above-the-line. Above-the-line media included mainstream advertising on press, cinema, commercial radio and TV. Below-the-line media generated no agency commission and included sales promotion, public relations and direct mail. Through-the-line campaigns utilised combinations of above- and below-the-line media.

Account manager   The role responsible for client liaison and the general business management of an account.

Account planner   The account team role responsible for research and strategy.

ACORN   A Classification of Residential Neighbourhoods: a form of geodemographic segmentation that categorises consumers on the basis of the residential neighbourhood where they live.

Adspend   The monetary expenditure on advertising and promotion.

Advergaming   The use of interactive games via the internet or mobile as an advertising device.

Advertainment   Advertisements that entertain by relating a dramatic narrative or by engaging consumers in an interactive process such as a game.

Affiliate marketing   Co-operative ventures, often e-based, with, for example, host websites carrying other brands' material for click-through business.

AIDA   Acronym for Attention–Interest–Desire–Action, a sequence of states through which a direct salesperson should take the prospect, popularised by Strong in *The Psychology of Selling and Advertising* (1929). AIDA was designed to model personal selling but is often used to model the alleged effects of mass media advertising.

Ambient media   Promotional messages inserted into traditionally non-promotional spaces in the consumer environment, such as the back of car parking tickets, farmers' fields, the sides of buildings and printed on toilet tissue.

Appeal   the creative content of advertisements can be categorised by the kind of appeal, e.g. humour, sexuality, fear, peer approval, social status … etc.

Audience   The number of people or households exposed to a given communication in a specified time period.

Awareness   The extent to which consumers have heard of or seen and recall a brand or a particular promotion, often measured by surveys.

Biometrics   A consumer research approach that entails measuring central nervous system response to external marketing stimuli via heart rate, brain activation, or sweat.

Brand engagement   No agreed definition but the concept revolves around the volitional and active attention of consumers, elicited by making promotions more interesting and, especially, by making them interactive.

Buzz marketing   Aims to generate WOM (word of mouth) and/or media coverage through a event, viral or pop-up event.

Buzz word   Briefly popular term.

Client   The brand manager or brand marketing director who works with the advertising agency in the development of the campaign.

Client brief/advertising strategy/creative brief   Internal agency documentation charting and guiding the development of communication.

Connote, connotation   A term referring to the secondary meanings that may subsist in a given text. For example, a car advertisement might highlight the car, but the imagery might connote happiness, attractiveness and an exciting lifestyle.

Consequentialist, consequentialism   The doctrine that the ethical status of acts should be judged according to the actual or possible consequences. In other words, if an advertisement may have good consequences, it is judged ethically acceptable. Many charities and public-service campaigns that try to shock people into driving more safely, drinking less alcohol and so on, are allowed to do so based on these implicit grounds.

Consumer communities Consumer groups whose only commonality is their mutual interest in a particular set of consumption values or practices. Some advertising agencies use the phrase 'brand communities' to indicate that heterogeneous social groups who share only a mutual interest in a particular brand can be defined as a group on this basis. The 'values' that are integral to the brand are, implicitly, shared by the group. An example might be the Manchester United Supporters' Club, a widely diverse group in terms of age, sex, ethnicity, nationality and social status, which is united only in their interest in the soccer club (and its merchandise).

Consumer practices Also social practices, or cultural practices: things consumers do, that may entail elements of ritual and make use of symbolism.

Content A term for any and all media content. Content marketing entails movies, games, blog pieces or anything else that can be viewed for entertainment or information, shared on social media, and branded.

Copy-testing A quasi-experimental group of research approaches usually conducted to test creative executions before a campaign launch. Copy-testing measures attitudes towards an advertisement and its different visual or other components.

Cost-per-thousand A media planning term denoting the cost per thousand consumers reached through a given medium, e.g. website banner ad, direct mail shot, TV ad.

Covert communication Covert communication in advertising occurs where the absence of a clearly designated communication source facilitates meanings that are implicit. For example, the promotional motive of content marketing is usually covert.

Creative Used as a noun to designate one member of the creative team, as in 'a creative'.

Creative execution The finished advertisement.

Creative team Since the 1960s it has been convention for advertising agency creative work to be done in teams of two.

Creative advertising development process The term used in some advertising agencies for the process of developing advertising.

Creative hot shops/boutiques It is common in the marketing communications field for successful professionals to break away from their employing agency to form new partnerships known as creative hot shops or boutiques. They are normally small partnerships of experienced professionals who seek a more responsive and rewarding environment than a large agency can offer.

Database mining software Data mining entails using large databases of customer information to generate new segments to target with direct marketing initiatives. Software packages can be useful in allowing marketing analysts to create contact lists of consumers from larger customer databases grouped according to any given criterion.

Deontological, deontology The doctrine that acts should be judged on their intrinsic rightness or wrongness regardless of the consequences. For example, consumers sometimes object to particular advertisements on the grounds that they are offensive: this is implicitly a deontological, ethical position.

Deprivation studies A technique used in anthropological studies that requires research participants to forego an item for a period of time and to record their feelings about its absence in a diary. The feelings of deprivation endured (and expressed) can be a measure of the importance and role of the item in the person's life. One such study conducted for a global audio equipment manufacturer examined the role of audio equipment in people's lives by getting a panel of consumers to do without their audio equipment for a month.

Discourse Anything that can be described in words: a category of social text that entails accepted or conventional communicative practices.

DRTV Direct-response television.

Embedded marketing Marketing initiatives presented in the context of entertainment vehicles such as movies, TV shows or sponsored media events. The key element of embedded marketing is that the audience is not necessarily explicitly aware that the brand exposure is a paid-for promotion.

Ethics The study of the good life, including the exploration of questions of what good conduct is conducive to living the good life.

Eye tachistoscope test A technique of advertising research in which a camera device tracks the movement of a viewer's eye over a creative execution.

Focus group Generic name for informal discussion groups often used by agencies for exploratory research.

Fragmentation of media audiences Mass media audiences have fragmented as the number of media vehicles has multiplied.

Frame of reference The norms and assumptions through which we interpret the world.

Full-service agency An advertising agency that offers the full range of communications services to clients. In practice most agencies rely to a greater or lesser degree on the sub-contracting of specialist services.

Generalisation   A truth or fact that holds under any circumstances in any culture.

Geodemographics   A technique of consumer segmentation that combines demographic with geographical information.

Glocalisation   Casting global advertising campaigns in terms of the local consumer cultural and linguistic idiom.

Guerrilla marketing   Marketing that does not use conventional media and may have its true intent deliberately obscured.

Hierarchy-of-effects theories   Theories of persuasive communication that conceive of a passive and indifferent consumer who must be persuaded to buy the brand by the accumulated effect of a number of ad exposures.

High involvement   a purchase of such importance that it requires a high order of processing, including, for example, an information search and evaluation of alternatives. Purchases such as a house, car or family holiday might be characterised thus. Many purchases that take a lower proportion of disposable income are thought to be more spontaneous and subject to a lower order of rational processing (i.e. low involvement). This binary construct loses its explanatory effectiveness when purchases have a powerful, symbolic value for consumers, e.g. spending months evaluating alternatives for the purchase of a new pair of shoes.

Household data   Market research focusing on the household unit, contrasts with panel data, which often focuses on the store or region.

Integrated marketing communications (IMC)   A management initiative to link and coordinate brand communications through all media channels. IMC is often only partially achieved because of functional divisions within organisations between different communications disciplines.

Integrated solutions   Advertising and promotional campaigns that use co-ordinated creative executions through different media channels.

Interpretive community   A group that shares certain cultural reference points and therefore a sense of meaning in some situations. For example, intertextual references in ads to scenes from Hollywood movies or to sports events will be most quickly understood by, respectively, movie buffs and sports fans.

Intertextuality   A characteristic of discourses whereby they adapt, copy or refer to other discourses, for example where ads refer to movies, or movies refer to brands.

Likert scales   The original form of attitude measurement scale; usually in the form of a statement and a five-item response scale ranging from 'strongly negative' to 'strongly positive'.

Linear information processing [theories of communication] Theories (or models) that draw an analogy between human and machine information processing. Also known as consumer information processing (CIP).

Magnetic resonance imaging (MRI) A medical technique for scanning the brain also used in neurological consumer research (neuro-marketing).

Managerial managerialist The genre of business writing and research devoted to solving the problems of managers without reference to wider social scientific or ethical issues and values.

Marketing mix The four Ps of marketing management: Price, Product, Promotion and Physical distribution. Subsequent versions have added People and Processes.

Media channel Any means by which a message can be communicated, such as TV, radio, OOH (out of home), print, digital, mobile. (See also *media vehicle*)

Media planner A specialist whose responsibility it is to see that a given campaign reaches the largest number of targeted consumers possible within the allocated budget.

Media-neutral planning Campaign planning that is not biased toward mass media.

Media vehicle A specific outlet within a given media channel: for example print is a media channel, the *Daily Telegraph* is a media vehicle; TV is a media channel, *The X Factor* is a media vehicle.

Native advertising Advertising that is 'native' to the consumer's environment, especially in digital and print in which sponsored content is included in editorial. Native advertising has been called 'a new name for advertorial', and another name for 'content marketing'. Print publications like *The Guardian* and *Huffington Post* have invested much effort in developing revenue streams from native advertising.

Neuro-marketing A biometric consumer research method based on magnetic resonance imaging (MRI) of brain activity under stimulation, to test emotional engagement. For example, some advertising straplines or creative executions will be tested using volunteers in MRI conditions to measure emotional engagement. The rationale for neuro-marketing is twofold: (1) consumer responses to marketing stimuli are primarily emotional, driven by physiological responses; (2) research methods based on self-reporting, such as questionnaire surveys, are unreliable instruments.

Operant conditioning In behavioural psychology, operant conditioning changes behaviour in response to repeated stimuli administered by an operator.

Ostensive communication   Communication that is explicit and has an identifiable source, usually contrasted with communication that is covert or implicit.

Panel data   Continuous data that are collected from a panel of consumers to monitor regular household purchases.

Peer group   People like us in age and outlook with whom we associate.

Penetration   The percentage of a market that is reached by a given medium or an individual promotional communication.

Pitching   The pitching or pitch process is the traditional method by which advertising agencies get new business. They 'pitch' their ideas to a prospective client in response to the client's brief, in competition with other agencies.

Polysemy   The capacity of a social text such as an ad to have multiple meanings. The meanings inferred will depend on such things as the cultural context and the interpretive strategy of the reader.

POS   Point of sale can refer to sales promotions at the cash till of a store or to any in-store promotion, such as free sample stalls and LCD screen advertising.

Positioning   A marketing concept indicating the values or ideas that are associated with a given brand and which differentiate the brand from competition. For example, the Nestlé KitKat chocolate confection is positioned (in the UK) as an excuse to have a break (that is, a rest) from work; the Marlboro cigarette brand is associated (through the image of the Marlboro cowboy) with individualism and toughness.

Positivistic   A term borrowed from the philosophy of logical positivism (Ayer, 1936) but referring in management and business research to approaches that model their methods and assumptions on those of natural science.

Primary research   The generation of new data. Contrasts with secondary research, which refers to the use of data sets already in existence.

Product placement   The practice of placing branded products or services in TV, radio, movie or other forms of entertainment.

Projective techniques   A psychological technique used in qualitative consumer research. It can take the form of a story-completion or picture-completion task. It originated in the psychiatric technique of asking a respondent to interpret Rorschach ink blots.

Promotional mix   The various promotional techniques. The term 'communications mix' is often used to indicate the differing communication channels that are deployed to reach the targeted audience.

Prompted and un-prompted recall   Brand recall can be measured with prompted and un-prompted tests: e.g. unprompted – 'Which brands do you recall seeing in TV advertising this week?'; prompted – 'Do you recall seeing brand X in TV advertising this week?'

Psycho-galvanometer tests   Tests carried out by a machine that measures the stimulation of the central nervous system by measuring the activity of sweat glands, thereby indicating the degree of interest a viewer has in a creative execution.

Psychographics   A lifestyles and attitudes-based approach to consumer segmentation.

Qualitative research   non-numerical research to seek insight into the quality of a group or person's experience of a given phenomenon.

Quantitative research   Research that generates numerical data.

Reach   The number of individuals or households within a target audience reached by a given promotional communication over a certain time period. Often expressed as a percentage.

Representative   A sample of people that, for research purposes, is assumed to have the same characteristics as the whole population of interest.

Segmentation   Aiming marketing interventions at a defined group of consumers who share certain demographic or lifestyle characteristics.

Semiology   The study of linguistic signs. Associated with the work of Ferdinand de Saussure.

Semiotics   The science of all signs and their meaning in communication, associated with Charles Sanders Pierce.

Socio-economic group   An approach to classifying groups of individuals based on the occupation of the main household wage earner. Devised by the UK civil service in the late 1940s and still used in audience analysis.

Split-run studies   A technique of measuring advertising effect by comparing two differing creative executions in two different but demographically similar regions.

Sub-culture   A non-mainstream group characterised by shared attitudes, lifestyles, symbols and ritual.

Sub-text   Texts that subsist beneath the main text, in other words, implied meanings, additional or subordinate to the primary meaning of a text.

Synergy   A coined word indicating the mutually reinforcing promotional effect of portraying a brand in a similar style on two or more media channels.

Targeting   The task of reaching the chosen segment of consumers by placing creative executions on carefully chosen media channels.

Tracking studies   Research studies that monitor the effect of a campaign after its launch against the objectives set for it.

Traffic controller   An administrative role within agencies responsible for keeping track of the progress of different accounts. Today, the traffic controller may be called project management.

Viral marketing   Originally the establishment of Hotmail was the model for viral marketing since word spread via email. Viral is now used to describe any content that is shared rapidly and widely on social media.

WOM   Word of mouth (promotion) is the spontaneous exchange of ideas within peer groups about a brand or advertisement.

References

Aaker, D.A (2004) *Brand Portfolio Strategy: Creating Relevance, Differentiation, Energy, Leverage and Clarity*. New York: Free Press.

Alvesson, M. (1998) 'Gender relations and identity at work: a case study of masculinities and femininities in an advertising agency', *Human Relations*, 51: 969–1005.

Amis, J., Slack, T. and Berrett, T. (1999) 'Sport sponsorship as distinctive competence', *European Journal of Marketing*, 33 (3/4): 250–72.

Ayer, A.J. (1936) *Language, Truth and Logic*. London: Victor Gollancz. (Reprinted by Penguin Books, 1990.)

Bagozzi, R., Tybout, A.M., Craig, C.S. and Sternthal, B. (1979) 'The construct validity of the tripartite classification of attitudes', *Journal of Marketing Research*, 16 (February): 88–95.

Bakhtin, M. (1989) 'Discourse in life and discourse in art (concerning sociological poetics)', in R. Davis and R. Schleifler (eds), *Contemporary Literary Criticism*. New York: Longman. pp. 392–410.

Balasubramanian, S.K. (1994) 'Beyond advertising and publicity: hybrid messages and public policy issues', *Journal of Advertising*, 23 (4): 29–47.

Balasubramanian, S.K., Karrh, J.A. and Patwardhan, H. (2006) 'Audience response to product placements: an integrative framework and future', *Journal of Advertising* 35 (3): 115–141.

Barnard, N. and Ehrenberg, A. (1997) 'Advertising: strongly persuasive or nudging?', *Journal of Advertising Research*, 37 (1): 21–31.

Barry, T.E. and Howard, D.J. (1990) 'A review and critique of the hierarchy of effects in advertising', *International Journal of Advertising*, 9: 121–35.

Barthes, R. (2000) *Mythologies*. London: Vintage.

Bassiouni, D. and Hackley, C. (2014) 'Generation Z children's adaptation to digital consumer culture: a critical literature review', *Journal of Customer Behaviour* (in press).

Belk, R.W. (1988) 'Possessions and the extended self', *Journal of Consumer Research*, 15 (2): 139–68.

Belk, R.W. and Pollay, R.W. (1985) 'Images of ourselves: the good life in twentieth century advertising', *Journal of Consumer Research*, 11: 887–97.

Berger, P.L. and Luckman, T. (1966) *The Social Construction of Reality*. London: Penguin.

Binet, L. (2009) 'Payback calculations: how to make sure you get your sums right', in N. Dawson (ed.), *Advertising Works 17: Proving the Return on Marketing Investment*. Henley-on-Thames: World Advertising Research Centre. pp. 19–22.

Blake, A., MacRury, I., Nava, M. and Richards, B. (eds) (1996) *Buy This Book: Studies in Advertising and Consumption*. London: Routledge.

Broadbent, T. (2009) 'Effectiveness and two-thirds of the human race', in N. Dawson (ed.), *Advertising Works 17: Proving the Return on Marketing Investment*. Henley-on-Thames: World Advertising Research Centre. pp. 3–6.

Brown, S. and Ponsonby-McCabe, S. (2013) 'They're great!' Introduction to the Special Issue. *Journal of Marketing Management*, 29 (1–2). doi: 10.1080/0267257X.2012.762184.

Brown, S. and Jensen-Schau, H.J. (2008) 'Writing Russell Belk: excess all areas', *Marketing Theory*, 8 (2): 143–65.

Brown, S., Stevens, L. and Maclaran, P. (1999) 'I Can't Believe It's Not Bakhtin!: literary theory, postmodern advertising, and the gender agenda', *Journal of Advertising*, 28 (1): 11–24.

Brownlie, D., Saren, M., Wensley, R. and Whittington, D. (eds) (1999) *Rethinking Marketing: Towards Critical Marketing Accountings*. London: Sage.

Burr, V. (1995) *An Introduction to Social Constructionism*. London: Routledge.

Buttle, F. (1994) 'Marketing communications theory – what do the texts teach our students?', *International Journal of Advertising*, 14: 297–313.

Calfee, J.E. and Scherage, C. (1994) 'The influence of advertising on alcohol consumption: a literature review and an econometric analysis of four European nations', *International Journal of Advertising*, 13 (4): 287–310.

Campbell, N. (2013) 'Signs and semiotics of advertising', in J. Schroeder, S. Warren and E. Bell (eds), *The Routledge Companion to Visual Organisation.* London: Routledge. pp. 258–79.

Chada, R. and Husband, P. (2006) *The Cult of the Luxury Brand: Inside Asia's Love Affair with Luxury*. London and Boston: Nicholas Brearley.

Chong, D. (2009) *Arts Management*. London: Routledge.

Cook, G. (2001) *The Discourse of Advertising*. London: Routledge.

Cook, W.A. and Kover, A.J. (1998) 'Research and the meaning of advertising effectiveness: mutual misunderstandings', in W.D. Wells (ed.), *Measuring Advertising Effectiveness*. Hillsdale, NJ: Lawrence Erlbaum Associates. pp. 13–20.

Cornelissen, J.P. and Lock, A.R. (2002) 'Advertising research and its influence upon managerial practice: a review of perspectives and approaches', *Journal of Advertising Research*, 42 (3): 50–5.

Cornwell, B.T. (2014) *Sponsorship in Marketing*. London: Routledge.

Cova, B., Kozinets, R. and Shankar, A. (2007) *Consumer Tribes*. London: Butterworth–Heinemann.

Cronin, A.M. (2004) 'Regimes of mediation: advertising agencies as cultural intermediaries', *Consumption, Markets and Culture*, 7 (4): 349–69.

Cronin, A.M. (2008) 'Gender in the making of commercial worlds: creativity, vitalism and the practices of marketing', *Feminist Theory*, 9 (3): 293–312.

Danesi, M. (1994) *Messages and Meanings: An Introduction to Semiotics*. Toronto: Canadian Scholar's Press.

Dawson, N. (2009) 'The evolution of commercially effective communication', in N. Dawson (ed.), *Advertising Works 17: Proving the Return on Marketing Investment*. Henley-on-Thames: World Advertising Research Centre. pp. 27–34.

d'Astous, A. and Seguin, N. (1999) 'Consumer reactions to product placement strategies in television sponsorship', *European Journal of Marketing*, 33 (9/10): 896–910.

De Chernatony, L., McDonald, M. and Wallace, E. (2010) *Creating Powerful Brands*. London: Routledge.

Dermody, J. (1999) 'CPM/HEM models of information processing', in P.J. Kitchen (ed.), *Marketing Communications – Principles and Practice*. London: Thomson Learning. pp. 156–71.

De Saussure, F. (1974) *Course in General Linguistics*. London: Collins.

Deuze, M. (2007) *Media Work*. Cambridge: Polity Press.

deWaal Malefyt, T. and Moeran, B. (2003) *Advertising Cultures*. London: Berg.

Diamond, N., Sherry, J.F., Muniz, M.A., McGrath, M.A., Kozinets, R. and Borghini, S. (2009) 'American girl and the brand gestalt: closing the loop on socioculture branding research', *Journal of Marketing*, 73: 118–34, and at www3.nd.edu/~jsherry/pdf/2009/American%20Girl.pdf.

Dichter, E. (1949) 'A psychological view of advertising effectiveness', *Journal of Marketing*, 14 (1): 61–7.

Dichter, E. (1966) 'How word-of-mouth advertising works', *Harvard Business Review*, 44 (6): 147–57.

Eagle, L., Kitchen, P.J. and Bulmer, S. (2007) 'Insights into interpreting integrated marketing communications: a two-nation qualitative comparison', *European Journal of Marketing*, 41 (7/8): 956–70.

Eagleton, T. (1991) *Ideology*. London: Verso.

Edwards, D. and Potter, J. (1992) *Discursive Psychology*. London: Sage.

Ehrenberg, A., Barnard, N., Kennedy, R. and Bloom, H. (2002) 'Brand advertising and creative publicity', *Journal of Advertising Research*, 42 (4): 7–18.

Elliott, R. (1998) 'A model of emotion-driven choice', *Journal of Marketing Management*, 14: 95–108.

Elliott, R. and Jankel-Elliott, N. (2002) 'Using ethnography in strategic consumer research', *Qualitative Market Research: An International Journal*, 6 (4): 215–23.

Elliott, R. and Ritson, M. (1997) 'Post-structuralism and the dialectics of advertising: discourse, ideology, resistance', in S. Brown and D. Turley (eds), *Consumer Research: Postcards From the Edge*. London: Routledge. pp. 190–248.

Elliott, R. and Wattanasuwan, K. (1998) 'Brands as symbolic resources for the construction of identity', *International Journal of Advertising*, 17 (2): 131–44.

Erdogan, B.Z. (1999) 'Celebrity endorsement: a literature review', *Journal of Marketing Management*, 15 (4): 291–314.

Feldwick, P. (2002) *What Is Brand Equity Anyway?* Henley-on-Thames: World Advertising Research Centre.

Feldwick, P. (2007) 'Account planning: its history and significance for ad agencies', in G. Tellis and T. Ambler (eds), *The Sage Handbook of Advertising*. London: Sage. pp.184–98.

Fill, C. (2002) *Marketing Communications: Contexts, Strategies and Applications*, 3rd edn. Harlow: Prentice Hall.

Fill, C. (2009) *Marketing Communications: Interactivity, Communities and Content*. London: FT/Prentice Hall.

Firat, Fuat A. and Venkatesh, A. (1995) 'Liberatory postmodernism and the re-enchantment of consumption', *Journal of Consumer Research*, 22 (3): 239–67.

Forceville, C. (1996) *Pictorial Metaphor in Advertising*. London: Routledge.

Fowles, J. (1996) *Advertising and Popular Culture*. London: Sage.

Fox, Stephen (1984) *The Mirror Makers: A History of American Advertising and Its Creators.* New York: William Morrow.

Foxall, G.R. (2000) 'The psychological basis of marketing', in M.J. Baker (ed.), *Marketing Theory: A Student Text.* London: Thomson Learning. pp. 86–101.

Gardner, B. and Levy, S. (1955) 'The product and the brand', *Harvard Business Review*, March–April: 33–9.

Gilmore, C., O'Donohoe, S. and Townley, B. (2011) 'Pot Noodles, placements and peer regard: creative career trajectories and communities of practice in the British advertising industry', *British Journal of Management*, 22 (1): 114–31.

Goffman, E. (1959) *The Presentation of Self in Everyday Life*. New York: Anchor Books.

Goffman, E. (1979) *Gender Advertisements*. New York: Harper & Row.

Griffin, C., Bengry-Howell, A., Hackley, C., Mistral, W. and Szmigin, I. (2009) 'Every time I do it I absolutely annihilate myself': loss of (self)-consciousness and loss of memory in young people's drinking narratives', *Sociology*, 43 (3): 457–77.

Griffin, C., Szmigin, I., Bengry-Howell, A., Hackley, C. and Mistral, W. (2012) Inhabiting the contradictions: hypersexual femininity and the culture of intoxication among young women in the UK. *Feminism and Psychology*, 23(2): 184–206.

Gronhaug, K. (2000) 'The sociological basis of marketing', in M.J. Baker (ed.), *Marketing Theory: A Student Text*. London: Thompson Learning.

Hackley, C. (1999) 'The communications process and the semiotic boundary', in P.J. Kitchen (ed.), *Marketing Communications: Principles and Practice*. London: Thomson Learning. pp. 135–55.

Hackley, C. (2000) 'Silent running: tacit, discursive and psychological aspects of management in a top UK advertising agency', *British Journal of Management*, 11 (3): 239–54.

Hackley, C. (2002) 'The panoptic role of advertising agencies in the production of consumer culture', *Consumption, Markets and Culture*, 5 (3): 211–29.

Hackley, C. (2003a) 'IMC and Hollywood: what brand managers need to know', *Admap*, November: 44–7.

Hackley, C. (2003b) 'How divergent beliefs cause account team conflict', *International Journal of Advertising*, 22 (3): 313–32.

Hackley, C. (2003c) '"We are all customers now" rhetorical strategy and ideological control in marketing management texts', *Journal of Management Studies*, 40 (5): 1325–52.

Hackley, C. (2003d) 'Divergent representational practices in advertising and consumer research: some thoughts on integration', Special Issue on representation in consumer research, *Qualitative Market Research: An International Journal*, 6 (3): 175–84.

Hackley, C. (2003e) *Doing Research Projects in Marketing, Management and Consumer Research*. London: Routledge.

Hackley, C. (2003f) 'Account planning: current agency perspectives on an advertising enigma', *Journal of Advertising Research*, 43 (2): 235–45.

Hackley, C. (2003g) 'From consumer insight to advertising strategy: the account planner's integrative role in creative advertising development', *Marketing Intelligence and Planning*, 21 (7): 446–52.

Hackley, C. (2007) 'Marketing psychology and the hidden persuaders', *The Psychologist*, 20 (8): 488–90.

Hackley, C. (2008) 'UK alcohol policy and market research: media debates and methodological differences', *International Journal of Market Research*, 50 (4): 429–31.

Hackley, C. (2009a) *Marketing – A Critical Introduction*. London: Sage.

Hackley, C. (2009b) 'Parallel universes and disciplinary space: the bifurcation of managerialism and social science in marketing studies', *Journal of Marketing Management*, 25 (7–8): 643–59.

Hackley, C. (ed.) (2009) *Advertising*. Sage 'Library in Marketing'. London: Sage. 3 volumes: Volume 1: *Advertising Management*; Volume 2: *Advertising Culture*; Volume 3: *Advertising Science*.

Hackley, C. (2010) '"Theorizing advertising: managerial, scientific and cultural approaches", Chapter 6 in Pauline MacLaran, Michael Saren, Barbara Stern and Mark Tadajewski (eds), *The Sage Handbook of Marketing Theory*. London: Sage. pp. 89-107.

Hackley, C. (2013a) *Marketing in Context: Setting the Scene*. London: Palgrave Macmillan.

Hackley, C. (2013b) 'Marketing psychology', in R. Bayne and G. Jinks (eds), *Applied Psychology: Training, Practice and New Directions*, 2nd edn. London: Sage. pp. 108–24.

Hackley, C. and Hackley, R.A. (2013) 'Television product placement strategy in Thailand and the UK', *Asian Journal of Business Research*, 3 (1): 97–110.

Hackley, C. and Hackley, R.A. (2014) 'Branding Narcissus: marketing myths in contemporary celebrity', in Nora Campbell, John Desmond, James Fitchett, Donncha Kavanagh, Pierre McDonagh, Aidan O'Driscoll and Andrea Prothero (eds), *Myth and the Market*. UCD Business School, Dublin, Ireland, pp. 309–20.

Hackley, C. and Hackley née Tiwsakul, R.A. (2012) 'Unpaid product placement: the elephant in the room in the UK's new paid-for product placement market', *International Journal of Advertising*, 31 (4): 703-18.

Hackley, C. and Kitchen, P. (1997) 'Creative problem solving as a technology of expert behaviour within marketing management', *Creativity and Innovation Management*, 6 (1): 45–59.

Hackley, C. and Kitchen, P.J. (1999) 'Ethical perspectives on the postmodern communications Leviathan', *Journal of Business Ethics*, 20 (1): 15–26.

Hackley, C. and Kover, A. (2007) 'The trouble with creatives: negotiating creative identity in advertising agencies', *International Journal of Advertising*, 26 (1): 63–78.

Hackley, C. and Tiwsakul, R. (2008) 'Comparative management practices in international advertising agencies in the UK, Thailand and the USA', in C. Smith, B. McSweeney and R. Fitzgerland, (eds), *Remaking Management: Between Global and Local*. Cambridge: Cambridge University Press. pp. 586–626.

Hackley, C., Bengry-Howell, A., Griffin, C., Mistral, W., Szmigin, I. and Hackley née Tiwsakul, R.A. (2013) 'Young adults and "binge" drinking: a Bakhtinian analysis', *Journal of Marketing Management*, 29 (7–8): 933–49.

Hackley, C., Brown, S. and Hackley, R.A. (2012) 'The X Factor enigma: Simon Cowell and the marketization of existential liminality', *Marketing Theory*, 12 (4): 451–69.

Hackley, C., Tiwsakul, R. and Preuss, R. (2008) 'An ethical evaluation of product placement – a deceptive practice?', *Business Ethics – A European Review*, 17 (April): 109–20.

Harbor, C. (2007) 'Pervasive and persuasive: advertisements for concerts in London 1672–1750'. Conference Paper: Marketing theory into practice. Academy of Marketing conference, Kingston Business School at Royal Holloway University of London, 3–6 July.

Head, V. (1981) *Sponsorship: The Newest Marketing Skill*. Cambridge:Woodhead–Faulkner, in association with the Chartered Institute of Marketing.

Heath, R.G. (2012) *Seducing the Subsconscious: The Psychology of Emotional Influence in Advertising*. Chichester: Wiley–Blackwell.

Heath, R. and Feldwick, P. (2008) 'Fifty years using the wrong model of advertising', *International Journal of Advertising*, 50 (1): 29–59.

Hirschman, E. (1986) 'Humanistic inquiry in marketing research: research, philosophy, method and criteria', *Journal of Marketing Research*, 23 (August): 237–49.

Holbrook, M. (1995) *Consumer Research: Introspective Essays on the Study of Consumption.* London: Sage.

Holbrook, M. and Hirschman, E. (1982) 'The experiential aspects of consumption: consumer feelings, fantasies and fun', *Journal of Consumer Research*, 9 (September): 132–40.

Holbrook, M.B. and O'Shaughnessy, J. (1988) 'On the scientific status of consumer research and the need for an interpretive approach to studying consumption behaviour', *Journal of Consumer Research*, 15: 398–403.

Holt, D. (2002) 'Why do brands cause trouble?', *Journal of Consumer Research*, 29 (June): 70–90.

Holt, D. and Cameron, D. (2010) *Cultural Strategy: Using Innovative Ideologies to Build Breakthrough Brands*. Oxford: Oxford University Press.

Horkheimer, M. and Adorno, T.W. ([1944] 2002) *Dialectic of Enlightenment* (trans. Edmund Jephcott). Stanford, CA: Stanford University Press.

Iser, W. (1978) *The Act of Reading*. Baltimore, MD: Johns Hopkins University Press.

Jefkins, F. (2000) *Advertising.* Harlow: Pearson Education.

Jenkins, H. (2008) *Convergence Culture: Where Old and New Media Collide*. New York: New York University Press.

Jones, J.P. (1990) 'Advertising: strong force or weak force? Two views an ocean apart', *International Journal of Advertising*, 9: 233–46.

Katz, E. and Lazarsfeld, P.F. (1955) *Personal Influence*. Glencoe, IL: Free Press.

Kelly, A., Lawlor, K. and O'Donohoe, S. (2005) 'Encoding advertisements – the creative perspective', *Journal of Marketing Management*, 21: 505–28.

Kennedy, John E. (1904) *ReasonWhy Advertising Plus Intensive Advertising*. Terre Haute, IN: TWI Press, Inc.

Kitson, H.D. (1921) The Mind of the Buyer. New York: Macmillan.

Klein, N. (2000) *No Logo.* London: Flamingo.

Kotler, P. and Roberto, E.L. (1989) *Social Marketing: Strategies for Changing Public Behaviour*. New York: The Free Press.

Kotler, P. and Zaltman, G. (1971) 'Social marketing: an approach to planned social change', *Journal of Marketing*, 35: 3–12.

Kover, A.J. (1995) 'Copywriters' implicit theories of communication: an exploration', *Journal of Consumer Research*, 21 (March): 598–611.

Kover, A.J. (1996) 'Why copywriters don't like research – and what kind of research might they accept', *Journal of Advertising Research*, 36 (2): RC8–12.

Kover, A.J. and Goldberg, S.M. (1995) 'The games copywriters play: conflict, quasi-control, a new proposal', *Journal of Advertising Research*, 35 (4): 52–68.

Kozinets, R.V. (2009) *Netnography – Doing Ethnographic Research Online*. Thousand Oaks, CA: Sage.

Lash, S. and Lury, C. (2007) *Global Culture Industry – The Mediation of Things.* London: Polity.

Lasswell, H.D. (1948) 'The structure and function of communication in society', in L. Bryson (ed.), *The Communication of Ideas*. New York: Harper.

Lavidge, R.J. and Steiner, G.A. (1961) 'A model for predictive measurements of advertising effectiveness', *Journal of Marketing*, 24 (October): 59–62.

Lazarsfeld, P.F. (1941) 'Remarks on administrative and critical communications research', *Studies in Philosophy and Science*, 9: 3–16.

Lears, J. (1994) *Fables of Abundance: A Cultural History of Advertising in America*. New York: Basic Books.

Lee, N. and Lings, I. (2008) *Doing Business Research: A Guide to Theory and Practice*. London: Sage.

Lehu, J.M. (2007) *Branded Entertainment: Product Placement and Brand Strategy in the Entertainment Business*. London: Kogan Page.

Leiss, W., Kline, S. and Jhally, S. (1997) *Social Communication in Advertising: Persons, Products and Images of Well-Being*. London: Routledge.

Leiss, W., Kline, S., Jhally, S. and Botterill, J. (2005) *Social Communication in Advertising: Consumption in the Mediated Marketplace*. London: Routledge.

Lemle, R. and Mishkind, M. (1989) 'Alcohol and masculinity', *Journal of Substance Abuse Treatment*, 6: 213–22.

Levitt, T. (1983) 'The globalisation of markets', *Harvard Business Review*, April/May: 92–107.

Levy, S. (1959) 'Symbols for sale', *Harvard Business Review*, 37 (July): 117–24.

Loo, B.K. and Hackley, C. (2013) 'Internationalisation strategy of iconic Malaysian high fashion brands', *Qualitative Market Research: An International Journal* 16 (4): 406–20.

Lu, P.X. (2008) *Elite China: Luxury Consumer Behaviour in China*. Singapore: Wiley.

Lutz, R.J. (1977) 'An experimental investigation of causal relations among cognitions: affect and behavioural intention', *Journal of Consumer Research*, 3 (March): 197–208.

McCracken, G. (1986) 'Culture and consumption: a theoretical account of the structure and movement of the cultural meaning of consumer goods', *Journal of Consumer Research*, 13 (1): 71–84.

McCracken, G. (1987) 'Advertising – meaning or information?', in M. Wallendorf and P. Anderson (eds), *Advances in Consumer Research*, Vol. 14. Provo, UT: Association for Consumer Research. pp. 121–4.

McCracken, G. (1989) 'Who is the celebrity endorser? cultural foundation of the endorsement process', *Journal of Consumer Research*, 16 (3): 310–21.

McCracken, G. (1990) *Culture and Consumption: New Approaches to the Symbolic Character of Consumer Goods and Activities*. Bloomington, IN; Indiana University Press.

McCracken, G. (2005) *Culture and Consumption 11: Markets, Meaning and Brand Management*. Bloomington, IN: Indiana University Press.

McDonald, C. and Scott, J. (2007) 'A brief history of advertising', in G. Tellis and T. Ambler (eds), *The Sage Handbook of Advertising*. London: Sage. pp. 17–34.

McFall, L. (2004) *Advertising: A Cultural Economy*. London: Sage.

McKeil, J. (1985) *The Creative Mystique*. London: John Wiley and Sons.

McLeod, C., O'Donohoe, S. and Townley, B. (2009) 'The elephant in the room? Class and creative careers in British advertising agencies', *Human Relations*, 62 (7): 1011–39.

McLuhan, M. (1964) 'Keeping upset with the Joneses', in *Understanding Media*. London: Routledge and Kegan Paul. pp. 226–33.

McQuarrie, E.F. and Phillips, B.J. (2005) 'Indirect persuasion in advertising: how consumers process metaphors presented in pictures and words', *Journal of Advertising*, 34 (2): 7–21.

Manning, N. (2009) 'The new media communications model: a progress report', in N. Dawson (ed.), *Advertising Works 17: Proving the Return on Marketing Investment*. Henley-on-Thames: World Advertising Centre. pp. 7–14.

Marchand, R. (1985) *Advertising and the American Dream: Making Way for Modernity, 1920–1940*. Berkeley, CA: University of California Press.

Marchand, R. (1998) *Creating the Corporate Soul: The Rise of Public Relations and Corporate Imagery in American Big Business*. Berkeley, CA: University of California Press.

McSweeney, B. (2002) 'Hofstede's model of national cultural differences and their consequences: a triumph of faith – a failure of analysis', *Human Relations*, 55 (1): 89–118, also at www.uk.sagepub.com/managingandorganizations/downloads/Online%20articles/ch05/4%20-%20McSweeney.pdf.

Meenaghan, T. (1991) 'Sponsorship: legitimising the medium', *European Journal of Marketing*, 25 (11): 5–10.

Meenaghan, T. and Shipley, D. (1999) 'Media affecting sponsorship', *European Journal of Marketing*, 33 (3/4): 328–47.

Melewar, T.C. and Wooldridge, A. (2001) 'The dynamics of corporate identity: a review of a process model', *Journal of Communication Management*, 5 (4): 327–40.

Mick, D.G. (1986) 'Consumer research and semiotics: exploring the morphology of signs, symbols and significance', *Journal of Consumer Research*, 13: 196–213.

Mick, D.G. and Buhl, K. (1992) 'A meaning based model of advertising', *Journal of Consumer Research*, 19 (December): 317–38.

Moeran, B. (1996) *A Japanese Advertising Agency: An Anthropology of Media and Markets*. London: Curzon.

Muñiz, Albert M. Jr and O'Guinn, Thomas C. (2001) 'Brand community', *Journal of Consumer Research*, 27: 412-32.

Nelson, J.P. and Young, D.J. (2001) 'Do advertising bans work? An international comparison', *International Journal of Advertising*, 20: 273–96.

Nightingale, D.J. and Cromby, J. (eds) (1999) *Social Constructionist Psychology: A Critical Analysis of Theory and Practice*. Buckingham: Open University Press.

Nixon, S. (2003) 'Re-imagining the advertising agency: the cultural connotations of economic forms', in P. DuGay and M. Pryke (eds), *Cultural Economy*. London: Sage.

O'Donohoe, S. (1994) 'Advertising uses and gratifications', *European Journal of Marketing*, 28 (8/9): 52–75.

O'Donohoe, S. (1997) 'Raiding the postmodern pantry – advertising intertextuality and the young adult audience', *European Journal of Marketing*, 31 (34): 234–53.

Ogilvy, D. (1963) *Confessions of an Advertising Man*. New York: Atheneum.

Ogilvy, D. (1983) *Ogilvy on Advertising*, 2nd edn. London: Multimedia Books.

O'Shaughnessy, J. (1997) 'Temerarious directions for marketing', *European Journal of Marketing*, 31 (9/10): 677–705.

O'Shaughnessy, N. and O'Shaughnessy, J. (2004) *Persuasion in Advertising*. London: Routledge.

Packard, V. (1957) *The Hidden Persuaders*. New York: McKay.

Parsons, E. and Maclaran, P. (2009) *Contemporary Issues in Marketing and Consumer Behaviour.* London: Elsevier.

Pateman, T. (1983) 'How is understanding an advertisement possible?', in H. Davis and P. Walton (eds), *Language, Image, Media*. Oxford: Blackwell. pp. 187–204.

Peirce, C.S. (1958) *Collected Papers*. Cambridge, MA: Harvard University Press.

Peng, N. and Hackley, C. (2007) 'Political marketing communications planning in the UK and Taiwan – comparative insights from leading practitioners', *Marketing Intelligence and Planning*, 25 (5): 483–98.

Peng, N. and Hackley, C. (2009) 'Are voters, consumers? A qualitative exploration of the voter–consumer analogy in political marketing', *Qualitative Market Research: An International Journal*, 12 (2): 171–86.

Percy, L. and Elliott, R. (2009) *Strategic Advertising Management*, 3rd edn. Oxford: Oxford University Press.

Percy, L., Rossiter, J.R. and Elliott, R. (2001) *Strategic Advertising Management*. Oxford: Oxford University Press.

Pickton, D. and Crosier, K. (2003) 'Marketing intelligence and planning', *Account Planning*, special issue, 21 (7): 410–15.

Pollitt, S. (1979) 'How I started account planning in agencies', *Campaign*, 20 (April): 29–30.

Potter, J. and Wetherell, M. (1987) *Discourse and Social Psychology: Beyond Attitudes and Behaviour*. London: Sage.

Powell, H. (ed.) (2013) *Promotional Culture in an Era of Convergence*. Abingdon: Taylor and Francis.

Punyapiroje, C., Morrison, M. and Hoy, M. (2002) 'A nation under the influence: the creative strategy process for advertising in Thailand', *Journal of Current Issues and Research in Advertising*, 24 (2): 51–65.

Quickenden, K. and Kover, A.J. (2007) 'Did Boulton sell silver plate to the middle class? A quantitative study of luxury marketing in late eighteenth-century Britain', *Journal of Macromarketing*, 27 (March): 51–64.

Richards, B., MacRury, I. and Botterill, J. (2000) *The Dynamics of Advertising*. London: Routledge.

Ritson, M. and Elliott, R. (1999) 'The social uses of advertising: an ethnographic study of adolescent advertising audiences', *Journal of Consumer Research*, 26 (3): 260–77.

Robinson, N., McWilliams, H., Bullinger, F. and Schouest, C. (2009) 'Dove's big ideal: from real curves to growth curves', in N. Dawson (ed.), *Advertising Works 17: Proving the Payback on Marketing Investment.* Henley-on-Thames: World Advertising Research Centre. pp. 335–70.

Rosch, E. (1977) 'Human categorization', in N. Warren (ed.), *Advances in Cross Cultural Psychology*, Vol. 1. New York: Academic Press. pp. 1–49.

Rossiter, J.R., Percy, L. and Donovan, R.J. (1991) 'A better advertising planning grid', *Journal of Advertising Research*, October–November: 11–12.

Sawchuck, K. (1995) 'Semiotics, cybernetics and the ecstasy of marketing communication', in D. Kellner (ed.), *Baudrillard: A Critical Reader*. Oxford: Blackwell. pp. 89–116.

Schlosser, E. (2002) *Fast Food Nation*. New York: Penguin Books.

Schor, J. (1998) *The Overspent American: Upscaling, Downshifting and the New Consumer.* New York: Basic Books.

Schramm, W. (1948) *Mass Communication*. Urbana, IL: University of Illinois Press.

Schroeder, J.E. (2002) *Visual Consumption*. London: Routledge.

Schroeder, J.E. (2005) 'The artist and the brand', *European Journal of Marketing*, 39 (11/12): 1291–305.

Schroeder, J. and Salzer-Morling, M. (eds) (2005) *Brand Culture*. London: Routledge.

Schultz, D.E., Tannenbaum, S.I. and Lauterborn, R.F. (1993) *Integrated Marketing Communications*. Lincolnwood, IL: NTC Business Books.

Schultz, D., Tannenbaum, S. and Lauterborn, R.F. (1996) *The New Marketing Paradigm: Integrated Marketing Communications*. Lincolnwood, IL: NTC Business Books.

Scott, L. (1990) 'Understanding jingles and needledrop: a rhetorical approach to music in advertising', *Journal of Conusumer Research*, 17 (September): 223–36.

Scott, L. (1994a) 'The bridge from text to mind: adapting reader–response theory to consumer research', *Journal of Consumer Research*, 21: 461–80.

Scott, L. (1994b) 'Images in advertising: the need for a theory of visual rhetoric', *Journal of Consumer Research*, 21: 252–73.

Shankar, A. (2000) 'Lost in music? Subjective personal introspection and popular music consumption', *Research: An International Journal*, 3 (1): 27–37.

Shankar, A. and Horton, B. (1999) 'Ambient media – advertising's new media opportunity?', *International Journal of Advertising*, 18 (3): 305–21.

Shannon, C.E. (1948) 'A mathematical theory of communication', *Bell System Technical Journal*, 27 (3): 379–423.

Sharma, C., Herzog, J. and Melfi, V. (2008) *Mobile Advertising – Supercharge Your Brand in the Exploding Wireless Market*. Hoboken, NJ: Wiley.

Sherer, P.M. (1995) 'Selling the sizzle: Thai advertising crackles with creativity as industry continues to grow', *The Asian Wall Street Journal Weekly*, 1: 6–7.

Sherry, J.E. (1983) 'Gift giving in anthropological perspective', *Journal of Consumer Research*, 10 (September): 157–68.

Sherry, J.F. (1987) 'Advertising as cultural system', in J. Umiker-Sebeok (ed.), *Marketing and Semiotics*. Berlin: Mouton. pp. 441–62.

Sherry, J.F. (1991) 'Postmodern alternatives – the interpretive turn in consumer research', in T.S. Robertson and H.H. Kasserjian (eds), *Handbook of Consumer Behaviour*. Englewood Cliffs, NJ: Prentice-Hall. pp. 548–91.

Shimp, T.A. (2009) *Integrated Marketing Communications in Advertising and Promotion*, international edition. Cincinatti, OH: South Western College.

Smith, R.E. and Yang, X. (2004) 'Toward a general theory of creativity in advertising: examining the role of divergence', *Marketing Theory*, 4 (1/2): 41–58.

Steel, J. (1998) *Truth, Lies and Advertising: The Art of Account Planning*. New York: John Wiley and Sons.

Stern, B.B.(1993a) 'A revised communication model for advertising: multiple dimensions of the source, the message and the recipient', *Journal of Advertising*, 23: 25–16.

Stern, B.B. (1993b) 'Feminist literary criticism and the deconstruction of ads: a postmodern view of advertising and consumer responses', *Journal of Consumer Research*, 19: 556–66.

Stevens, R. (1996) 'Ten ways of distinguishing between theories in social psychology' and 'Trimodal theory as a model for interrelating perspectives in psychology', in R. Sapsford (ed.), *Issues for Social Psychology*. Milton Keynes: Open University. pp. 45–66, 77–84.

Strong, E.K. (1929) *The Psychology of Selling and Advertising*. Chicago, IL: American Library Association.

Supharp, S. (1993) *Thai Culture and Society: Values, Family, Religion and Tradition*, 8th edn. Bangkok: Thai Watanapanich [in Thai].

Svensson, S. (2007) 'Producing marketing: towards a social-phenomenology of marketing work', *Marketing Theory*, 7: 271–90.

Szmigin, I. (2003) *Understanding the Consumer*. London: Sage.

Szmigin, I., Bengry-Howell, A., Griffin, C., Hackley, C. and Mistral, W. (2011) 'Social marketing, individual responsibility and the "culture of intoxication"', *European Journal of Marketing*, 45 (5): 759–79.

Szmigin, I., Griffin, C., Mistral, W., Bengry-Howell, A., Weale, L. and Hackley, C. (2008) 'Re-framing "binge drinking" as calculated hedonism: empirical evidence from the UK', *International Journal of Drug Policy*, 19 (5): 359–66.

Tanaka, K. (1994) *Advertising Language: A Pragmatic Approach to Advertisements in Britain and Japan*. London: Routledge.

Thompson, C.J., Locander, W. and Pollio, H. (1989) 'Putting consumer experience back into consumer research: the philosophy and method of existential phenomenology', *Journal of Consumer Research*, 17: 133–47.

Thompson, C., Pollio, H. and Locander, W. (1994) 'The spoken and the unspoken: a hermeneutic approach to the understanding the cultural viewpoints that underlie consumers expressed meanings', *Journal of Consumer Research*, 21: 431–53.

Tirakhunkovit, V. (1980) 'Why Thais do not like Thai products', *Monthly Business Journal*, February: 22–9.

Tiwsakul, R. (2008) 'The meaning of Kod-sa-na-faeng: an interpretive exploration of consumers' experiences of television product placement in the United kingdom and Thailand', PhD Thesis, University of London, Royal Holloway and Bedford New College.

Tiwsakul, R., Hackley, C. and Szmigin, I. (2005) 'Explicit, non-integrated product placement in British television programmes', *International Journal of Advertising*, 24 (1): 95–111.

Umiker-Sebeok, J. (ed.) (1997) *Marketing and Semiotics*. Amsterdam: Mouton de Gruyter.

Vakratsas, D. and Ambler, T. (1999) 'How advertising works: what do we really know?', *Journal of Marketing*, 63 (January): 26–43.

Vaughn, R. (1986) 'How advertising works – a planning model revisited', *Journal of Advertising Research* (February–March): 57–66.

Veblen, T. ([1899] 1970) *The Theory of the Leisure Class*. London: Unwin Books.

Watson, J. (1924) *Behaviorism*. Chicago, IL: University of Chicago Press.

Weaver, W. and Shannon, C.E. (1963) *The Mathematical Theory of Communication*. Champaign, IL: University of Illinois Press.

Wells, W.D. (1975) 'Psychographics: a critical review', *Journal of Marketing Research*, 12 (May): 196–213.

Wernick, A. (1991) *Promotional Culture – Advertising, Ideology and Symbolic Expression*. London: Sage.

West, D. (1993) 'Cross-national creative personalities, processes and agency philosophies', *Journal of Advertising Research*, 33 (5): 53–62.

West, D.C. and Paliwoda, S.J. (1996) 'Advertising client–agency relationships: the decision-making structure of clients', *European Journal of Marketing*, 30 (8): 22–39.

Williamson, J. (1978) *The Semiotics of Advertising*. London: Sage.

Wilmshurst, J. and Mackay, A. (1999) *The Fundamentals of Advertising*, 2nd edn. Oxford: Butterworth–Heinemann.

Wolf, M. (1999) *The Entertainment Economy: How Mega-media Forces are Shaping Our Lives*. New York: Crown Business Books.

World Health Organization (WHO) (1988) *Alcohol and the Mass Media*. Copenhagen: WHO.

Young, M. (1995) 'Getting legless, falling down pissy-arsed drunk', *Journal of Gender Studies*, 4 (1): 47–61.

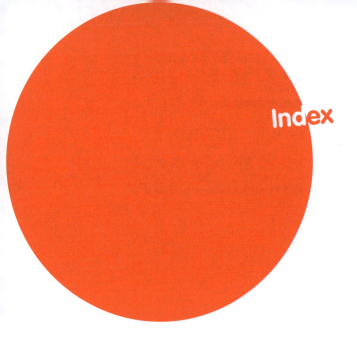

Index

NOTE: page numbers in *italic type* refer to figures and tables, page numbers in **bold type** refer to glossary entries.